The Best Places to Go

A GUIDE TO PLANNING ANY TRIP

WEST
SIDE
PUBLISHING

Factual Verification by: Daniel Spellerberg

Interior Illustrations: Linda Howard Bittner, Erin Burke, Dan Grant, Jupiter Images, Robert Schoolcraft, Shutterstock, Shavan Spears, John Zielinski

All of the "10 Great Places" and sidebar content was originally published in USA TODAY or Gannett properties between 1987 and 2010.

CONTENTS

✳ ✳ ✳ ✳

WHEN ONLY THE BEST WILL DO

✳ ✳ ✳ ✳

The best restaurant. The best hotel. The best natural landmark. These and other travel-related "bests" can mean different things to different people. So while there may not be one "best" to suit each and every person, *Armchair Reader™: USA*

Today—The Best Places to Go offers list after list of "10 Great Places" to help you plan your next trip, whether you're seeking an adventure-filled, action-packed family excursion or a high-end couples retreat for the travel industry's version of the three R's—rest, romance, and revitalization. What's more, these lists were created by experts in all areas of travel and

leisure. Renowned chef Mario Batali's 10 great Little Italys? It's safe to say he knows what he's talking about on the Italian food front. Top spots to hear jazz music? Chances are noted musician Wynton Marsalis's picks will be good ones.

Divided into eight logical chapters, the book offers travel tips on:

- **Entertainment:** Read about the country's top tiki bars, where to go fly a kite, what you'll discover at the world's best festivals, and more.

- **Dining:** From roadside pit stops and neighborhood joints to organic markets and regional wineries, the places featured in this section will take the guesswork out of eating on the road.

- **Arts and Culture:** Whether your idea of "culture" is kitschy roadside statues or highfalutin museums, you'll find plenty of artsy options to add to your itinerary.

- **History:** Travel to the past by visiting the historical sites suggested in this chapter, from early settlements to war memorials to presidential haunts.

- **Holidays:** This section covers travel tips to help you survive the harried holiday season as well as unique holiday-related destinations, such as the best places to ring in the New Year and where to get good and spooked on Halloween.

- **Sports:** Sports lovers will be giddy over the lists of "10 Great Places" in this chapter, which offer winning spots for spectators of all sports as well as suggestions for those who want to get in on the action.

- **The Great Outdoors:** Camping, bike riding, boating—if it's outdoorsy, this section covers it. But you'll also find tips on the best places to view fall colors and various wildlife as well as where to kick back and relax on a beach, lake, or other open-air spot.

- **Places to Stay Awhile:** This catchall chapter leads you to great destinations around the world, from detoxifying spas to pet-friendly hotels to off-the-beaten-path locales.

Even if your next trip is many years away, you'll delight in reading about the hundreds of incredible places to go from the comfort of your armchair. And who knows? Your perfect vacation may be hidden among these pages!

ENTERTAINMENT

* * * *

ADVENTURE AND LEARNING

10 great places to unleash
your inner Indy

Fans of the Indiana Jones flicks—or anyone ready to up the adventure ante—will enjoy these intrepid getaways, courtesy of National Geographic's Boyd Matson. (Just try to avoid dangling above snake pits and being chased by boulders.)

Mount Everest, Tibet and Nepal
To really flex your explorer muscles, trek to the Mount Everest base camp, about 17,000 feet up the 29,000-foot mountain on the Tibetan side. If climbing isn't your cup of tea, you may be more comfortable sipping something warm at the Rum Doodle Bar in Kathmandu, Nepal, in the shadow of the monster mountain. "The ceiling is covered with banners and T-shirts signed by trekkers, but behind the bar is a board reserved for the signatures of those who have made it to the top" of Everest. *therumdoodle.com*

Djemaa el-Fna Square, Marrakech, Morocco
For a scene that could be plucked straight out of one of the films, check out the palaces, mosques, and Djemaa el-Fna Square in Marrakech. "To up the adventure component, head into the Atlas Mountains for a little four-by-four travel and then spend a night in a traditional Berber tented camp in the desert."

Petra, Jordan
"Hike or ride donkey-drawn carts through a slot canyon to arrive at this ancient city carved out of the sandstone cliffs. Petra offers the chance to hook up with nomadic tribesmen and do either a one-day or multiday camel

safari in the desert." Now a UNESCO World Heritage Site, this once-vibrant Nabataean city was an oasis where Greeks, Romans, and Arabs met for caravan trading.

Valley of the Whales, Wadi al-Hitan, Egypt
From the tomb of Tutankhamen to the Pyramids, Egypt is filled with mystical quests. Head off the beaten trail for Wadi al-Hitan, the Valley of the Whales. "You can hike around a small area in the desert that was once under the sea and is now filled with the fossils of prehistoric whales."

Cloud Forest, Monteverde, Costa Rica
Hike through Cloud Forest and see the rain forest as the birds do while you glide along a series of zip lines strung through the canopy. "You're strapped into a harness and then clipped onto a pulley system attached to a cable. You can easily imagine yourself making a daring escape while being chased by some lost tribe firing arrows at you."

Anasazi ruins, Colorado and New Mexico
"A visit to Anasazi ruins is like an Indiana Jones expedition in search of a lost civilization that mysteriously disappeared. Start in Durango, Colorado, with a visit to the cliff dwellings at Mesa Verde, then drive down to Chaco Canyon in New Mexico." Explore the trails, climb over the boulders, and play archaeologist here. *nps.gov/meve; nps.gov/chcu*

Machu Picchu, Agua Caliente, Peru
Gain some explorer creds by hiking the Inca Trail through the Andes Mountains to Machu Picchu, about 8,000 feet above sea level. With a guide, the trek can take four days. For a less-treacherous experience, take a train through the Sacred Valley to get a taste of the Lost City of the Incas. "You'll be amazed how anyone could build such a place in a relatively short period of time without the arch, the wheel, or the written word." Top off your trip with a "hike up the steep peak that overlooks Machu Picchu, where you'll discover other ruins."

Sepic River, Papua New Guinea
"Visiting Papua New Guinea can be like stepping into a time machine." It's easy to fancy yourself an explorer of medieval ruins

when surrounded by men still carrying spears and bows and arrows with elaborately painted faces. "Travel up the Sepic River in a dugout canoe and visit the villages along the way. You just know there must be a crystal skull hidden somewhere in these jungles that are the home of former head hunters."

Jungle trek, Bumthang, Bhutan

"This place offers amazing trekking opportunities through jungles in a mountain kingdom." Wind through meadows and valleys, then meander through a mixed forest of bamboo and magnolia. Vacationers beware: This trek is not for the faint of heart. Himalayan bears have a high population here, so it's best to stick with guided tours.

ATM Cave, Belize

For the ultimate archaeological experience, check out the Actun Tunichil Muknal (ATM) Cave for skeletal remains aplenty. "Just like in Indiana Jones, all the artifacts are still in place." Grab a guide for the one-hour drive from San Ignacio, Belize, then hike the remaining distance for another hour. "There is a place to break and swim and swing off jungle vines. Arriving at the entrance to the cave, you discover a deep pool of water—so the only way in is to swim."

10 great small towns with huge backyards

Get a glimpse of the simpler life—and get in shape at the same time. Small towns can offer big outdoor adventures all year long. Sarah Tuff, coauthor of 101 Best Outdoor Towns: Unspoiled Places to Visit, Live & Play, *shares her picks.*

Salida, Colorado

"This is the place for white-water paddling action. Downtown Salida even has two of its own 'playholes' in an all-natural, white-water park on the Arkansas River. Plan a visit around the annual FIBArk (First in Boating on the Arkansas River) Whitewater Festival. Landlubbers can find 15 Fourteeners (mountains more than 14,000 feet high) nearby."

Haines, Alaska

"Some 20 million acres of wilderness surround this unhurried town on the longest fjord in the United States. One of the best ways to explore is by kayak: Put in at Bartlett Cove at Glacier Bay National Park. In the fall, you'll want to be at the Alaska Chilkat Bald Eagle Preserve to see the congregation of thousands of bald eagles that feast on spawning salmon."

Livingston, Montana

"They weren't lying when they named this place Paradise Valley. Livingston is an Eden along the Yellowstone River, just 52 miles north of Yellowstone National Park. Galleries share space with bars, gear shops, and breakfast spots in the historic downtown. Anglers have the Yellowstone or nearby Gallatin and Madison rivers, which teem with thousands of fish per mile. Some 2,000 miles of trails beckon backpackers and bikers to the Gallatin National Forest."

Bethel, Maine

"You'd never guess that this picture-perfect town, complete with covered bridges and a village common, is host to one of the most unusual outdoor adventures in the country: the annual North American Wife Carrying Championships that take place at Sunday River Ski Resort every October."

Hood River, Oregon

Fresh fruit and produce from the Hood River Valley, as well as incredible local brews and regional wines, are as rewarding as the outdoor activities here. Bike trails surround the town, and there's rafting and kayaking on the nearby Columbia River's swift tributaries. "Hood River's recreational resources blow away even people who are deathly afraid of kiteboarding and windsurfing. A multitude of instructors make it easier to learn than you think."

Lake Placid, New York

"Though famous for the Olympic Winter Games, this unspoiled town is actually a year-round outdoor haven. You can't beat the setting on two jewel-like lakes, surrounded by the six-million-acre Adirondack Park. Hike the summits of the Adirondacks or just paddle on Lake Placid, then sink into a suite at the Mirror Lake Inn and Spa. Go shopping on Main Street, then set out for the swimming hole and sparkling cascades of Rocky Falls."

Ely, Minnesota
"For those who fantasize about paddling a canoe on pristine waters, surrounded by pine trees and listening to the cry of the loon from a lakeside tent, there's simply no better place to make that fantasy come true than Ely. The town, at the edge of the 1.1-million-acre Boundary Waters Canoe Area, teems with friendly outfitters who will provide every level of service, from a point in the right direction to a fully guided canoe trip complete with meals." Another highlight: seeing wolves at the International Wolf Center.

Davis, West Virginia
Leaf-peepers can get a jump start on fall foliage viewing in this Appalachian town where, because of the high elevations, peak foliage season is usually late September. Winter's not a bad time to visit either. "Believe it or not, this town gets 150 inches of snow a year—more than some places in Vermont. That makes for surprisingly good skiing at Canaan Valley and Timberline ski resorts."

McCall, Idaho
This mountain town is on shimmering Payette Lake. "Summer visitors enjoy waterskiing and wake-boarding, plus rock-climbing routes, mountain-biking trails, fishing holes, and the 2.3 million acres of the Payette National Forest. A highlight of every year is the Winter Carnival (January–February) for snow-sculpting, tubing races, and snowshoe golf."

Boone, North Carolina
"Boone has a built-in air conditioner for the summer months that turn the rest of the South sticky: the Blue Ridge Mountains, which keep temperatures at a lovely 75 degrees in August. The town, 100 miles north of Asheville, stays hip, thanks to Appalachian State University. Get jazzed at Espresso News before heading into the Pisgah National Forest for hiking, mountain biking, and rock climbing. Rafters rollick along the Nolichucky and French Broad rivers."

Talk to the Expert

TRUE ADVENTURE HARDER TO FIND

Inveterate traveler and author Richard Bangs is a founding partner of Mountain Travel Sobek, which helped launch the adventure-travel industry more than 40 years ago. We asked him to chart some of the industry's changes and look ahead to its new frontiers.

Q: You once defined adventure travel as travel without a map, an itinerary, or a tether. Does that still apply in an era when Mount Everest has traffic jams and aging baby boomers think roughing it includes cell phones and cappuccino?

A: From my perspective, adventure is something that really is wild and takes unknown turns. And that sliver of the population who wants to really explore and be out there experimenting still exists. But the adventure-travel industry has taken a left turn and watered itself down to become much more mainstream and accommodating. Trips are shorter and have become more like an amusement park: There's a little bit of thrill, but everything lives up to expectations.

Q: What kinds of trips have struck out over the past 40 years?

A: When the geopolitical landscape changes, there very often is a rush of interest to a new destination. When Russia and the former Soviet republics became available as destinations, there was an enormous flood of interest; China was the same. But at both destinations, the interest has waned considerably.... Adventure-travel companies have retooled themselves to address the soft adventure market, and infrastructures don't exist in back-country Russia and China to accommodate that type of travel.

Q: And which trips have stood the test of time?

A: The sheer, awesome power and beauty of places like the Himalayas will always attract people. The same goes for wildlife—this primal connection takes place when you are not very far from a mountain gorilla or a lion or a grizzly bear. The places that offer a glimpse into the past, like Easter Island, Machu Picchu, and Angkor Wat...and the thrill of challenging yourself by running wild rivers like the Zambezi or climbing mountains that always have an element of objective danger.

10 great places to catch a fish in action

Once a ho-hum field-trip destination, many of the underwater zoos in the United States have been upgraded, renovated, and redesigned. "Most people never get to explore the ocean depths, so aquariums become our best way to observe and understand the complexity and beauty of the sea," says John Grant, author of Window to the Sea. *He shares some aquariums "that enable us to get close to the oceans without getting wet."*

John G. Shedd Aquarium, Chicago, Illinois
"Promoting itself as the 'world's aquarium,' the Shedd lives up to the title. The three-million-gallon tank in the Oceanarium is home to rare beluga whales and white-sided dolphins, and visitors watch as trainers work with and care for the popular mammals. The 750,000-gallon Wild Reef exhibit re-creates a Philippine coral reef, one of the ocean's richest habitats." *sheddaquarium.org*

New England Aquarium, Boston, Massachusetts
"The Giant Ocean Tank, with its 52 large viewing windows, is the main attraction here. Myrtle, a giant green sea turtle, is one of the tank's most popular animals, along with sharks, rays, and more than 100 other species. The Aquarium Medical Center is a working animal hospital/exhibit that allows visitors to observe veterinarians examining and treating sea creatures." *neaq.org*

Tennessee Aquarium, Chattanooga, Tennessee
"This is a unique aquarium in that a large portion of its collection features freshwater species and it specializes in fish, amphibians, and reptiles from the southwestern part of the country. The River Journey exhibit transports visitors from the Appalachian highlands through ponds, rivers, and swamps, all the way to the seacoast. The Ocean Journey exhibit allows visitors to sample a variety of saltwater environments." *tennesseeaquarium.com*

Waikiki Aquarium, Honolulu, Hawaii
"Many exhibits from this aquarium use Hawaii's abundant natural daylight. This allows Waikiki to display only live coral, which creates

beautiful exhibits. It's also a world leader in the propagation of live coral. The aquarium features some unusual and rarely seen species, including the chambered nautilus and the endangered Hawaiian monk seal." *waquarium.org*

New York Aquarium, Brooklyn, New York
"The oldest continuously operated aquarium in the country features 630 species and more than 8,000 animals," Grant says. "The walruses are especially popular," and visitors can witness the feeding of the aquarium's reef sharks, nurse sharks, and sand tiger sharks. *nyaquarium.com*

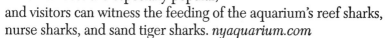

Monterey Bay Aquarium, Monterey, California
"Located along the shoreline in beautiful Monterey, MB focuses on the rich and diverse habitat of the bay. The one-of-a-kind Kelp Forest exhibit features swaying giant kelp and a host of fish and other marine animals. Visitors also can observe sea otters and a beautiful sea jelly exhibit." *montereybayaquarium.org*

North Carolina Aquarium on Roanoke Island, Manteo, North Carolina
"The Graveyard of the Atlantic exhibit reflects the aquarium's proximity to the state's Outer Banks, where thousands of ships have run aground over the centuries. Divers in the exhibit carry on a conversation with visitors outside the tank." *ncaquariums.com*

National Aquarium, Baltimore, Maryland
"Located in the Inner Harbor area, and well known for its dolphin demonstrations, this is one of Maryland's most popular tourist attractions. Animal Planet's [exhibit] *Australia: Wild Extremes* depicts survival stories in an extreme environment and features 1,800 Australian animals." *aqua.org*

Georgia Aquarium, Atlanta, Georgia
One of the country's newest aquariums, the Georgia Aquarium "bills itself as the largest in the world, holding more than 100,000 animals representing 500 species. It is the first in the United States to display whale sharks, the largest fish in the world." *georgiaaquarium.org*

Oregon Coast Aquarium, Newport, Oregon
"Celebrating the beauty and diversity of Oregon's coastline, many exhibits are outdoors, including harbor seals, sea lions, and sea otters. Inside, a 200-foot underwater tunnel snakes through the Open Ocean, Halibut Flats, and Orford Reef exhibits, providing a nearly 360-degree view of sharks, batfish, and giant octopi."
aquarium.org

Day trips turn to night at museum sleepovers

Some of the hottest events at museums these days are a real snooze. Sleepovers are taking place nationwide at museums, zoos, and aquariums as they open "camp-in" programs to the public that traditionally have been tailored for Scout groups and the like. Sleepovers "are an opportunity for museums to deepen the experience of a day visit," says Janet Rice Elman of the Association of Children's Museums.

All-nighters also generate revenue. And because they frequently tie into current exhibits, they can help build future visitation. Among the programs:

- The Maritime Museum of San Diego offers overnight sailings aboard the schooner *Californian* and 18-hour "voyage of the imagination" programs on the *Star of India*.

- At the Adventure Aquarium in Camden, New Jersey, overnight guests sleep with the fishes—actually, near a 760,000-gallon tank that houses sharks and other fish.

- At Philadelphia's Franklin Institute, visitors bed down on weekends from October to May around the museum's walk-through human heart and elsewhere.

- The Battleship New Jersey, one of the U.S. Navy's largest and most decorated warships and now a waterfront museum in Camden, has staged overnight outings for groups since 2002.

At many zoos and aquariums the programs are "hugely popular," and offerings have doubled in the past several years, says Jane Ballentine of the American Zoo and Aquarium Association.

10 great places to have s'more adventure

Sign up for playfulness at these multigenerational camps that have activities geared for all ages and abilities. "The camp experience benefits everyone, from the very young to the young at heart," says Peg Smith, CEO of the American Camp Association. She shares her list of great places to go to camp with the kids.

Medomak Camp, Washington, Maine
"Unplug, relax, and reconnect with what's important: family, community, and the environment" at this camp on coastal Maine. Adults and children enjoy counselor-led activities such as archery, sailing, sculling, arts and crafts, tennis, and photography. Adults can also enjoy massage, yoga, and local Maine beer and cheese tastings. *medomakcamp.com*

Camp Motorsport, Adult/Child Sampler Weekends, Alton, Virginia
"Enjoy the excitement of driving or riding together in the cars and carts" of this camp at the Virginia International Raceway. No experience is required, as half the participants, from grandparents to kids, have never done it before. Stay in traditional camp dorms or opt for the resort hotel on the property. *campmotorsport.com*

Cheley Colorado Camps, Estes Park, Colorado
"Families stay in covered wagons that sleep four people per wagon" at this camp near Rocky Mountain National Park. "Activities include a movie-making day with camper screenings in the evening, technical climbing, riflery, crafts, horseback riding, and day hiking." *cheley.com*

Camp Tecumseh YMCA, Brookston, Indiana
"In addition to Family Camp, Tecumseh offers Grand Camp, a weekend just for grandparents and their grandchildren." Soar into the lake on a Huck Finn–style rope swing, learn to play the popular Ga Ga game, or visit Three-house Treehouse, a hiking destination for an away lunch or overnight stays. The camp's private cabins have carpeting, a bathroom, and built-in bunks. *www.camptecumseh.org*

Fairview Lake YMCA Camps, Newton, New Jersey
"From hiking the Appalachian Trail and boating on the 110-acre lake to making candles and pressing apple cider, there's something for the entire family here. Join other families who want to develop or renew an appreciation for each other, while enjoying the peace and tranquility of beautiful Fairview Lake." The head chef is sensitive to vegetarian preferences and campers with special dietary needs. *fairviewlakeymca.org*

Bishop Stoney Camp & Conference Center, Santa Fe, New Mexico
"Located on 216 acres in the majestic forested countryside east of Santa Fe, Camp Stoney offers a variety of options in an enchanting setting." Plan a mini family reunion and stay in cabins, which are divided into two rooms, or tepees, which are popular with the kids. *campstoney.org*

Camp Lakamaga, Scandia, Minnesota
"Accommodations are in troop houses, cabins, yurts, or platform tents" at this camp owned by the Girl Scouts. Take the grandkids geo-caching—an outdoor treasure hunt using GPS coordinates—or go with your mate. Get in touch with your inner child and play relay games and obstacle courses on the lawn. Sign up for horseback riding, archery, biking, and boating. *girlscoutsrv.org*

Big Lake Youth Camp, Sisters, Oregon
"Enjoy the natural beauty of central Oregon while mountain biking through hemlock and fir trees" at the family camp sessions here. "Do a hike on the Pacific Crest Trail; canoe and wakeboard on the clear, clean lake; then eat delicious meals." Campers young and old rave about the homemade bread and pasta sauces served here. *biglake.org*

Lake of the Woods Camp for Girls and Greenwoods Camp for Boys, Decatur, Michigan
"Every night there's a different evening program here, from singing around the campfire to family talent shows. It's about spending quality time together." Adults have as much fun as the kids with golf, waterskiing, fishing, climbing, windsurfing, archery, riflery, tennis, and sailing—together or solo. *lwcgwc.com*

Camp Alleghany, Lewisburg, West Virginia
"This is an affordable, fun family camp in the Allegheny Mountains. Registration includes a three- or four-day stay, a platform tent with cots for each family, and three buffet meals each day." Swim and canoe on the Greenbrier River, or bring bikes and ride along the Greenbrier River Trail. The nearby town of Lewisburg has antique stores, and there's live, professional theater at the Greenbrier Valley Theatre. *campalleghany.com*

10 great places to get your motor running

Auto aficionados and those just in the need for speed can fill up their adventure tank at the adrenaline-boosting racing schools recommended by Larry Webster, Car and Driver *magazine's technical director. "You won't believe what it's possible to do in a car."*

Skip Barber Racing School, various locations
"Run at tracks all over the country, [the school] offers a one-day course where students drive miniature Indy cars that accelerate like a Corvette. There are also new-driver programs and a high-performance class where students drive 500-horsepower Dodge Vipers. My pick: the three-day racing pro-gram. Go for it." *skipbarber.com*

Smiley Sitton's Outlaw Driving School, Dallas, Texas
"Imagine piloting a car that looks no bigger than a go-kart but has a 700-horsepower engine, and you'll get the idea behind this school." *outlawdrivingschool.com*

Bobby Ore Stunt Driving School, Camarillo, California
"Yes, you can learn to be a stunt driver, and Ore's school teaches *Dukes of Hazzard*–style slides and also how to drive a car on two wheels. Now you can watch a movie chase scene and think, 'Hey, I can do that!' " *bobbyoresports.com*

Richard Petty Driving Experience, various locations
"You won't learn a whole lot in this one, but you will get to experience what it's like to zoom around an oval like a NASCAR driver—either as a passenger or in the driver's seat of a stock car." *1800bepetty.com*

Land Rover Experience, Asheville, North Carolina
Land Rover "courses that teach extreme off-road driving are held at some of the swankiest grand hotels in the country, like this one at the Biltmore Estate," where competing teams vie for the Biltmore Cup.

Team O'Neil Rally School, Dalton, New Hampshire
"Located in gorgeous northern New Hampshire, the O'Neil Rally School offers one- and two-day car-control schools and three-day rally schools where students learn how to effortlessly slide cars over gravel roads." *team-oneil.com*

Porsche Driving Experience, Birmingham, Alabama
"Held at the Barber Motorsports Park outside of the city, the PDE runs one-day courses or an advanced program. The best parts: You get to learn in Porsche 911s, and the instructors are legendary drivers like Hurley Haywood. There's also an off-road class where drivers pilot Porsche Cayennes." *porschedriving.com*

Roy Hill's Drag Racing School, various locations
"If the idea of driving a 1,200-horsepower drag racer down a quarter-mile track sounds good to you, Roy Hill will teach you how" at various tracks. "It's not cheap, but we're talking rocketlike acceleration." *royhillsdragracingschool.com*

Jim Hall Kart Racing School, Ventura, California
"Most professional drivers got their start in karts, and you'll be amazed at how much you can learn in a pint-size vehicle that's about the size of a shopping cart." *jimhallkartracing.com*

Wide Open Baja Adventure, Baja California, Mexico
"This one is for serious adrenaline junkies, because you drive two-seat dune buggies over the same Mexican desert routes used in the Baja 500 and 1,000 races." *wideopenbaja.com*

10 great places to die for, figuratively speaking

Take a break from the ordinary—just don't wait. "The desire to escape normal life and do something different that engages the mind, body, and spirit is in all of us," says Clare Jones, coauthor with Steve Watkins of Unforgettable Things to Do Before You Die. *From their book, Jones shares unforgettable spots to savor long before you pass.*

Skeleton Coast, Namibia, Africa
"Lashed by fierce surf, littered with shipwrecks, and backed by towering two-story-high sand dunes, Africa's loneliest stretch of coast is a world apart. The only way to really explore the immense Namib Desert and its wild mountain interior is via a unique flying safari. Recognized as a national park in 1971, this narrow tract of coastal desert stretches north toward Angola and the Kunene River and southward toward the Ugab River." *skeletoncoastsafaris.com*

Backwater Canals, Kerala, India
"If you want to find laid-back luxury, then idly cruising Kerala's backwater canals in a converted rice boat, past swaths of palm trees, vast paddy fields, and small villages, is a fabulous way to discover this unique part of India. Often described as the country's 'rice bowl,' this is a lush green corner of the country where smiling faces and wonderful food greet visitors throughout the journey."

Espiritu Santo, Baja California, Mexico
"With cactus-studded desert mountains plunging into tranquil turquoise bays, gliding manta rays, and pods of migrating orca whales, this uninhabited island in the Sea of Cortez, which separates mainland Mexico and the fingerlike Baja peninsula, is every bit the paradise island you dream of escaping to. It's also the perfect place to explore by sea kayak; warm water and sunshine are almost guaranteed from October to May."

Arena of Verona, Verona, Italy
"Immortalized by Shakespeare's *Romeo and Juliet,* Verona now trades as the city of romance. You can even visit that famous balcony for a reenactment, but for more blazing passion and highly charged

emotions, open-air opera is offered at one of the oldest Roman sites in the world. The outdoor Arena amphitheater, at the heart of the ancient Italian city, is where this veritable extravaganza of color, light, and sound takes place." *arena-verona.com*

Marrakech, Morocco
"It might sound like a long way to go for a spot of shopping, but the vivid colors of its bustling souk; the red of its medina walls; the mingling aromas of a thousand spices; and the sounds of storytellers, fire-eaters, and snake charmers certainly make Marrakech one of the world's most exotic locations to try your hand at bargain hunting."

Vallée Blanche, Chamonix, France
"Hidden among the high mountains of the French Alps above Chamonix, the Vallée Blanche is Europe's longest off-piste ski run, offering unique access to a wild, snow-swept, ice-carved landscape. For intermediate skiers, remote towering Alpine peaks, including Mont Blanc; crevasse-strewn glaciers like Mer de Glace; and limitless powder snow await."

Milford Track, Fiordland, New Zealand
"Hailed as the 'world's greatest walk,' the Milford Track traverses the heart of South Island's dramatic wild fiord country, winding through native bush and rain forest, glaciated valley systems, and up into the high mountains at the Mackinnon Pass. It then skirts majestically downward past rivers and waterfalls, including the awesome Sutherland Falls, to Milford Sound crowned in scenic splendor by the jagged Mitre Peak."

Golden Circle, Iceland
"Iceland is a living geological masterpiece, a peerless volcanic land of dramatic skies, bubbling earth, thundering waterfalls, and thermal lagoons. If you want an insight into how the planet was sculpted by the forces of Mother Nature, exploring the Golden Circle will provide many answers."

Princess Royal Island, Canada
"This rain-forest paradise of moss-laden trees and tumbling rivers off the west coast of Canada is one of the few places in the world where you may have the privilege of encountering a spirit bear (whitish-

colored black bears spiritually important to the Kitasoo/Xaixais people). Think *Lord of the Rings* film sets and you may come close to picturing the tangled, mossy web of old trees that makes exploring here so magical."

Arches National Park, Moab, Utah
"Embedded deep within the Colorado Plateau where it sprawls into Utah, Moab is the center of a quintessential North American outdoor playground. Set in a desertlike arena of canyons, natural rock arches, white-water rivers, and imposing sandstone towers, it boasts access to a unique collection of otherworldly landforms. There is no shortage of activities here, but the easily reached and expertly managed hiking trails of the national park offer the best snapshot of this grand spectacular landscape." *arches.national-park.com*

Healthy travel

There's nothing worse than becoming ill during your long-anticipated vacation. Instead of just hoping for the best, there are ways to increase your chances of having a happy, healthy trip, according to travel experts.

Traveler's diarrhea is one of the biggest culprits when it comes to putting a damper on a getaway. It often results when tourists eat from "beautiful buffets set up in the sun in tropical islands," says Dr. Martin Wolfe of Traveler's Medical Service of Washington. His advice: Avoid ice cubes, cold salads, foods from buffets and street vendors, diluted fruit juices, and milk. Best bets often are hot, cooked foods; fruits that can be peeled; and carbonated beverages. And even a little bit of water can do damage: Sometimes people refuse to drink local tap water but then make the mistake of brushing their teeth with it, Wolfe says. Instead, use bottled water for everything.

A good traveler has no fixed plans, and is not intent on arriving.
—Lao Tzu

10 great places to savor the wild blue yonder

From early stick-and-canvas constructions to the Saturn V's *7.5 million pounds of thrust, the exhibits at aviation museums are over the top. Pat Trenner, a pilot and senior editor at* Air and Space *magazine, shares her favorites.*

Old Rhinebeck Aerodrome, Rhinebeck, New York
Some people plan their vacations around the Aerodrome's 20-minute open-cockpit biplane tours above the lush Hudson Valley. They also come for the vast collection of early airplanes and to watch air shows. *oldrhinebeck.org*

Fantasy of Flight Museum, Polk City, Florida
Veterans get VIP treatment here; requests to sit in the cockpit are granted whenever possible. It's "a classy presentation of the history of flight, civil and military, through the 1950s." There's a portly Grumman Duck, a *Spirit of St. Louis* replica, and a Bell 47G helicopter. "Buy a hot-air-balloon ride for dessert." *fantasyofflight.com*

EAA Airventure Museum, Oshkosh, Wisconsin
"The Experimental Aircraft Association has a huge group of 'homebuilders'—pilots who eschew the conventional and choose to build their own craft, from scratch or from a partially prebuilt kit." The family-friendly museum holds a variety of eclectic aircraft, including 2004's *SpaceShipOne,* the first privately financed, crewed spaceflight. *airventuremuseum.org*

Flying Heritage Collection, Everett, Washington
"Gazillionaire Paul Allen has collected 20th-century military aircraft and restored them to pristine condition using only original materials." A number are flown regularly for visitors, including a North American P-51 Mustang and "a Curtiss Jenny from the barnstorming era." Oral histories from those who flew the aircraft give visitors the stories behind the planes. *flyingheritage.com*

National Museum of the United States Air Force, Dayton, Ohio
The collection of *Air Force One* jets is a big draw here. Visitors can board and "see the desks and beds in FDR, Truman, Eisenhower,

and JFK presidential planes." Plus, there's "an A-to-Z collection of international airpower," from early balloons to modern-day craft. *nationalmuseum.af.mil*

Evergreen Aviation Museum, McMinnville, Oregon
"This is the final resting space of Howard Hughes's behemoth flying boat." Hughes "loathed the 'Spruce Goose' nickname bestowed by the press; it was constructed of birch." *sprucegoose.org*

National Air and Space Museum, Washington, D.C.
Billed as the world's most-visited museum, it's on the Mall and in the Steven F. Udvar-Hazy annex near Dulles airport outside Washington, and it's "a no-kidding must-see. Touch a moon rock, see Charles Lindbergh's *Spirit of St. Louis,* Chuck Yeager's Bell X-1 that broke the sound barrier in 1947, and—holiest of holies—the Wright Brothers' Flyer that started it all in 1903." At the annex, enter a mock control tower; also, you'll see the *Enola Gay* and the space shuttle *Enterprise. nasm.si.edu*

Kennedy Space Center Apollo/Saturn V Center, near Titusville, Florida
Named for the president who was focused on putting a man on the moon and located near NASA's actual launch area, this museum is
dedicated to astronauts
and all things Apollo.
"Relive the first manned
Saturn V launch in a
reconstructed 1960s
Apollo control room."
kennedyspacecenter.com

Museum of Flight, Seattle, Washington
It's the only place where civilians can sit in the cockpit of a U.S. SR-71 spy plane. It's also where a pioneering fighter aircraft, a 1914 Italian Caproni, is displayed after having been walled up in a monastery for more than a half century. Start your tour in the Red Barn, "where William E. Boeing took his first steps to becoming one of the world's aerospace giants." Check out historic Lear jets and the Concorde. *museumofflight.org*

Air Force Flight Test Center Museum, Edwards Air Force Base, California

"This is where military experimental planes first went supersonic: Mach 1, 2, 3. Lots of exotic stuff here." Future military aircraft are tested on this site; it's like going on an aircraft safari, because you never know what's winging overhead. *edwards.af.mil/index.asp*

NIGHTLIFE
10 great places to forge fun

Nightlife spots are playing off the do-it-yourself trend by inviting partiers to create their fun. Zagat editor Eric Grossman suggests these haunts that encourage participation.

Stats Sports Bar, Atlanta, Georgia

"Conveniently located a Hail Mary [pass] from the Georgia Dome and Phillips Arena, this huge bar is a sports fan's dream thanks to not only the plethora of giant TVs but because it was the first bar in the United States to feature self-service beer taps. Each of the four state-of-the-art 'beer tables' feature two personal beer taps, ensuring thirsty fans never have to flag down a server again." *statsatl.com*

Karaoke Duet 48, New York, New York

"With 16 private rooms, this establishment lets armchair [*American*] *Idol* contestants be the star of their own concert without worrying about performing in front of strangers. The encyclopedic song library is updated monthly and includes more than 100,000 tunes in a variety of languages." *karaokeduet.com*

Dan's Café, Washington, D.C.

"College types, interns, and post-grads love Dan's approach. For less than the cost of a couple of cocktails at one of the trendier options down the street, customers get their own small bottle of booze, plus mixers, and make their own drinks."

W.I.N.O., New Orleans, Louisiana

The Wine Institute of New Orleans is "an oenophile's dream. This Warehouse District establishment—a sophisticated respite from the nearby Bourbon Street madness—combines a wine bar, shop, and school. The main attraction is a state-of-the-art Italian-made wine serving system that, upon inserting a prepaid store debit card, allows customers to pour an ounce's taste or a half or full glass." *winoschool.com*

Castro Theatre, San Francisco, California

"This historic movie theater—linchpin of the colorful Castro neighborhood—reminds us that not all interactive nightlife options must include alcohol. Scores of revelers pack this grande dame for its frequently held singalong nights, where crowds participate by doing their best to keep up with the stars of *Grease* and *Hairspray,* among others, on the big screen." *castrotheatre.com*

Middlesex Lounge, Cambridge, Massachusetts

"Cool without being pretentious, this popular Cambridge hangout takes on a different shape nightly—literally—as lounge lizards customize the room's low, movable benches and tables to suit their fancy." The rocking rotation of entertainment, from hedonistic dance parties to techno/house DJs, reigns here, so the rhythm rules the furniture placement. DJs keep things jumping, "occasionally encouraging revelers to move their tables aside to form an impromptu dance floor." *middlesexlounge.us*

Billy Bob's, Fort Worth, Texas

"Since opening in 1981, the world's largest honky tonk has offered up a truly unique assortment of nightlife options, all under one roof. At night, guests can catch a big-name country music act, shoot some pool, join in a line dance, take a dance lesson, watch live bull riding, chow on some authentic BBQ, or shop for cowboy gear—all with a drink in hand." Space is rarely an issue: At 127,000 square feet, Billy Bob's can handle more than 6,000 guests at a time. And with more than 30 bars, patrons rarely have to wait for a drink. *billybobstexas.com*

Beauty Bar, San Diego, California

"This small national nightlife chain provides the beautiful and beauty-minded with a stylish spot in which to enjoy a mani/pedi or other salon service while partying with the cool crowd. Vintage hair dryers and other atmospheric accoutrements make for a retro-chic setting." *beautybar.com*

Bar at Times Square, New York New York Casino, Las Vegas, Nevada
"It may sound kitschy, but this always—and often rowdy—Vegas homage to NYC is a must-visit for fans of dueling-piano bars. After a drink or two, most patrons find themselves pouring their hearts out while singing along with a kaleidoscopic array of tourists from all over the world." A pair of pianists rip into everything from classic rock to rap. *nynyhotelcasino.com*

24:London, London, England
"In a city full of scene-chasing options, London's 24 ups the ante when it comes to futuristic nightlife." This club dubs itself the world's first interactive bar, and nearly every aspect can be controlled by scene-seekers. Interactive projection screens allow bargoers to choose the images on the floor-to-ceiling backdrops in private booths, as well as on the tabletops. "Even the tables are interactive, as an empty glass, when placed down, sends out an alert to the bartender." *24london.eu*

10 great places to cozy up to a warm winter drink

"Nothing beats the cold like a piping-hot drink," says Nick Mautone, master mixologist and author of Raising the Bar: Better Drinks, Better Entertaining. *"Whether your taste runs to nogs, grogs, toddies, or tonics, there's a potent potable to warm body and spirit." Mautone shares some super hot spots serving tasty winter warmers.*

The Peak, Four Seasons Hotel, Jackson Hole, Wyoming
While you're in snow country, order "a Corbet's Toddy, a grown-up hot chocolate made with Cointreau and Kahlua. The steaming brew is named after Corbet's Couloir," a well-known and difficult Jackson Hole run.
fourseasons.com/jacksonhole/dining/the_peak.html

Mondo Mocha Cafe, Doubletree Hotel Atlanta NW/ Marietta, Atlanta, Georgia
After working out in the pool or the fitness center, relax at the hotel's Mondo Mocha Cafe for "a Mondo

Mocha Toddy, made with rich dark rum, mocha-flavored cocoa-coffee, and whipped cream." *mondomochacafe.com*

DYLAN Prime, New York, New York
Warm up in the Big Apple with a tempting concoction called "Hot Buttered Apples, a mix of chunked fruit, apple schnapps, Drambuie, brown sugar, cinnamon, water, and butter." Want something a little spicier? Go for "the house specialty, a warm and wonderful sangria." *dylanprime.com*

Turner Fisheries Restaurant & Bar, Boston, Massachusetts
Tame chilly Beantown winters with the innovative drink called Chocolate Orange Truffle. "It's a dark and delicious hot chocolate swirled with Stoli orange vodka and Grand Marnier, garnished with a dark-chocolate-dipped blood-orange wedge." *turnersboston.com*

W Bar, W Hotel, Seattle, Washington
Visitors and locals alike stop in at this urbane urban tower of a hotel (check out the much-talked-about steel-and-mesh pyramid on top) for the "Goldfinger, a surefire warm-up created with Grey Goose vanilla vodka, Goldschlager, and Oregon chai tea." *earthocean.net/wbar.html*

Tosca Cafe Bar, San Francisco, California
"Choose from more than ten delicious Irish coffees at this well-known coffeehouse and bar," one of the city's oldest, known for its ambience and array of tasty java drinks. The house specialty, "a cappuccino spiked with brandy and Ghirardelli chocolate, is memorable." *toscacafesf.com*

Westin La Paloma Resort & Spa, Tucson, Arizona
The sun may blaze during the day, but cool Arizona nights beg for a "Sonoran Monk, made with Frangelica and Amaretto, topped with a mound of whipped cream, which is then drizzled with Chambord." A decadent dessert to sip in the desert. *westinlapalomaresort.com*

Rooftop Lounge, Triple Creek Ranch, Darby, Montana
Before or after your stroll in the snow at "this awesome Montana getaway, situated adjacent to the wilds of the Bitterroot Wilderness, try the ranch's Not-So-Classic Hot Buttered Rum, which combines

rum and hot water with vanilla ice cream, butter, brown sugar, cinnamon, cloves, and allspice." *triplecreekranch.com*

Fonda San Miguel Restaurant, Austin, Texas
Stop in at this stunning hacienda for the unique "Coconog Batida, an amazing warm Latin eggnog that is part piña colada, part eggnog made with white and dark rum, Coco Lopez, milk, guava nectar, and fresh mint." *fondasanmiguel.com*

Eleven, Pittsburgh, Pennsylvania
"Served in a contemporary yet extremely warm and beautiful lounge, Eleven's Hot Buttered Rum has an interesting twist, combining Captain Morgan Spiced Rum and butterscotch candy." This drink provides a smooth and creamy antidote to a frigid night.
bigburrito.com/eleven/eleven.shtml

10 great places for margaritas and more

Margaritas have that way of making everyone feel like having a fiesta any time of year. Kate Krader, editor of Food & Wine Cocktails 2009, *and Jim Meehan, deputy editor and master mixologist, share the best places to have one— or two—of these cool, tasty concoctions.*

Tommy's, San Francisco, California
For the best margaritas in the country, Krader and Meehan suggest a stop at this West Coast bar, where the bartender makes a classic concoction with tequila, lime juice, and agave nectar. "The bar is nothing fancy, but their tequila selection is incredible." *tommystequila.com*

Jimmy's Bar, Aspen, Colorado
"Colorado consumes more tequila than any other state besides Texas and California. Jimmy's, hidden in a fancy mall in the middle of glitzy Aspen, has a huge selection of tequilas and agave spirits, and they make terrific margaritas." *jimmysaspen.com*

Oyamel, Washington, D.C.
This D.C. eatery serves up a traditional margarita with a twist: "a topping of salt-air foam." *oyamel.com*

Rivera, Los Angeles, California
"In the late 1980s, John Sedlar put haute Mexican food on the map in the United States. Now he's back with a Los Angeles pan-Latin restaurant, where they have a mix of premium and seasonal tequilas on tap." For some serious royal treatment, take a turn in the bronze-and-leather chairs dedicated to tequila tastings—the chairs have special holders for tequila flights. *riverarestaurant.com*

Petrossian Bar at the Bellagio, Las Vegas, Nevada
Sin City is rarely referred to as the home to anything purist, but Vegas bartenders know their stuff. "The best margaritas around the country are often found at purist cocktail establishments. Petrossian Bar, the swank cocktail bar at Las Vegas's Bellagio, is one of those establishments." *bellagio.com*

Nacional 27, Chicago, Illinois
"The margaritas are hyper-seasonal and fresh-ingredient driven." The seemingly endless menu here can confuse a novice, so try one of their regular margaritas, like the breakfast margarita or the luxe margarita, or pick a seasonal creation such as the smoky passion-fruit margarita. *n27chicago.com*

Mayahuel, New York, New York
This mescal and tequila bar is owned by star mixologist Philip Ward, "one of the most creative drink makers in the country." *mayahuelny.com*

Tequilas, Philadelphia, Pennsylvania
With a name like Tequilas, there's no doubt the duo behind this elegant hacienda-style restaurant knows its stuff. "Restaurateur David Suro, who grew up near agave fields in the Mexican state of Jalisco, serves drinks by mixologist Junior Merino." There's no shortage of tequilas behind the bar here, which serves up around 100 variations. *tequilasphilly.com*

Lonesome Dove, Fort Worth, Texas
You know what they say: "Don't mess with Texas." Apparently, that applies to their margaritas as well. Lonesome Dove evokes the American West with its inventive menu of big food like Texas elk sausage and wild boar ribs. "The rustic Fort Worth favorite, located in the historic Stockyards District, is also creative with its signature cocktails such as the jalapeño-cucumber margarita." *lonesomedovebistro.com*

Mercadito Cantina, New York, New York
"The exceptional margaritas range from traditional to Tres Cítricos, made with orange and habanero chile." Or try a mentirosa, featuring "tric-quila," a sake-based blend that imparts a crisper taste and smoother finish than regular tequila. *mercaditorestaurants.com*

Hotels: Take the soap but leave the TV

An OAG Travel Solutions survey says more than 60 percent of travelers admit to taking toiletries from hotel rooms. But do hotels mind if you stuff unopened bottles of soap and shampoo into your bag before you clear out?

"We don't say please don't take the amenities, but we find that people do," says a Ritz-Carlton spokesperson.

When does harmless souvenir grabbing become theft? A general manager of the Doubletree Guest Suites in New York won't ever forget the guest "who cleaned out pretty much everything in the suite." The loot included drinking glasses, a tray and ice bucket from the wet bar, the coffee maker, the bathroom scale and hair dryer, and all the clothes hangers.

That kind of theft is rare at upscale hotels among credit-card-carrying customers, says a loss prevention representative at Marriott. "They have to present identification rather than going under an assumed name."

Some travelers are conscientious. One traveler from St. Louis called the front desk where she was staying because she wasn't sure if a jar of mints with a bow on it was a gift. "They said the jar's not for you, but the mints are," she says. She collects hotel bathrobes from around the world and makes sure the hotel charges the robe to her bill.

10 great places to see the stars come out

A visit to Los Angeles often comes with a celebrity sighting or two. Where can you expect to see some of those stars unwind in L.A. or elsewhere across the United States? Tara de Lis, nightlife editor for Citysearch.com, lists favorite celeb watering holes.

Tao, New York, New York
Years after becoming a household name on *Sex and the City,* this Asian-fusion-eatery-cum-sizzling-nightspot is still a no-brainer for celeb spotting. "Though it's technically a restaurant, the bar scene is just as important, and after 10 P.M., it's hard to tell the difference." Don't let the 16-foot Buddha mislead you. "Tranquility does not reign supreme. It's loud, and last-minute tables can be difficult to finagle." *taorestaurant.com*

Polo Lounge, Los Angeles, California
This place "is an L.A. institution. It's a class act—no guest list, no attitude. And unlike many bar scenes that don't get going till after 10 P.M., it's open throughout the day for midweek power lunches and weekend brunches. So your chances of seeing a star are always high." *beverlyhillshotel.com/the-polo-lounge*

Mansion, Miami Beach, Florida
"True to its name, this expansive, 40,000-square-foot concept club features a Robin Leach–meets–South Beach party vibe—design elements include crystal chandeliers, Venetian-glass mirrors, and impressive dance-floor laser lights. A custom-designed sound system carves heavy hip-hop and electronic beats." *mansionmiami.com*

J-Bar, Aspen, Colorado
The Hotel Jerome's famous watering hole is a charming Old West–style saloon that, since opening in 1889, has been everything from a silver miners' haven to a celeb-studded après-ski retreat. "There's a saying in town that 'if you haven't been to J-Bar, you haven't been to Aspen.' " *hoteljerome.rockresorts.com*

Playboy Club, Las Vegas, Nevada

This club, on the 52nd floor of the Fantasy Tower of the Palms resort, sets itself apart from others in Vegas in that celebs are not tucked away in VIP rooms. "The retro factor is big. Most patrons never experienced Hef's originals—not that they'll care after seeing the sexy new Roberto Cavalli–designed Bunny outfits. Plus, there are high-stakes gaming tables. Getting in isn't easy or cheap, but here's the trick: Pay your cover at 8 P.M., get a reentry stamp, then dine at Nove Italiano, one floor below. Afterward, take the dedicated elevator back up to the 52nd floor, skipping the line—and get access to Moon after-hours lounge." *palms.com/playboy_club_1.php*

Marquee, New York, New York

"It's not a question of who has been there, but who hasn't. With a capacity of only 600 people and a tight door policy, your best bet is to get there early, dress to impress, and/or opt for bottle service." *marqueeny.com*

Area, Los Angeles, California

SBE Entertainment's Sam Nazarian is the hottest nightlife impresario in L.A. "He builds it, and celebs come. Six months later, he rebuilds it, and they come back. When once-hot nightspot Prey began to lose steam, he redesigned it to create Area, a lighter, more open lounge-y space with an expanded dance floor." The club often hosts A-list parties; keep an eye out for promoted nights and get there early. *sbeent.com*

Redwood Room, San Francisco, California

Sometimes derided by locals as being "too L.A.," the Clift Hotel's trendy Redwood Room is equal parts glamour and whimsy—and a mainstay for celebrity sightings. "First-timers can't get enough of the signature wall portraits, with eyes that seem to follow you around the room à la Scooby-Doo." Hotel guests are given preferential entry. *www.clifthotel.com/default.aspx#/explore/?id=redwoodroom*

NoMI Lounge, Chicago, Illinois

The NoMI Lounge is a low-key space adjacent to the Park Hyatt's acclaimed restaurant of the same name. "For many, it's a nice pre-dinner drink spot; for others it's a destination in its own right."

Located on the seventh floor, the lounge also offers spectacular views. "Best of all, no cover charge, no unruly crowds or queues." *nomirestaurant.com/gallery/nomi/setting/lounge.html*

Antone's, Austin, Texas
This is where Stevie Ray Vaughn launched his career and where thousands of bands hope to do the same every year at the annual South by Southwest music festival. Named after late owner and legendary bluesman Clifford Antone, the venue has hosted late-night jam sessions with everyone from Bonnie Raitt to U2. "It's a down-home, laid-back joint with a fun crowd of serious music lovers of all ages." *antones.net*

10 great places to carry a torch for tiki bars

Slip on your grass skirt and turn a road trip into a tiki adventure. "Starting in the 1930s and picking up steam after World War II, we had this pop-culture phenomenon where people were interested in things that were exotic," says James Teitelbaum, author of Tiki Road Trip. *"People started opening up Polynesian-themed bars." Teitelbaum shares his top tiki locales.*

Alibi Lounge, Portland, Oregon
You can't get much more tiki than this. The Alibi Lounge, which was transformed into a tiki bar in the late '40s, features such tiki standards as neon torches, fountains, and a Day-Glo mural of dancing hula girls.

Hala Kahiki, River Grove, Illinois
Located in suburban Chicago, the Hala Kahiki is a dimly lit restaurant filled with tiki artifacts and the sounds of soothing tropical music. "When I think of what a tiki bar should be, this place comes to mind. More than anything, tiki is about escapism. It's about wanting to step away from the smog, your car, your job, money worries, and step into a tropical paradise where you can get away." *hala-kahiki.com*

Tiki-Ti, Los Angeles, California
This tiny, family-run bar, opened along the Sunset Strip in the '60s, features noteworthy tiki drinks. "People who are into tiki are very into drinks. There's a misconception that they are fruity and sweet and will give you a stomachache. That's true in the second-rate places, but the guys at Tiki-Ti squeeze their fruit juices fresh and use quality rum. They put a lot of care into each drink. They're not too sweet." *tiki-ti.com*

Tonga Room, San Francisco, California
Tucked into the Fairmont Hotel in San Francisco is a vintage tiki restaurant built around what used to be a pool. "There's a lagoon in the middle of the restaurant, and every half hour there's a rainstorm. There's a soundtrack of thunder and lights to make it seem like lightning. You go for the atmosphere." *fairmont.com/sanfrancisco*

Jardin Tiki, Montreal, Quebec, Canada
Jardin Tiki, near Montreal's Olympic Village, has been a huge tribute to tiki since the 1970s. "Visually, it's beautiful. There's a huge atrium filled with tropical plants and strategically placed tikis. And they have a turtle pond with real turtles."

Forbidden Island, Alameda, California
Forbidden Island's decor includes blowfish lamps, private bamboo booths, and a wall of spears and clubs. "There's no TV in the place. I feel strongly about that. It distracts from the lounge; the bright, blue glow ruins the mysterious lounge feel. There are a lot of new tiki places open, but very few are willing to go whole hog with the vibe. Forbidden Island does." *forbiddenislandalameda.com*

Trader Vic's, Atlanta, Georgia
Donn Beach and Victor Bergeron really made tiki culture popular in the '30s and '40s with their restaurant chains Don the Beachcomber and Trader Vic's. "Don the Beachcombers are gone, but Trader Vic's is thriving." The Atlanta locale is one of the earliest still around and "exemplifies what the tiki vibe is all about." The restaurant, in the lower level of the Atlanta Hilton, is a labyrinth of dark rooms stuffed with artifacts. "The drinks are amazing. Trader Vic invented most of the drinks, and his recipes have been preserved." *tradervicsatl.com*

Kowloon, Saugus, Massachusetts
Outside Boston is one of the largest tiki restaurants in the United
States. The Kowloon is guarded by a 15-foot tiki carving. Inside is a
lagoon, a room composed entirely of half of a schooner, and lots of
tikis. "There are thousands of islands in the Pacific, so there are thousands of styles and reasons for a tiki. Some were tributes. Some were
fertility symbols, and some were just art." *kowloonrestaurant.com*

Mai-Kai, Fort Lauderdale, Florida
"It's the last of its kind," Teitelbaum says of this restaurant, which
opened in 1956. "It's crammed to the gills with tikis, some of which
were carved in the Pacific. Every night there's a floor show with a
band, traditional dances, and a DJ. The bar is amazing; they make
some of the best drinks." *maikai.com*

Omni Hut, Smyrna, Tennessee
The Omni Hut, outside Nashville, is the oldest Chinese restaurant
in Tennessee. It has two dining rooms, a waterfall, ceiling fishnets,
and lots of tikis. The best part is owner Polly Walls. "She has a smile
and a warm welcome for everyone. Southern hospitality meets tiki
culture at the Omni Hut." *omnihut.com*

10 great places to slip
into a modern speakeasy

*Prohibition ended back on December 5, 1933, but the
intrigue of those days remains in secret hangouts across the
country. Derek Brown, ambassador to the Museum of the
American Cocktail, offers his list of great (legal) speakeasies.*

PDT, New York, New York
Historically, speakeasies were illegal operations—the owners were
avoiding taxes, serving illegal immigrants, or pouring cocktails during
Prohibition. So mum was the word, and secrecy still prevails at many
of today's speakeasies. At PDT in the East Village, patrons enter
through a phone booth in an adjoining hot dog shop. "You have to go
through some effort to get in there. Once you do, the cocktails are
outstanding. They have cocktails you would find pre-Prohibition, as
well as ones they've created themselves."

The Velvet Tango Room, Cleveland, Ohio
"They research their drinks and try and bring you back to another era of cocktails. They even have a glass for almost every drink. It's similar to how there's a Burgundy glass, a Champagne glass, and a port glass for wine. It's the same thing with cocktails. You can have different glasses to emphasize different cocktails."
velvettangoroom.com

The Swizzle Stick Bar, New Orleans, Louisiana
The bar at Cafe Adelaide "is not a speakeasy in the traditional sense. They do have these terrific, artisanal cocktails." Hard to overlook among the surroundings: a giant block of ice in the middle of the room. "Most bars use regular ice. It's like a chef cooking with Sterno. Bartenders blend and mix by chilling things down with ice. Being able to control that and having the proper ice is very important. Speakeasies tend to pay attention to those details." *cafeadelaide.com*

Bourbon & Branch, San Francisco, California
The decor is one factor that really differentiates many of today's speakeasies from other bars. "Historically, they weren't all that beautiful and elegant, but there's an emphasis on that now." Besides great cocktails, Bourbon & Branch has "a handsome environment.... It's masculine and elegant." *bourbonandbranch.com*

PX, Alexandria, Virginia
PX has all the trappings of a speakeasy—secretiveness, elegant decor, and creative cocktails. "There's no sign, just a blue light indicating when it's open. It has a gorgeous interior. There are chandeliers hanging from the ceiling and vintage shakers around the bar. There's an expectation that gentlemen would wear a jacket. It's not strictly enforced, but you'd feel out of place without it."
eamonnsdublinchipper.com

The Violet Hour, Chicago, Illinois
This speakeasy's name references a quote by the writer Bernard DeVoto, who described that quiet, magical time at dusk as "the violet hour, the hour of hush." It's the perfect time for a cocktail, and the Violet Hour aims to be incredibly relaxing. "They have hush tones, a fireplace, and great pre-Prohibition cocktails."
thevioleurhour.com

Apothecary, Philadelphia, Pennsylvania
"This isn't a tiny, discreet bar by any means, but guests are asked to
abide by rules." Apothecary's rules include, "No shouting, scream-
ing, yelling, howling, hollering, yollering, or other loud vocalizations
unless necessary to warn the rest of us of some impending calamity."
apothecarylounge.com

The Florida Room, Miami, Florida
The bar in South Beach's Delano hotel "is more contemporary; it's
not referencing pre-Prohibition. Like a lot of today's speakeasies,
it's an elegant cocktail lounge. They have a beautiful piano, a Lucite
grand piano, food on the bar, and then amazing cocktails."
delano-hotel.com

Drink, Boston, Massachusetts
There's no cocktail list here. Instead, patrons request a flavor
and a liquor, and the bartenders whip up something on the spot.
"Sometimes, people say the drinks at a speakeasy take too long, that
they're too labor-intensive. It's a trade-off. It might take a couple
extra minutes, but you don't have to pace up and down the bar. And
the drinks are worth it." *drinkfortpoint.com*

The Edison, Los Angeles, California
This lounge and cabaret-style bar "isn't exactly a speakeasy. But it
has a classic aura and great cocktails." *edisondowntown.com*

AND ANOTHER THING . . .

Al Capone's haunts

Modern-day speakeasies not enough for you? Just 40 miles west
of Chicago, Al Capone's Hideaway & Steakhouse still stands at
35W337 Riverside Drive in St. Charles, Illinois. The notorious gangster operated in the Windy City from 1919 until his arrest for tax evasion in 1931. According to David Borgenicht, editor of *Crime Scene
USA: A Traveler's Guide to the Locations of Famous and Infamous
Murders, Robberies, Kidnappings, and Other Unlawful Acts,* "a sign by
the urinal reads, 'Big Al hung out here.' "

FESTIVALS

10 great places to celebrate food

Americans love their hot-weather food festivals—tasty celebrations of regional specialty cooking spiced up with local fun and entertainment. "These festivals are somewhat kitschy, somewhat obsessive, and a whole lot of fun," says Dana Cowin, editor in chief of Food & Wine *magazine. "For every food obsession, there seems to be a festival and a huge number of avid fans." Cowin offers a sumptuous sampling of gastronomic events.*

Gilroy Garlic Festival, Gilroy, California
"Garlic in every guise, savory and sweet, is the reason 13,000 people trek to Gilroy, the heart of California garlic-growing country. Food vendors sell over two tons of garlicky dishes to visitors who come for the food, live music, shopping, and the cook-off." *gilroygarlicfestival.com*

Maine Lobster Festival, Rockland, Maine
In addition to thousands of visitors downing tons of lobster, this summer festival features a cooking contest, live music, a lobster-crate race, and more. "Don't miss the Coronation of the Maine Sea Goddess." *mainelobsterfestival.com*

Hatch Valley Chile Festival, Hatch, New Mexico
"Chile fanatics come to little Hatch Island, the self-described Chile Capital of the World, to feast on fiery burritos, enchiladas, chile con carne, tacos, chiles rellenos, and chile-topped burgers and to buy top-quality dried chiles and chile powder." *hatchchilefest.com*

National Hard Crab Derby, Crisfield, Maryland
"At this Labor Day tribute to all things crabby, thousands of spectators come to watch crustaceans race—and eat them. Crabs are considered one of the meanest creatures on land or water, but don't let that deter you. Pros will be on hand to give tips on extracting crabmeat from the shell." *crisfieldevents.com/crabderby.aspx*

Okra Strut Festival, Irmo, South Carolina

"Who knew there were so many okra lovers in the world? This two-day festival, celebrating the oft-maligned green vegetable and launched as a way to raise money to build a new town library, now attracts more than 50,000 aficionados. There's a parade, a petting zoo, rides, a street dance, and plenty of okra in an array of dishes." *irmookrastrut.com*

Apple Squeeze Festival, Lenox Village, Massachusetts

"To celebrate the cider season's first apple pressing, Lenox Village is transformed into a country fair, with sidewalk sales, bands, crafts demonstrations, face painting, a giant pumpkin weigh-off, a children's dog show (with canine costumes), and lots and lots of apples."

Marion County Country Ham Days, Lebanon, Kentucky

A festival to celebrate country ham, bourbon, and tobacco? Why not? "Visitors can participate in a pig-calling contest or pipe-smoking competition, bid on a champion ham at auction, or dive into a Southern breakfast of scrambled eggs, sliced tomatoes, fried apples, biscuits, and, of course, ham." *hamdays.com*

Monterey Bay Strawberry Festival, Watsonville, California

"From beautiful plump strawberries eaten plain to strawberry tamales, this festival is a strawberry extravaganza that attracts more than 74,000 visitors. Hallmarks include the Gooey Contest, involving a strawberry-pie-eating competition, a strawberry relay race, and more." *mbsf.com*

Oyster Bay Oysterfest, Long Island, New York

Attendees of this October festival "consume bivalves in every conceivable form.... There's also a shucking contest, a 5K run, an exhibit of historic boats, and an oyster-eating competition." *theoysterfestival.org*

Barbecue Festival, Lexington, North Carolina

"Lexington probably has more barbecue joints per capita than any other town. At the festival, visitors can eat pulled-pork sandwiches; watch the Tour de Pig or Hawg Run; or enjoy gospel music, square dancing, and blues performances. The Carolina-style barbecue in a vinegar-based sauce is worth trying." *barbecuefestival.com*

Pulses race at Monaco

In the world of lavish spending, Monaco is a renowned tax haven and watering hole. In the world of fairy-tale glamour, it's where a movie star named Kelly turned into a princess named Grace. In sports, it's a car race—the car race of all car races for some and a delightful anachronism to others.

Here are the top 10 things to look for and listen to at the Monaco Grand Prix:

1. The scenery. There is no more glamorous racecourse on the planet.

2. Who wins the pole. Because there is so little passing, whoever wins the pole is nearly guaranteed to win the race—unless he or his team screw up.

3. The in-car camera shots. Cars speeding from sunlight, into the tunnel (the fastest portion of the course, at about 186 mph), and back into the sunlight at 174 mph along the harbor...it's a treat.

4. The yachts. The shots might only be a second or two long, but surely the sharp eyes of aficionados can pick up the really expensive ones berthed in the harbor.

5. The exuberance of the SPEED commentating crew. They not only love the sport but also possess vast and intimate knowledge.

6. The cars. True technological wonders.

7. The glam drivers whose status in Europe, Asia, and Latin America places them in a stratosphere some rock stars would envy.

8. The strategy. How many pit stops? Light fuel load or heavy? When to race with soft tires and when to race with hard tires? Teamwork—or the lack thereof. And the heavy rain showers forecast to drench the principality could exacerbate everything.

9. The start. Every Formula 1 green flag is a prescription for chaos and destruction.

10. The finish. Just how large will the winning margin be?

10 great places to keep the party going worldwide

*Keep your noisemakers handy for these fab festivals.
Martin Dunford, publishing director of* Rough Guides *and
contributing editor of* World Party: Rough Guide to the
World's Best Festivals, *shares his picks.*

Junkanoo, Nassau, the Bahamas
Howl into a conch shell or ring a cowbell and take to the streets with half the island population on New Year's Day. This celebration dates back to the 16th century, when plantation slaves were given a few days off to whoop it up. The excitement of extravagant costumes and colorful, mile-high headdresses is intensified by West African drumbeats and brass bands. "Parades flood the streets in a reeling mass of singing and dancing—it's a celebration not to be missed." *caribtickets.com*

Carnival, Port of Spain, Trinidad
Don your costume and join the steel bands and bikini-clad masqueraders marching in the streets. "There's nothing like this pre-Lenten orgy of feasting and dancing. Rio is still the daddy of them all, but this year try somewhere different, like Trinidad, where this joyful, rum-soaked celebration is the biggest in the Caribbean. It's a national obsession." *ncctt.org*

Monaco Grand Prix, Principality of Monaco
People-watching is as much fun as this May event that draws the world's elite. Raise a glass of bubbly with the high rollers at the Hotel de Paris bar. "Pack your best clothes, especially if you want to risk your shirt at the city-state's famous casino. It's hard but not impossible to get seats for the race, which is the highlight of the grand prix calendar." *yourmonaco.com/grand_prix*

Las Fallas, Valencia, Spain
This fiery festival, held in March, originated with the ancient practice of carpenters welcoming spring by burning the wooden candelabras used to light their shops in winter. "It's a party of ferocious proportions, with firecrackers and bonfires and the *fallas* themselves—

hundreds of doll-like effigies are carried on the final day in a parade and put to the torch—a fantastic spectacle." *fallasfromvalencia.com*

São João Festival, Porto, Portugal
This coastal city celebrates its saints' day (São João, or St. John, is the most important) each year on June 23. "Fireworks, bonfires, and roaming bands of hammer- and leek-wielding lunatics keep the crowds entertained until the first rays of dawn appear on the beach."

Queen's Day, Amsterdam, the Netherlands
Already known as a party paradise, this Dutch city has an all-nighter on the queen's birthday, April 30. "Lots of drink is consumed, and everyone goes berserk on the water—rowboats, barges, and old fishing vessels crammed with people, crates of beer, and sound systems pound their way around the canals. Get on a boat or just watch from the comfort of a nearby bridge—or bar." *amsterdam.info/queensday/*

Wine War, Haro, Spain
Wear white and bring a water gun, then fill it with free wine, compliments of the city council, for this super-soaker spectacle. "Held annually at the end of June, it's a modern-day remnant of the feuds between rival towns of this wine-producing area in which everyone drenches everyone else in Rioja."

Naadam, Ulaanbaatar, Mongolia
"This event is less about participation, focused as it is on the national sports of archery, wrestling, and horsemanship. It's an experience you won't forget, especially once you've squeezed into a nomad's tent [and] swilled Genghis Khan vodka with 300-pound wrestlers while a woman in silk robes serves you platters of sheep innards." *naadam-festival.mn*

La Tomatina, Buñol, Spain
During this summer festival in the small town of Buñol in eastern Spain, truckloads of tomatoes are unloaded in the square, a rocket is fired, and thousands of festive food-fighters reduce the fruit to a juicy explosion of seeds, skin, and pulp. "It's all about joining in, and most

people find that chucking around 130,000 kilos (286,000 pounds) of tomatoes at each other is a strangely liberating experience. It's the one party at which you can say that you've painted the town red." *cyberspain.com/life/tomatina.htm*

Day of the Dead, Mexico
"Celebrated on the first two days of November, this is both a time of remembrance for the dearly departed and a celebration of the eternal cycle of life. Favorite dishes are placed on flower-bedecked altars, and, come nightfall, graveyards resemble roadside restaurants, as picnic tables and chairs are arranged, tortillas are fried, and tequila is consumed in memory of the deceased. Truly, an absorbing and culturally fascinating way to end a year of festivals."

10 great places for hot fun in the wintertime

Snowbirds fly south. Snow animals head north and west, where the white stuff is welcomed by hearty souls eager to celebrate the real essence of winter at seasonal festivals. "Winter doesn't last long enough for those who like their parties outside," says Greg Ditrinco, executive editor of SKI *magazine. Here, Ditrinco shares some hot cold spots to spice up the season.*

Wintersköl, Aspen, Colorado
"Gone are the days of the bawdy wet-T-shirt contest, but with a parade, canine fashion show, snow sculptures, fireworks, and general carousing, Aspen still strips off its pretensions for its winter celebration.... The annual community bash dates back to a quiet January in 1951, when a few locals organized a *skol* (or toast) to winter to liven things up." *stayaspensnowmass.com/p-winterskol-festival.php*

St. Paul Winter Carnival, Minneapolis/St. Paul, Minnesota
"Like a large state fair held in winter, this big-deal carnival attracts half a million visitors to its famous ice palace alone. Billed as the largest and oldest winter festival in America, it features scores of events, including car racing on ice, fireworks, torchlight parades, a frozen 5K race, ski and hockey competitions, and more." *winter-carnival.com*

Sundance Film Festival, Park City, Utah
"This very cool event" offers viewings, parties, and thrills—both inside and out. No coincidence that "the most famous film festival in America is held smack in the middle of ski country." *festival.sundance.org*

Polar Bear Jump Off, Seward, Alaska
"One of the bigger events in this town, the festival includes a variety of homespun events (a parade, oyster-slurping contest, used-book sale, a dog show, even a hair cutoff), along with the costumed jump into icy Resurrection Bay." *sewardak.org/news-events/polarbear.htm*

Telus World Ski & Snowboard Festival, Whistler/Blackcomb, British Columbia, Canada
"Many events claim to be the biggest party on snow. In this case, it looks to be true as hordes of skiers, boarders, and revelers head to Whistler for a ten-day adieu to winter. The lineup includes the World Skiing Invitational, Filmmaker Showdown, World Snowboard Invitational, and free concerts with 30 bands." *wssf.com*

International Snow Sculpture Championships, Breckenridge, Colorado
"Sculptors from all corners of the globe carve massive works of art from 12-foot-tall, 20-ton blocks of ice and snow. Sixteen teams chisel, shape, water, and freeze their creations for a week in this juried competition."

Primitive Biathlon, Smugglers' Notch, Vermont
"It's hard not to love a competition in which the rules address the misfiring of single-barrel muzzle-loaders. . . . Participants race on wooden snowshoes and fire at targets in a timed competition." The biathlon is part of the Heritage Winterfest, which features sleigh rides, ice-skating, and fireworks. *primitivebiathlon.com*

International Horse Races, St. Moritz, France
"Racing on snow first began here in 1907. See and be seen at this feast of entertainment and elegance, the social highlight of the season."

Shovel Racing Championships, Angel Fire, New Mexico
"Angel Fire Resort workers discovered that riding their shovels

down the mountain was the quickest way to the lodge bar. That blue-collar commute has evolved into the Shovel Racing Championships, in which competitors ride contraptions that you won't find in any hardware store." *angelfireresort.com*

National Ski-Joring Finals, Red Lodge, Montana
"Enjoy thrills and skills as horse and rider tow skiers at breakneck speed around slalom gates and over jumps for the fastest times. If that's not enough, how about skiers launching off jumps for distances of over 60 feet!" *redlodge.com/ski-joring*

Sundance "summer camp"

Each January, hundreds of Hollywood trendsetters, media types, and everyone who is anyone descend upon the Sundance Film Festival to wallow in the hype of the latest must-see movie, get a whiff of the next big thing, and ski a little on the company dime.

But Sundance—an empire begun by Robert Redford in 1981—is much more than a trendy film festival. Far from the media glare, Hollywood bigwigs mingle with aspiring filmmakers in an atmosphere of mutual respect and camaraderie. In a pine-dotted hideaway tucked deep in the Rocky Mountains—the nearest store a good 15 miles away—is the Sundance Filmmakers Laboratory. No chance of finding cell phones or sycophants here. Entertainment consists of a hike up to Stewart Falls or a creekside stroll.

Each year, 10 to 12 novice filmmakers—out of 3,000 applicants worldwide—are chosen to spend a month at the Sundance Resort, all expenses paid, to work on key scenes in their scripts. Based on the merits of one submitted screenplay, lab participants, some of whom have no hands-on directing experience, are given the keys to Hollywood: advice from industry experts, high-tech equipment, and links to producers and financing.

Though we travel the world over to find the beautiful, we must carry it with us or we find it not.
—Ralph Waldo Emerson

SPORTS AND LEISURE

10 great places to putt up or shut up

There's nothing quite like making a hole-in-one through an alligator's mouth or under a waterfall. Bob Detwiler, owner of the Hawaiian Rumble course in North Myrtle Beach, South Carolina, established the U.S. ProMiniGolf Association and turned the game into a legitimate sport. He shares his picks for top putting spots.

Pirates' Pier Mini Golf, Santa Monica, California
"Putters can hear real waves below as they navigate through a shipwreck and other swashbuckling themes on this mini golf course 40 feet above the Pacific Ocean." The course is part of Pacific Park, a two-acre theme park on the historic Santa Monica Pier. Save time for a ride on the solar-powered Ferris wheel. *pacpark.com*

Deer Run Golf Center, Woodstock, Illinois
Out in the country, ten miles south of the Wisconsin border, this prairie-themed course is incorporated into the natural landscape. Balls are driven through logs, up and around hills, and over a stream. "Watch for the wolf on top of the waterfall." This mini golf course is part of a family-oriented golf learning center and driving range. *deerrungolfcenter.com*

Mini-Golf America, Williamsburg, Virginia
"This is a great place to visit. The course is only two miles from the historic area." All-day passes are available, and hole placements change daily. The course is set in flowering gardens with hundreds of shrubs, azaleas, and perennials. In fall the foliage is vibrant. *minigolfamerica.com*

Premiere Country Club, Sedona, Arizona
Located high in the desert on the grounds of Los Abrigados Resort and Spa, you won't find any giraffes or windmills on this eco-course, where philosophical postings at each hole remind players to respect the environment. "This course rewards the skilled player. Luck is not much of a factor here."

Golf Gardens, Avalon, California
Originally a garden, this beautiful course on Catalina Island is half a block from the beach. Palms, a coral tree, and eucalyptus provide plenty of shaded areas. "There are lots of ups and downs as well as tunnel shortcuts and loop-the-loop holes."

Dolphin Mini Golf, Boothbay, Maine
"Shoot a hole-in-one through a fisherman's house or into a whale's eye at this nautical-themed course where the ship's wheel turns and buoys bounce." The greens have dolphin, whale, and anchor shapes, and colorful goldfish share nearby pools with frogs and lily pads. *dolphinminigolf.com*

Grand Country Indoor Mini-Golf, Branson, Missouri
Live music brings more than seven million visitors a year to this small town in the hills of the Ozarks with 40 theaters and 60,000 theater seats. Putters will pass the world's largest fiddle with flashing neon strings as they walk through the lobby to the 36-hole indoor golf area of the Grand Country Square complex. "The climate-controlled environment is a welcome relief from the summer humidity and winter weather." *grandcountry.com*

Fantasia Gardens Miniature Golf, Walt Disney World Resort, Florida
"Hippos dance, Pan plays the flute, broomsticks leap, and water shoots out of their buckets at this unique course based on the Disney animated film *Fantasia.* It's a golfing fantasy." *disney.go.com*

Par-King Skill Golf, Lincolnshire, Illinois
An easy drive into the northern suburbs of Chicago, this course is also a trip back in time with a '50s-era turtle, clown, and carousel. "Designed to test your skill, the course has many moving pieces and mechanical objects, hence the 48-inch height requirement for kids." There's a roller-coaster hole where you hit the ball into an elevator and it goes up a tall tower and does a big loop. At the orbiter hole, players hit their ball from a rotating platform. *par-king.com*

Bay View Golf Park, Kaneohe, Hawaii
"This 36-hole course in Kaneohe Bay has long, sloping hills with lots of banks and angles." The tropical setting includes a giant banyan tree, grass huts, rivers, canyons, and waterfalls.

10 great places to shop haute

*Couldn't make it to New York fashion week this year—
or any year? Fear not, fashionistas. Lucky magazine
editor at large Elise Loehnen shares her list of
favorite upscale shopping spots nationwide.*

West Village, New York, New York
Whether you're looking for one-of-a-kind pieces or designer duds,
Manhattan's West Village is the place to be. "Arguably
New York's most charming neighborhood, the
area is also host to some of the best independent
women's clothing boutiques in the city, most of
which are housed in cozy townhouses. Bleecker
Street, which cuts through the heart of the
neighborhood, has more well-known chains."

Abbot Kinney Boulevard, Venice, California
Chic-seekers in search of big-name shops aren't
going to find them along this beachside stretch of boho boutiques—
Abbot Kinney Boulevard has an ordinance against chains setting
up shop. "No longer just for surfers, this thoroughfare is laden with
great independent boutiques. It's totally laid-back and really fun to
walk, particularly because it's dotted with loads of great coffee shops
and restaurants." *abbotkinneyonline.com*

Williamsburg, Brooklyn, New York
High-end meets low-key in this cool neighborhood where those in
the know hunt for hot deals. "Home to a significant population of
young artists and creative types, this Brooklyn neighborhood is over-
run with great, offbeat shopping."

Bal Harbour, Miami, Florida
For shoppers who want to see and be seen, this glamorous garment
emporium in super-stylish Miami really ups fashion's Fahrenheit.
"When it comes to depth of options and shopping ease, it's hard to
beat a mall, particularly when it's a lushly landscaped, gorgeously
appointed outdoor space. Every conceivable desirable brand is represented here." *balharbourshops.com*

Bucktown and Wicker Park, Chicago, Illinois
Located along Damen Avenue, "these abutting neighborhoods are the heart of Chicago's shopping scene and offer everything from the very best in up-and-coming designers to more established lines. It's one of those streets that has something for everyone."

Newbury Street, Boston, Massachusetts
This swank street is steps from Copley Square, where you'll find high-end houses such as Louis Vuitton, Gucci, and Chanel.

West Third Street, Los Angeles, California
"Spanning about ten blocks, you can easily while away an entire day snapping up evening gowns, smock tops, and organic T-shirts—it's all here, which means you just have to hunt for a parking spot once. Plus, it's only a stone's throw away from the celeb-trafficked Robertson Boulevard, where you'll find big chains like Lisa Kline and Kitson."

Northpark Center, Dallas, Texas
"This brand-new, posh development is a multitiered complex of apartments, hotels, restaurants, spas, and shops. The most notable is Lifestyle Fashion Terminal, a 21,000-square-foot department-store-style space that has pieces from a long roster of designers."
northparkcenter.com

Buckhead, Atlanta, Georgia
Well-heeled window shoppers know they've hit the luxe lottery in this central Atlanta district. Two malls—Phipps Plaza and Lenox Square—along with a slew of small shops make up this chic district.

Russian Hill, San Francisco, California
"San Francisco's Union Square has all the tony flagships—Prada, Barneys, Goyard, Marc Jacobs—and big outposts of style like Banana Republic and Levi's. But Russian Hill and nearby Chestnut Street serve up boutiques like Dress and Dylan, where labels like Diane von Furstenberg are always in." Consignment shops and up-and-comers rule in Russian Hill, and flea-market fans will find style sanctuary.

10 great places to let the good times roll

In an age of X-Games and elaborate theme parks, roller-skating rinks may seem somewhat antiquated. Not so. With high-tech lighting and sound systems, live DJs, theme events, and vibrant new skating styles, today's rinks are not your traditional roller domes. Budd Eversman of Roller Skating Association International shares his list of favorite venues.

Skatetown USA, West Chester, Ohio
This facility outside Cincinnati is really two rinks in one. "Skatetown has a large hardwood rink for regular skaters and a dedicated roller-hockey rink complete with locker rooms, benches, penalty boxes, and a scorekeeper's box." Roller-hockey enthusiasts can join leagues of varying age groups, and "open hockey" (the roller-hockey version of pick-up hoops) is offered as well. *skatetownusa.us*

Interskate 91 North, Hadley, Massachusetts
Located on the second floor of a large shopping mall, this popular New England rink boasts an unusual skating floor. "Most roller-skating rinks are oval in shape, like a racetrack. But the floor here is hourglass-shape, so skaters make right and left turns coming around each end." *interskate91.com*

United Skates of America, Tampa, Florida
This popular skating center is known as one of the top "jam skating" venues in the country. "Jam skating—today's version of roller disco—combines elements of skating, dancing, and gymnastic moves set to music." The rink also offers workshops for elementary and middle school students, where instructors use roller-skating to illustrate math and science concepts. *unitedskates.com/tampa*

Sparkles, Hiram, Georgia
"Located just northwest of Atlanta, this skating center includes a multilevel indoor playground, a live DJ spinning tunes, a full-service café, and wireless Internet throughout." *sparklesrollerrinks.com*

Skate Daze, Omaha, Nebraska
This 45,000-square-foot skating center has something for just about everyone. "In addition to a first-class skating rink, Skate Daze has a huge arcade with a roller coaster, bumper cars, a rock-climbing wall, and a laser-tag arena." *skatedaze.com*

Oaks Park Amusement Park and Skating Rink, Portland, Oregon
"Opened in 1905, this is one of the oldest continuously operating skating centers in the country. The skating floor is the largest on the West Coast, and the rink boasts its own Wurlitzer pipe organ." *oakspark.com*

Skate Galaxy, Baton Rouge, Louisiana
"Skate Galaxy includes all the elements that make up an exciting modern skate center. They have a first-class skating floor, a special

Tips for air travel with children

No one said traveling with kids was easy. But with a little patience and planning, we can all get along in the skies. Barbara Rowley, author of *Baby Days: Activities, Ideas, and Games for Enjoying Daily Life with a Child Under Three,* offers these tips for parents:

- Be prepared. Bring plenty to do, such as a favorite storybook and some new ones, crayons and paper, and handheld games (with headphone jacks). Pack a favorite stuffed animal and a few familiar toys.

- But don't overdo it. Don't bring every toy, book, and entertainment gizmo from home.

- Watch a movie or listen to a story. Consider bringing your own DVD or CD player and a stash of movies, stories, or songs your kids will enjoy.

- Eat. Bring plenty of snacks, even if your flight promises a meal and you've ordered one for the kids.

- Tire them out. Ideally, your kids will take advantage of their time in the air by catching up on sleep. Wear them out by walking around and exploring the airport before your flight.

skate-and-play area for small children, and a great laser-tag arena and rock-climbing wall." *skategalaxy.com*

Roll Arena, Midland, Michigan
A huge skating facility with an attached full-service restaurant, Roll Arena has an unusual claim to fame: its own inline speed-skating team, the Midland Rockets. *rollarena.net*

Skate Center of Brentwood, Brentwood, Tennessee
"Where fun meets fitness" is the motto of this skating center in the Nashville area. Fittingly, the facility offers four party rooms, along with live DJs and an elaborate lighting and sound system. One amenity that harried parents may appreciate: supervised childcare during daytime sessions. *skatecenter.com*

Northridge Skateland, Northridge, California
This family-owned skating center, in operation for more than 50 years, has hosted more than seven million skaters over that time. "Up to three generations of families have skated here, including countless Hollywood celebrities." The 12,000-square-foot hardwood skating floor is surrounded by seven giant video screens, complemented by a state-of-the-art lighting and sound system. Several films, TV shows, commercials, and videos have been shot at Skateland over the years. *skateland.net*

10 great places to take a cue from pool pros

Like poker, pool is a cool, "new" pastime. Although billiards has been around since medieval times, the game is being popularized as it becomes more high-end. "More than 40 million people play pool in America," says Mason King, managing editor at Billiards Digest *magazine. "And the expectations, in terms of entertainment, dining, and amenities, are higher than ever." King suggests some interesting spots to rack 'em up.*

Continental Modern Pool Lounge, Arlington (Rosslyn), Virginia
"Probably the most imaginatively designed room in America. The inspiration is equal parts *The Jetsons,* Disneyland, and *Barbarella.*

Each signature space is its own little movie set, stocked with kitschy furniture and doodads. The decor and exotic cocktails make it perfect for a fun, social game." *modernpoollounge.com*

Amsterdam Billiard Club, New York, New York
"ABC is a rarity among the high-end pool halls. It's fancy enough to host corporate parties and still boast more street cred among die-hard players than most rooms on the East Coast. If you're a serious player in NYC, you've played at ABC." *amsterdambilliardclub.com*

The Corner Pocket, Williamsburg, Virginia
"This handsome, red-brick rebuild, on the outskirts of Colonial Williamsburg, carries strong whiffs of Italianate architecture along with more relaxed Southern styles. Throw in outdoor dining, an eclectic menu, and an open floor plan—with defined areas for shooting pool, live music, drinking, and nonsmoking dining—and CP can please just about any clientele." *thecornerpocket.us*

Trick Shots Billiards, Waterford Lakes, Florida
Just outside Orlando, "Trick Shots' tri-level open floor plan gives a great feeling of space, so it's easy to relax. The crowd is a real melting pot, and most of the play is social. And check out the upside-down pool table hanging over the bar." *trickshotsbilliards.com*

Boston Billiard Club, Boston, Massachusetts
"BBC is a favorite spot of Red Sox fans—it's a block from Fenway Park and elbow-to-elbow on game days. So don't expect to sit much. But this is a pretty serious poolroom, with the split personality of a sports bar and martini lounge." *bostonbilliardclub.com*

JOB Billiards Club, Madison, Tennessee
Billed as "one of the nation's true players' rooms," JOB is also "a great place for neophytes to play. There are smaller 'bar tables' for easy shooting, as well as high-quality, tournament-size tables." *jobbilliards.com*

Hard Times Billiards, Bellflower, California
"If pool were a religion, this could be its cathedral. It's spacious and the atmosphere is smoke- and alcohol-

free, so followers can spend all their time (and money) practicing their chosen devotion. A lot of pros have come up through this room, so you'll probably cross sticks with a future star. Recreational players also are welcome, but be careful about 'friendly' wagers." *hardtimesbellflower.com*

Slate, New York, New York
Sophisticated Slate "has hosted *Saturday Night Live* cast parties and other galas." King describes it as "equal parts lounge, restaurant, and pool hall. It's the place you're most likely to spot a celebrity shooting some stick in a private room." *slate-ny.com*

Clicks Billiards, Houston, Texas
"Here's an upscale room (a sports bar and poolroom in one), where the testosterone is still pretty thick—it's Texas, of course—and you can watch your team, shoot pool, or play darts." *clicks.com*

Shakespeare's Pub & Billiard Room, Denver, Colorado
"Designed with players in mind, it offers space between tables, a smoke-eating system, good food, and good instructors. And it scores high in the three attributes that separate the good from the great poolrooms: quality of equipment, style of decor, and respect for the game."

10 great places around
the world to go fly a kite

Scott Skinner is a master kite maker and the executive director of the Drachen Foundation, a Seattle-based nonprofit group devoted to advancing the pastime of kite flying worldwide. He lists special places where devotees of this whimsical sport can take their kites to the skies.

Mission Bay, San Diego, California
"Picturesque Mission Bay is one of the country's best kite-flying venues. The very active San Diego Kite Club gathers here. It's a great place to watch skilled four-line kite fliers practice individual and team maneuvers." *sandiegokiteclub.com*

The Wildwoods, New Jersey
"The wide, long beach and brisk winds here make it a wonderful place to fly kites." Each year on Memorial Day weekend, the Wildwoods hosts one of the premier American kite festivals, drawing participants from around the world. One of the highlights is a "night flight" during which the kite-filled skies are lit up by strobe lights. *wildwoodsnj.com/index.cfm*

Fano Beach, Fano Island, Denmark
This small island off the west coast of Denmark is home to Europe's largest informal kite conclave, held each year during the third

---

AND ANOTHER THING...

KITE FLYING—WITH A TWIST

Kiteboarding combines the thrill of board sports with the simplicity of kite flying.

Enthusiasts on both American coasts and on waterways in between are slipping into a harness, strapping their feet to a kiteboard (similar to a wakeboard), and skimming across the water, propelled by an inflatable kite. With practice, they can go airborne.

The sport has been popular in parts of Europe but didn't begin to take off in U.S. waters until the late 1990s with the development of an inflatable kite that floats and is easy to relaunch from the water. Kiteboarding requires less wind and physical strength than windsurfing— maneuvering the kite is about as strenuous as steering a car. And after 12 hours or so of instruction, a person with absolutely no boarding or kite-flying skills can be up and riding, says Cori Bison of New Wind Kiteboarding in Hood River, Oregon.

As one of the fastest-growing water sports, kiteboarding now has a pro circuit and several magazines dedicated to it. The pros focus on freestyle jumps and aerial turns and can hit speeds of up to 40 mph. But new, more advanced lightweight equipment is propelling the sport from extreme to mainstream. And many of those novice boarders are content to just cruise and stick to smaller jumps.

weekend in June. Started as an impromptu gathering of kite-flying friends, it now draws more than 8,000 enthusiasts from around the world. "Many come to camp, others to enjoy the ten-mile-long white-sand beach, but all come to fly kites. At its peak, the kites form a solid wall of color dancing above the beach."

Jaipur, India

Kite flying is a hugely popular pastime in this ancient northeastern Indian city. "Families and friends often gather on rooftops to eat, drink, and fly kites. During festival times, the skies are filled with kites as far as you can see." Some fly *patangs*—single-line, maneuverable "fighting kites" that employ glass-coated lines. "These kites (depicted in the best-selling novel and film *The Kite Runner*) are flown to engage one another and 'fight' until one line is cut."

Cervia, Italy

Situated on the east coast of Italy near the city of Ravenna, Cervia may be the ideal kite-flying location. "The eight- to ten-mph breeze typical of Cervia makes kite flying here a true pleasure." The town's "formal" kite festival is held at the end of April, before the big crowds and hot weather set in, but kite enthusiasts gather here all year long. *artevento.com*

Ivanpah Dry Lake Bed, Primm, Nevada

"Ivanpah is not a spot for traditional kite flying but a marvelous gathering place for kite buggying." In this unusual sport, participants race around in high-tech, three-wheeled go-karts powered by kites. "Ivanpah is the perfect spot to learn this skill. There are miles of smooth, hard lake bed, with fickle and sometimes frustrating winds." *nabx.net*

Long Beach, Washington

Home to the World Kite Museum and Hall of Fame, Long Beach is one of the finest kite-flying venues along the Northwest Coast. "All summer long there are kite festivals here. The largest is the Washington State International Kite Festival, held annually during the third week of August. This is a great spectacle as well as a wonderful flying site." *worldkitemuseum.com*

Brenton Point State Park, Newport, Rhode Island
"This is just a fine place to fly kites. The sprawling park is on the water, but trees and bushes
make natural breaks in the terrain. It's easy to
find a secluded space to picnic, fly, and enjoy
nature. The seascape is always changing, with
a variety of sailboats and motorboats out on the
water. There are pleasant walks and bike paths,
and the breeze is perfect for kites."
riparks.com/BRENTON.htm

Dieppe, France, and **Dieppe,** Canada
Sister cities, the two Dieppes are both excellent kite-flying venues that stage biennial, world-class kite festivals. Dieppe, France,
holds forth in September on even-numbered years, while the
Canadians stage theirs every odd-numbered year, usually in
August. "The small beach town of Dieppe, France, on the country's north coast, is charming and caters to tourists with a variety
of restaurants and bars. Dieppe, Canada, is in the heart of Acadian
Canada. It's like a slice of Cajun Louisiana in eastern Canada, with
great music, dancing, and food. Both towns are great places to see
kites and to fly them." *dieppe-cerf-volant.org/dccv/ukaccueil.html;
cerf-volant.ca/english/home/*

10 great places to watch thoroughbreds gallop by

*To horse-racing fans, the first Saturday in May means
one thing: the running of the Kentucky Derby at Louisville's
Churchill Downs. Of course, horse-racing is a year-round sport,
and there's nothing quite like experiencing the thunder of charging
thoroughbreds live and up close. Marlene Smith-Baranzini, coauthor
of* Horse Racing Coast to Coast: A Traveler's Guide to the Sport of
Kings, *shares a list of her favorite racing venues.*

Churchill Downs, Louisville, Kentucky
"The Kentucky Derby is the biggest mint-julep-and-elegant-hat
party of the year. The whole city of Louisville goes all out, with

a fireworks festival, theater and music events, and plenty more." Racing at the legendary track starts one week before the Derby and continues into early July. *churchilldowns.com*

Saratoga Race Course, Saratoga Springs, New York

Located in upstate New York, Saratoga Springs is a charming, historic cultural arts enclave known for its curative hot springs. For six weeks each summer—from late July through Labor Day—it is also one of the nation's premier horse-racing venues. "The track and its famous striped-umbrella picnic grounds sprawl within walking distance of tony eateries, Victorian inns, and historic Revolutionary War landmarks." *nyra.com/index_saratoga.html*

Lone Star Park, Grand Prairie, Texas

"Lone Star Park delivers big, Texas-style racing entertainment in this vast, relatively new facility west of Dallas. Along with live racing and a 1,200-seat simulcast center, Lone Star also serves up top musical events during night racing." *lonestarpark.com*

Santa Anita Park, Arcadia, California

Located just north of Los Angeles, 320-acre Santa Anita Park's oval has a backdrop of palm trees, red tile-roofed homes, and the San Gabriel Mountains. "It's quintessential Southern California—right down to the lush paddock gardens that overflow with spectators before every race." Racing opens each December 26 and continues through late April. *oaktreeracing.com*

Arlington Park, Arlington Heights, Illinois

"Less than an hour northwest of Chicago by car, Arlington Park offers patrons a range of lovely interior and terrace dining facilities, as well as lively cabana-party areas and outdoor concerts on its grassy trackside lawns. Toss in the racetrack's grand central stairway and its signature white fences, and Arlington Park stacks up as a handsome and sophisticated racing destination." *arlingtonpark.com*

Keeneland, Lexington, Kentucky

In the heart of bluegrass country, Keeneland spells high tradition unlike any other racetrack in the United States. "Its impeccably kept grounds, with ivy-covered stone buildings and handsome spectator areas, are set among beautiful groves of oak and sycamore. The surrounding countryside is checkered with some of the most prestigious horse farms in the country." Racing seasons are each April and October. *keeneland.com*

Pimlico Race Course, Baltimore, Maryland
With Kentucky Derby excitement still reverberating, the winning horse and jockey will have settled in at Pimlico to prepare for the Preakness Stakes, the second leg of the Triple Crown. "Pimlico, opened in 1870, is the second-oldest racetrack in America. It's a truly prestigious sporting facility with a storied history." *pimlico.com*

Gulfstream Park, Hallandale, Florida
"Combine South Florida's warm winter climate, beaches, boutiques, and nightlife with Gulfstream Park's Mediterranean-style racetrack, and the tourist appeal borders on the endless." Gulfstream, about ten miles north of Miami Beach, hosts a winter meet (early January to mid-April). "The road to the Kentucky Derby often starts right here." *gulfstreampark.com*

Del Mar Thoroughbred Club, Del Mar, California
"Just a mile inland from the ocean, the Del Mar Thoroughbred Club epitomizes the California dreamer's perfect race park. It's a lush,

romantic, Spanish-styled paradise, vibrant with tropical flowers and soft pastel archways." *dmtc.com*

Oaklawn Park, Hot Springs, Arkansas
With a season running from January into mid-April, Oaklawn offers plenty of Kentucky Derby–qualifying action. "Area residents stay and socialize over Oaklawn's popular dinner fare, now a track institution." *oaklawnpark.com*

10 great places to cut a fine figure eight

"I'm always excited to watch Olympic skating," says Kristi Yamaguchi, 1992 Olympic women's figure skating gold medalist. "Skating has so much emotion in it. It's not an athlete crossing a finish line. It's more theatrical, and the personalities on the ice make it thrilling and dramatic. Now, looking back on it, I'm more in awe of it than ever." She shares some favorite public spots to glide across the ice.

Oakland Ice Center, Oakland, California
Featuring two huge indoor rinks—an Olympic-size figure-skating rink and an NHL-size one—the OIC offers public skating, hockey programs, and figure-skating instruction year-round. "My Olympic coach is here, and when I'm home in California, I still skate here." *oaklandice.com*

RecZone, Raleigh, North Carolina
This indoor ice rink offers public hockey and skating, plus instruction for both. "And it's the official practice rink for the Carolina Hurricanes." *www.reczone.net*

Ice Rink at Rockefeller Center, New York, New York
Billed as the world's most famous outdoor ice-skating rink, "this obviously is an icon, and a beautiful, special place to skate. On my first trip to New York, I was 14 years old and I just had to skate here—had to. It's an incredible experience." *rockefellercenter.com*

Incredible ICE, Coral Springs, Florida
This 75,000-square-foot facility, "with an indoor Olympic figure-skating rink (and adjoining NHL-size rink), is a great place to practice." The official home of the Florida Panthers offers lessons, public skating, adult and youth hockey programs, and competitive figure-skating programs. *incredibleice.com*

The Depot Skating Rink, Minneapolis, Minnesota
"Located right downtown, this building was once an old train station. It's a unique place featuring a beautiful indoor rink with glass windows so skaters can see outside and onto the street. It's also one of the warmer rinks with a decent temperature." *thedepotminneapolis.com/icerink/*

International Skating Center of Connecticut, Simsbury, Connecticut
This twin-rink facility caters to competitors as well as to the public. "It's a great indoor rink featuring a high level of competitive ice"— the comprehensive figure-skating program focuses on freestyle, pairs, and dance and includes off-ice classes and conditioning. *isccskate.com*

Riverfront Park Ice Palace, Spokane, Washington
Open from October to March, this accessible, 100-acre urban park's outdoor rink is located in downtown Spokane. "It's a perfect place for families to skate together, very pretty, and not too different from Wollman in New York." *spokaneriverfrontpark.com*

Wollman Rink, New York, New York
Located outdoors in Central Park and ringed by Manhattan's skyscrapers, this 33,000-square-foot rink opened in 1950. "It's a beautiful and a very different skating experience because you have to deal with the cold, the wind, uneven ice, and other elements." *centralparknyc.org*

Sun Valley Skating Center, Sun Valley, Idaho
"There is an indoor rink open year-round in this beautiful ski community, but the outdoor rink is situated right near the lodge so you can see the mountains and skiers as you skate." *sunvalley.com*

Alltel Ice Den, Scottsdale, Arizona
"The Phoenix Coyotes practice here, but this large (120,000-square-foot), two-rink indoor facility allows more ice time for everyone." In addition to public skating, Den staffers offer hockey programs, private figure-skating instruction, and group lessons.
coyotesice.com/publicskating/index.php

10 great places to be a tourist— and a shopper

Bring home authentic, high-quality handmade goods as souvenirs—and get a jump on holiday shopping. Laura Morelli, author of Made in Italy, Made in the Southwest, *and* Made in France, *shares her favorite places to shop.*

Spanish Market, Santa Fe, New Mexico
"For seasoned collectors and curious tourists alike, the Spanish Market as well as the annual Indian Market are excellent sources for Native American and Hispanic handmade goods, from turquoise bracelets to hammered-tin Christmas ornaments." The Spanish Market is held twice a year, in July and December.
spanishmarket.org

Little's Boots, San Antonio, Texas
"In the birthplace of the cowboy boot, a few old-fashioned shoe-makers have elevated this once-humble footwear to high art," and Little's Boots, established in 1915, is "among the best." The handsome, high-quality dress boots are strictly made to order.
davelittleboots.com

Kinngait Co-operative Ltd. (West Baffin Eskimo Co-op), Cape Dorset, Canada
This Arctic town is in the new Canadian territory of Nunavut. "Native Inuit carvings of soapstone, bone, and antlers make wonderful portable collectibles. Buy from community cooperatives such as the ones you'll find in Cape Dorset, on the southwest tip of Baffin Island, and other small communities across Nunavut. The Canadian government uses an igloo trademark to indicate authentic origin and craftsmanship."

Night Market, Chiang Mai, Thailand
"Thailand's second-largest city is famous for its craft traditions. Numerous 'factories' filled with individual silver and bronze smiths, embroiderers, and jewelry makers cluster along Sankampaeng Road. Crafters also can be found at the Night Market, named for its odd hours, 6 P.M. to midnight. If you have time, venture into the surrounding hill towns such as Tohn Pao, Bor Sarng, and Pa Bong, where you can explore artisan studios and find fantastic bargains on unique embroidered textiles, ceremonial masks, Buddhas, and exquisite woodcarvings."

International Antiques and Fine Arts Biennale, Florence, Italy
"Whether someone is a well-heeled arts buyer or a budget traveler, this event has something for everyone. The modest entrance fee allows visitors to view the many museum-quality antiques and fine-art works on display while touring the fair's home, the Palazzo Corsini." *biennaleantiquariato.it*

African Heritage, Nairobi, Kenya
"Wooden carvings, sisal baskets, and colorful ceramic beads are among Kenya's most traditional wares. This gallery on Banda Street features carved wooden bowls and sculpture, jewelry, textiles, and more, all of impressive quality." *africanheritage.net*

Rinck, Paris, France
"This and other shops located in the Bastille quarter in the 11th arrondissement offer a no-frills alternative to glitzy Right Bank boutiques. The specialty here is handcrafted furniture, mostly fancy period pieces that require the collaboration of several craftspeople experienced in working wood, marquetry (inlaid veneer), stone, and metal." *rinck.fr*

El Mercado de Artesanias, Oaxaca City, Mexico
"Shops selling quality handcrafted Zapotec rugs cluster in the streets between the zócalo (town square) and Santo Domingo de Guzman Church, and the craft specialty market known as El Mercado de Artesanias. In outlying villages, especially Teotitlan del Valle, a town known for its colorful, handwoven rugs, you can buy directly from some 150 weavers and witness them work firsthand."

Crafts Museum, New Delhi, India

"Handcrafted goods—from textiles to jewelry and carving—are the lifeblood of India's economy and one of the pillars of its cultural identity. This excellent museum is a good place to grasp the rich history of Indian craft. In the museum shop, you can choose among high-quality saris, papier-mâché masks, ornaments, carved boxes, and other treasures, as well as watch craftspeople demonstrating their work." *travelgodelhi.com/delhi-museum/delhi-craft-museum.htm*

Kyoto Handicraft Center, Kyoto, Japan

"One of Japan's richest cultural cities, Kyoto is also home to many masters of clay, paper, and wood. You can get a big-picture view of the region's traditions at this seven-story extravaganza, where you can watch artisans at work and even try your hand at making cloisonné jewelry or woodblock prints." *kyotohandicraftcenter.com*

Travel safety tips

Help is available on the Internet for advice on traveling safely abroad. Here are some suggested Web sites:

- The State Department posts country-by-country travel warnings, crime and security information, health conditions, and minor political disturbances. Travel safety information can also be requested via e-mail at travel.state.gov.
- Keep up on natural disasters at usatoday.com or weather.com.
- You can find out about necessary vaccinations and disease outbreaks at cdc.gov, drwisetravel.com, or travelhealthline.com.
- Corporate Travel Safety (corporatetravelsafety.com) offers seminars and audio books on avoiding travel scams.

I have found out that there ain't no surer way to find out whether you like people or hate them than to travel with them.

—Mark Twain

DINING

* * *

RESTAURANTS

10 great places to sup and sip in the summertime

Toast the first weekend of summer and celebrate the season with a glass of wine. Barbara Fairchild, editor in chief of Bon Appetit, *shares her list of top spots for warm-weather sips.*

Auberge du Soleil, Rutherford, California
"Sit on the terrace at Auberge du Soleil in Napa Valley and you can look at the grapevines below while enjoying the result." When you're maxed out on an infinite supply of foie gras and other rich foods on your wine-country vacation, the restaurant's vegetarian tasting menu paired with different wines is a refreshing alternative. *aubergedusoleil.com*

MC Perkins Cove, Ogunquit, Maine
"Ask for a window table and order sauvignon blanc or chardonnay." You can see the ocean from every window in this restaurant. Watch lobster traps bob in Perkins Cove below as sailboats glide by. Live it up and order the Sticky Toffee Pudding for dessert. *mcperkinscove.com*

Ristorante Da Delfina, Artimino, Italy
"The terrace of this restaurant, in a medieval hamlet less than half an hour north of Florence, overlooks the Tuscan countryside. Nothing could be better—except the superb food from veteran chef and owner Carlo Cioni." Feast on wild mushrooms and locally made sausage, then digest your meal with a stroll through the olive grove. *dadelfina.it*

CanoeHouse Restaurant, Kohala Coast, Hawaii
"This restaurant at Mauna Lani Resort has nice wines by the glass, but their mai tai and a sunset on the outdoor patio are the perfect combination." Enjoy Pacific Rim specialties, three miles of secluded shoreline, a meditation pavilion, and outdoor spa treatments at this Big Island getaway. *maunalani.com*

The Terrace at the Peninsula Chicago, Chicago, Illinois
"Only open in summer, this fourth-floor terrace is surrounded by spectacular views of the city's skyscrapers, including the iconic John Hancock building. It's a great place to enjoy a glass of wine." It's also a popular refuge for the city's power players, as well as acquisitive fashionistas toting shopping bags from luxury stores on Michigan Avenue. *chicago.peninsula.com*

Pacific's Edge, Carmel, California
"Located at Highlands Inn, this bar and dining room has bay views framed by the area's famed Monterey Pines. If you're lucky, you might also spot whales in the water below." Binoculars are standard issue in all the rooms, and local fish from Monterey Bay is often on the menu. *pacificsedge.com*

Barcibo Enoteca, New York, New York
"Crowded and fun, this neighborhood wine bar on the Upper West Side has great Italian 'small plates' to go with their lovely selection of wines by the glass." The wines—red, white, and sparkling—are strictly Italian. They even have grappa, the fiery Italian distillation. Join one of the communal-style tables and toast the joys of being part of the city's hip scene. *barciboenoteca.com*

St-Laurent Bar & Lounge, Quebec City, Quebec, Canada
It's worth coming here just to go inside Fairmont's landmark Le Chateau Frontenac, the hotel that looks like a storybook castle towering above Old Quebec City. "You can sip away while enjoying the view of the St. Lawrence River. Besides some nice wines by the glass, there are also fun cocktails and interesting local beers available." Savor smoked salmon on a ciabatta roll while watching ferryboats cruise over to lush Île d'Orléans. *fairmont.com/frontenac*

Dukes Bar, London, England
"People-watching at its best, British-style, at Dukes Hotel in St. James's." If you are in the mood for a secluded oasis but want to enjoy the same bar menu and hospitality, head for the hotel's Zen Garden courtyard. Located next to the Drawing Room, it feels like a secret garden and features wicker furniture and an Oriental fountain. *campbellgrayhotels.com/dukes-london*

Le Comptoir du Relais, Paris, France
"Sit at a sidewalk table and watch the constantly changing scene on this vibrant corner of the Left Bank. The three-course menu of owner/chef Yves Camdeborde is some of the finest—and the most reasonably priced—cooking in a city filled with great food."

10 great places to take an exit to good eatin'

He makes no claim to being a dining critic, but Mark Watson has done his share of eating at restaurants—especially those just off the highway. He drives about 25,000 miles each year to put together The Next Exit, *his guide to what's at every interstate exit across the United States. "Clean windows and a busy parking lot" are what Watson says he looks for when first picking a place to eat. Here are some of his favorites.*

Prejean's, near Interstate 10 at I-49, Exit 2 (traveling north), Exit 4 (traveling south), Lafayette, Louisiana
"Upscale seafood" is how Watson describes the eating at this colorful restaurant. The menu features what you'd expect in Cajun country—crawfish, shrimp, oysters, crabs, catfish, even alligator, which probably makes "Big Al," a 14-foot stuffed alligator that presides over the dining room, none too happy. Live music every night. *prejeans.com*

Lambert's Cafe, I-55, Exit 67, Sikeston, Missouri
Claiming to be "The Only Home of Throwed Rolls," this bustling place features mostly country cookin' (fried chicken, catfish, and the like) as well as what they call "pass arounds" (fried potatoes and onions, fried okra, black-eyed peas, etc.) and cinnamon rolls so big they're called "hubcaps." Those "throwed rolls"? Back in 1976,

a customer impatient for his bread roll hollered out, "Throw the damn thing!" and they're still doing it. *throwedrolls.com*

Lena's Seafood Restaurant, I-95, Exit 60, Salisbury, Massachusetts
"Good fish sandwich and chowder." The chowder is homemade, as is the coleslaw at this no-nonsense New England establishment that also features fresh scallops and fried clams. Order from the counter. *lenasseafood.com*

El Rodeo, I-90, Exit 176 North, Moses Lake, Washington
"Just plain Mexican. And the fajitas are flaming hot when they come to the table." The decor, too, is South of the Border, and the place is small (only about 20 tables, including those on the patio).

Bubba's Bar-B-Q & Steakhouse, I-45, Exit 251, Ennis, Texas
Belly up to Bubba's might be more like it. "Plates piled high with all varieties of barbecue, including huge briskets. Look for a place to take a nap after this."

Steamboat Bill's Restaurant, I-10, Exit 29 (traveling east), Exit 30A (traveling west), Lake Charles, Louisiana
"Crawfish galore. Very busy, not fancy." The menu offers crawfish fixed every which way, as well as gumbo, po' boys, and jumbo fried shrimp. The owners started selling shrimp by the side of the road and now have three restaurants in Lake Charles. *steamboatbills.com*

In-N-Out Burger, various locations
OK, it's a chain, but a very special chain. "The menu is simple ... hamburgers, three kinds of shakes, and fries. The fries are cut from fresh potatoes right there in front of you." Decorated in '50s-style red-and-white tiles, In-N-Outs are "how hamburger joints ought to operate." *in-n-out.com*

Shellhouse Restaurant, 1-95, Exit 94, near Savannah, Georgia
"Good interstate-highway seafood if you don't want to make it all the way to the beach." Just don't expect the seafood to be from Georgia—the menu features, almost overwhelmingly, Alaskan snow crab legs. The decor is nautical, the atmosphere is casual (shorts and flip-flops are OK), and the food can be eaten with your fingers. "Ask for plenty of paper towels." *shellhousesav.com*

Parker's Barbecue, I-95, Exit 119 (traveling south), Exit 107 (traveling north), Wilson, North Carolina

"It's probably ten miles or so off I-95 but well worth the drive for the world's best eastern-style North Carolina barbecue." Not much has changed at Parker's since it opened in 1946—including the recipe for its pork barbecue, less sweet and more vinegary than that served in the western part of the state. Plenty of traditional sides too—from Brunswick stew to coleslaw and boiled potatoes.

Gaido's Seafood Restaurant, I-45, Exit 1A, Galveston, Texas

Watson says this is his "very favorite." Founded in 1911, the place is now run by the fourth generation of Gaidos—and they still peel shrimp, shuck oysters, and fillet fish the old-fashioned way. "Best scallops I've ever eaten." *gaidosofgalveston.com*

10 great places to start your day sunny-side up

It's often said that breakfast is the most important meal of the day, so we asked Eddy Chavey, food historian, breakfast expert, and creator of the Web site mrbreakfast.com, to share his favorite places.

Ken's House of Pancakes, Hilo, Hawaii

"Open 24 hours a day, Ken's is very popular among breakfast lovers on the Big Island of Hawaii. The menu features multiple variations of a signature Hawaiian dish called Loco Moco—a beef patty, gravy, and an egg over rice. If you order the largest version, called the Sumo Moco, the staff will all yell 'Sumo!' Also try the homemade coconut syrup on their Hawaiian-style pancakes." *kenshouseofpancakes-hilohi.com*

Pete's Kitchen, Denver, Colorado

From the guy walking in off the street to the couple arriving by limousine, customers come from all over Denver to slide into the cozy tan booths of this Greek diner. "Open 24 hours, seven days a week, all year long, this is the place to grab breakfast after a long night of partying. Their breakfast burritos, smothered in chili, are the best in town." *petesrestaurantstoo.com*

The Flying Biscuit Cafe, Atlanta, Georgia
"For a healthy, hearty breakfast served all day and the fluffiest biscuits you'll get anywhere, try this hip restaurant in the Candler Park community of Atlanta. Biscuits and gravy or biscuits with [the café's] own homemade cranberry-apple butter are the don't-miss items on the menu." *flyingbiscuit.com*

Keltic Kitchen, West Yarmouth, Massachusetts
Children who grew up feasting at this Cape Cod cottage near Nantucket Sound now bring their own families to the restaurant

Talk to the Expert

THE DOUGHNUT "WHOLE" STORY

Doughnut, anyone? Of course you want one, maybe two if they're hot. Fact is, the United States is a nation of glazed gastronomes who gobble 10 billion doughnuts—that's $2 billion worth of fried dough—each year. "It's not a big mystery," says Sally Levitt Steinberg, author of *The Donut Book: The Whole Story in Words, Pictures & Outrageous Tales.* Here, she demystifies the doughnut.

Q: What is the enduring appeal of doughnuts?
A: The answer is not in their taste; it's about their shape. The circle is so universal, and the doughnut is very appealing physically and metaphorically. Of course, there are doughnuts that are not shaped in circles, and fritters are really doughnuts, but we don't categorize them like doughnuts. The doughnut is in a class by itself; it transcends mere food appeal.

Q: Can you explain the increase in consumption at a time when many people are trying to eat healthier and decrease their fat and carb intake? Why is the doughnut impervious to diets?
A: Doughnuts represent a time-out from dietary considerations. They are not a staple; they're a treat. And sometimes, diet or not, you just have to have a doughnut.

Q: Do doughnut machines produce better doughnuts than those made by hand?

A: No, not better, but a doughnut machine is more efficient in terms of standardization of doughnuts produced and quantity.

Q: Can home bakers buy doughnut machines?

A: Yes, there is a company called Lil' Orbits (lilorbits.com), which offers home doughnut-making equipment such as fryers and cutters that can be used with the machine that mixes the mix, cuts the dough and the hole, drops the doughnut in oil, fries it, then places it on a conveyor belt.

Q: You say in the book that doughnuts are very persnickety, needing perfect humidity and temperature for just-right rising and frying. How can home cooks ever hope to create them?

A: It's really so hard, I don't even do it. My kids and husband made them once, and it was a huge mess. Back in the old days on American prairies, women cooked and baked constantly and then did it so many times they got good at it. Frying doughnuts in vegetable oil is tricky (old-timers use lard) because the dough is so delicate yet it has to absorb so much.

Q: What is your favorite kind of doughnut?

A: I love a glazed raised (yeast) doughnut, provided it doesn't have too much sugar in it. It's easier to find good raised doughnuts. But if you can get a good cake doughnut, it's an amazing and wonderful experience.

Q: There's a lot of controversy over the origin of the doughnut's hole. Is there a definitive answer?

A: There are many stories, and in the 1940s, a big debate erupted between two camps: Did a whaling captain stick a piece of dough on his ship's wheel to create the hole? Or was it a Native American who shot a doughnut out of a pioneer woman's hand? All I know is that the hole has been around for a long time, and there is evidence in paintings that round cakes with holes existed in Europe in the 17th century. In America, there has been a doughnut with a hole since the 19th century.

to sit in the seats they call their own. "Come for a traditional Irish breakfast, including black-and-white pudding (aka blood sausage), brown bread, beans, and thick Irish bacon. Expect to hear some Irish accents; a lot of customers come here to get a taste of home." *thekeltickitchen.com*

Saddle Ranch Chop House, West Hollywood, California

"Watch fellow brunchers ride the mechanical bull while you enjoy huge portions of steak and eggs. The building and decor are right out of a 1930s cowboy movie—an unlikely gem in the middle of the glitz and glam of the L.A. Sunset Strip." Serious breakfast slingers can down Bottomless Bloody Marys and tasty mimosas. Campfires are aglow outdoors for everyone to make s'mores. *srrestaurants.com*

The Breakfast Klub, Houston, Texas

"Known for the combinations of Wings & Waffles and Katfish & Grits, it's the best place for a traditional Southern-style breakfast in Houston. They also have the best cheese grits west of the Mississippi." The jazzy red, yellow, and orange walls match the music played here. The day starts with gospel music and eases into jazz. On Saturdays, you can sing along to oldies. *thebreakfastklub.com*

Good Enough to Eat, New York, New York

New York City chefs come here for breakfast because everything on the menu, from the dill-onion bread to the sausage, is homemade. "You get a comfortable vibe when you see their white picket fence on the busy Upper West Side. It's a cool, relaxing joint to get a hometown-style breakfast. The Gramercy Park omelet, made with apple slices and Vermont cheddar, is a standout." *goodenoughtoeat.com*

Cadillac Cafe, Portland, Oregon

"The pink '61 Cadillac on display in this restaurant is an attraction for some, but it's the thick hazelnut-crusted French toast and the Bunkhouse Vittles Sampler (chicken-apple sausages, seasoned fried potatoes, eggs, and a slice of hazelnut French toast) that are the real draw."

Cafe Du Monde, New Orleans, Louisiana

"This historic French Quarter coffee shop, unscathed during Hurricane Katrina, was closed for two months after the storm due to lack of water or power. It offers up the best beignets in the nation. They are simply fried dough covered with powdered sugar. The café also serves up notoriously smooth chicory coffee." Tables are set under a huge green-and-white awning in the first building of the French Market. *cafedumonde.com*

Pancake Pantry, Nashville, Tennessee

You may have to wait in line, but it's worth the time to get inside for a Southern welcome that feels like home. "Their sweet potato pancakes are highly recommended. Be sure to order the traditional buttermilk pancakes or French toast just so you can try their home-made cinnamon syrup." *thepancakepantry.com*

10 great places to snack at a seafood shack

Nothing says summer like fresh-as-can-be ocean delights from a seafood shack. Starting in Connecticut and heading north, Elizabeth Bougerol, author of New England's Favorite Seafood Shacks, *offers some of her favorites.*

The Place, Guilford, Connecticut

This is "the coolest clambake in Connecticut." Clams, lobsters, bluefish, and corn on the cob pepper a long ramshackle grill, smoke billowing overhead, as coowners Gary and Vaughn Knowles work fast (and with fireproof gloves) to deliver your dinner. "Everything is caught locally and roasted, grilled, or steamed to order over the hickory and oak fire." Best of all: the Clam Special, littlenecks roasted until dabs of cocktail sauce and butter melt into the brine.

Costello's Clam Shack, Noank, Connecticut

Costello's is a cheery double-decker shack right on the water in Noank Shipyard, "serving up all things golden and crunchy. Try the fried whole Canadian clams or the center-cut cod, with a side of Costello's excellent onion rings. For die-hards, there's even fried ice cream." *costellosclamshack.com*

Aunt Carrie's, Point Judith, Narragansett, Rhode Island
Local legend has it that when Carrie Cooper spent summers at
Point Judith with her family almost a century ago, the picnic lunches
she packed smelled so good that other families asked for a taste.
"Nowadays, Aunt Carrie's legacy lives on in every order of perfectly
crunchy belly clams, steamers, Rhode Island–style (broth-based)
clam chowder, and clam cakes, which, as most Rhode Islanders will
tell you, Carrie Cooper invented." For dessert, try Indian pudding
with molasses, topped with vanilla ice cream. *auntcarriesri.com*

Arnold's Lobster & Clam Bar, Eastham (Cape Cod), Massachusetts
By day, it's a boisterous, kid-friendly spot that doles out lobster rolls
and fried seafood to families straight from (or headed to) the beach;
by night, it's a laid-back watering hole/raw bar. "The thin onion rings
are almost worth a trip by themselves." *arnoldsrestaurant.com*

J.T. Farnham's, Essex, Massachusetts
Clam fans refer to this stretch of Cape Ann as "Clam Alley" because
it's home to so many restaurants known for fried clams (dug at the
nearby Ipswich flats). Among them: Farnham's, housed in a non-
descript marshside cottage. "Fried seafood rules, from haddock
and scallops to oysters and, of course—just like the big yellow sign
says—'Farnham's Famous Clams.' "

Brown's Seabrook Lobster Pound, Seabrook, New Hampshire
This big, drafty barn just across the Massachusetts border has been
serving seafood classics for more than 50 years. "The atmosphere is
strictly summer-camp mess hall: Line up here for steamers; there for
lobster; and head outside for fried clams, shrimp, scallops, and oysters. After all that, you still have to stake out one of the in-demand
picnic tables, but it's all part of the experience." *brownslobster.com*

Middlebay Lobster, Cundy's Harbor, Maine
The vibe is roadhouse-meets-bait-shop at Middlebay, tucked in a
grove of pines in Maine's bucolic Cundy's Harbor. Middlebay is all
about "spanking-fresh seafood done simply—and addictively. Try
the sweet, briny steamers; a cool, fresh-picked crab roll (a Maine
specialty hardly found outside the state); or a bowl of Elizabeth's
stratospherically good lobster stew."

Five Islands Lobster Co., Georgetown, Maine
"Get your lobster steamed or boiled, or try the Jenny Special (a crab-cake-and-haddock sandwich) and wash it down with the booze you BYO'd as fishing boats come and go." *fiveislandslobster.com*

Bet's Famous Fish Fry, Boothbay, Maine
Blink and you'd miss it—a glorified trailer on a quiet patch of Route 27. Owner Bet Finocchiaro catches all the haddock and cod herself, prepares it according to her grandmother's recipe, and serves it with a side of her legendary Down East sassiness. "She crams more than a pound of fish into each sandwich, ensuring that you won't possibly leave hungry."

Waterman's Beach Lobster, South Thomaston, Maine
"The menu's just a few items long, and you're out of luck if it rains (seating is outdoor picnic tables), but none of this matters when you're perched at the water's edge and chowing down on one of the sweetest, most succulent lobsters of your life." Indeed. Waterman's Beach is a past winner of the James Beard Foundation's America's Regional Classics Award. *watermansbeachlobster.com*

10 great places to welcome the Chinese New Year

The Chinese New Year, or Lunar New Year, typically begins on the first day of the first month of the Chinese calendar and ends on the 15th day. Master chef Martin Yan, a professional cooking instructor and host of Yan Can Cook, *shares his list of places to celebrate the occasion.*

Koi Palace, Daly City, California
"When it is Chinese New Year, booking a table at a good teahouse is a top priority for Cantonese families." Order the dim sum at this teahouse, which reminds Yan of one in his Canton hometown. "You can choose top-quality teas to go with your dim sum or order dishes that are typical of southern China." *koipalace.com*

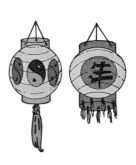

Yangming, Bryn Mawr, Pennsylvania
"Chef Michael Wei's restaurant has great Peking duck." The restaurant has dedicated customers who often request favorite servers and tables. *yangmingrestaurant.com*

Fung's Kitchen, Houston, Texas
"If you like seafood, this is the place to go. Fresh live seafood, including Alaska king crab, Australian egg crab, New Zealand mussels, as well as Maine and Pacific lobster, is served here." During the Chinese New Year, Fung's serves traditional dishes said to provide "good fortunes and wealth to every generation" in the new year. *eatatfungs.com*

Bo Ling's, Kansas City, Missouri
Bo Ling's has been providing authentic Chinese food in America's heartland for more than 30 years. "The food is always fresh and good." *bolings.com*

Grand Sichuan, New York, New York
"For anyone who loves hot and spicy dishes, this is a great choice for an authentic Sichuan experience in the Big Apple." *thegrandsichuan.com*

Empress Dim Sum Seafood Restaurant, Denver, Colorado
"In southern China, we celebrate the Chinese New Year by roasting a whole pig and sharing it with our neighbors and relatives. Here, the roast pork is from a whole pig roasted in-house, making Empress a truly unique dining experience." *empressseafoodrestaurant.com*

Chef Lee's Peking Restaurant, Columbus, Georgia
"Mongolian Beef is one of the best-selling dishes on the menu. But chef/owner Joe Lee's hand-pulled noodles win my vote, hands down. He is a master noodle chef—a rare find these days." The elegant restaurant has dining rooms with large windows and a view of their beautiful garden.

East Restaurant & Lounge, Wells, Maine
"Lobster is the star in this Chinese restaurant. You can also order from their Pan-Asian menu in case your mate has a sudden craving for Japanese sushi or Thai cuisine." *eastdining.com*

Hunan Taste, Denville, New Jersey
"Hunan Taste in northern New Jersey has walls of aquariums filled with exotic fish as room dividers. It's also a great place to impress someone with a classic Chinese banquet. Another reason to go there is the restaurant's Chinese name. *Wan Fu Yuan* literally means 'ten thousand fortune in the garden.' " *hunantaste.com*

Wong's King Seafood Restaurant, Portland, Oregon
"This restaurant is Portland's hidden treasure." It's not unusual to see weddings and other important occasions being celebrated at this popular spot, especially on weekends.

10 great places to make a meal out of salad

Go green at any of the myriad cafés and restaurants that feature salads. Wiley Mullins, author of Salad Makes the Meal: 150 Simple and Inspired Salad Recipes Everyone Will Love, *shares his list of favorite places.*

Ching's Table, New Canaan, Connecticut
"There are salads, and then there is the Vietnamese salad, a culinary wonderment all on its own. Shredded jicama (a sweet, crunchy Mexican root vegetable), mango, thin dried-rice noodles, ground peanuts, and a touch of jalapeño earn this salad a place on my list of favorites. The flavorful duck dressing adds the finishing touch to this masterpiece." *chingsrestaurant.com*

City Grocery Cafe, Oxford, Mississippi
"Tossed in a mildly sweet dried-fig vinaigrette dressing, the delightful spinach walnut salad, made here with baby spinach leaves, grilled pear slices, crumbled Maytag blue cheese, bits of red onion, sourdough croutons, and walnuts, awakens all of your taste buds." The restaurant, on Courthouse Square, is two blocks from Rowan Oak, the house where William Faulkner wrote many of his novels. *citygroceryonline.com*

Blue Hill at Stone Barns, Pocantico Hills, New York

The intensely flavorful heirloom tomatoes in the salad are grown on a working farm at Stone Barns Center for Food and Agriculture, where visitors can walk through the fields and observe the animals. "This heirloom tomato salad is certain to capture the imagination of any food connoisseur. Flavorful tomatoes are definitely the hero. Dried comfit, sorbet, and ricotta cheese complete this amazing creation." *bluehillfarm.com*

Chez Panisse, Berkeley, California

"One of the many benefits of living in California is the year-round availability of fresh produce. Recipes including native citrus appear on many restaurant menus, but the citrus salad from Chez Panisse captures the refreshment and the relaxed atmosphere often associated with living in the West." *chezpanisse.com*

84 High Street, Westerly, Rhode Island

"Don't be fooled by the generic name of the mesclun salad here. It's so much more than the name suggests. In fact, it's perhaps the most satisfying salad I've ever eaten. It's piled with what appears to be hundreds of crunchy, caramelized walnut pieces; you'll savor every bite. The delicious homemade balsamic vinaigrette dressing simply makes this salad experience special." *84highstreet.com*

Cafe Pasquals, Santa Fe, New Mexico

The salad at this festive restaurant—hearts of romaine with Maytag blue cheese, toasted chile pecans, and roasted beets—celebrates the culture and tradition of the Southwest. "It's practically a complete meal." *pasquals.com*

Columbia Restaurant, Tampa, Florida

This restaurant is in Ybor City, Tampa's lively Latin Quarter. "The 1905 Salad is famous throughout Florida, and salad lovers travel near and far to enjoy it. No wonder it's trademarked! Tossed and created at your table, this masterpiece of a meal includes the juiciest beefsteak tomatoes you've ever tasted; lettuce; tender, baked ham; Romano and Swiss cheeses; olives; and a deliciously smooth garlic dressing." *columbiarestaurant.com*

Firefly, Lenox, Massachusetts
"This isn't your grandmother's Caesar salad. After you've tasted the grilled Caesar salad, with homemade croutons and a romaine heart that is grilled over the flame together with the chicken, the standard old reliable Caesar just won't suffice." *fireflylenox.com*

Hall Street Grill, Beaverton, Oregon
"The remarkable Asian chicken salad here is simply magnificent! The tender, roasted chicken melts in your mouth. The delicious hoisin vinaigrette dressing makes this salad fit for a king. Other ingredients include mandarin oranges, colorful julienne peppers, toasted almonds, and shredded carrots." Ask for an outside table and sit on the tented patio near the creek for a garden view. *hallstreetgrill.com*

True, Mobile, Alabama
"You'll want to stand up and cheer after tasting the roasted shrimp salad, made with fresh grilled Gulf of Mexico shrimp, delicately cured zucchini noodles, lemon-marinated mushrooms, arugula, and braised artichoke hearts. Citrus-tomato vinaigrette adds the finishing touch." *truedine.com*

10 great places for solo diners to pull up a chair

Table for one, or would you prefer the counter?
Marya Charles Alexander, editor and founder of solodining.com, shares her list of favorite eat-alone places.

Bar Boulud, New York, New York
This casual bistro, across from Manhattan's Lincoln Center, is named for the owner and chef of several eponymous restaurants, including the city's famed Daniel. "It has a charcuterie bar (specializing in traditional house-made terrines, pâtés, and cured ham) with casual seating for 21 diners wrapped around it. Solo diners are also welcome to enjoy their meal at the round tasting table that seats 14." *danielnyc.com*

801 Steak & Chop House, Des Moines, Iowa
The surroundings and amenities at this elegant downtown establishment are solo-friendly with a full menu available at the bar. "Luckily,

half orders of sides are permissible. A full order is ample for two."
Choose from a selection of wines by the glass, splits, and half bottles.
801steakandchop.com

Miss Mary Bobo's Boarding House, Lynchburg, Tennessee
"Lynchburg is known as the home of Jack Daniel's Distillery
and—drumroll!—this restaurant, where 12 guests sit together at a
single table in each of the eight dining rooms. Southern regional
food is served family-style at this former boardinghouse." The ease
with which solos blend into the scene of taking "dinner"—rural
Tennessee's midday meal—with 11 strangers creates instant
camaraderie.

Mesh, West Chester, Ohio
Solo diners are as welcome to a table for one in the main dining
room as they are in the adjoining lounge area of this sleek restaurant
outside Cincinnati. "The bar, a freestanding rectangle in the lounge,
is also a draw, as are the high-top tables, inviting couches, and live
entertainment."

Lynn's Paradise Cafe, Louisville, Kentucky
"How do you characterize a restaurant that describes its location as
'behind the giant red coffeepot on Barret Avenue' and hosts an Ugly
Lamp Contest? Quirky, of course. Off-the-wall fun? Absolutely. Is it
a magnet for solo diners? Yes!" The counter is where the action is.
Regulars welcome newcomers; conversations flow easily over such
specialties as Bourbon Ball French Toast. *lynnsparadisecafe.com*

Rosemary's Restaurant, Las Vegas, Nevada
"A respite from the Strip, a warm welcome, and fine dining await
solos here. The chef is acutely aware of solo guests, whether they
reserve seating at the 8-seat food bar located midrestaurant that
overlooks the open kitchen or opt for the 30-seat bar/lounge area
that features high-top tables or dine comfortably in the main dining room." Signature dish: Hugo's BBQ shrimp with Maytag Blue
Cheese coleslaw. *rosemarysrestaurant.com*

Cafe Pasqual's, Santa Fe, New Mexico
"Getting your green on is easy at this boisterous restaurant, where
95 percent of the ingredients in the Mexican/Southwest/Asian-

I'm No Expert, But...

SOLO TRAVELING

Finding the perfect travel companion may be easier than you think: Just look in the mirror. Fans of solo travel say venturing out alone can be the best way to see the world. "It's not just a different way to travel," says Lea Lane, author of *Solo Traveler: Tales and Tips for Great Trips*. "I think it's the ultimate way."

Here are Lane's tips for traveling solo:

- Accept help. Let the concierge map out your route.

- Smile and ask questions. The easiest is: "Where are you from?"

- Take lots of photos. This will give you a fun activity and lots of memories to reflect on.

- Savor every experience. Lasting memories require focus and contemplation.

- Above all, be flexible. Your freedom to deviate from or ditch the entire plan on a whim is what makes soloing the ultimate way to go.

inspired menu are organic. Securing one of the dozen coveted places at their old oak 'Joiner's Table' is more of a challenge because this small café draws crowds of locals and visitors at all meals." *pasquals.com*

Pagliacci Pizza–Queen Anne, Seattle, Washington
"Some simply assume that Seattle is best known for coffee. The locals know better. Pagliacci Pizza—six dine-in locations strong—has embraced the Seattle area with its style and comfort food for almost 30 years." Visit its Queen Anne locale, where the tables are close together and conversation is easy. Additional seating is at the counter along the window. *pagliacci.com*

Ina's, Chicago, Illinois
"Proprietor Ina Pinkney knows how to show her appreciation for solo diners' business. She promises no seats in 'Siberia' or near the kitchen door, no 'invisibility,' and no rude service. Chicago's

Breakfast Queen also does the other meals. Here's your chance to revel utensil-free in her incredible finger-food fried chicken at dinnertime." *breakfastqueen.com*

Hot and Hot Fish Club, Birmingham, Alabama
"A seat at the chef's counter in the main dining room promises a view of the bustling kitchen plus the company of fellow diners. The bar offers friendly company and an opportunity to order from the full menu. However, your very own table may prove to be the best choice of all." Try their tasting menu with wine pairings that can be customized to each diner's preferences. *hotandhotfishclub.com*

ETHNIC AND REGIONAL CUISINE

10 great places to discover Italy— in America

It seems the United States has much amore for Italian neighborhoods, considering how many there are in cities big and small. Mario Batali, award-winning chef, TV personality, and restaurateur, shares his favorite Little Italys.

Murray Hill, Cleveland, Ohio
"Corbo's Bakery has the best cassata (cake) I have tried in the United States. Every August, the Feast of the Assumption is celebrated in Little Italy with a four-day party." *littleitalycleveland.com*

Little Italy, New York, New York
"Even though it no longer resembles its 19th-century heyday, there is still a great deal that is authentic here. On Grand Street, stop by Di Palo Fine Foods for a Ph.D. lesson in the various ages of Parmigiano Reggiano. Stroll down the street to Caffe Roma on Broome Street for the ultimate Italian pastry and a perfect caffe corretto— a shot of espresso with a shot of liquor, usually grappa, brandy, or sambuca." *littleitalynyc.com*

Federal Hill, Providence, Rhode Island
"Stop by Scialo Brothers Bakery and then head to Venda Ravioli for a beautiful lunch with fresh pasta made every day from scratch, all served in a delightful little piazza with opera music blaring from tiny speakers in a Fellini-style setting."

North Beach, San Francisco, California
"Palermo Delicatessen has imported foods from Sicily and other regions of Italy. Folks line up for the Dungeness-crab-salad sandwich and toasted focaccia. Stella Pasticceria e Caffe, also in the neighborhood, was a favorite of (Luciano) Pavarotti. Have the prized sacripantina cake, a sponge cake made with rum. Two other local favorites: Mario's Bohemian Cigar Store, which serves delicious meatball focaccia sandwiches, and Molinari Delicatessen, famous for its salami and other dried meats." *sfnorthbeach.org*

Arthur Avenue, New York, New York
"Less touristy than its downtown counterpart, here are a few great spots you must try in this vibrant Little Italy. Many of the city's best chefs buy their seafood at Cosenza's Fish Market, where people enjoy the outdoor clam bar and oyster bar. Biancardi's butcher shop sells everything from prime steaks and chops to whole baby goats and tripe. Around the corner on 187th Street at De Lillo Pastry Shop, the anise-scented biscotti are among my faves." *arthuravenuebronx.com*

Little Italy, Chicago, Illinois
"All along Taylor Street, the main thoroughfare here, you'll find a bunch of Italian restaurants—from bakeries and sandwich shops to fine dining. Taylor Street also has the National Italian American Sports Hall of Fame. The Original Ferrara Bakery on Taylor Street is still here. Sixteen-year-old Salvatore Ferrara brought the art of Italian pastry-making and confectionery with him when he emigrated in 1900. Ferrara's has some of the best cannoli in the city." *littleitalychicago.com*

Ninth Street Italian Market, Philadelphia, Pennsylvania
"This outdoor market epitomizes the quintessential foods we associate with Little Italy, with stalls selling roasted red peppers, fresh

mozzarella, cannoli, fresh pasta. John's Water Ice, two blocks over on Seventh and Christian Street, is a South Philadelphia institution. It's a favorite spot for water ice, a combination of fruit or syrup and shaved ice." *phillyitalianmarket.com*

The Hill, St. Louis, Missouri
"After playing a round of bocce ball at the courts in Berra Park, stop by Adriana's on Shaw Avenue for poetic caponata (a Sicilian eggplant dish), the famous pasta pie with a meat crust special, and other Sicilian delights. Then find the deep-fried city treasure, toasted ravioli, at Mama Toscano's." *hill2000.org*

Little Italy, San Diego, California
"Assenti's Pasta on India Street makes their pasta fresh here on a noisy contraption in the back room, and Roberto and Luigi Assenti will sell you any one of 44 varieties." The annual Little Italy Precious Festa in October features music, food, and more. *littleitalysd.com*

North End, Boston, Massachusetts
"The best and most acclaimed café in the area is the deluxe Caffe Vittoria on Hanover Street. The decor is a mixture of pretension and authenticity. The coffee is remarkable, and the gelati are superior. Coconut and chocolate are top-selling flavors. Mike's Pastry, down the street, is another great spot." Order the lobster tail, a crusty baked pastry shell with a sweet, creamy filling named for its shape. *northendboston.com*

10 great markets to cultivate organic farmers

As more and more people eat organic, it's a good idea to celebrate the farmers and markets that include organic growers. And who better to ask for directions than Alice Waters, chef, author, and coowner of Chez Panisse in Berkeley, California? Waters, who is credited with spearheading the sustainable- and organic-food movement in the United States, shares her market picks.

Portland Farmers Market, Portland, Oregon
"Produce is the backbone of this market, but you'll also find buffalo,

wild salmon, oysters, clams, and artisan cheeses." The Saturday market on the campus of Portland State University has about 140 stalls and includes vendors from organic farms in the fertile Willamette River Valley. Patrons range from college students to local chefs. *portlandfarmersmarket.org*

Crescent City Farmers Market, New Orleans, Louisiana
This downtown market near the French Quarter has fresh shrimp and fish, along with a huge variety of flowers and produce. "Go to the Saturday market early, because things tend to sell out as the day goes on." The prices are good, and there's often free entertainment, from string quartets to jazz singers. *crescentcityfarmersmarket.org*

Green City Market, Chicago, Illinois
This market near Lake Michigan in Lincoln Park is noteworthy because it's a whole-day event with shopping, chef demonstrations, and local vendors selling prepared food from products sold at the market. "The focus here is on sustainable and organic agriculture." *chicagogreencitymarket.org*

Union Square Greenmarket, New York, New York
"The Greenmarket connects New Yorkers to the natural world and to the people who grow their food." *cenyc.org*

Santa Monica Farmers Market, Santa Monica, California
Organic is the emphasis at the Saturday market at Arizona Avenue and Third Street. You'll find Asian pears, pomegranates, grapes, and peaches, as well as an international crowd. The local Persian population favors the green pistachios, Oaxacans like the fresh shell beans, and flavorful greens will satisfy every culinary taste. *smgov.net/farmers_market*

Coconut Grove Organic Farmers Market, Coconut Grove, Florida
Blue and white tents and shady live oaks provide a canopy for this Miami-area market. "You'll find several kinds of avocados here, as well as heirloom organic tomatoes." The huge selection of produce also includes papaya, pineapple, and other tropical fruits, plus a full line of organic dried fruit and nuts. There's a raw-food

salad bar and a variety of juices and creamy nut milks. *glaserorganicfarms.com*

Santa Fe Farmers Market, Santa Fe, New Mexico
"This market is huge, with lots of local, organic produce. You'll find every kind of dried and fresh chile imaginable." Customers build relationships with the growers and may even visit them on the farm. Everything at the market comes from northern New Mexico—right down to the wheat baked in the bread. Events include chefs demonstrating techniques with ingredients from the market. *santafefarmersmarket.com*

City Farmers Market Wooster Square, New Haven, Connecticut
"It's important that healthy food is accessible to the entire community. Food stamps are accepted here, as are WIC coupons, enabling low-income women and children access to wholesome food. Vendors include students from the Yale Sustainable Food Project, selling produce they've grown themselves at Yale Farm." Look, too, for oysters, clams, and lobsters from Long Island Sound. *cityseed.org*

Eating energy efficiently

With Americans looking to reduce their carbon footprints, food seems an obvious place to start. Adopting a diet with a smaller carbon footprint means choosing foods that are processed in ways that emit less carbon dioxide into the atmosphere.

The chart below shows the number of miles you would have to drive to generate the same amount of carbon dioxide emitted in the production of one pound of each type of food listed.

	lbs of CO_2	miles
Beef	14.8	19.62
Pork	3.8	5.04
Chicken	1.1	1.46
Soybeans	0.26	0.36

Dane County Farmers Market, Madison, Wisconsin
Organic farming is widely supported in Wisconsin, a major agricultural producer, and it really wouldn't be Wisconsin without cheese.
"There are many fine artisan cheese makers at this market." But
that's not all. Pick up wild mushrooms, squash, and Brussels sprouts,
as well as any kind of steak—emu, elk, ostrich, pheasant, duck,
goose, pork, bison, venison, and rabbit. The market is beautifully
situated in a state park around the square near the State Capitol.
dcfm.org

Ferry Plaza Farmers Market, San Francisco, California
"This is the place I go on Saturdays to meet many of my friends,
selling extraordinary jams, bread, and organic produce." The food at
the market, located in a renovated 1898 ferry terminal that survived
all the city's major earthquakes, is exceptional in quality. And the
customers are so enthusiastic that farmers tend to pick their best for
this venue. *cuesa.org/markets*

10 great places to flag down a fabulous feast

*Eager chefs have taken the wheel, and they are steering
food in a whole new direction. The growing demand for
fresh local bounty has led to more food trucks and carts
working the streets nationwide, especially during
summer. Dana Cowin, editor in chief of* Food & Wine
magazine, shares her favorite movable feasts.

Skillet, Seattle, Washington
"Joshua Henderson, a former private chef, and
Danny Sizemore tool around Seattle in their
silver 1962 Airstream, which they've turned
into a kitchen-on-wheels. There's a
devoted following for the edgy, eclectic food they serve at various locations
around the city. (A weekly schedule is posted on their Web site.)
Favorites include poutine (a Canadian dish combining french fries
with cheese curds and gravy); hazelnut-crusted chicken; and Skillet's

pride and joy, a juicy Kobe beef burger topped with Cambozola cheese and bacon jam." *skilletstreetfood.com*

Chef Shack, Minneapolis, Minnesota
"This upscale street-food trailer, which can be found Saturday mornings at Minneapolis's Mill City Farmers Market, is a party on wheels: A live DJ provides the music, and there's a go-go dancer on the trailer's rooftop for entertainment. The Chef Shack serves "locally sourced dishes, including pulled-pork sandwiches, beef-tongue tacos, Indian-spiced doughnuts, and handmade ice-cream sandwiches." *millcityfarmersmarket.org*

RoliRoti, San Francisco, California
"Swiss-born Thomas Odermatt introduced his popular rotisserie-stocked trucks in 2001 with a single truck. He excels at anything spit-roasted, including pork rib roast, chicken, leg of lamb, and porchetta. Odermatt's chefs-on-wheels wear professional uniforms and bring high-end food to several locations in the Bay Area." *roliroti.com*

Green Truck, Culver City, California
"Fueled by used vegetable oil and biodiesel, stocked with locally grown, 100 percent certified organic ingredients and biodegradable containers and utensils, Green Truck company operates two trucks in various locations around the city and serves salads, grilled tuna tacos, and signature 'Mother Trucker' vegan burgers to L.A.'s health- and eco-conscious eaters." *greentruckonthego.com*

Flip Happy Crepes, Austin, Texas
"Austin just might be America's food-truck capital. If it is, Flip Happy Crepes's 1966 Avion trailer, where long waits are common, is its city hall. Flip Happy's owners use giant crepes like tortillas, wrapping them around a variety of sweet and savory fillings—from shredded pork with caramelized onions to smoked salmon with herbed cream cheese to lemon curd with blueberry dressing." *fliphappycrepes.com*

Que Crawl, New Orleans, Louisiana
"Located on the corner of Tchoupitoulas Street and Napoleon Avenue, just outside of Tipitina's, a popular live-music club, this K&B purple truck serves weekend music lovers long into the night.

Chef and owner Nathanial Zimet offers classic barbecue and creative Cajun sides, including ribs, pulled pork, po' boys, and duck gumbo, along with grits fries and fried boudin balls, homemade from the traditional Cajun sausage." *quecrawl.com*

DessertTruck, New York, New York

"Stationed near the New York University campus, this truck serves restaurant-quality desserts created by Jerome Change, a former pastry chef at New York's heralded Le Cirque restaurant. It's quickly become one of the city's most popular sweet stops, thanks to its rotating selection of desserts, including peanut-butter-and-milk-chocolate-mousse parfaits topped with caramel corn. One of its more adventurous (and memorable) creations is chocolate bread pudding topped with bacon crème anglaise." *desserttruck.com*

Ned's Groceria, Gloucester, Massachusetts

This is truck food with a twist. It comes delivered to your door with groceries, wine, and beer. "This mobile food market is stocked with local and imported foods such as grass-fed beef from Maine, Turkish figs, and loaves of locally baked bread. The owners deliver these specialty foods to your door, along with meals they prepare at their sister storefront, including calamari salad, roast beef, and stuffed tomatoes." *nedsgroceria.com*

Moxie Rx, Portland, Oregon

"Fruit juice and smoothies are the specialties here, but you'll also find inventive breakfast and brunch items like cheddar biscuits and buckwheat Belgian waffles." Grapefruit juice with basil and soda as well as the Rx—a smoothie made with bananas, dates, and almond butter—are top sellers.

Food Shark, Marfa, Texas

"This silver Ford delivery truck serves owners Adam Bork and Krista Steinhauer's excellent Mediterranean street food, including kebobs, hummus, and the ultra-popular Marfalafel (a playful way of describing their falafel)." Food Shark is parked across the street from the Marfa Book Store in a public pavilion. *foodsharkmarfa.com*

10 great places to nosh on authentic Jewish deli food

The classic Jewish deli was born of homesickness. Eastern European immigrants who flooded into New York from 1881 to 1924 brought with them a yearning for the Old Country. And they found it by sharing food and conversation in neighborhood eateries. Sadly, many of the time-honored Jewish delis are gone. How to identify the real deal? "The ambience isn't fancy. The menus always stay the same," says Sheryll Bellman, author of America's Great Delis: Recipes and Traditions from Coast to Coast. *She steers hungry deli-searchers to the following classic Jewish delis.*

Canter's Deli, Los Angeles, California
This old-fashioned deli in the heart of Los Angeles looks much as it did when it opened at its Fairfax Avenue location in 1953 (though it's been in business since 1931). "The booths are the same. Even the waitresses seem pretty much the same. And they have the best bakery in the city: babka, rugelach, cheese Danish, cheese blintzes. The best." *cantersdeli.com*

Stage Deli, New York, New York
Established in the heart of the theater district in 1937, the restaurant drew actors and theatergoers and continued to attract those loyal customers after it moved in 1943 to Seventh Avenue and 54th Street. The original owner, Russian immigrant Max Asnas, was the first to put a celebrity sandwich on the menu, a tradition that continues today, with creations such as the Dolly Parton (pastrami and corned beef on twin rolls). *stagedeli.com*

Shapiro's Delicatessen, Indianapolis, Indiana
Indianapolis isn't exactly where you'd expect to run across a classic deli, but this one has been in the Shapiro family for four generations. The cafeteria-style restaurant seats 250, who flock there to dine on traditional fare such as sour cream egg noodles and potato pancakes. *shapiros.com*

Zingerman's Delicatessen, Ann Arbor, Michigan
Owners Ari Weinzweig and Paul Saginaw couldn't find decent deli food in this Midwest college town, so they solved the problem by

opening their own place. "It's not that old—they opened in the '80s—but they've developed into a famous place where people go for the reason people go to delis—good, plentiful food." *zingermans.com*

Attman's Delicatessen, Baltimore, Maryland

Three generations of the Attman family have been serving up delicatessen delicacies at this institution on Baltimore's "Corned Beef Row." Try the traditional corned beef sandwich, washed down with a can of R.C. Cola. *attmansdeli.com*

Rose's Restaurant and Bakery, Portland, Oregon

Portland isn't exactly a hotbed of Jewish cooking, but Rose's has been an off-and-on fixture since 1956, when Rose Naftalin opened her place on NW 23rd Avenue. It has changed and expanded, but all rely on Naftalin's original recipes. People come from all over for the cinnamon rolls. *eatatroses.com*

Nate 'n Al Delicatessen Restaurant, Beverly Hills, California

The whitefish is delicious; the lox, divine. And the celebrity-spotting at this vintage deli isn't half bad either. Regulars include Larry King, Robert Wagner, and Neil Diamond. Even so, "it's not as touristy as some New York delis. It's more of a locals' place." Little has changed since opening day in 1945. "The waitresses have been there forever. The menu hasn't changed." And even in weight-conscious Beverly Hills, "on Sundays there's a line out the door." *natenal.com*

Corky & Lenny's, Woodmere Village, Ohio

This suburban Cleveland restaurant remains "*the* Jewish deli in the area," years after Corky Kurland and Lenny Kaden opened it. It's still family-run and still known for its chocolate phosphates—"what we in New York call an egg cream. There are no eggs and no cream. It's milk and chocolate syrup and seltzer." *corkyandlennys.com*

Carnegie Delicatessen, New York, New York

The sandwiches are huge. The waitstaff is surly. The tour buses line up outside. "It's the quintessential New York deli. You eat at these long tables and everything's delicious. It's a huge tourist place, but [diners] get their money's worth." *carnegiedeli.com*

Langer's Deli, Los Angeles, California
Patrons rhapsodize about the pastrami sandwiches, on the menu since 1947 at this downtown Los Angeles restaurant. Office workers routinely climb on the city's abbreviated subway system and take the "pastrami express"—the red line train to the Westlake/MacArthur Park stop—for one of these tender creations. *langersdeli.com*

Travel globally, eat locally

One of the tastier trends to emerge from the cookie-cutter realm of airport dining is that more vendors are attempting to add local flavor to their menus. Adventurous eaters who cruise the concourses will increasingly find iconic regional foods mixed among generic fare, as well as branches of popular area restaurants. Here's a sampling of options around the country.

Comida Buena Gourmet Deli and Bakery, Albuquerque (New Mexico) International Sunport
Regional food find: Green-chile chicken soup
Description: Green chiles, tomatoes, celery, and Southwest spices in a rich chicken broth

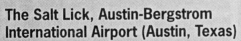

The Salt Lick, Austin-Bergstrom International Airport (Austin, Texas)
Regional food find: Barbecued-beef-brisket sandwich
Description: Slices of slow-smoked brisket on a sesame-seed bun, topped with barbecue sauce and served with a sour pickle on the side

Oaxaca Restaurant & Cantina, Sky Harbor International Airport (Phoenix, Arizona)
Regional food find: Tostada
Description: A fried corn tortilla filled with lettuce, cheese, and tomatoes

Jasper White's Summer Shack, Logan International Airport (Boston, Massachusetts)

Regional food find: Ipswich whole-belly-clam dinner

Description: Crispy fried clams with coleslaw and french fries

Gold Star Chili, Cincinnati-Northern Kentucky International Airport (Cincinnati, Ohio)

Regional food find: Cincinnati-style "five-way" chili

Description: Spaghetti topped with chili, onions, beans, and cheddar cheese

Andy Jackson's Tavern, Nashville (Tennessee) International Airport

Regional food find: Jack Daniel's Old No. 7 Tennessee Whiskey

Description: A mellow, charcoal-filtered whiskey from nearby Lynchburg

Shipyard Restaurant, Portland (Maine) International Jetport

Regional food find: Lobster wrap

Description: A whole-wheat wrap filled with lobster meat, lettuce, and tomato

Yankee Pier, San Francisco (California) International Airport

Regional food find: Dungeness crab cake

Description: Fresh crabmeat rolled in bread crumbs; flavored with onion, garlic, Tabasco, and hollandaise sauce; deep-fried; and served with cocktail and tartar sauces

Anthony's Restaurant & Fish Bar, Seattle-Tacoma (Washington) International Airport

Regional food find: Alder-planked silver salmon

Description: Roasted salmon fillets topped with smoked red pepper and white butter sauce

10 great places to harvest a bounty of artisan breads

A golden, fresh-baked loaf of bread can make a meal go from good to great. Peter Reinhart, author of Peter Reinhart's Whole Grain Breads: New Techniques, Extraordinary Flavor, *shares his recommendations for artisan bakeries nationwide.*

Acme Bread Co., San Francisco, California
"Acme, the first of the new-generation bakeries to consistently produce world-class hearth bread, is the most important artisan bread bakery in America. Every time I visit, the quality actually seems to improve." *ferrybuildingmarketplace.com/acme_bread_company.php*

Amy's Bread, New York, New York
"There's no shortage of terrific bakeries in New York, but Amy's Bread has distinguished itself for its commitment to quality products and community involvement. The semolina fennel raisin twists are a signature item, but all of the breads and pastries, such as the wonderful muffins, scones, and cakes, are baked with the same attention to detail and traditional craft techniques." *amysbread.com*

Clear Flour Bread, Brookline, Massachusetts
"Try the French Ancienne, a ciabattalike rustic bread with a crisp crust and creamy large-holed crumb. They also make dense, complex German rye breads. Check the Web site for their daily bread menu." *clearflourbread.com*

Village Bakery Cafe, Amarillo, Texas
"The ciabatta breads are beautifully holey, the croissants are flaky, and the fresh-fruit danishes are to die for. They also make seeded and red-curry lavash cracker breads, focaccia, and various country breads with nuts and cheeses, as well as gorgeous desserts." *villagebakerycafe.com*

Bit of Swiss Pastry Shoppe, Stevensville, Michigan
This bakery "makes you feel like you're in Europe, with extraordinary almond croissants, whole-wheat scones and pastries, along with

Bavarian-cream cakes, buttercream tortes, wedding cakes, and the finest-quality hearth and sandwich breads of all styles." *bitofswiss.com*

Companion, Clayton, Missouri
"Owner Josh Allen serves up great baked goods and also one of my favorite all-time breakfasts—custardy baked eggs with various fillings. The café also makes fabulous sandwiches on their ciabatta, New York rye, croissants, and Parisian and specialty breads. There is also an inspiring array of moist cakes, colorful tarts, and petits fours." *companionstl.com*

Pearl Bakery, Portland, Oregon
"The huge, four-pound pillowy Pugliese loaves are, alone, worth a special trip. The pastries are every bit as good as the breads." *pearlbakery.com*

Mrs. London's, Saratoga Springs, New York
"Whether it's meringues and macaroons; custard-filled Saint-Tropez Beret; or soups, salads, and sandwiches—everything is done with a spectacular flair for both presentation and flavor. The food here will transport you to Paris—and Saratoga Springs isn't too shabby in its own right." *mrslondons.com*

King Arthur Flour Bakery, Norwich, Vermont
"One of America's greatest bakers, Jeffrey Hamelman, presides at this destination bakeshop on the scenic Vermont/New Hampshire border, where you can take classes in the showcase bakeshop at the headquarters of the famous King Arthur Flour Catalog. No point in listing the products—you will want everything—but the rye breads and pastries are definitely not to be missed." *kingarthurflour.com*

Seven Stars Bakery, Providence, Rhode Island
"Hearty, crusty, European-style breads come flying out of the giant round brick oven built at this shop just blocks from Brown University on Providence's East Side. The baguettes are terrific, but so is the crusty olive bread—difficult choice, so get them both." *sevenstarsbakery.com*

10 great places to eat regionally, eat well

This country's most unique foods are best experienced in native settings. Jane and Michael Stern's book 500 Things to Eat Before It's Too Late *is a state-by-state guide to must-eats across America. Michael shares his favorites.*

Hell's Kitchen, Minneapolis, Minnesota
"Chef Mitch Omer got the idea for mahnomin porridge while reading the Lewis and Clark diaries. Explorers described a Cree Indian dish based on the region's hand-parched wild rice. To the native Minnesota grain he adds enough cream to give it an oatmeal-like consistency, then he flavors it with roasted hazelnuts, dried berries, and maple syrup. It is deeply satisfying, fascinating, and just plain delicious." *hellskitcheninc.com*

Frank Pepe Pizzeria Napoletana, New Haven, Connecticut
"This is the daddy of all pizza. Pepe's signature is white-clam pizza, invented half a century ago when a clam vendor in an alley near the pizza parlor convinced Frank Pepe that the two of them could make sweet music together." They have succeeded. The combination of fresh clams and garlic is worth the wait. *pepespizzeria.com*

Keaton's, Cleveland, North Carolina
"There is fried chicken, which is crunchy-chewy-juicy bliss, and there is hot fried chicken, which just might make you swoon, not only because it is dizzyingly delicious but because it is thermonuclear. Here, after being fried to a golden crisp, the parts are dipped in simmering barbecue sauce for a hot-pepper zest. It belongs in a food group of its own." *keatonsoriginalbbq.com*

Frontier Restaurant, Albuquerque, New Mexico
"Carne adovado, pork marinated in liquefied chiles until it absorbs the flavor and heat, is a dish that celebrates pepper power. The great-bargain carne adovado... is a burrito at the Frontier. It doesn't contain any extras, just chile-infused meat intense enough to turn the tortilla that wraps it the color of a sunset." *frontierrestaurant.com*

Eating on the cheap while traveling

Frugal travelers are finding creative ways to get more bang for their buck at mealtime. Here are some ways to save money and feel satisfied:

- Stay in hotels where meals are included in the room rate. Check into hotels that offer complimentary continental breakfasts or happy hours.

- Pick up extra bagels and fruit on your way out. That way you'll save breakfast and lunch money.

- Depending on where you stay, dinner could be on the hotel as well. Fill up on the free food served during happy hour.

- Cook your own meals. Some travelers on longer trips check into hotel rooms with kitchens, such as at Residence Inns and Embassy Suites.

- The hotel ice bucket can serve as a small temporary fridge. Put the ice on top of your sealed food, then wrap the entire bucket in the numerous towels provided.

- Avoid eating at airport lounges and hotel restaurants. Their prices are usually steep. Ask residents for recommendations in the suburbs. Out-of-the way local restaurants are sometimes cheaper and tastier.

- Look for restaurants on the Internet, in travel guidebooks, or in reviews in local papers. Ask the hotel concierge for recommendations within your price range.

- Use hot water from the in-room coffeemaker for "instant" meals such as oatmeal, soup, noodles, etc.

- Don't pass up airline snacks if you're not hungry—stash them in your carry-on bag for later.

Hansen's Sno-Bliz, New Orleans, Louisiana
"New Orleans is known for food that is hot and spicy. Hansen's Sno-Bliz is cool and soothing. The shaved-ice machine was invented here. Theirs makes ice that is neither crushed nor crystals but more like newly fallen snow. Flavored syrups are added in layers, so you

taste them all the way to the bottom of the cup." Live large and top it off with a rich layer of condensed milk. *snobliz.com*

Cherry Hut, Beulah, Michigan

"Northern Michigan is cherry country, and starting in June, roadside stands sell bags of washed cherries ready to enjoy while you drive. A first-rate cherry pie is more than happy and delicious. It has mystique. It is fresh, bright, and innocent. It is the purest of pies. The Cherry Hut uses only just-picked local cherries in its first-rate pies." The flaky crust is made the old-fashioned way, with pure lard. *cherryhutproducts.com*

Louie Mueller Barbecue, Taylor, Texas

"Mueller's brisket is celestial. As the inherently fatty cut of cow basks in wood smoke, its marbling melts and turns the once-tough cut recklessly tender, more like warm butter than beefsteak. Its exterior, blackened by time in the pit, has some crunch and an even more concentrated flavor." The smoke-tinged walls in this former school gym provide a peeled-paint backdrop for the gold standard of Texas barbecue. *louiemuellerbarbecue.com*

Sahagun, Portland, Oregon

"The primary purpose here is to tell you that Elizabeth Montes's hot chocolate is as rapturous as love itself. But please note a few other heartthrob specialties in this earnest little sweetshop. You will also find lavender truffles, candied Meyer lemon peels, chile-lemon soda, roasted cocoa beans, and hazelnut sour cherry bark here. As for the hot chocolate . . . it almost feels illicit." *sahagunchocolates.com*

McClard's Bar-B-Q, Hot Springs, Arkansas

"Like humans, french fries come in all shapes and sizes. Attractive french fries are dressed in so many different ways, from slender, honey-brown twigs to thick spud logs. Southern barbecues use potatoes as dressing for a pork plate. At McClard's, [the fries] top slabs of hickory-cooked ribs. As you dig into these platters with fork or fingers, the meat sauce and potatoes mingle in wanton rapture." *mcclards.com*

Red's Eats, Wiscasset, Maine
"A whole lobster requires concentrated effort to eat, but a lobster roll is trouble-free. It is the simplest sandwich, basically lobster meat surrounded by bread. The best lobster roll on Earth is served at an extremely humble shack known as Red's Eats. Red's primacy is a legend among lobster lovers, who flock to it in such numbers (summer only), the wait in line can be up to an hour."

POPULAR FOODS

10 great places to give yourself a cookie

Chocolate chip? Sugar? Peanut butter? That's right— it's cookie time! Veteran cookie baker Judy Rosenberg, owner of Rosie's Bakeries in the Boston area and author of Rosie's Bakery Chocolate-Packed Jam-Filled Butter-Rich No-Holds-Barred Cookie Book, *shares the bakeries she happily frequents when away from her own.*

William Greenberg Jr. Desserts, New York, New York
Growing up in New York, Rosenberg says this local institution's flavors and textures inspired her to create her first desserts. It's a mix of "American and unpretentious Eastern European" pastries "dripping with butter." Her favorites are the raspberry thumbprints, the pecan cookies, and the "to-die-for Linzer tarts." Don't miss the cinnamon babka—"you will never find anything" like it. *wmgreenbergdesserts.com*

City Bakery, New York, New York
Owner Maury Rubin melds a "down-home and gourmet feel" seamlessly in his original New York bakery. The "absolutely delicious" cookies are worth the trip, especially the sugar domes and melted chocolate-chip cookies. *thecitybakery.com*

Miette Organic Patisserie, San Francisco, California
These mostly organic cookies and baked goods were first sold under a pink tent at the Berkeley Farmers Market before the operation

moved into a tiny boutique. The chocolate sables (French butter cookies) and walnut shortbreads are "outstanding," as are the jam thumbprints "with jam made from seasonal organic or unsprayed fruit." *miettecakes.com*

Macrina Bakery and Cafe, Seattle, Washington
Owner Leslie Mackie creates "earthy, great-tasting cookies made with high-quality ingredients." Standouts include chocolate-chip-espresso-apricot cookies with ground espresso beans and unsulphured fruit and brown-sugar shortbreads "imprinted with seasonal designs." *macrinabakery.com*

Bittersweet, Chicago, Illinois
Patrons will enjoy watching through the "viewing window as these artisans prepare their French-inspired desserts" in this Lakeview bakery café. It's best known for its sable and "beautiful" butter cookies cut in shapes like "butterflies or hearts and decorated with colored icings." She recommends pairing them with a "cup of their half coffee, half hot chocolate concoction." *bittersweetpastry.com*

Sophia's Bakery, Portland, Maine
Owner and *Diet Code* author Stephen Lanzalotta has "come up with a selection of totally healthy cookies that actually taste good and are pretty much guilt-free." Based on Leonardo da Vinci's Golden Ratio, Lanzalotta's recipes—such as flourless chocolate-chip cookies with spelt and whole-grain oats and his "shortbreadlike" ricciarelli that is flour- and dairy-free—stick to a 52 percent carb, 20 percent protein, and 28 percent fat ratio.

Rene's Bakery, Indianapolis, Indiana
Baker A. Rene Trevino's Chocolate Chewiest, a flourless and butter-free chocolate cookie with walnuts, are "decidedly delicious." The bakery also offers "the best lemon-curd tartlets I have ever tasted." *renesbakery.com*

Downtown Bakery and Creamery, Healdsburg, California
This nearly all-organic Sonoma County bakery, "with its great smells and open kitchen," makes "California-American with European influence" cookies that are "just like homemade." Don't miss its

"staples"—crisp ginger wafers, oatmeal raisin with nuts and chocolate, and crisp chocolate-chip cookies. *downtownbakery.net*

Susina Bakery & Cafe, Los Angeles, California

Stepping into this Art Nouveau patisserie and surveying the European-inspired cookies, chocolates, and tarts feels like a trip to the Continent. There is no "other bakery where you can find beautiful Italian cookies made only with pure butter—no shortening whatsoever." *susinabakery.com*

Jean-Paul Hevin Chocolatier, Paris, France

When in Paris, Rosenberg samples the local bakeries. Extensively. And "after tasting the classic macaroon" all over the City of Light, Hevin's are the best. "Moist and chewy and intensely chocolate." *jphevin.com*

10 great places to chow down on barbecue

The toughest thing about declaring the nation's top barbecue joints? Winnowing the list, says Karen Adler, author of several books on barbecuing, including The BBQ Queens' Big Book of Barbecue. *Indeed, there is no shortage of smokin' 'cue in this land, and in her travels Adler has sampled some of the tastiest regional specialties, from brisket to short ribs. She directs us to her favorite joints.*

Dreamland Drive-In Bar-B-Cue, Tuscaloosa, Alabama

This shanty-style roadhouse serves one thing and one thing only: spareribs with a side of white bread. "No fries, no slaw, no pulled pork, or brisket. They do one thing, and they do it to perfection. These ribs are fabulous, with a sauce that's in between vinegary and sweet." *dreamlandbbq.com*

Big Bob Gibson Bar-B-Q, Decatur, Alabama

The family-owned restaurant is known for its Alabama white sauce, made of thin mayonnaise, apple cider vinegar, and pepper, served with hickory-smoked chicken. "It's very different. But people have been raving about it since the 1920s, when they opened." *bigbobgibsonbbq.com*

Hickory Hollow BBQ, Ellenton, Florida

The restaurant, located between St. Petersburg and Sarasota, serves delicious North Carolina–style barbecue (pulled pork with a vinegar-based sauce). But the seasonal vegetable dishes, such as corn pudding, collards, and black-eyed peas, pack them in too.

R.U.B., New York, New York

The initials stand for Righteous Urban Barbecue, and world championship barbecuer Paul Kirk serves just that at his restaurant in the city's Chelsea neighborhood. The menu features traditional slow-smoked baby back and spareribs, brisket, and pulled pork, along with nontraditional offerings such as Szechwan smoked duck and pastrami that's smoked in-house.

Wilber's Barbecue, Goldsboro, North Carolina

Wilber's serves eastern North Carolina–style barbecue—they smoke the whole hog. "This is one of those places with an old-fashioned wood fire pit." It's known for its pulled pork, served on a plate or as a sandwich, chopped and dressed with peppery vinegar sauce. "When peaches are in season, there's a farmer selling outside, and people leave and eat ripe peaches for dessert in the parking lot." *wilbersbarbecue.com*

Goode Co. Bar-B-Q, Houston, Texas

"It's a typical Texas barbecue place with rough barnwood interior" serving delicious slow-smoked mesquite barbecue. *goodecompany.com*

Kreuz Market, Lockhart, Texas

"Kreuz, like several other butcher/barbecue places, serves beef-shoulder clod. Most places outside of Texas do not serve this cut. They serve all their meats in brown butcher paper." *www.kreuzmarket.com*

The Bar-B-Q Shop, Memphis, Tennessee

The signature dish at this midtown eatery is the pork sandwich on Texas toast—chopped or pulled pork with a vinegar-based sauce. It also serves ribs, and as is typical in Memphis barbecue joints, customers have a choice of "wet" (slathered in sauce) or "dry" (with additional spice rub sprinkled over them). Look for the two dancing pigs on the sign out front. *dancingpigs.com*

Fiorella's Jack Stack Barbecue, Kansas City, Missouri
"They do one thing better than anyone else in Kansas City, and that's burnt ends. They cut off the crusty ends of the meat (brisket, pork roast, and ham) and chop it up nice and sauce it (tomato-based sauce with a little vinegar, but not too sweet) and serve it as their signature sandwich, the Poor Russ." Don't miss the barbecued baked beans, made with leftover meat—brisket, pork, and sometimes chicken—flavored with meat juices from the smoker. *jackstackbbq.com*

BB's Lawnside Bar-B-Q, Kansas City, Missouri
For those who enjoy a side of blues with their brisket, this roadhouse is the place, presenting live music Wednesday through Sunday. The restaurant adds a dash of New Orleans to the menu with its signature dish, Smokey Jo's Gumbo, made of smoked sausage, chicken, turkey, and ham in a tomato-based stock. "They also serve rib tips, which is sort of a lost art. They're a great appetizer." *bbslawnsidebbq.com*

10 great places to get your licks in

Ice cream is the perfect sweet to be savored all summer—or all year—long. Mark DeCarlo, host of Travel Channel's Taste of America, *shares some favorite places. "Nothing beats chasing the neighborhood ice-cream truck,' DeCarlo says, "but around this country, there are frozen confections that are worth a detour."*

Pinkberry, Los Angeles, California
Pinkberry "is so trendy that the West Hollywood location's celebrity-watching factor ranks the shop practically as a tourist attraction in itself." The zero-fat, low-sugar treat is topped with a choice of healthful fresh berries. *pinkberry.com*

Angelo Brocato's, New Orleans, Louisiana
"If you can withstand the gelato temptation, go for the light, delicious, and cold lemon ice" in the airy dining room at Angelo Brocato's in the lush Garden District. All of their ices are made from scratch—"though they won't say exactly how."
angelobrocatoicecream.com

Graeter's, Cincinnati, Ohio
There are those who say Graeter's ice cream is reason enough to visit the Queen City. "Graeter's still uses the same French pot process the founders brought from Europe in the 19th century. The result is indescribable creaminess." *graeters.com*

Leon's Frozen Custard, Milwaukee, Wisconsin
"Home of the World's Favorite Frozen Custard" is the claim, and Leon's sells more than 100,000 gallons every year. "The 1950s-style establishment—the inspiration for the original Arnold's in the TV sitcom *Happy Days*—is still a drive-up, but the carhops are gone, so you fetch your own soft-serve." *foodspot.com/leons*

Ghirardelli, San Francisco, California
In recognition of the oldest continuously operating chocolate factory in the country, an entire historic city square was named after the Ghirardelli Chocolate Company. "You can always take Ghirardelli's premium chocolate squares home, but it is advisable to eat the hot fudge sundae on the premises." *ghirardelli.com*

OTTO, New York, New York
"As many times as we see New York's Washington Square in the movies or on TV, nothing beats the real thing, especially when you can do your people-watching while licking gelato from OTTO's old-fashioned cart." Adventurous tasters swear by the unusual flavors, such as olive oil, roasted cinnamon, or pumpkin and ginger.
ottopizzeria.com

Ted Drewes, St. Louis, Missouri
"Treat yourself to a Ted Drewes signature 'concrete'—custard blended with any of dozens of ingredients and served so thick that

AND ANOTHER THING . . .

GELATO GOODNESS

Traditional ice cream may be in for a licking. Or at least a little healthy competition. More Americans are turning to gelato as the newest form of cool—not only in culinary-hip Los Angeles and New York but also in less likely locales such as Baltimore.

These gelaterias make small batches with premium ingredients:

- **Gelato Bar:** Studio City, California. Besides Italian classics such as Nocciola, Stracciatella, and Gianduia, flavors include English toffee, cinnamon-basil, and rosemary-lemon. *gelatobar-la.com*

- **Bulgarini:** Pasadena, California. Highlights include Valrhona chocolate-rum and zabaglione made with marsala from Sicily. *bulgarinigelato.com*

- **Pitango Gelato:** Baltimore, Maryland. Uses organic ingredients and traditional Italian methods. Flavors include Italian chocolate-hazelnut and roasted pistachio, as well as kiwi yogurt and chocolate infused with hot peppers. *pitangogelato.com*

- **Grom:** New York, New York. Uses all-natural, premium ingredients. The most popular is Grom Cream—an egg-cream base mixed with corn biscuits from Italy and chocolate flakes from Colombia. *grom.it/eng*

when the large yellow cup is turned upside-down, neither the contents nor the spoon and straw fall out." *teddrewes.com*

Bobtail Ice Cream Company, Chicago, Illinois
"At dusk in the Windy City, head to Buckingham Fountain to be there when it lights up. Enjoy the cooling spray, then walk over to the Bobtail Ice Cream Company for Grandpa Wilcoxon's Signature Sunset: Merlot ice cream studded with chocolate chunks. Eat it on the patio overlooking Lake Michigan, the Chicago skyline, and Millennium Park." *bobtailicecream.com*

Valentino, Las Vegas, Nevada
"Sit down to a gourmet meal and indulge in a frozen delight for dessert—either a delicate seasonal-fruit sorbet and fruit composition or frozen mousse, with a smooth texture and flavor that melts straight into your taste buds." *venetian.com*

Waiola Shave Ice, Honolulu, Hawaii
"At Waiola Shave Ice, they go out of their way to make sure you say it right: shave ice, no 'd.' Gallon-size frozen chunks of fresh local water are shaved by a machine that works like a circular sander; tiny flakes of ice (not slush) are packed into a cone with adzuki beans and drenched with handcrafted syrups in tropical mango, pineapple, and guava flavors."

10 great places to get jazzed about great java

Whether you're a coffee lover or trying to cut back, every cup should count. Kenneth Davids—author of books on coffee, editor of coffeereview.com, and a respected taster and consultant— recommends spots where he gets a great one.

Bay View Farm, Honaunau, Hawaii
The Big Island's famed Kona is "the only coffee grown [commercially] in the United States, and this is a good place to taste the best." The farmers drive here from the higher altitudes where coffee is grown. Bay View processes and roasts it. *bayviewfarmcoffees.com*

Caffe Dante and Caffe Reggio, New York, New York
"The Italian Americans hung out here and played cards," Davids says of Caffe Reggio, which claims to have made the first cappuccino in the United States. The small room is "authentic and simple," with a vintage chrome-and-bronze espresso machine. One of those beauties adorns Caffe Dante too. Both Greenwich Village stalwarts "make a rough, old-fashioned Italian coffee—a robust, sharp, dark roast. You're experiencing espresso as it was early in the century, before it became a mall drink." *caffe-dante.com; cafereggio.com*

Caffe Trieste, San Francisco, California
Grant Avenue in North Beach "has kept its bohemian, funky atmosphere," and Trieste patrons have "held down the fort against pure tourism. They roast their own coffee...kind of a rough, robust, 'take no prisoners' espresso." *caffetrieste.com*

Peet's, Berkeley, California
The original store, where Alfred Peet "used to roast coffee in the back," is a landmark in coffee history: Many industry people "feel it started the specialty-coffee movement," because it pioneered small-batch, in-store roasting. "The way they brew, the roast style, and the coffees they choose are a...treasure: strong, heavy-bodied drip coffee." *peets.com*

Zoka, Seattle, Washington
Zoka's espresso is "hearty but more refined" than that served by older places like Trieste. It's "full-bodied" without tasting sharp or bitter. Paladino is its signature espresso; Tangletown is the popular drip blend. *zokacoffee.com*

Stumptown Coffee Roasters, Portland, Oregon
"They're extremely serious: They serve coffee in French presses only." They buy prize-winning beans and "treat coffee like wine." Stumptown is representative of "a new wave of young people who entered the business seven to ten years ago and are now industry leaders." *stumptowncoffee.com*

Intelligentsia Coffee Roasters, Chicago, Illinois
As serious about its coffee as Stumptown, this company serves "amazing coffees, some of the world's finest." Itelligentsia "hired a young guy just to go around the world picking out small lots of exceptional coffee." Its celebrated espresso blend, Black Cat, is "robust. People who like intensity will like it." *intelligentsiacoffee.com*

Cafe Beignet, New Orleans, Louisiana
This "cute, tucked-away place" near the French Quarter's police station is also "cool for people-watching. It's real New Orleans" and makes its beignets in-house. "The coffee is produced by Coffee

Roasters of New Orleans.... All their coffees are excellent; the chicory is refined, not too overpowering." *cafebeignet.com*

News Cafe, Miami Beach, Florida
This 24-hour Ocean Drive hot spot surrounded by neon-lit Art Deco hotels is "more an outdoor café-bar than a coffee place...a people-watching scene any time of day." You can order a regular cup or a thick, sweet Cuban coffee. *newscafe.com*

True Grounds, Somerville, Massachusetts
This "classic neighborhood café" in the Boston area showcases local artists and serves Terroir, "one of the finest, most refined aficionado coffees." All coffees are from one farm in Brazil, "light-roasted, emphasizing the natural sweetness." *truegrounds.com*

10 great places to make a beeline for the honey

If you've heard the buzz on declining honeybee populations, then you may enjoy treats made with honey more than ever. Bruce Boynton, CEO of the National Honey Board, shares his list of sweet places to enjoy the fruits of honeybees' labor.

Buzz Bakery, Alexandria, Virginia
Buzz Bakery uses honey in a variety of products throughout the year. Specials include wildflower-honey ice cream, Bee Hive sugar cookies, and Tupelo honey panna cotta. *buzzonslaters.com*

Elixir, San Francisco, California
This speakeasy in the Mission district creates cocktails that often play up organic, local, and homemade ingredients, including house-infused honey syrups that "water down" the honey to adapt it to a drink. *elixirsf.com*

Carolina's Restaurant, Charleston, South Carolina
This landmark Lowcountry restaurant regularly uses honey from a beekeeper located on one of the coastal islands in a variety of dishes,

including a smoked-honey ice cream amuse-bouche and a honey panna cotta. *carolinasrestaurant.com*

Delicious! Bakery & Cafe, Valley, Nebraska

This tiny bakery outside Omaha, which focuses on organic, hormone-free ingredients, created a hit when it started making honey-caramel sticky buns.

Cultural Center, Chicago, Illinois

Chicago is one of the few cities that allows beekeeping, and several beehives are located atop the roofs of City Hall and the Cultural Center in Chicago. The bees pollinate the flowers along Michigan Avenue and in Grant Park, rewarding the beekeepers with a few hundred jars of honey, which are sold at the center to support a job-training program.

The Plantation House Restaurant, Kapalua, Hawaii

Located on Maui, the Plantation House Restaurant dishes up a scallop skewer appetizer that is wrapped in apple-smoked bacon and finished with a Lehua-honey-and-guava glaze. Made from the blossoms of the native Hawaiian ohia tree, Lehua honey has a light, floral taste. *theplantationhouse.com*

Panzano, Denver, Colorado

This Northern Italian restaurant in the Hotel Monaco serves up a charcuterie platter with hazelnuts, melon, and pecorino cheese that's drizzled with clover honey. *panzano-denver.com*

Cambridge Brewing Co., Boston, Massachusetts

In a refurbished mill, the Cambridge Brewing Co. encourages customers to take a long sip of their Arquebus, a summer barley wine. One of the ingredients that makes the brew special is the honey, produced by bees kept within five miles of the brewery. *cambrew.com*

Gracie's, Providence, Rhode Island

Gracie's features honey regularly on the ever-changing tasting menu. The chef drizzles wildflower honey from Massachusetts on a beet salad with roasted pecans and dishes up a honey beer bread, made from Smuttynose India pale ale and honey. The restaurant also roasts stone fruits with honey from Honig Vineyard in Napa Valley. *graciesprov.com*

Sky River Meadery, Sultan, Washington
In the Cascade Mountains, Sky River brews mead, an alcoholic drink made from honey. Legend has it that honey descended from heaven as dew and was gathered by bees. The mead, created from the nectar, bestowed health, strength, and virility to the drinkers. Sky River brews several styles of mead, including a sweet and dry, which are available to sample in their tasting room. *skyriverbrewing.com*

Children are hardier than you think

Maureen Wheeler and her husband, Tony, founded Lonely Planet, the Australia-based adventure and budget guidebook publisher, in 1973. "Travel is Tony's and my identity. We couldn't quit when I had babies." Her book *Travel with Children* was among the first family-adventure guidebooks.

- **Key advice:** "Americans are so timid. Don't be. Don't underestimate children. They will take on more challenges than you imagine." Still, she says, "you have to meet kids halfway to make a great trip." Upgrade to hotels with modern plumbing and restaurants with chairs; trade days of cultural enlightenment with days at the beach; let children eat Western junk food when they find it.

- **Hot spots:** "If you have two weeks, take your kids to Nepal, not Disney. It will be so much richer for all of you." Her children first went when one was three years and the other was eight months old. The kids trekked when they were preschoolers. "And these are kids who use a remote to change TV channels."

- **New directions:** "Asia is the best. They welcome children everywhere, unlike England, Australia, or America where a restaurant owner looks with horror when your children walk in."

Bread to feed our friendship,
Salt to keep it true,
Water is for a welcome,
And wine to drink with you.
—French blessing

ARTS AND CULTURE

✳ ✳ ✳ ✳

ARCHITECTURE

10 great places to be dazzled by humans' labor

Just as man "does not live by bread alone," humankind does not toil merely to eat. Barry Goldsmith, professor of architectural history at New York University, shares his picks of tremendous achievements created by the brains and brawn of people through the ages.

Pyramids of Giza/Abu-Simbel, Egypt
The Great Pyramid, dating to the 25th century B.C., is the only one of the Seven Wonders of the Ancient World to survive and is part of a complex that includes other pyramids and the Sphinx. Located near Cairo, the giant tomb was built for the Pharaoh Khufu (Cheops) by thousands of human beings. "Even today, the proportions are dazzling." Farther south near Aswan, a modern-day feat of engineering in the 1960s moved the Abu-Simbel temple and its four gigantic statues of Ramses to save it for posterity.

Hoover Dam, Nevada/Arizona border
"The Hoover Dam was the largest concrete structure ever built when it was constructed between 1931 and 1936. In fact, the amount of concrete used could pave a two-lane highway from San Francisco to New York." New technology had to be developed for such a huge mass of concrete to set and dry evenly. Unfortunately, building the dam claimed 100 lives. *usbr.gov/lc/hooverdam*

Angkor Wat, Cambodia
Angkor Wat is the world's most extensive temple complex: It's made up of more than 70 Buddhist temples primarily built from the 9th through the 12th centuries. Its 77 square miles were lost

until the temples were rediscovered by the French in the 19th century. "Almost every inch of these stone temples is covered with exquisite carving. These masterpieces are ever more amazing because they were created in the middle of an unbearably hot, steamy jungle."

Panama Canal, Panama

The country was carved out of Colombia by the administration of President Theodore Roosevelt so the United States could build this canal linking the Atlantic and Pacific oceans. "For ten years, up to 45,000 men at a time dug through swamps infested by mosquitoes carrying yellow fever and malaria. Their wages, at least, were considered high: 30 cents a day, plus meals." *www.pancanal.com*

Golden Gate Bridge, San Francisco, California

There are longer suspension bridges than the Golden Gate Bridge, but none have held the record for being the longest longer: 27 years, from 1937 to 1964. And it held the record for the world's tallest suspension towers for even longer. "The Art Deco aesthetics of this beautiful bridge are enhanced by the artfully positioned lighting. No wonder the Golden Gate is the most photographed bridge ever." *goldengate.org*

Great Wall of China, People's Republic of China

It took the Chinese 1,800 years (from the 2nd century B.C. to the 16th century A.D.) to complete the world's longest structure. "What makes it so spectacular is that it follows the varying topography of China for thousands of miles, from straight, barren deserts to riding up the crests of mountains and down to valleys. Contrary to popular myth, it cannot be seen from space." *greatwall-of-china.com*

Channel Tunnel, the English Channel

Great Britain joined the European Union in 1973, but it took until 1994 for the British Isles to be physically linked to the Continent with the completion of the "Chunnel," the 31-mile tunnel under the

English Channel. The Eurostar high-speed train now connects Paris with London in less than three hours. "Modern technology has fulfilled this age-old dream, and by connecting Britain to France, it has indirectly fulfilled another dream—getting better food to England." *eurotunnel.com*

Mount Rushmore National Memorial, Black Hills of South Dakota
The largest work of art in the world, Mount Rushmore is the culmination of 14 years of combining engineering and sculpting skills
with the muscle of 400 men detonating explosives and wielding huge drills. (Remarkably, there were no fatalities.) "The face of each of the four presidents is 60 feet tall, more than three times the size of the head of the Statue of Liberty."
nps.gov/moru

Machu Picchu/Sacsayhuaman, Peru
Machu Picchu is another of the world's wonders that was hidden and forgotten until its rediscovery in the early 20th century. The 15th-century Inca city was entirely self-sufficient: Manmade terraces literally supported farming. "We still do not know how they got the huge chiseled stones up the steep mountain. Nor did the Incas use mortar: The massive hewn boulders—even larger at nearby Sacsayhuaman—were intricately stacked and fitted together like pieces in an enormous jigsaw puzzle."
machupicchu.org

Peterhof, St. Petersburg, Russia
"One of the world's most beautiful palace complexes has the world's most magnificent display of artistic waterworks: dozens of cascading fountains, as far as the eye can see, propelled only by gravity. This would be an engineering marvel today, let alone when it was created in the early 18th century." Almost destroyed by the Nazis, the palace and fountains were meticulously restored and replicated after World War II.

AND ANOTHER THING...

SPECTACULAR SPANS

These bridges were picked by *Engineer* magazine as tops in the United States:

- The Golden Gate Bridge, San Francisco, California. Almost everyone's favorite. In a word, "magnificent."

- Houston Ship Channel Bridge, Texas. Great shortcut, always a plus in Texas.

- Glenwood Canyon I-70 Bridges, Colorado. "Scenic wonder and an engineering masterpiece."

- Clark Bridge, Alton, Illinois. Cable-stayed design, "an elegant solution to an engineering challenge."

- Tom Moreland Interchange, Atlanta, Georgia. "Six major bridges, a four-level interchange. And it looks good."

- Yaquina Bay Bridge, Newport, Oregon. "Classic, nicely detailed concrete arch bridge, one of the few left on the West Coast."

- Father Louis Hennepin Bridge, Minneapolis, Minnesota. Links artistry and engineering. "A concrete sculpture."

- Roosevelt Lake Bridge, Roosevelt, Arizona. "Longest (1,080 feet) two-lane arch bridge in the United States."

- Rainbow Bridge, Niagara Falls, New York. "Named for the rainbow that's always over Niagara Falls."

- Brooklyn Bridge, New York, New York. "You grab the suspender cables and feel the vibration of traffic. It's alive!"

- Wire Bridge, New Portland, Maine. "May be the oldest (1866) suspension bridge in the country."

- Varina-Enon Bridge, Richmond, Virginia. "Example of how straight lines can work."

10 great places to revel in cinematic grandeur

There's more to going to the movies than just the movie, says Ross Melnick, coauthor with Andrea Fuchs of Cinema Treasures: A New Look at Classic Movie Theaters. *"Experience the theater as art," says Melnick, who shares these gorgeous historic gems, perfect for viewing today's first-runs.*

Academy of Music Theatre, Northampton, Massachusetts
"Built for $125,000 in 1890, the Academy of Music showed its first motion picture here eight years later. Harry Houdini, Mae West, and a host of celebrities appeared on its stage, and scores of others graced its screen. Located in this college town, one of the oldest movie theaters in the country still boasts its original 19th-century balcony, lounge, and private boxes." *academyofmusictheatre.com*

Fargo Theatre, Fargo, North Dakota
"The snow outside is white, but the delightful Art Deco/moderne interior of this theater, featuring multicolored Deco mirrors and mahogany-wood accents, shines in the blue-neon splendor of the 1937 remodeling." *fargotheatre.org*

Galaxy Lafayette Theatre, Suffern, New York
This theater, "which celebrated its 80th anniversary in 2004 restored and renovated, is in many ways better than ever."

Grauman's Chinese Theatre, Hollywood, California
"As the most famous movie theater in the world, the May 1927 palace received a $7 million renovation in time for its 75th birthday." Check out the famous handprints and footprints in the forecourt before catching a blockbuster inside. *manntheatres.com/chinese*

Landmark's Mayan Theatre, Denver, Colorado
"Before its November 1930 opening as part of the Fox Theatres circuit, this theater was exorcised of evil spirits by members of a local Native American tribe. Although it closed down in 1980,

it was reopened as a triplex in 1985 by Landmark Theatres, the nation's largest art-house theater circuit."
landmarktheatres.com/market/Denver/MayanTheatre.htm

Loews Uptown Theatre, Washington, D.C.

"Originally opened by Warner Bros. in 1936, the Uptown is one of the oldest (and most lauded) theaters in the Loews Cineplex empire. This John Zink–designed Art Moderne classic, which features a massive screen, has been an event-film mecca for Washington, D.C.-area audiences for decades."

Panida Theatre, Sandpoint, Idaho

"If you feel a cool breeze after sitting down in this Spanish Mission–style auditorium, opened in 1927, it may not be the air conditioning. Rumor has it that original owner F. C. Weskil still walks the aisles. He dedicated his theater 'to the people of the panhandle of Idaho,' and movies and live performances still bring in the crowds." *panida.org*

Clearview Cinemas Ziegfeld Theatre, New York, New York

"As multiplexes have conquered Manhattan, this 1,195-red-velvet-seater, opened in 1969, remains the last of its kind in the borough: a single-screen movie house, opulent with crystal chandeliers and gold and marble accents. Named for Broadway showman Florenz Ziegfeld, the theater features displays with programs and photos from his famous Ziegfeld Follies." *clearviewcinemas.com*

Tampa Theatre, Tampa, Florida

"If you've ever wanted to know what it feels like to see a film inside a vintage atmospheric movie palace, this theater is at the top of a short list. Opened in October 1926 by architect John Eberson, it still is delighting local audiences with first-run and classic films, concerts, and other live performances." *tampatheatre.org*

Watts Theatre, Osage, Iowa

" 'Your key to Watts of entertainment, Watts of comfort . . .' the opening program promised. After 28 years in the good care of Jim and Millie Watts, it is run today by Robert Williams and his family, who maintain this 1950s showcase. Recently, the son of the man who installed the original neon marquee restored it."
wattstheatre.com

Budget Travel Tips *from the* USA TODAY Archive

TRANSPORTATION

We asked several well-traveled experts how to save on such vacation expenses as lodging, transportation, shopping, and more. Of course, no one has a monopoly on the best advice, but...before you make a move, read what they have to say.

Put it in writing, nicely

When asking for an upgrade from an airline, let them know you're going to write a nice letter. Airline employees can't take monetary tips, but a letter can be very important to them. It goes into their personnel file and becomes very important when it comes time for merit raises and promotions.

—Joel Widzer, *The Penny Pincher's Passport to Luxury Travel*

10 great places to tour Swedish America

Plenty of options exist for travelers who want to celebrate the Swedish American experience. Alan H. Winquist and Jessica Rousselow-Winquist, authors of Touring Swedish-America: Where to Go and What to See, *offer suggestions.*

Holy Trinity (Old Swedes) Church, Wilmington, Delaware
Delaware was originally settled by Swedes arriving in 1638 at what is today Wilmington. "In 1697, three Church of Sweden missionaries arrived, and shortly Holy Trinity (Old Swedes) Church was built. The sanctuary contains significant features dating from the early 1700s." *oldswedes.org*

Swedish American Museum Center, Chicago, Illinois
During the past 20 years, the center "has become one of the three largest museums in the United States focusing on the Swedish immigration experience." *samac.org*

American Swedish Institute, Minneapolis, Minnesota
This Indiana-limestone mansion was built for newspaper owner
Swan J. Turnblad at the turn of the 20th century. After the death of
his wife, he established what would become the American Swedish
Institute and endowed his home to the organization. "The richly
decorated two-story grand hall and several spectacular ceramic-
tiled *kakelugnar* (stoves) are among its most imposing features."
americanswedishinst.org

Birger Sandzen Memorial Gallery, Lindsborg, Kansas
Swedish-born Birger Sandzen immigrated to Lindsborg in 1894,
joined the faculty of Bethany College, and over six decades produced hundreds of oil and watercolor paintings. He is noted for his
landscapes of Kansas and Colorado, many of which can be seen in
the gallery. *sandzen.org*

Bishop Hill, Illinois
Bishop Hill began as a religious commune in 1846 on the northwestern plains of Illinois. Twenty large commercial buildings were
erected, many in classical style, and some 15,000 acres of land
were farmed. The colonists excelled in producing linen, furniture,
wagons, brooms, and farm products. "A number of the original
buildings are open to the public, including the impressive Colony
Church, the Steeple Building, and the Bjorklund Hotel."
bishophill.com

Gammelgården, Scandia, Minnesota
"One of the loveliest Swedish American sites in Minnesota is the
complex of six pioneer structures called *Gammelgården,* or the Old
Farm." Among the buildings: the oldest existing Swedish Lutheran
Church and parsonage in the state. *gammelgardenmuseum.org*

"Spirit of Nebraska's Wilderness," Omaha, Nebraska
Swedish-born Kent Ullberg's wildlife sculptures can be found
throughout the United States, but a favorite is his monumental
fountain installation depicting 58 Canada geese taking off from a
pond, flying through the air, circling an intersection, and ending in
the glass-enclosed atrium of the First National Bank in downtown
Omaha. "The geese dramatically transition from bronze to stainless

steel to symbolize the evolution from the open range to the modern cityscape."

Gustavus Adolphus College, St. Peter, Minnesota

The hilltop campus of Gustavus Adolphus College, founded by Swedish immigrants in the 1860s, overlooks the town of St. Peter in south-central Minnesota. "A number of buildings and markers underscore the school's Swedish heritage. Old Main is on the National Register of Historic Places. The Jussi Bjorling Recital Hall, Nobel Hall of Science, and Linnaeus Arboretum also bear Swedish names." *gustavus.edu*

Cranbrook Art Academy, Bloomfield Hills, Michigan

From 1931 to 1951, the internationally acclaimed Carl Milles was the resident sculptor at Cranbrook. "A number of his works are housed in the [academy's] gallery, but there are also several Milles fountains on the grounds." *cranbrook.edu*

Rika's Roadhouse and Landing, Big Delta State Historical Park, Delta Junction, Alaska

Rika Wallen, born in Sweden, emigrated to Minnesota in 1891 and eventually made her way to Alaska, where she managed a roadhouse on the Tanana River during the gold rush. She was a natural farmer who understood the cold Alaskan climate. "She designed and supervised the construction of a Swedish-style barn with a unique ventilation system, making it possible to winter cows, sheep, oxen, mules, and poultry. The Roadhouse is the oldest non-refurbished building in Alaska, and Rika's barn is now a museum." *alaskafursandgifts.com/roadhouse.html*

As the traveler who has been once from home is wiser than he who has never left his own door step, so a knowledge of one other culture should sharpen our ability to scrutinize more steadily, to appreciate more lovingly, our own.

—Margaret Mead

10 great places to share history of the Jewish faith

"The Jewish community has contributed a wealth of fine architecture to the American scene," says Samuel Gruber, author of American Synagogues: A Century of Architecture and Jewish Community. *"Most of these synagogues are listed on the National Register of Historic Places. Many contain exhibitions that explain the role of Jews in local and national history."*

Shearith Israel, New York, New York
"This is the fourth home of America's oldest Jewish congregation. Its classically inspired building, built in 1897, faces Central Park and is the first and best of many Roman-temple-type synagogues. It combines a monumental exterior with a more subtle interior, featuring restored Tiffany windows and an excellent exhibition of 350 years of the Orthodox Congregation's history."
shearithisrael.org

Lloyd Street Synagogue, Baltimore, Maryland
"The history and architecture of this restored 1845 synagogue, open as a historic site by the Jewish Museum of Maryland, sums up some of the dramatic changes in American Judaism and in American taste before and after the Civil War. Built for the Baltimore Hebrew Congregation in Greek-temple design, it has served many congregations, not all Jewish."
nps.gov/history/nr/travel/baltimore/b30.htm

B'nai Abraham, Brenham, Texas
"My great-grandfather helped found and build (in 1893) this simple little shul, an Eastern European Orthodox manifestation deep in Texas. Though not used regularly, the sole local Jewish resident maintains this clapboard building, typical of small-town synagogues of the time." *smallsynagogues.com/brenham.htm*

Stone Avenue Temple, Tucson, Arizona
"This small synagogue, built in 1910 as Temple Emanu-El, is the oldest synagogue in Arizona, built several generations after the first Jews arrived in the mid-19th century. Local preservationists have

restored this structure, a one-story sanctuary combining elements of classical high style and Mission architecture, to create a bit of grandeur." *templeemanueltucson.org*

Temple Beth Israel, Portland, Oregon
"After World War I, Jewish architects developed a new style based, perhaps surprisingly, on Byzantine Christian church designs. For many Jews, this style combined a sense of history with bold new geometrics and more centralized, dome-topped worship spaces. Now housing Congregation Beth Israel, it also boasts spectacular stained-glass windows." *bethisrael-pdx.org*

Touro Synagogue, Newport, Rhode Island
"Built in 1763, it is the oldest surviving synagogue in North America. Still in use, the building combines an intimate elegance with classical grandeur in the best tradition of Georgian architecture. It is also a National Landmark, the highest designation given to an American building." *tourosynagogue.org*

Wilshire Boulevard Temple, Los Angeles, California
"Rabbi Edgar Magnin ('rabbi of the stars') oversaw the creation of this opulent Reform Temple from 1928 to '29. His synagogue has all the drama of a Cecil B. De Mille spectacular: Of special note are murals by sometime silent-film director Hugo Ballin, depicting the history of the Jews." *wilshireboulevardtemple.org*

Park Synagogue, Cleveland, Ohio
"Built from 1948 to 1953, this is one of the first great modern American synagogues. German-Jewish refugee Erich Mendelsohn created a building with a Byzantine essence that is dynamic from outside and awe-inspiring within. The spaces of this Conservative Jewish Synagogue-Center are connected in a balanced way that is symbolic and practical." *parksyn.org*

North Shore Congregation Israel & Perlman Sanctuary,
Glencoe, Illinois
"The grand sanctuary, built in 1964, was designed by Minoru Yamasaki, architect of the World Trade Center. It is a dramatic, awe-inspiring space but hard to use by a congregation, so a smaller

sanctuary was built in 1979. Together, the two connected buildings create a portrait of Jewish aspirations in the late 20th century." *nsci.org*

Jewish Center of the Hamptons, Easthampton, New York
"In 1989, Norman Jaffe created a warm, inviting space for prayer, filled with natural wood, with a view of trees. Jaffe also reintroduced more traditional elements into a Reform synagogue, such as a more central table from which to read the Torah." *jcoh.org*

10 great places to feel dwarfed by kitsch

When it comes to roadside attractions, there's a time-honored American tradition to go big or go home. Before the sprawling Wal-Marts and Target Greatlands dotted the interstates, towering kitschy statues reigned supreme. Brian and Sarah Butko, coauthors of Roadside Giants, *share their favorite oversize icons.*

The Big Duck, Flanders, New York
"One term for buildings shaped as other things is a 'duck.' Here's the inspiration for it, a duck-shape stand, built in 1931, that was its own giant sign, needing no words to announce what was sold inside: ducks and duck eggs." Once a staple in the area, the 20-foot-high stand stopped selling quackers in 1984. Now visitors can buy all manner of duck souvenirs.

Dinosaur Land, White Post, Virginia
There are no gentle giants at this park in Virginia's Shenandoah Valley, where 40 dinosaurs battle it out and eat the heads off small game. Visitors can walk through a 60-foot-long shark, and children can sit in King Kong's paw. Other random animals join the mix, like the 20-foot-tall king cobra and a giant praying mantis. But the favorite is the souvenir shop that gets you both coming and going with everything you never knew you needed. *dinosaurland.com*

Gatorland, Orlando, Florida
For more than 40 years, kids and grown-ups alike have been
awed by the entrance to Gatorland, a massive concrete replica of
an alligator's head. But that isn't the only giant at this 110-acre
theme park: The preserve also plays host to Alf, a rare American
crocodile that weighs more than 1,000 pounds. The park offers
extensive wildlife-education programs too; crowds love the Gator
Jumparoo show, where the reptiles lunge for their food.
gatorland.com

Albert the Bull, Audubon, Iowa
More than 20,000 people a year visit Albert the Bull, a 30-foot-
tall, 35-ton Hereford bull. Audubon's Junior Jaycees raised
$30,000 in 1963 and rounded up steel rods from abandoned wind-
mills to build the frame of the statue. Layers of sprayed concrete
were added to give Albert a "hairy" appearance, and more than
60 gallons of paint completed the look.
auduboncounty.com/attractions.asp

Coney Island Hot Dog, Bailey, Colorado
The biggest Coney Island dog in the United States isn't found in
Coney Island, New York, but in Bailey, Colorado. The 42-foot-long,
14-ton, hot-dog-shape restaurant—complete with condiments—
was built in Denver, moved to the shadow of the Rockies in Aspen
Park, and finally relocated to the banks of the South Platte River.
Owners Ron Aigner and Diane Wiescamp have been cooking up a
renovation, "but it's hard to get anything done when tourists stop
every few minutes to gawk."

Paul Bunyan Land, Brainerd, Minnesota
"You'll find Paul Bunyan and Babe the Blue Ox from coast to coast,
but he thrives best in the upper Midwest." The best-known pairing is in Bemidji, Minnesota, but an animated one from 1949 steals
the show at Paul Bunyan Land, a small amusement park at This
Old Farm Pioneer Village. This 36-foot-tall Paul moves his head,
mouth, and arms while talking to visitors. "Kids get spooked when,
through the magic of helpful ticket takers, Paul greets them by
name." *paulbunyanland.com*

The World's Largest Jackalope, Douglas, Wyoming

The legend of the jackalope started as a joke when some local
hunters mounted deer antlers on a jackrabbit. For decades, while
the myth of the hybrid animal grew, jackalope souvenirs were one
of the staples of this small Wyoming town. The Douglas Chamber
of Commerce honored the fabled creature with an eight-foot-tall
jackalope sculpture that was destroyed by an errant pickup truck.
A larger sculpture was later erected in the center of the city, and a
traveling jackalope pops up around town, complete with saddle for
visitors to hop on for photo ops. *jackalope.org*

The Coffee Pot, Bedford, Pennsylvania

Back when the Lincoln Highway (U.S. 30) was the main New
York–San Francisco artery, this giant coffeepot caught the eye of
weary drivers headed through Pennsylvania. Built in 1927, the
building was originally a lunch spot attached to a gas station. After
a bypass diverted congestion and customers, it fell into disrepair.
Things perked up in 2004, when the Lincoln Highway Heritage
Corridor moved it across the road to the county fairgrounds and
restored it.

Gemini Giant, Wilmington, Illinois

In 1965, at the dawn of the Space Age, John and Bernice Korelc
set out to find something to distinguish the Launching Pad Cafe
from the countless other restaurants along Route 66. They found
the answer in the form of a 28-foot tall, 500-pound fiberglass giant.
Originally a lumberjack, the giant was painted green and refitted
with a space helmet and Styrofoam rocket, which has been stolen
and replaced several times over the years. The restaurant mascot
was named the Gemini Giant after NASA's Gemini space program.

Randy's Donuts, Inglewood, California

Built in the 1950s as part of the Big Do-Nut Drive-In chain and
located near Los Angeles International Airport, the giant doughnut
is popular for photos ops of planes spied through its hole. Though
most sources estimate it's about 22 feet across, it seems much
bigger.

10 great places to study skylines of the world

After nearly 20 years photographing skylines, James Blakeway, author of Skylines of the World, *remains fascinated by how a "collection of unique buildings comes together to create a city." He shares his list of favorite viewing spots.*

Duquesne Incline, Pittsburgh, Pennsylvania
One of Pittsburgh's more interesting architectural elements is the plethora of bridges that span the city's three rivers: the Allegheny and the Monongahela rivers, which meet to form the Ohio River. "They're not your usual flat-deck bridges but these beautiful older bridges that have been rebuilt." Take the Duquesne Incline up Mount Washington for a sweeping view of the city, rivers, and bridges. *incline.pghfree.net*

Sydney Ferries, Sydney, Australia
Sydney Harbor is ringed with some of the most recognizable architecture in the world, including the uniquely designed Opera House. The distinctive architecture, the natural beauty of the  water, and the abundance of boats create an impressive skyline. Take a ferry ride away from the city and enjoy the city views from the boat's deck. *sydneyferries.info*

Kerry Park, Seattle, Washington
"You see it all here. You go from the snowcapped Cascade Mountains to Puget Sound with the city right in the middle of it." Head to Kerry Park on Queen Anne Hill, a steep hill on the north side of downtown. "If the air is clear, you can see Mount Rainier." *seattle.gov/parks*

Point Bonita, Marin County, California
"The real unique features of the San Francisco skyline are the two massive bridges, the Golden Gate and the Oakland Bay Bridge,

which shoot out from opposite ends of the city." For great views, head toward Point Bonita, part of the Golden Gate National Recreation Area in nearby Marin County, across the Golden Gate. "It's a fantastic area to watch the sunset as the fog rolls into the bay. Often, you'll see just the top of the Golden Gate Bridge peeking out of the fog." *nps.gov/goga/pobo.htm*

London Eye, London, England
London's skyline features a surfeit of architectural beauties, including palaces, the Tower Bridge, the Houses of Parliament, and Big Ben. "The best view is from the London Eye," the 443-foot Ferris wheel along the Thames. "At the top, you can see for miles and miles." *londoneye.com*

Hamilton Park, Weehawken, New Jersey
"A 50-story building is giant, and they are everywhere in New York City." Some of the best views, however, are found outside Manhattan. "There's a park (Hamilton Park) in Weehawken, New Jersey, on a cliff overlooking the Hudson. The sun sets behind you, so the sunset reflects off the buildings' windows like mirrors."

Adler Planetarium, Chicago, Illinois
Chicago's modern skyline, dominated by the Willis (formerly Sears) and John Hancock towers, lines Lake Michigan. For sweeping views of city and lake, drive out to Adler Planetarium and then walk along the water. "You're looking across the water, back at the city. The breakwaters keep the water calm, so you have a really great chance of seeing the city reflect in the water." *adlerplanetarium.org*

Montparnasse Tower, Paris, France
Paris boasts some of the world's most recognizable architecture, such as the Eiffel Tower, the Louvre, and the Basilica of Sacre-Coeur. "It's also not a tall city. Most of the buildings are ten stories or less." For a breathtaking view of the city, head to the Montparnasse Tower on the Left Bank. The 689-foot tower is one of the few skyscrapers in Paris, and the rooftop terrace is open to the public. *tourmontparnasse56.com/uk*

Stratosphere, Las Vegas, Nevada
"There's no place on earth that has this incredible lighting. Into the night, every building is lit with amazing colors." Take it all in from an observation deck atop the 1,149-foot-high Stratosphere tower, hotel, and casino—though any number of other rooftop bars or restaurants in Las Vegas might also do as well. *stratospherehotel.com*

Mount Fløyen, Bergen, Norway
This small city is an old fishing and shipping village on the shores of a Norwegian fjord, with steep hills surrounding the city center. Bergen preserved some of its centuries-old commercial buildings. On a clear day, which can be rare, take the Floibanen, a funicular that rises from the city center, to the top of Mount Fløyen for an amazing panoramic view. "You can see the fjords, the ferries, and the beautiful old buildings." *floibanen.com*

10 great places to behold
Frank Lloyd Wright's vision

Frank Lloyd Wright, who is considered America's greatest architect, defied gravity and building codes in his quest for harmony with nature. Victor Sidy, dean of the Frank Lloyd Wright School of Architecture, shares his list of Wright's greatest buildings to visit.

Hollyhock House, Los Angeles, California
"This house, built in the '20s for an oil heiress with a passion of the arts, is beautifully sited in an olive grove on a hill overlooking Hollywood." Known for blurring the lines between the indoors and outdoors, Wright even used the roof of this 6,000-square-foot house as living space, embracing the ocean views and the Southern California climate. *hollyhockhouse.net*

Price Tower, Bartlesville, Oklahoma
"I had the delight of staying in one of the rooms at the Inn at Price Tower here," Sidy says of this multiuse skyscraper, where seven floors are now dedicated to hotel space. "It's one of the best experiences of an FLW building you can get." *pricetower.org*

Taliesin West, Scottsdale, Arizona

Sidy's personal favorite, "it's the perfect counterexample of the evils of suburban sprawl and our lack of sensitivity to the environment." In addition to being an experimental laboratory (Wright tested new materials and methods on his own buildings), this was the headquarters of Wright's innovative architecture school as well as his winter home. *franklloydwright.org*

Pope-Leighey House, Alexandria, Virginia

"The idea Wright was after with the Usonian projects was to provide something affordable for the common man," Sidy says of this and the many other Usonian homes built for middle-income families. "Later in his life, he felt that architecture needed to address the ideas of democracy." *popeleighey1940.org*

Darwin Martin House, Buffalo, New York

"This is an incredibly pure example of his early work. The great thing about Buffalo is it also has examples of Louis Sullivan's work, the architect with whom Wright apprenticed and worked." *darwinmartinhouse.org*

Wright's Chicago home

The nation's largest, most impressive collection of Frank Lloyd Wright buildings is in Oak Park, Illinois, ten miles west of downtown Chicago.

The renowned architect lived and worked in this suburb from 1889 to 1909. Wright's home and adjacent studio (951 Chicago Avenue) now form a museum where visitors can view his living areas, office, library, drafting room, and a chain-suspended balcony. The Ginkgo Tree Bookshop specializes in architectural-design texts and sells souvenirs of Wright's designs. Up the road (at 1019, 1027, and 1031 Chicago Avenue) are three early Wright houses; seven Wright-built homes along adjacent Forest Avenue, the Unity Temple on Lake Street, another dozen Wright buildings throughout Oak Park, and six in nearby River Forest trace the evolution of Wright's Prairie School of Architecture. Escorted group tours and maps for self-guided tours are available at the Oak Park Visitors Center.

Johnson Wax Buildings, Racine, Wisconsin
"Wright was fascinated by the quality of light in a forest. When you walk into the Administration Building here, with its slender columns, you have the same dappled light as in a forest. It's remarkable for its structural expressiveness." *racinecounty.com/golden*

Beth Sholom Synagogue, Elkins Park, Pennsylvania
"Wright designed buildings for every type of religion. Later in his life he embraced all religions as having nature as their source. Light is the real key in this building. The entire roof is translucent during the day, and at night it has a beautiful, lanternlike glow." *bethsholomcongregation.org*

Fallingwater, Mill Run, Pennsylvania

"This was Wright's coming-back-out party after everyone thought he was a has-been. He had a remarkable career, then the Depression came and his career dipped. More than any of his other buildings, this represents the perfect balance between man and nature." An iconic structure, complete with waterfall, it's fixed in our collective imaginations. *fallingwater.org*

Taliesin, Spring Green, Wisconsin
"This was his ancestral home, where his maternal grandparents settled. It is where he worked on the farm as a boy and where his first architectural commission was realized, a school building for his aunts. Later, he founded his architecture school here before starting Taliesin West." There are a number of remarkable structures on this campus, including his drafting studio where some of his most important work was created. *taliesinpreservation.org*

Frank Lloyd Wright Home & Studio, Oak Park, Illinois
"This offers a window into FLW's early work and life." It is in this studio that Wright found his own niche and designed the Robie House (in Chicago), the quintessential Prairie-style house. Many of his commissions were in Oak Park. Walking tours are available in the area, now a historic district. The Cheney house, featured in the book *Loving Frank,* is in the same neighborhood. *gowright.org*

The new Frank Lloyd Wright?

He's unassuming, low-key, a little rumpled, grandfatherly. Frank O. Gehry doesn't look like a guy who might be chased through airports by autograph-fevered fans.

But these days everybody is chasing Gehry. He is besieged by billionaires and corporate pooh-bahs, badgered by university grandees and museum chiefs. Presidents—of countries—importune him. You see him on TV and read about him in newspapers. So, who is this guy?

He's the Canadian-born, Los Angeles–raised, prize-winning, internationally acclaimed architect—the most important architect of the last half of the 20th century, according to the culture czars who decide these kinds of things.

Gehry is the go-to guy these days if you want to put your city, your museum, your university, or your corporate image on the culture map.

Gehry's buildings are startling, unconventional—even radical and off-putting to those not ready for his curves and surprises. But his recent works seem to function the way Europe's medieval cathedrals functioned in their day: They attract crowds of art and architecture pilgrims and pump millions of dollars into municipal economies. Even if the locals don't "get" Gehry's architecture, they certainly get the ringing cash registers.

Some of his recent accomplishments:

- A $100 million museum paean to American popular music for Microsoft cofounder Paul Allen in Seattle
- A distinctly un-Jeffersonian addition to the Corcoran Gallery of Art in Washington, D.C.
- A fantastical $230 million Disney Concert Hall in downtown Los Angeles
- Vontz Center, a $46 million molecular science laboratory at the University of Cincinnati Medical Center
- The Jay Pritzker Pavilion, an outdoor music venue in Chicago's Millennium Park

10 great places for studied relaxation

Many old schoolhouses nationwide have been converted into comfortable bed-and-breakfast inns—where the three R's stand for rest, romance, and relaxation. Sandy Soule of bedandbreakfast.com shares her list of favorites.

Noftsger Hill Inn B&B, Globe, Arizona
Built in 1907, this onetime elementary school lists several notable Arizonans among its alumni, including former governor Rose Mofford. "The old classrooms are now spacious guest rooms, each with a sitting area and fireplace. Guests can leave their thoughts and comments on the original chalkboards." *noftsgerhillinn.com*

Carr Manor, Cripple Creek, Colorado
"What was once the Cripple Creek High School is today a delightfully appointed boutique inn." One of the region's original Mining District schools, the inn served as a school for more than 70 years before being converted into a small hotel in 1983. "The ballroom still sports the stage where students performed, and the grand central staircase brings back the days when kids scrambled to get to class." *carrmanor.com*

Davie School Inn, Anna, Illinois
This elegant, three-story brick schoolhouse, opened in 1869 and closed in 1996, sat empty until its rebirth as a hostelry in 2002. "The inn has all the modern comforts and conveniences you would expect—including double whirlpool tubs in the bathrooms. But the atmosphere of the old schoolhouse has been delightfully retained." *davieschoolinn.com*

Chambery Inn, Lee, Massachusetts
Tucked away in the Berkshire Hills, this 19th-century parochial school reopened as a country inn in 1990. "Spacious, 500-square-foot suites with canopied beds, 8-foot windows, and warming fireplaces contribute to the ambience of this gracious inn." *chamberyinn.com*

School House B&B, Rocheport, Missouri
In the quaint Missouri River town of Rocheport, between St. Louis and Kansas City, this former schoolhouse is listed on the National Register of Historic Places. "The building dates to 1914 and served as a school until 1972. Reopened as a B&B in 1988, it is beautifully restored and decorated, with all the amenities guests expect. Its old-fashioned schoolhouse charm inspired Hallmark to choose this B&B for a series of greeting cards." *schoolhousebb.com*

Washington School Inn, Park City, Utah
The original schoolhouse, built in 1889 and containing three large classrooms, was considered one of the finest schools in the state at the time. "The limestone building was one of the few structures in town to survive a major fire in 1898. It was renovated in 1984 and converted into an elegant bed-and-breakfast inn. The building's original coal cellar—now housing a spa and ski-locker facility—was said to be a popular place for student mischief." *washingtonschoolinn.com*

Old Schoolhouse B&B, Fort Davis, Texas
About 60 miles north of Big Bend National Park in South Texas, this former small-town schoolhouse was built in 1904. "Now a comfortable inn situated in a pecan grove, the building sports 22-inch-thick adobe walls and ceiling-high windows." The inn's three cozy guest rooms are aptly named the Reading, 'Riting, and 'Rithmetic Rooms. *schoolhousebnb.com*

Barclay Cottage, Virginia Beach, Virginia
Built in 1895, Barclay Cottage is one of two remaining original beach cottages in Virginia Beach. In 1916, schoolteacher Lillian Barclay moved in—and for the next 50 years ran a combination lodging house and primary school. "Lillian closed the school in 1972 when she turned 80, but she continued to host guests in the Victorian-style inn until she passed away in 1989." *barclaycottage.com*

Lebanon Schoolhouse B&B, Cortez, Colorado
Just north of the town of Cortez in the scenic Four Corners Region, this 1907 Greek Revival–style schoolhouse was reborn as a

B&B in the 1980s. "The playground still sports the original merry-go-round." Five antiques-furnished guest rooms complement a large common area that features the school's original grandfather clock. *lebanonschoolhouse.com*

The Old Schoolhouse B&B, Waukau, Wisconsin
This former schoolhouse, built in 1926, bills itself as a place where "not only can you sleep in class—we encourage you to do so!" Each of the four guest rooms is named for a teacher who taught here. "The original hardwood floors remain throughout the inn, as do some of the old desks and chairs." A cozy loft library overlooking the main sitting area is stocked with books, puzzles, and board games, and a large yard and nearby nature preserve provide outdoor options. *theoldschoolhouse.biz*

Budget Travel Tips *from the* USA TODAY Archive

TRANSPORTATION

Don't pay as you go
When traveling in cities that have a good public transportation system, purchase a several-day/week pass in lieu of paying each time you board the bus, subway, etc. It is almost always a better deal.
—Lysa Allman-Baldwin, senior travel writer, SoulOfAmerica.com

Go with the flow
Look at rental car fleets as flocks of migrating birds. In November, there are deals driving cars to Florida; in July, bringing cars up to San Francisco from Southern California.
—Peter Greenberg, *The Travel Detective*

Shift to an automatic
While I normally rent a standard-shift car because they cost far less than an automatic, I prefer an automatic in countries like Britain, since sitting on the right and shifting with your left hand takes some getting used to.
—Jens Jurgen, founder, *Travel Companion Exchange*

ARTS AND CRAFTS

10 great places for a hands-on crafts experience

Celebrate the joy of making things at crafts events throughout the year. Victor Domine, spokesman for the nonprofit Craft & Hobby Association, shares his list for hands-on fun.

Indie Craft Experience, Atlanta, Georgia
"The Indie Craft Experience (ICE) is not your grandmother's kind of craft fair. The crafts at ICE have a hipper edge or an ironic playfulness not usually associated with traditional crafts." Vintage fabrics or repurposed material might be incorporated into designs for cell-phone and iPod covers. Crafting workshops, vegan baked goods, and live bands are all part of the mix. *ice-atlanta.com*

Maker Faire Bay Area, San Mateo, California
"This two-day family-friendly event in the Bay area is one of the largest DIY craft festivals in the country. Described as craft-fair-meets-science-fair-meets-county-fair, it attracts more than 80,000 people." Creations from past events have included robots, costumes, and cupcake-shape electric cars, complete with icing and sprinkles. *makerfaire.com*

Great American Scrapbook Convention, Arlington, Texas
"Just outside Dallas, this is one of the largest public scrapbooking events in the country. Thousands of scrapbooking, card-making, and rubber-stamping enthusiasts come to try new tools and practice their craft." The event features classes, cropping parties (rooms full of people who bring their supplies and do scrapping together), door prizes, shopping, and free demonstrations. *greatamericanscrapbook.com*

BUST Spring Fling Craftacular, Brooklyn, New York
"Indie designers and crafters enjoy taking crafting to the next level. This event is a celebration of their handmade goods and edgy designs." The annual BUST Spring Fling Craftacular is created by

BUST Magazine, a hip, women's lifestyle magazine. It's an all-day party, jam-packed with the best in indie crafters, plus dancing, DJs, and drinks. *bust.com/craftacular/craftacular-home.html*

Creativ Festival, Toronto, Ontario, Canada

"Join creative enthusiasts together with top instructors at this event in the heart of Toronto's entertainment district. Learn techniques from the experts, then put your own one-of-a-kind stamp on everything from clothes and curtains to greeting cards and accessories." *creativfestival.com*

Bead & Button Show, Milwaukee, Wisconsin

"No event in the country celebrates jewelry-making better than this annual show. Anyone with a passion for jewelry, fashion, or art should experience it." *beadandbuttonshow.com*

Creating Keepsakes Scrapbooking Conventions

"More than a dozen of these popular scrapbooking venues are held at locations around the country. They're very affordable, and scrapbookers can easily find one for a girlfriends getaway or family fun." *creatingkeepsakes.com*

Learning & Products Expo: Art!, Chicago, Illinois

"You can take a single class or a whole weekend's worth at these art events. The flexible class schedules let you explore your favorite medium or experiment in something new, from airbrush to pastels." *learningproductexpo.com*

STITCHES

"Loyal knitters fly in from all over the country to share their passion with others at these large consumer shows." Learn from the stitching gurus, shop, and get inspired at these regional events, sponsored by *Knitter's Magazine. knittinguniverse.com*

International Quilt Festival/Chicago, Rosemont, Illinois

"Even if you can't thread a needle, you will enjoy seeing the amazing quilts, from antiques to avant-garde designs, on display here. Quilt

collectors, quilt artists, and quilt lovers can shop, take exciting classes, and view amazing special exhibits." Other crafts are also represented at the festival. *quilts.com*

Who knew?

Quilting was brought to America by Dutch, English, and Welsh immigrants, but slaves soon adapted the tradition, infusing quilts with uniquely African designs and color schemes.

10 great places for famous photography

Follow in the path of photographer Robert Frank's famous 1958 road trip The Americans. *Jeff Rosenheim, curator of the Metropolitan Museum of Art's department of photographs, shares his suggestions of modern-day places to discover.*

New Orleans, Louisiana
"The cover photo of Frank's book was the streetcar in New Orleans. Pick up the streetcar on Canal Street and ride it to the end of the line, then come back. It's a great way to see the world and this city." *neworleanscvb.com*

Charleston, South Carolina
"What's appealing today about Charleston is that so much of the 19th-century feeling is still present here," Rosenheim says of the antebellum architecture and Southern hospitality. "This is where Frank got his first vision of the South and the social conditions of the time." *charlestoncvb.com*

Detroit, Michigan
"Frank chose Detroit as a destination because of the auto industry. He got permission to take photos at the Ford factory because he felt the industry was driving America at the time." Frank also took pictures at Belle Isle, a 983-acre island park, designed by Frederick Law Olmsted, with a botanical garden. *visitdetroit.com*

Butte, Montana
The 19th-century copper-mining boomtown "is in a state with beautiful natural landscapes. You can stay in the Finlen Hotel,

where Frank stayed and took pictures from the window." *buttecvb.com*

Memphis, Tennessee
"Memphis today is an interesting place to visit—not just because of the music. Frank listened to the radio and was drawn to the sounds coming out of Memphis. Johnny Cash, one of his favorite musicians, got his start there in the '50s, and Elvis recorded there." Visitors can tour Beale Street blues clubs, the National Civil Rights Museum at the Lorraine Motel, and Graceland. *memphistravel.com*

Santa Fe, New Mexico
"Frank experienced this vibrant city's strong Spanish and Native American heritage. Today's visitor will find many galleries available for viewing photography." The alluring landscape and light of Santa Fe have drawn many artists and photographers here. *santafe.org*

Las Vegas, Nevada
"Frank went out of his way to visit this endlessly fascinating place." Today's visitor can enjoy world-class hotels, art, dining, and entertainment. Take photos of the Bellagio fountains or Mirage volcano. *visitlasvegas.com*

Hoboken, New Jersey
"Sinatra's hometown and the site of the first recorded baseball game is also the subject of the first two photos in Frank's book," Rosenheim says of this lively community across the Hudson River from Manhattan. "It has a great panorama of the city." *hobokenchamber.com*

San Francisco, California
"Like so much of California, this is a great place to photograph. Frank spent two months photographing in and around San Francisco. The vibrancy of Chinatown today makes it a very special place." Walk across the Golden Gate Bridge and take photos of the San Francisco skyline, or go to Lombard Street for incredible vistas. *onlyinsanfrancisco.com*

Miami Beach, Florida
Miami, the city Frank captured so well, "is a vibrant city with great hotels and a fascinating culture. There is a convergence of influences from the Americas." The Art Deco District on Ocean Drive in Miami Beach "is one of the most visually rewarding areas, and the light there provides a great opportunity for photographers." *miamiandbeaches.com*

10 great places to introduce children to art

What do you get when you mix art with the NBA? Answer: former Dallas Maverick Tariq Abdul-Wahad. A proud supporter of the arts, he shares some family-friendly galleries.

San Jose Museum of Art, San Jose, California
"Free and full of amazing modern art (check out the colorful Dale Chihuly chandeliers), this is the coolest urban museum in the United States—an atmosphere not lost on hard-to-impress teens." *sjmusart.org*

Legion of Honor, San Francisco, California
Children will love "the view of the Golden Gate Bridge, Pacific Ocean, and all of San Francisco at this beautiful Beaux-Arts building in Lincoln Park. It's renowned for...a collection spanning 4,000 years of ancient and European decorative arts and paintings." *famsf.org*

Los Angeles County Museum of Art, Los Angeles, California
"The LACMA is the Met of the West Coast, covering virtually every angle of a classic museum. Collections, from the colorful textile collection to the gorgeous Asian art collection, vary enough to keep little ones' interest." *lacma.org*

Portland Art Museum, Portland, Oregon
There's a "depth and diversity of the Native American art collection, filled with stunning objects crafted by more than 200 indigenous groups from throughout North America, including prehistoric, historic, and contemporary works. This collection alone is worth a

family trip to the oldest museum in the Pacific Northwest."
portlandartmuseum.org

Metropolitan Museum of Art, New York, New York
"The benchmark of museums in America, the imposing but accessible Met has something for everyone in the family, including the most extensive and complete permanent collection on the continent, plus daily programs and resources for students and teachers."
metmuseum.org

Indianapolis Museum of Art, Indianapolis, Indiana
"Although IMA is not overwhelming in size, it more than compensates in content and substance. A balanced collection, a great setting, and a passionate staff add to the kid-friendly environment. It's also a special treat for lovers of European Neo-Impressionists."
imamuseum.org

Denver Art Museum, Denver, Colorado
"A family museum par excellence housed in a Gio Ponti–designed building that itself is a work of art. Although it is underrated on the American museum scene, Denver boasts the best youth art program in the country. Everything in it is designed to please youngsters and to make art fun and accessible, often with popular exhibits that sell out quickly." *denverartmuseum.org*

Art Institute of Chicago, Chicago, Illinois
"The 'big boy' of the Midwest, the institute houses a museum, a school, a variety of art programs for kids, and more than 300,000 works of art, including a large collection of 19th-century French paintings. Also fascinating is the modern and contemporary wing housing Georges Seurat's classic painting *Un Dimanche à la Grande Jatte.*" *artic.edu*

Dallas Museum of Art, Dallas, Texas
"The best museum in the Southwest, it features modern architecture, activities, and programs that have transformed the city of Dallas into a place suited for art lovers. Kids will be impressed with the size of the building, plus the special activities and the permanent collection of Western art, from impressionism to contemporary sculpture." *dm-art.org/index.htm*

Smithsonian American Art Museum, Washington, D.C.
"The American Art Museum is one of the many museums that make up the Smithsonian Institution. Several exhibits, including some 19th-century paintings, have been moved to the smaller Renwick Gallery." *americanart.si.edu*

Art museums paint a fun picture for kids

Art museums often fail to make kids' "fun list" because they're filled with...art. There are no dinosaurs or spaceships or Egyptian mummies or adorable pandas—the things that make natural history and science museums and zoos so popular with millions of families.

Yes, kids still do the traditional "walk and gawk" tours of art museums. Every day, school buses pull up outside museums, and hordes of children disembark to wander the galleries with varying degrees of interest or boredom, understanding or befuddlement.

But museums know they have to do more—and they have. Educators in museums around the country have crafted a variety of creative programs to draw kids and families into galleries, establish close working relationships with local schools, and generally make art institutions more friendly, accessible, and fun. For instance:

- At the Denver Art Museum, youngsters are issued backpacks filled with games, objects, and activities connected to specific artworks or exhibits. The Baltimore Museum of Art offers similar interactive kits; one contains costumes that kids can try on to help them imagine what life was like for people depicted in the museum's paintings and portraits.

- At the Whitney Museum of American Art in New York, teens are trained as junior docents and tour guides to help their peers connect with art.

- Staffers from the Norton Museum of Art in West Palm Beach, Florida, teach scores of at-risk kids in after-school art classes held three times a week in their neighborhoods.

Besides all this, most museums offer special tours and audio guides for children, free entrance for kids on some days, and elaborate "family fun" centers where youngsters can play with and make art.

In short, museums have figured out what many parents know: Kids learn more when they're having fun.

10 great places with arts-filled spaces

From coastal New Hampshire to the desert Southwest, a new generation of artists, performers, writers, and musicians is settling into once-sleepy villages and turning them into great places for arts-filled action. John Villani, author of The 100 Best Small Art Towns in America, *directs art enthusiasts to some favorites.*

Athens, Ohio
This college town is home to the Dairy Barn Arts Center, "one of the nation's best. Its extensive yet affordable shop is loaded with fine-crafts bargains, as well as local quilts and beadwork." *athensohio.com*

Carrboro, North Carolina
"Artists and musicians seeking a relaxed, low-cost alternative to nearby Chapel Hill and Durham have turned Carrboro into a refuge of art galleries, coffee shops, and friendly taverns." *chapelhillcarrboro.org*

Bay St. Louis, Mississippi
"Slipping away from the Big Easy's hustle and bustle is as simple as driving an hour east along the Gulf Coast to this historic town on St. Louis Bay. Art and fine-crafts galleries line the streets of Old Town." *hancockcountyms.org*

Ashland, Oregon
Host to one of the nation's most prestigious Shakespearean theaters (Oregon Shakespeare Festival), Ashland's gallery-filled downtown "has a decidedly Elizabethan flavor. Import shops, selling everything from Portuguese ceramics to South African furniture, lend Ashland a special cachet." *ashlandchamber.com*

Key West, Florida
"America's slice of the Caribbean has long been a favored retreat for artists, writers, and arts-loving urban refugees, and that's why more than 40 art galleries, selling primarily local arts, are tucked along Duval, Front, and Greene streets. There's also lots of Cuban and Haitian art and a new contemporary art district on White Street." *fla-keys.com*

Portsmouth, New Hampshire

Just an hour's drive from Harvard Square in Cambridge, Massachusetts, this maritime community "has a lovingly preserved historic downtown that's home to crafts shops, coffee bars, and a half dozen art galleries" and is known for its summer music festivals and year-round theater. *portsmouthnh.com*

Lanesboro, Minnesota

When the first paved section of the Root River State Trail opened, this once-obscure community three hours south of Minneapolis turned into a year-round destination for bicyclists and other outdoors enthusiasts. "Cornucopia Art Center sells fine crafts from across the state, while Commonweal Theatre Company stages plays year-round. Shops sell locally crafted Amish furniture, and Das Wurst Haus dishes up homemade brats." *lanesboro.com*

Berkeley Springs, West Virginia

With homeopathy, hot springs, an art gallery inside a restaurant, and a movie theater that posts its popcorn recipe on the Internet, "Berkeley Springs lives up to its reputation as a fun-loving place filled with quirky characters." Less than 90 minutes west of the Washington, D.C., Beltway, it's "loaded with antiques stores, fine-crafts galleries, and shops specializing in bath and spa items." *berkeleysprings.com*

Chico, California

This "affordable gem," a three-hour drive northeast of San Francisco, boasts more than leafy streets and a vibrant college. "Artist studios fill the second stories of downtown's quaint storefronts," and the former train depot is an art gallery. *chicochamber.com*

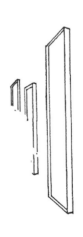

Prescott, Arizona

"Like many of the West's small art towns, this mountain community in north-central Arizona has a mining history. Today, miners' shacks in the McCormick Street Arts District are filled with galleries and studios, while new galleries have popped up near downtown's Courthouse Plaza." *prescott.org*

LITERATURE

10 great places to become well versed in poets

Take the fork in the road and see the landscapes that inspired some of America's best-loved poets. J. D. McClatchy— poet, editor of the Yale Review, *and author of* American Writers at Home—*shares his recommendations.*

Henry Wadsworth Longfellow National Historic Site, Cambridge, Massachusetts
"The most popular and beloved poet of his era, even Queen Victoria was an admirer. His handsome house on Brattle Street, Washington's headquarters during the Siege of Boston, has a rich collection of furnishings, mementos, and writings. The study has a chair carved from the 'spreading chestnut tree' Longfellow made famous in his poem ('The Village Blacksmith')." *nps.gov/long*

Carl Sandburg Home, Flat Rock, North Carolina
"The son of Swedish immigrants, Sandburg was born in Illinois and made his name with poems about Chicago. He won the Pulitzer Prize twice, was friendly with presidents and movie stars, but he never forgot his humble beginnings." Hence, his somewhat baronial estate, 30 miles from Asheville, North Carolina, may seem out of character to some visitors. A herd of goats is a reminder of the dairy farm his wife once ran here. *nps.gov/carl*

Dunbar House, Dayton, Ohio
"Paul Laurence Dunbar, the son of freed slaves, was only 33 when he died of tuberculosis but already had achieved fame as one of the first important African American poets." The Italianate, turn-

of-the-20th-century home has been restored, and a visitors center contains interpretive panels chronicling Dunbar's life. *ohsweb.ohiohistory.org/places/sw03/index.shtml*

Emily Dickinson Museum, Amherst, Massachusetts
The site consists of two historic homes—The Homestead, where Dickinson was born and lived, and next door, The Evergreens, where her brother and his family lived. "Eventually, she (Dickinson) rarely emerged from her second-floor bedroom (in The Homestead), where she wrote at a table by the window and secretly kept her poems in a bureau drawer." *emilydickinsonmuseum.org*

Robert Frost, Stone House Museum, South Shaftsbury, Vermont
A man of contradictions, Frost sat at the dining room table here on a hot June morning and wrote his most famous poem, "Stopping by Woods on a Snowy Evening." "He lived in this Colonial house in the '20s and is buried nearby in Old Bennington Cemetery behind the Old First Congregational Church." *frostfriends.org*

Edgar Allan Poe House and Museum,
Baltimore, Maryland

"No American poem is better known than 'The Raven,' Edgar Allan Poe's haunted romance. Because he was impoverished and an alcoholic, Poe moved around restlessly. Several of his homes have been preserved, the best of them in Baltimore. He and his wife are buried in the nearby Westminster Graveyard." *eapoe.org/balt/poehse.htm*

Tor House, Carmel, California
"Robinson Jeffers was a fiercely independent spirit, determined to live as close to nature as possible. Five years after he and his wife, Una, first saw the Carmel coastline from a stagecoach, he bought land on a bluff facing the sea and built a house, stone by stone." *torhouse.org*

Walt Whitman House, Camden, New Jersey

Considered by many to be America's greatest poet, the author of *Leaves of Grass* lived here from 1884 until his death eight years later. "The house has a rustic appearance because it's the only wooden house on the block. Whitman would sit by the front window in the mornings chatting with passersby." His original letters, personal belongings, the bed in which he died, and the death notice that was nailed to the front door have all been preserved. *state.nj.us/dep/parksandforests/historic/Whitman*

Steepletop, Austerlitz, New York

"Edna St. Vincent Millay was the toast of the town in 1925, when she and her husband bought a former dairy farm in upstate New York. It was here that she wrote the sonnets that secured her fame." Visitors can see her writing cabin and stroll along the Poetry Trail leading to the family gravesites. *millaysociety.org*

Sidney Lanier Cottage, Macon, Georgia

"One of the best Southern poets of the 19th century, Sidney Lanier is most remembered for his shimmering 'Marshes of Glynn' [poem], about the coastline of Georgia. His childhood home preserves many family belongings and mementos, including the poet's alto flute." *historicmacon.org/slc.html*

10 great places to get on the road and feel the Beat

On the Road author Jack Kerouac and his friends spawned a current of rebellious creativity that still sparks artists, musicians, and all walks of life. Renowned Beat scholar Ann Charters—whose books include the first Kerouac biography and the two-volume Beats: Literary Bohemians in Postwar America—*reminisces about seminal Beat places.*

Lowell, Massachusetts

Kerouac Park downtown "honors the writing he did" with granite plaques bearing words from his books. Kerouac was born in this town among "red-brick factories and the river." Visit the town

cemetery too: His grave is "a loving place" festooned with flowers, wine bottles, and poems left as tributes. "His widow installed a headstone that says, 'He honored life.' "
nps.gov/lowe/historyculture/Kerouac.htm

New York, New York

Manhattan is rife with Beat landmarks. Allen Ginsberg lived in a full-floor condo at 405 East 13th Street, a building owned by artist Larry Rivers. In Greenwich Village, one of the few women Beats, Diane di Prima, read poetry at the Gaslight Cafe. On the West Side, Kerouac and then-wife Joan Haverty lived at 454 West 20th Street, where he began writing her a long letter about his recent travels while she waited tables to support them: The letter became *On the Road,* "the bible of the Beat generation." He wrote the book itself at the Hotel Chelsea, later the home of the so-called unsung Beat, Herbert Huncke. But the seminal spot is the newsstand at Broadway and West 66th Street, where Kerouac and his girlfriend Joyce Johnson "walked just after midnight, on September 5, 1957," to read the *New York Times'* glowing review of *On the Road.* "By morning, Jack was famous."

The French Quarter, New Orleans, Louisiana

"Lots of bohemians hung out" at the French Market and Jackson Square, and there were "people in the square selling cheap art," even in the Beat era. "Jack passed through when he went there to visit (*Naked Lunch* author William S.) Burroughs, who lived in Algiers across the river," and Kerouac wrote about the Quarter in *On the Road.*

San Francisco, California

The Beats frequented the North Beach area, and Lawrence Ferlinghetti's City Lights bookstore on Columbus Avenue—replete with warrens of Beat books—is still a haven for readers and writers who look the part. Ferlinghetti "not only published the Beats but paid royalties." The rug store at 3119 Fillmore Street was once Six Gallery, where Ginsberg first read part of his poem "Howl" on October 7, 1955, "a defining moment for the Beats. About 100 people were there" for readings by five poets: Ginsberg,

Michael McClure, Gary Snyder, Philip Whalen, and Philip Lamantia. "It set everyone alight. Kerouac was too shy to read, but he passed a hat" to collect donations for the poets.

Denver, Colorado
Kerouac's friend Neal Cassady (aka Dean Moriarty in *On the Road*)—"the one who galvanized Kerouac and gave him his style"—lived with his father in Denver's Skid Row, an area "in the middle of town. It's still pretty derelict." Young Neal stole cars, but in reform school he read widely, including the Harvard Classics, and he became a self-taught thinker. He met Ginsberg in New York and was introduced to Kerouac in 1946. Cassady "was Kerouac's ticket to the West; he opened up the continent for him."

Mount Tamalpais, Marin County, California
Gary Snyder and Kerouac climbed this mountain, which was sacred to the area's Native Americans. "Jack described the climb in *The Dharma Bums.* Gary tells Jack he has to 'live pure' and turns him into an environmentalist." *mttam.net*

Bixby Canyon, near Big Sur, California
Kerouac stayed at Lawrence Ferlinghetti's "little cottage" in the canyon, about 13 miles south of Carmel on Highway 1. By then drinking heavily, Kerouac hid from the world there "while he wrote *Big Sur."*

Washington State
In the early and mid-1950s, Kerouac, Snyder, and Whalen served as fire lookouts for the National Park Service in the North Cascades. Kerouac couldn't wait to leave remote Desolation Peak, in the park's Ross Lake National Recreation Area. *nps.gov/noca*

Davenport, Iowa
"This is where Jack felt his first feelings for America" as a whole. "This is when he really left the East Coast." When Kerouac traveled across the country in the summer of 1947, he crossed Iowa along Highway 6. In *On the Road,* he wrote that Davenport smelled of sawdust and the farmers looked at him with suspicion.

Rocky Mount, North Carolina
Kerouac "practiced his Buddhism" here while staying with his sister, Caroline Blake, in a household that also included their mother, Gabrielle, and Blake's husband and child. Kerouac "took along the family dog when he meditated in the woods."

"They were like the man with the dungeon stone and gloom, rising from the underground, the sordid hipsters of America, a new beat generation that I was slowly joining."

—Jack Kerouac, *On the Road*

10 great places to get write with the word

"Reading and writing are solitary pursuits, so it's rewarding to be with people who share your passion," says Pam Houston, author of Sight Hound *and* Cowboys Are My Weakness *and director of creative writing at the University of California-Davis. Here, she talks about inspiring literary events.*

Aspen Summer Words Writing Retreat and Literary Festival, Aspen, Colorado
"The Sundance Film Festival of literary publishing" brings together "first-rate writers, some of the brightest lights from New York's publishing community, in a town that has been among the writer-friendliest since Hunter Thompson showed up a half century ago." *aspenwritersfoundation.org*

Fine Arts Work Center, Provincetown, Massachusetts
"The Fine Arts Work Center is the oldest continuous art colony in the country, where writers and visual artists compare notes in one of the most accepting and inspiring locales on earth." *fawc.org*

Iowa Summer Writing Festival, Iowa City, Iowa
"Along the Iowa Avenue Literary Walk, bronze panels celebrate the voices that have come together at the renowned Iowa Writers

Workshop, from Flannery O'Conner and Kurt Vonnegut to John Irving and James Tate." *continuetolearn.uiowa.edu/iswfest*

Sewanee Writers' Conference, Sewanee, Tennessee
"Tennessee Williams specified in his will that a memorial fund be established to encourage creative writing, and many years later his wishes are carried out each July." *sewaneewriters.org*

Centrum's Port Townsend Writers Conference, Port Townsend, Washington
"Held each year in this beautiful town, Centrum hosts the most impressive summer literary gathering in the Northwest." *centrum.org/writing/writers-conference.html*

Taos Summer Writers' Conference, Taos, New Mexico
"Held each July in a charmingly weathered adobe inn, this conference feels like a family reunion, as everyone catches the relaxed spirit of the desert that has been inspiring artists in northern New Mexico for years." *unm.edu/~taosconf/*

Squaw Valley Community of Writers, Squaw Valley, California
"If you like your literature mixed with mountain hikes, bungee jumping, and a swim in the blue waters of Lake Tahoe, this event offers poetry and fiction, nonfiction, memoir, and screenwriting, along with inspiring scenery." *squawvalleywriters.org*

Bread Loaf Writers' Conference, Middlebury, Vermont
"The granddaddy of all literary gatherings," Bread Loaf brings "writers, students, and lovers of words together in the Green Mountains of Vermont. There is nowhere in America where you can hear more great writers reading more great work in such a short space of time."
middlebury.edu/blwc

Hawaii Writers' Retreat/Conference, Maui, Hawaii
"If you are a fan of genre writing (mysteries, thrillers, romances, science fiction) but want a little mainstream literature thrown in,

then this is the gathering for you. More commercially driven than the others—agents and editors come here to sign up writers—and significantly less highbrow." *hawaiiwriters.org*

Tomales Bay Workshops, Marshall, California
Workshops "promise writers such as Richard Bausch, Kim Barnes, and Brady Udall. Participants can let the drama of the Pacific Coast inspire them."

10 great places to bask in the glory of their stories

"If you love an author, then anything you can see about that author is terrific, even if the setting is so-so," says B. J. Welborn, author of Traveling Literary America: A Complete Guide to Literary Landmarks. *"On the other hand, some literary landmarks are amazing, regardless of the writer's status." Welborn shares some enlightening literary experiences.*

Edgar Allan Poe Museum, Richmond, Virginia
"Experience the mystery and madness of Edgar Allan Poe, master of the horror story. The museum, housed in the city's oldest surviving building (The Old Stone House, circa 1754), documents the dark genius's life" with letters, manuscripts, and personal memorabilia. *poemuseum.org*

Jack London Ranch, Glen Ellen, California
"John Griffith (Jack) London, the most popular and highest-paid American writer in the first decade of the 20th century, bought this ranch in 1905, where he lived until his death in 1916 at age 40. Visitors to the 1,413-acre Jack London Park can view exhibits, artifacts, early manuscripts, the charred ruins of London's dream house (Wolf House), and his grave." *jacklondonpark.com*

Alex Haley House Museum, Henning, Tennessee
"As a boy, Alex Haley sat on his front porch listening to stories about his ancestors. He left the bungalow in 1929, but the oral histories stayed with him, and in 1976 he finished his Pulitzer Prize–winning *Roots.* Haley died in 1992 and is buried in the

front yard. Inside, there is a display of family artifacts, including the writer's eyeglasses."
tennessee.gov/environment/hist/stateown/alexhale.shtml

Mark Twain Study, Elmira, New York
"Fans of Mark Twain, possibly America's greatest writer, can tour the octagonal study his brother-in-law built for him (and Twain dubbed 'The Cozy Nest') here on the campus of Elmira College. Twain's grave also is located in Elmira, hometown of his wife, Olivia."
elmira.edu/academics/distinctive_programs/twain_center/study

Ingalls Homestead, DeSmet, South Dakota
"Laura Ingalls Wilder wrote six of her nine Little House books about her young life in DeSmet, a prairie town that features The Surveyors' House (the family home for the winter of 1879), the Ingalls House ('The House that Pa Built'), and a memorial on the family's original homesteading property." *ingallshomestead.com*

National Steinbeck Center, Salinas, California
"The interactive, 37,000-square-foot center features seven galleries centered on themes from John Steinbeck's greatest novels. Walk into an *East of Eden* lettuce boxcar, smell sardines on Cannery Row, and tour the literary lion's boyhood bedroom and writing studio."
steinbeck.org

Rowan Oak, Oxford, Mississippi
"William Faulkner's longtime home contains a heady mix of personal memorabilia, including the outline of *A Fable* he wrote on the walls of his office. Outside, see the stable that the Nobel-winning novelist, a horse lover, designed and built near the Greek Revival–style house, sited on 32 acres." *rowanoak.com*

Erskine Caldwell Birthplace and Museum, Moreland, Georgia
"Visit the humble one-story house, called The Little Manse, where novelist Erskine Caldwell was born, located just off the central town square here. Caldwell's typewriter, watch, childhood books, and other personal belongings are on display."
newnan.com/ec

More ways to see what the writers saw

Here are a few more spots that go beyond the book—and in these cases, overseas—courtesy of bibliophile and author Joni Rendon.

Tennyson Trail, Isle of Wight, England

"Poet Alfred Tennyson once said the salty sea air on this windswept isle in the English Channel was 'worth sixpence a pint.' He regularly strolled along the 14-mile footpath above the chalky white cliffs of what is now known as Tennyson Down. Sweeping vistas of the Atlantic Ocean and mainland England can be found at the base of the Tennyson Monument. Nestled in the woods below is the poet's grand home, Farringford, today a luxurious hotel." *islandbreaks.co.uk*

Yasnaya Polyana Nature Preserve, Tula Province, Russia

"A lane of silver birch trees featured in *War and Peace* leads to the vast country estate where Leo Tolstoy penned the epic masterpiece. He regularly went on long walks and horseback rides around this densely wooded property, about 124 miles south of Moscow. Several shady footpaths lead to Tolstoy's charming birch bench, the orchard he lovingly cultivated, and his unmarked grave at the edge of a forested ravine." *yasnayapolyana.ru/english/index.htm*

Brontë Waterfall and Top Withens, Haworth, England

"The windswept Yorkshire Moors immortalized by the Brontës are one of the most eerily atmospheric places to hike in England. A 2½-mile walk from the sisters' former home, the Brontë Parsonage Museum, through heather-strewn hills, leads to their favorite destination, a gentle waterfall and stream. Rest on the stone slab known as the Brontë chair before walking a mile farther to see the ruins of an isolated farmhouse, Top Withens, the possible setting of *Wuthering Heights*." *haworth-village.org.uk*

Karen Blixen Museet/Museum, Rungsted, Denmark

"Just 15 miles north of Copenhagen, get a taste of the Danish countryside on the 14 acres of wilderness adjacent to the centuries-old farmhouse where Karen Blixen, who wrote under the pseudonym Isak Dinesen, penned *Out of Africa*." *karen-blixen.dk*

Walden Pond, Concord, Massachusetts
"In season, visitors can swim in the 103-foot-deep glacial pond or hike around it to view the flora and fauna about which Henry David Thoreau wrote during his two-year stay here. See where he built his one-room cabin, then fish, canoe, picnic, ski, or snowshoe at the state-run 333-acre park." *mass.gov/dcr/parks/walden/*

Booker T. Washington National Monument,
Franklin County, Virginia
"Booker T. Washington, author, statesman, and founder of Tuskegee Institute in 1881, was born a slave on this Virginia tobacco farm in 1856. On this plantation, once owned by the James Burroughs family, visitors can see stone slabs outlining the original site of Washington's boyhood cabin." *nps.gov/bowa*

10 great places to see through a novelist's eyes

Did you ever want to step into the rich scenery of a novel? "Many of my favorite places have inspired great authors, and their stories illuminate the destination," says Melissa Biggs Bradley, CEO of Indagare.com, a travel Web site whose destination reports include reading lists. She shares her list of favorite hotels for book lovers.

Resort at Paws Up, Greenough, Montana
"The Blackfoot River, which runs through this 37,000-acre ranch, is the river referred to in Norman Maclean's wonderful *A River Runs Through It.* The great open plains that lured the crew in Larry McMurtry's *Lonesome Dove* to the wilds of Montana still seem to go on forever. Accommodations here range from luxury tents to three-bedroom vacation homes, and activities include roping, riding, rafting, and fly-fishing." *pawsup.com*

Blantyre, Lenox, Massachusetts
"Edith Wharton wrote *The House of Mirth* at her grand estate, The Mount, in this tiny town. Down the road, Herman Melville penned *Moby-Dick.* Today, visitors can tour the gardens at The Mount and Melville's home, Arrowhead. The perfect base is Blantyre, an exquisite country-house hotel where every guest room has at least

one Edith Wharton book, a children's classic, and two volumes of poetry." *blantyre.com*

Twin Farms, Barnard, Vermont
"This special country estate in Vermont was once the home of Sinclair Lewis and his wife, journalist Dorothy Thompson. Though their farmhouse now boasts museum-quality art and there are ten sumptuously decorated cottages on the 300-acre property, the bucolic New England setting that drew Lewis in the first place remains the main draw." Guests can canoe on the lake or visit nearby Woodstock. *twinfarms.com*

Algonquin Hotel, New York, New York
"Since it opened in 1902, this hotel has drawn a slew of literary giants, including Gertrude Stein, Simone de Beauvoir, and most famously the Algonquin Round Table. Dorothy Parker and *New Yorker* founder Harold Ross were among the Round Table community of writers, critics, and tastemakers that lunched here for years." *algonquinhotel.com*

Kehoe House, Savannah, Georgia
"This restored mansion, now a premier historic inn, is less than a mile from Flannery O'Connor's childhood home," which is open to the public. "Each guest room is named after a historic Savannah figure, including singer Emma Kelly, a prominent character in John Berendt's *Midnight in the Garden of Good and Evil.* Still referred to only as 'The Book,' Berendt's award-winning novel put Savannah on the literary map in 1994." *kehoehouse.com*

The Study at Yale, New Haven, Connecticut
"Surrounded by Yale University's great literary tradition, this hotel is located in the heart of Yale, which has graduated the likes of Tom Wolfe and Ann Packer. The hotel has a football field's length of titles from New York City's legendary Strand bookstore." *studyhotels.com*

L'Hotel, Paris, France
"Oscar Wilde famously expired in this Left Bank property while complaining about the mortally ugly wallpaper. A makeover has

reenlivened the romance of Paris's literary quarter inside this memorabilia-filled 19th-century townhouse hotel." *l-hotel.com*

The Gardens, Key West, Florida
"Hemingway had a lifelong love affair with this island. 'It's the best place I've ever been anytime, anywhere,' he noted. Later he bought a grand Spanish Colonial home where he penned *A Farewell to Arms.* For proximity to his house, stay at The Gardens a few blocks away." *gardenshotel.com*

Canoe Bay, Chetek, Wisconsin
"You can retreat to your own lakeside hideaway in the woods with a book from Canoe Bay's library of more than 2,000 hardcover titles." This upscale resort with three private lakes is in the tranquil Big Woods of the upper Chippewa Valley, a region made famous by Laura Ingalls Wilder. *canoebay.com*

Hotel Rex, San Francisco, California
"The hotel, named for poet Kenneth Rexroth, has clubby interiors that are lined with antique typewriters, globes, and books. Readings and book signings are regularly hosted at its roundtable salon." *jdvhotels.com*

MUSIC AND THEATER

10 great places to see the lights way off Broadway

Searching for a little culture with your travel? Scattered across the nation, small-town, summer-stock theaters are like "hidden jewels that, unless you are specifically looking for them, often go unnoticed," says Beth Leonard, artistic director of Stephens College Okoboji Summer Theatre in Spirit Lake, Iowa. Leonard shares some favorite stages where "the heritage of American theater is kept alive."

The Little Theatre on the Square, Sullivan, Illinois
"Look carefully as you drive through or you'll miss it," Leonard

says of the town and its Little Theatre. It's "an amazing success story. Huge musicals are available in this tiny central Illinois town (summer season runs through August) that offers the theater an amazing amount of community support." *thelittletheatre.org*

Ogunquit Playhouse, Ogunquit, Maine
Considered one of the state's cultural treasures, "this well-known grande dame has survived and thrived" for more than 70 years, "with well-known Broadway stage plays and musicals." *ogunquitplayhouse.org*

Tibbits Professional Summer Theatre, Coldwater, Michigan
Held at the historic Tibbits Opera House, "this successful summer theater (through August), featuring musicals, nonmusicals, and children's theater, serves the Midwest well." *tibbits.org*

Lyric Theatre, Oklahoma City, Oklahoma
Founded in 1963, "the Lyric is a devoted musical theater with a reputation as the finest in the area." *lyrictheatreokc.com*

Coeur d'Alene Summer Theatre, Coeur d'Alene, Idaho
"Producing full-scale Broadway musicals through August, this Northwest powerhouse offers its productions at Schuler Auditorium on the North Idaho College campus" by Lake Coeur d'Alene. *cdasummertheatre.com*

Kentucky Repertory Theatre at Horse Cave, Horse Cave, Kentucky
"Situated in the middle of beautiful horse country, this company offers nonmusicals, classics, and new plays from June through December." *kentuckyrep.org*

Creede Repertory Theatre, Creede, Colorado
"This company was started from graduates of the University of Kansas, and it's one of the most successful reps in the country." Located in tiny Creede, "the company takes on really challenging material." *creederep.org*

Peterborough Players, Peterborough, New Hampshire
Founded in 1933, "this group is right up there with the great
Eastern Seaboard theaters." Through September, musicals and
nonmusicals, plus contemporary and Shakespearean plays, are
presented in an 18th-century barn at historic Stearns Farm, three
miles from downtown Peterborough. *peterboroughplayers.org*

Casa Manana Theatre, Fort Worth, Texas
"This very famous theater, introduced to the city in 1936 but
permanently built in 1958, is known for its aluminum dome and
intimate in-the-round configuration." *casamanana.org*

Bucks County Playhouse, New Hope, Pennsylvania
The historic playhouse, a grist mill built in 1790, was renovated
in 1938 and became known as "America's Most Famous Summer
Theater," thanks to its high-profile stars and pre-Broadway pre-
mieres. "Today Bucks is still known for its star draw and long
season, which runs from Easter to December."
buckscountyplayhouse.com

10 great places to get jazzed about great jazz

*Jazz music is rooted in African folk music traditions
and the American soil. Wynton Marsalis—trumpeter, composer,
and artistic director of jazz at Lincoln Center in New York—
shares his picks of top jazz clubs.*

Yoshi's, Oakland, California
With its corner stage and tables fanning out on tiered levels, there
isn't a bad seat in the house. "This place is a stalwart. It has been
through ups and downs but remains the essence of the '60s jazz
scene." There is sushi on the menu and live music every night of
the week. *yoshis.com*

Snug Harbor Jazz Bistro, New Orleans, Louisiana
"My daddy (Ellis Marsalis) has been swingin' here for years. It's
a good place for the younger musicians to play. They have good
fried-oyster sandwiches." *snugjazz.com*

Baker's Keyboard Lounge, Detroit, Michigan
Open since 1934, the longest-running jazz club in the world has
been a rite of passage for many jazz greats, including John Coltrane,
Ella Fitzgerald, and Charlie Parker. The low ceiling fills up the place
with sound; you can hear every instrument distinctly. The only thing
that beats the jazz is the Southern comfort food, ranging from collards and catfish to short ribs with mac and cheese.
bakerskeyboardlounge.com

Green Mill Jazz Club, Chicago, Illinois
"Al Capone had his own booth here." The place still looks much as it
did back in the days of Prohibition, when a trapdoor behind the bar
was used to smuggle in alcohol. The gangsters are gone, but much of
the art-nouveau interior, including the original banquettes, is intact.
greenmilljazz.com

El Chapultepec, Denver, Colorado
"This is a true neighborhood jazz club.
The beer is cheap, the burritos are great,
and the people are real hip." The name
and menu reflect the original clientele, Mexican migrants who came to
work in the mines. A dive bar located
in the older warehouse district, it was
always a jazz spot. There's no cover, no
dancing, and no Web site, just a pay phone
on the wall.

Blues Alley, Washington, D.C.
"Tables surround the stage in this very elegant and intimate club."
The Creole cuisine, named for musicians, includes McCoy Tyner's
Reddened Fish and Stanley Turrentine's Crab Cakes. *bluesalley.com*

Jazz at the Bistro, St. Louis, Missouri
"The bookings are impeccable at this classy club; it's one of the best-
managed places in the business." There are no age restrictions, so
everyone is welcome. Sit by the balcony rail upstairs and feel regal,
as if you have your own box seat. Or, sit downstairs, a few rows from
the stage, and feel like part of the music. *jazzstl.org*

50 years and counting

Motown has so deeply penetrated American culture that to define it simply as a "record label" is to commit a grave error of omission. At the very least, it's a "sound," and at most, it's a full-blown social movement.

More than a half century after its start on January 12, 1959, Motown's success and influence remain unmatched. The hit factory churned out countless classics ("Baby Love," "My Girl," "Papa Was a Rolling Stone") and mass-produced legends (Michael Jackson, Stevie Wonder, Marvin Gaye, Diana Ross).

This small, black-owned record label, which began with a measly $800 start-up family loan, somehow managed to change the face of music. And proof of the label's surprising humility is on display at Motown's original Detroit headquarters, known as Hitsville USA.

Motown's founder, Berry Gordy Jr., transformed a humdrum home on West Grand Boulevard into an American landmark. The living room became the company's reception area, where Martha Reeves and Diana Ross once answered phones. The kitchen was converted into a control room; the hallway, a makeshift sound booth; and the garage, a recording studio.

The cramped quarters forged a sort of camaraderie, a familial warmth. "When you hear about the Motown family, it really existed. We are all brothers and sisters," says Smokey Robinson, music giant and former Motown vice president.

In its heyday, Hitsville was a notoriously competitive record label. And with the likes of Marvin Gaye and Stevie Wonder pitted against each other, it was quite a fight.

In 1961, just two years after the label began, the Marvelettes' "Please Mr. Postman" topped the Billboard Hot 100—a feat that was to be repeated over and over again by Motown artists. Robinson remembers being on tour and looking out into the crowd, where he could see firsthand the label's cultural impact. He says that, at first, "the audience wouldn't be mingling. But after they started digging on the music, we'd go back [to the same venue], and they would be dancing and hanging together. The music bridged a lot of gaps. It brought people together. I'm proud of that."

Dakota Jazz Club & Restaurant, Minneapolis, Minnesota
On all sides, from Canada and Wisconsin to the Dakotas and Iowa, people cross the state line to enjoy the A-list performances at this Midwestern jazz oasis. "The open room is inviting, and there's live jazz every night." *dakotacooks.com*

Tula's, Seattle, Washington
Comfortable as a living room, Tula's is owned by a retired Navy band leader dedicated to local talent. It fills an important niche in town, and the lamb souvlaki, prepared by the Iraqi cook, adds to the attraction. *tulas.com*

Elephant Room, Austin, Texas
"They have a nice college scene that brings a lot of energy to the room." You'll find local beer from Live Oak Brewing Company but no food at this dependable basement jazz club. *elephantroom.com*

10 great festivals to cure the summertime blues

Music festivals are to summer what rock is to roll. If you haven't had a chance to beat the heat with your favorite legend, it's time to face the music. Here's the lowdown on late-summer and fall festivals from Rolling Stone *executive editor Jason Fine.*

Lollapalooza, Chicago, Illinois
"While most of the big festivals happen in remote or rural locations, from the Mojave Desert (Coachella) to rural Tennessee (Bonnaroo), the once-traveling Lollapalooza is now grounded in Grant Park in downtown Chicago, close to plenty of great hotels and restaurants." *lollapalooza.com*

Newport Folk Festival, Newport, Rhode Island
In addition to its reputation for launching the careers of major musicians—not to mention Bob Dylan's infamous first go with an electric guitar—this festival is now unabashedly pop-oriented, bringing in high-profile acts.

Austin City Limits, Austin, Texas
It's the after-hours parties on Sixth Street that make this hot festival cool. "Unlike Austin's other great music festival, South by Southwest, this one's not about the music industry—it's about music fans. It's a great place to check out the state-of-the-art in rock 'n' roll in one place." *aclfestival.com*

All Points West, Jersey City, New Jersey
The musical masterminds behind Coachella have set up shop on the East Coast with this fest, which features headliners galore, at waterfront Liberty State Park. *apwfestival.com*

All Tomorrow's Parties, Monticello, New York
"The weirdest, most experimental festival of the summer takes place at the old Borscht Belt resort, Kutshers, with a lineup heavy on indie rock and post-punk heroes." *www.atpfestival.com*

Virgin Festival, Baltimore, Maryland
Forget hot dogs and hamburgers, and eat like the natives do at this festival. Chesapeake crabs and local oysters are crowd pleasers, but don't spend too much time in concession-stand lines when there's so much good music going on. *virginfestival.com*

Outside Lands, San Francisco, California
If an awesome lineup and a splendid setting top your list for festival utopia, head to San Francisco. "Taking place in Golden Gate Park, where the Summer of Love was launched more than 40 years ago," this festival has a great musical lineup "plus tents for poetry, comedy, and even yoga." *sfoutsidelands.com*

Monolith Festival, Morrison, Colorado
"There's no more beautiful American venue than Red Rocks, high in the Rocky Mountains, so this is a great summer destination to see rising stars." Be sure to hike through Red Rocks Park and explore Dinosaur Ridge while you're in town. *monolithfestival.com*

Hardly Strictly Bluegrass, San Francisco, California
Free music fests are virtually unheard of—but not in San Francisco. Fine calls this weekend event "one of the greatest under-the-radar American festivals, filled with artists from across

a wide swath of American traditions, from blues and bluegrass to gospel, country, folk, and R&B." *strictlybluegrass.com*

Voodoo Experience, New Orleans, Louisiana
"As the weather starts to cool off in the Crescent City, the Voodoo festival mixes local artists and superstar acts for three days of music under the giant oak trees in City Park." Don't leave town without tasting the beignets and gumbo. *thevoodooexperience.com*

AND ANOTHER THING...

MORE OUTDOOR MUSIC FESTS

Pack your picnic baskets and feast on the sound of live music under the summer sky at these outdoor music festivals.

- Tanglewood, Lenox, Massachusetts (tanglewood.org)
- Aspen Music Festival, Aspen, Colorado (aspenmusicfestival.com)
- Santa Fe Opera Festival, Santa Fe, New Mexico (santafeopera.org)
- Vancouver Folk Music Festival, Vancouver, British Columbia, Canada (thefestival.bc.ca)
- GrassRoots Festival of Music & Dance, Trumansburg, New York (grassrootsfest.org)
- Quebec City Summer Festival, Quebec City, Quebec, Canada (infofestival.com)
- Summerfest, Milwaukee, Wisconsin (summerfest.com)
- Kaslo Jazz Etc., Summer Music Festival, Kaslo, British Columbia, Canada (kaslojazzfest.com)

HISTORY

✳ ✳ ✳ ✳

10 great places to dig deep into our human past

*To know where we're going, it's sometimes best
to know where those who went before us have been.
Brian Fagan, an archaeologist and the author of many
popular books on the topic, shares his list of finds.*

Historic Jamestowne, Virginia
"You can visit the excavations that recently exposed James Fort
at this first permanent English settlement in North America.
Founded by settlers on May 14, 1607, it was the capital of the
Virginia Colony for 93 years." A site museum documents the lives
of America's first colonists. *historicjamestowne.org*

L'Anse aux Meadows, Newfoundland, Canada
"Founded by the Norse in the 990s, this is the first European
settlement in North America. A museum and reconstruction provide a vivid impression of life in a remote encampment in an alien
land." *pc.gc.ca/lhn-nhs/nl/meadows/index.aspx*

Head-Smashed-In Buffalo Jump, Alberta, Canada
"For thousands of years, Plains Indians
hunted buffalo here, driving them into a
natural basin behind a precipitous cliff,
then stampeding them to their deaths
below. A beautifully designed site
museum reconstructs details of more
than 7,000 years of bison hunts and the
lives of those who killed and butchered
the great beasts. You also get to see

details of the excavations that exposed the thick layers of bison
bones under the cliff." *head-smashed-in.com*

Vindolanda, Northumberland, England
"Hadrian's Wall was the most remote frontier in the Roman Empire of the second century. Thanks to imaginative conservation, you can explore long lengths of the wall and its forts, notably around Housesteads. The nearby frontier post at Vindolanda offers an evocative impression of a Roman soldier's life in hostile country." View the ongoing excavations at Vindolanda and visit the Roman Army Museum. *vindolanda.com*

Cahokia Mounds State Historic Site, Collinsville, Illinois
"Climb to the top of what was once a temple mound, the height of a modern-day ten-story building and the largest ancient earthwork ever constructed in the Americas. A thousand years ago, a powerful chiefdom flourished in the Mississippi bottomlands in the area of present-day Collinsville," near St. Louis. Earth was carried in woven baskets to create the 100-foot-high Monks Mound and other mounds. *cahokiamounds.org*

Hopewell Culture National Historical Park, Chillicothe, Ohio
"The people of the Hopewell culture in what is now Ohio were hunter/gatherers who enjoyed an elaborate ceremonial life and burial rituals, reflected in mysterious and still little-understood earthworks and burial mounds built between 200 B.C. and A.D. 500. The site offers an excellent introduction to this remarkable Native American society." *nps.gov/hocu*

Fort Mose Historic State Park, near St. Augustine, Florida
"The first free African American community in North America, this fort outside St. Augustine was a settlement for people fleeing slavery in the British Carolinas. Storytellers and poets tell exciting stories of adventure and freedom in a Florida state park that is a wonderful adventure walk." Although the fort no longer exists, the park's visitors center offers a glimpse into various stages of the fort's history through exhibits and programs. *floridastateparks.org/fortmose*

Museum of Ontario Archaeology, Ontario, Canada
This museum is beside the Lawson archaeological site, a 500-year-old Neutral Iroquoian village that is still being excavated.

Arrowheads, pottery shards, and a prized antler comb are among
the artifacts on view. "Explore the history of this Iroquoian tribe by
visiting the reconstruction of their longhouse. The entire area is a
chronicle of fur-trading and missionary activity, which had profound effects on Native American culture." *uwo.ca/museum*

La Purisima Mission State Historic Park, Lompoc, California
Known as the "Williamsburg of the West," this mission is a jewel
in the California state park system. "The 11th mission of the
21 Spanish missions in California, La Purisima became a school
and training center for Chumash converts living on mission lands.
Nine buildings and their furnishings give an excellent impression
of mission life in early California." *lapurisimamission.org*

Pech Merle, Cabrerets, near Cahors, France
"One of the few Stone Age caves in France still open to visitors,
Pech Merle offers a vivid excursion into the world of more than
25,000 years ago. The paintings, including a famous spotted horse,
are so fresh, it was as if they were painted yesterday. The cave's
well-sited lights and excellent guides make this an evocative and
memorable experience. If you visit one ancient cave-art site, this
should be it." *pechmerle.com*

10 great places to walk amid Civil War history

*On July 21, 1861, spectators left Washington, D.C.,
for nearby Manassas, Virginia, to watch the Battle of
Bull Run, the first major land battle of the Civil War. They
never imagined that dozens of battles would follow. Today, this
battlefield site and many others draw spectators of another kind
to remember this chapter of U.S. history. Jeff Shaara, author of
several books about the Civil War, shares his battlefield picks.*

Shiloh, Shiloh Church, Tennessee
The peach orchard, pastures, forests, and fields of Shiloh, a couple
of hours from Memphis and Nashville, look exactly as they did in
1862. "It's so well-preserved you can physically feel connections to

what happened there. There's the mineral-rich, rust-brown water in 'Bloody Pond,' where wounded soldiers and horses went for water and their blood flowed into the pond." *nps.gov/shil*

New Market, Shenandoah Valley, Virginia
Cadets from the Virginia Military Institute marched 84 miles to fight at this battlefield, now owned by VMI. The campus and surrounding area are rich with war history. "There's a statue of Stonewall on VMI parade grounds with the remains of his horse buried beneath it. Four original artillery pieces he used to teach cadets at VMI are there too." *shenandoahatwar.org*

Wilderness, west of Fredericksburg, Virginia
This beautiful Virginia farm country has enough remaining wilderness to be used for military classes on how to fight the enemy when you can't see them. "You get that sense of blindness, of two armies stumbling toward each other." *nps.gov/frsp*

Fredericksburg, Virginia
Fredericksburg is packed with poignancy. Walk along the sunken road at the base of Marye's Heights and note the stone wall. "Confederate soldiers lined up four and six deep behind it so the man in front could shoot his musket, hand it back, and get another musket."
Note the two numbers on the headstones: One is for the grave and the other to indicate how many people are buried there. *nps.gov/frsp*

Antietem, Sharpsburg, Maryland
The landscape of Antietem was a major factor in causing the single bloodiest battle of the Civil War. Climb the lookout tower and you'll understand the soldiers' vulnerability as they moved across the rolling hills, unable to see the enemy just beyond the dips in the land. "It's easy to imagine men walking down into a depression, blind to what lay beyond, while their enemy moved in position beyond the next rise. You can see how they came face-to-face with each other." *nps.gov/anti*

Gettysburg, Pennsylvania
"There's no finer place, even if you have no interest in the Civil War. Stand at the High Water Mark where the Union soldiers watched Pickett's Charge. You can look across a mile of open ground to where Lee's army was. The woods are exactly where they were then. Imagine 12,000 troops, a line a mile wide, stepping out of those trees in one motion, and then the massacre." *nps.gov/gett*

Vicksburg, Mississippi
The deep ravines of this beautiful landscape high above the Mississippi made the Confederates feel secure. "Grant couldn't just attack. It's obvious why when you see the severe ground. Imagine soldiers rolling cannonballs down the hill. If the Union soldiers were close enough they'd try to catch them like a game of hot potato. Look for the Union's zigzag-shape trenches, dug to evade a clear shot." *nps.gov/vick*

Chickamauga, Chickamauga Creek, Georgia
More than 1,000 monuments and markers and 50 miles of hiking trails occupy the lush woodlands of north Georgia where this battle was fought. *nps.gov/chch*

Cold Harbor, Old Cold Harbor, Virginia
The enormous mound of dirt that Lee's soldiers built and hid behind is still here. "This was Ulysses Grant's worst day as a battlefield commander. The Union soldiers were ordered to march across the wide-open tabletop of flat ground. The ones that survived dug little bowls into the ground with their bayonets, little one-man potholes. I've actually curled myself up in one of these things. You can't help but feel the horror." *nps.gov/rich*

Petersburg, Virginia
Union coal miners dug a tunnel underneath the Confederate lines and dragged in gunpowder to blow it up. The crater is still there. "When the blast happened, an untrained unit was sent forward and they didn't know what to do. They filed into the crater because that was the safest place. They were packed in elbow-to-elbow, and nobody could get out of the way." *nps.gov/pete*

10 great places to remember D-Day's fallen heroes

On June 6, 1944, more than 156,000 American, British, French, Canadian, and other Allied forces landed on the beaches of Normandy to free occupied France from Nazi Germany's control. Historian and author Ronald J. Drez (Voices of D-Day, Remember D-Day) tells where to honor those who took part in this remarkable effort.

Normandy, France
"Second to none is to visit Normandy. The invasion beaches are all there, just as they were years ago." Small museums and memorials dot the invasion and paratroop-drop sites, including the Musée du Debarquement in Arromanches. It features models of the artificial harbors created off the town's coast to aid the invasion. Other important sites include Utah Beach, Cherbourg, and Quineville. *normandy-tourism.org*

D-Day Museum, Portsmouth, England
"The great armada set sail from there." Preparations for the invasion, code-named Operation Overlord and Operation Neptune, were centered in the southern English city of Portsmouth. Allied troops trained and gathered their huge force here. The museum says 6,939 landing craft and 2,395 aircraft (with 11,590 more in support) were deployed. A stunning 34-panel tapestry called the Overlord Embroidery depicts the four-year run-up to the invasion. *ddaymuseum.co.uk*

National WWII Museum, New Orleans, Louisiana
When historian and D-Day Museum founder Stephen Ambrose interviewed President Eisenhower in 1964, Ike said New Orleans shipbuilder Andrew Higgins, designer of Normandy landing craft, was "the man who won the war for us." Filled with interactive galleries about the D-Day era, the museum—which escaped major damage by Hurricane Katrina—is "first-class, with lots of artifacts and veterans' testimony." *nationalww2museum.org*

National D-Day Memorial, Bedford, Virginia

It's built in the U.S. town that suffered the worst loss per capita on D-Day—including 19 "Bedford Boys" of the 29th Division's 116th Regiment who were killed in the first minutes on Omaha Beach. The "centerpiece is this giant wall you see soldiers scrambling over under fire." The outdoor memorial's "statuary, water park, and ponds give the visitor the image and impression of this force coming from the sea." *dday.org*

National World War II Memorial, Washington, D.C.

Dedicated on Memorial Day 2004, the World War II Memorial on the National Mall features a main plaza, 56 granite pillars, a large central pool, fountains, and a commemorative wall with 4,000 stars representing the 400,000 Americans who died in the war. *wwiimemorial.com*

Arlington National Cemetery, Arlington, Virginia

A visit to pay homage to America's fallen soldiers is a short car or subway trip from the National World War II Memorial in Washington, D.C. *arlingtoncemetery.org*

Dwight D. Eisenhower Library, Abilene, Kansas

"The best place to learn about the supreme commander." Interactive computer kiosks, artifacts, and photos tell the story of Eisenhower's rise to supreme commander of the Allied forces in 1944 and presidential win in 1952. Visitors can hear recordings of his D-Day orders and Guildhall address in London after victory in Europe in 1945. *eisenhower.archives.gov*

Franklin D. Roosevelt Presidential Library and Museum, Hyde Park, New York

Visitors tour a replica of Roosevelt's secret White House map room, designed for round-the-clock updates during the war, and participate in an interactive exhibit on wartime decision making. *fdrlibrary.marist.edu*

Imperial War Museum's Churchill Museum and Cabinet War Rooms, London, England

This museum shows the war through "mostly British eyes." Remarkable permanent exhibits include Cabinet War Rooms nearly untouched since being sealed August 16, 1945, the day after V-J Day. Prime Minister Winston Churchill directed the British campaign from there, including the Royal Navy's crucial Operation Neptune. *cwr.iwm.org.uk*

Truman Presidential Museum & Library, Independence, Missouri "The man who ended the war" helped build a library and museum with an impressive collection of newspaper clippings, recordings, photos, and eyewitness accounts. *trumanlibrary.org*

AND ANOTHER THING...

WWII SITES

The list of poignant places connected with World War II is long. Here are just a few more.

- USS *Arizona* Memorial, Pearl Harbor, Hawaii (nps.gov/valr)
- Corregidor, the Philippines (corregidorisland.com)
- Memorial to the Fallen Heroes of Stalingrad, Volgograd, Russia
- Auschwitz-Birkenau Extermination Camp, Oswiecim, Poland (en.auschwitz.org.pl/m/)

If men could learn from history, what lessons it might teach us! But passions and party blind our eyes, and the light which experience gives is a lantern on the stern, which shines only on the waves behind us!

—Samuel Taylor Coleridge

10 great places to unwind like a president

Get away from it all, just like the nation's presidents, by visiting their special enclaves. "For more than two centuries, our nation's leaders have found rest, relaxation, and a measure of solace at their private hideaways and estates," says Kenneth T. Walsh, chief White House correspondent for U.S. News & World Report *and author of* From Mount Vernon to Crawford: A History of the Presidents and Their Retreats. *Walsh suggests sites "where we can literally walk in the presidents' footsteps."*

The Hermitage, Nashville, Tennessee
"Andrew Jackson is remembered in the popular imagination as a rough-and-ready general and a man of the people. He was actually a wealthy individual, and his 1,000-acre estate, which he lovingly restored, gives splendid insight into his life and times." *thehermitage.com*

Lincoln Cottage, Washington, D.C.

"Abraham Lincoln, faced with the trauma of the Civil War and the death of his young son, needed solace more than most other presidents. And he found it at the Soldiers' Home, a center for convalescing soldiers. Lincoln actually lived at the Soldiers' Home and commuted to the White House for one-quarter of his presidency." *lincolncottage.org*

Sagamore Hill, Long Island, New York
"Theodore Roosevelt's estate is perhaps the most unusual of any presidential retreat, filled with the heads or skins of buffalo, lions, and other big-game animals he had shot or been given as gifts in recognition of his prowess as a sportsman." *nps.gov/sahi*

LBJ Ranch, Stonewall, Texas
"Lyndon B. Johnson's outsized personality was nowhere more evident than on his ranch. He spent 484 full or partial days here during his five-year presidency. Today, visitors can take tour buses and hear guides relate how LBJ grew up in the area and how he always felt, even in the toughest of times, that his neighbors cared about him." *nps.gov/lyjo*

Poplar Forest, Bedford County, Virginia (near Lynchburg)
"Thomas Jefferson designed and built Poplar Forest in 1806 as a retreat from his visitor-plagued Monticello." Jefferson escaped to Poplar Forest to read, write, ride horses, and visit with his grandchildren. *poplarforest.org*

Truman Little White House, Key West, Florida
"Harry Truman relished the climate and simple surroundings. He enjoyed poker and bourbon but kept it secret so the country wouldn't know the president was gambling and drinking hard liquor." *trumanlittlewhitehouse.com*

Mount Vernon, Mount Vernon, Virginia

"George Washington's plantation, a short drive from the nation's capital, offers excellent tours that evoke the life of our first president when he was at home. Visitors can just sit on the back porch, where the father of our country frequently went to unwind, taking in the gorgeous view of the Potomac River." *mountvernon.org*

Springwood, Hyde Park, New York
"Franklin D. Roosevelt found spiritual refreshment at his family's posh estate in upstate New York, where he was born in 1882. FDR spent a total of 562 full or partial days here during his 12-year presidency. Roosevelt also made important decisions here: one was to plan the development and possible use of the atomic bomb

in a series of meetings, starting in June 1942, with British Prime Minister Winston Churchill in FDR's small, book-lined study that visitors can still see today." *nps.gov/hofr*

Warm Springs, Georgia

"One of the most poignant presidential stories was FDR's commitment to a ramshackle health resort here. He came for therapy for his polio-paralyzed legs in the 88-degree water that emerged from the ground. Roosevelt spent 175 days here during his presidency, hoping to motivate other polio patients. Visitors still can see the pools FDR used and the small pine-paneled house he built nearby. It's where he died on April 12, 1945." *warmspringsga.com*

Plains, Georgia

"Jimmy Carter used his tiny hometown to reinforce his image as a Washington outsider and a peanut farmer who promised not to lie. But his attachment to Plains is genuine; he moved back after losing his 1980 reelection bid. Visit the town to get a sense of Carter, still teaching at a local Baptist church, riding his bike, or walking the streets." *plainsgeorgia.com*

In "Plains" sight

Jimmy Carter's hometown is the site of a couple of peculiar moments. "While attending a meeting at the Lions Club in 1969, the future president saw a UFO and reported it," says Bill Fawcett, author of *Oval Office Oddities*. "The flying object, which witnesses (including Carter) described as being bright as a full moon, flew to within a third of a mile and then sped off."

Later, when he was president, Carter was on a fishing trip at a swamp a few miles outside of town when he met with what became known in the media as the "killer rabbit." "Basically, a swamp rabbit—and they do exist—threatened Carter," Fawcett says. "He used an oar to drive it away."

10 great places to remember Jewish heritage

For many, visiting sites of historical and religious significance throughout the world provides a connection to their family and faith, says Burton Visotzky, Appleman Professor of Midrash and Interreligious Studies at the Jewish Theological Seminary in New York, an academic and spiritual center of Conservative Judaism. He lists some places of meaning for the Jewish faithful.

Jerusalem, Israel
"Holy to the world's three major mono-theistic religions, this ancient city is the religious and historical homeland of the Jewish people. Home of the First and Second Temples, two of Judaism's holiest sites here are the Temple Mount and the Kotel (Western Wall)."

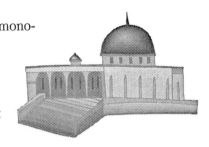

Ben Ezra Synagogue, Old Cairo, Egypt
"The 800-year-old synagogue is the site of the Cairo Genizah (depository). It is against Jewish law to destroy anything that contains God's name, so all deteriorating or no-longer-usable ritual documents must be buried or stored in a special room called a *genizah.* This treasure-trove of ancient documents has been a boon to scholars throughout the 20th century."

Baghdad, Iraq
"In addition to being the capital of Iraq, a little-known piece of this war-torn city's history includes being the final home of two of the greatest Talmudic academies in Jewish history, Sura and Pumbeditha. Judaism flourished in Iraq for more than two millennia."

St. Catherine's Monastery, Sinai, Egypt
"Set beneath Mount Sinai, the mountain where Moses is said to have received the Ten Commandments, this monastery houses the

oldest icons of Christ and a guarantee of safe passage signed by Muhammad's handprint." *interoz.com/egypt/Catherines.htm*

Old Jewish Cemetery, Prague, Czech Republic
"Created in the 15th century in the Jewish Quarter when Jews were forbidden to bury their dead outside their area, this cemetery is the final, and crowded, resting place of the great rabbinical authorities of central European Jewry and centuries of Jewish faithful." *jewishmuseum.cz*

Mount Nebo, Jordan
"Atop this mountain, Moses glimpsed the Holy Land spread before him but was denied entry. Deuteronomy reports Moses died here and was buried by God."

Cordoba and Grenada, Spain
"Cordoba is the home of Maimonides, arguably Judaism's most revered philosopher. Maimonides, who lived in the 12th century, was the first person to write a systematic code of all Jewish law, known as the Mishneh Torah. He also authored one of the great philosophic statements of Judaism, *The Guide of the Perplexed*; served as physician to the Sultan of Egypt; and led Cairo's Jewish community. Samuel Ibn-Naghrela of Grenada was a Spanish Jewish courtier who became Secretary to the Vizier and Nagid (Chief) of the Jewish community of Spain in the 11th century. Grenada and Cordoba were home to the Golden Age of Spanish Jewry under Muslim rule."

Jewish Museum, Berlin, Germany
"Designed by Daniel Libeskind, this museum has received worldwide attention for its unusual architecture that evokes strong emotions. Originally known as the Berlin Museum, it is now a memorial to the Berlin Jews who died in the Holocaust." *jmberlin.de/main/EN/homepage-EN.php*

Kairawan, Tunisia
"This ancient, sacred city of Islam is famed as a caravan city and was also home to a famous Talmudic academy in the 10th and 11th centuries."

Jewish Museum, New York, New York
"This museum was founded in the Library of the Jewish Theological Seminary. Its mission is to preserve, study, and interpret Jewish cultural history through the use of authentic art and artifacts. Its permanent collection, which has grown to more than 26,000 objects—paintings, sculpture, works on paper, photographs, ethnographic material, archaeological artifacts, numismatics, ceremonial objects, and broadcast media materials—is the largest and most important of its kind in the world." *jewishmuseum.org*

10 great places to declare your love of liberty

Clint Johnson, author of Colonial America and the American Revolution: The 25 Best Sites, *shares his choices of historic places best suited for contemplating the significance of our nation's struggle for independence.* "These colonial sites, from New England in the north to the Carolinas in the south and even the Midwestern frontier, evoke the sacrifices of those who fought in the defense of liberty."

Concord Bridge, Concord, Massachusetts
"The 'shot heard round the world' was fired here. Here too is the famous Minute Man statue, memorializing the common citizen willing to fight for freedom." *nps.gov/mima*

Fort Ticonderoga, Ticonderoga, New York
This stone fort sits on the shores of Lake Champlain, opposite the hills of Vermont. From here, after the British surrendered to Ethan Allen and Benedict Arnold's Green Mountain Boys, cannons were dragged 300 miles to Boston in the winter of 1775 to frighten the British into abandoning the city. "Even tourists who are not history buffs love this site. Its spectacular scenery proves that history can be beautiful." *fort-ticonderoga.org*

Moores Creek Bridge, Currie, North Carolina
"The short but dramatic battle that took place here between
Patriot rifles and Tory broadswords in February 1776 was a morale-
building first Revolutionary War victory for the colonists after the
Patriots' crushing defeat at Bunker Hill eight months earlier. The
reconstructed bridge and earthworks are on the original location of
the seldom-visited battlefield, where British rule over the colony
ended forever." *nps.gov/mocr*

National Archives, Washington, D.C.
"The boldly written Declaration of Independence; the brilliantly
structured United States Constitution; and the people's document,
the Bill of Rights, are displayed in the Rotunda for the Charters of
Freedom. It's worth the wait in line to read the original documents
that created and defined the United States." *archives.gov/dc-metro*

Independence Hall, Philadelphia, Pennsylvania
"The men who gathered from all over the colonies in this building
in the summer of 1776 risked their fortunes, their property, and
their lives to put their names on the Declaration of Independence
so future generations could call themselves Americans rather than
Englishmen." *nps.gov/inde*

Morristown National Historical Park, Morristown, New Jersey
"Although Valley Forge gets all the glory, Washington's army's winter camp here in 1779–80 was arguably even a greater testament
to his soldiers' loyalty and sacrifice. The snow was yards deep, and
sentries froze to death while standing guard in subzero weather."
nps.gov/morr

House of Burgesses, Williamsburg, Virginia
"In this chamber (in the colonial capital), commoners used to make
suggestions to help King George III rule the colony. Then, starting
in 1765, men like Patrick Henry began speaking out eloquently and
angrily about unfair taxation; his speeches would gradually favor
rebellion against the Crown."

George Rogers Clark National Memorial, Vincennes, Indiana
The murals here dramatically tell the story of 170 Virginians
and Kentuckians who marched for weeks—sometimes through

freezing, chest-deep water—to capture Fort Sackville in the Northwest Territories from the British in February 1779. When the Treaty of Paris was signed in 1783, England ceded what became the American Midwest. "Finding Revolutionary War history so far from the main theaters of battle lends special significance to this place." *nps.gov/gero*

Kings Mountain National Military Park, Blacksburg, South Carolina
"Both sides in the conflict agreed that the battle fought here in October 1780 was a critical turning point in the war. Thomas Jefferson called it 'the turn of the tide of success,' while one British general called it the 'first link in a chain of evils' that resulted in 'the total loss of America.' " *nps.gov/kimo*

Touro Synagogue, Newport, Rhode Island
"In 1790, the nation's second-oldest synagogue, founded in the colony established on the principle of religious freedom, sought the assurances of the country's first president that Jews could freely practice their religion. George Washington famously replied that the United States would 'give to bigotry no sanction, to persecution no assistance.' " Washington's pledge came a year before the Bill of Rights was ratified and made this non-Christian house of worship a symbol of enduring religious tolerance. *tourosynagogue.org*

The charm of history and its enigmatic lesson consist in the fact that, from age to age, nothing changes and yet everything is completely different.
—Aldous Huxley

AND ANOTHER THING...

PLACES STEEPED IN AMERICAN HISTORY

Need even more places to commemorate America's independence? Check these out:

- Old North Church, Boston, Massachusetts— Paul Revere's midnight ride to warn Samuel Adams and John Hancock that the British were arriving by sea began when the church's sexton hung two lanterns in its steeple. *oldnorth.com*

- Fraunces Tavern, New York, New York—George Washington bade his officers a final farewell here on December 4, 1783, after the last British soldiers had left American soil. *frauncestavern.com*

- Old South Meeting House, Boston, Massachusetts—Over 5,000 angry colonists met here on December 16, 1773, to discuss what would result in the Boston Tea Party. *oldsouthmeetinghouse.org*

- Fort McHenry National Monument and Historic Shrine, Baltimore, Maryland—While watching a British attack on this star-shape fort in 1814, lawyer Francis Scott Key penned our national anthem, "The Star-Spangled Banner." *nps.gov/fomc*

- Yorktown Battlefield, Yorktown, Virginia—Site of the last major battle in America's Revolutionary War, this is where George Washington teamed up with the French to defeat General Charles Cornwallis's British army in 1781. *nps.gov/colo*

10 great places to experience the first millennium

Historian Richard Landes, director of Boston University's Center for Millennial Studies, says that "a millennial year is historically a pilgrimage year, a time when the world is reordered in peace and people want to be in a holy place." Several of his recommendations were visitor magnets in the year 1000.

Angkor Wat, Cambodia
Built between the 9th and 13th centuries, the massive temples of the Khmer Empire represent a millennial culture "every bit as vigorous as that of Western Europe." At this eerie archaeological site in Siem Reap, "trees drape over the buildings and reach into the ground like fingers stuck in dough. It's a great place to meditate on the frailty of civilization."

Conques, France
Tucked away in the Massif Central area of south-central France, Conques owes its fame to Sainte Foy, a 12-year-old girl who converted to Christianity in the third century and became the heroine of the popular Peace of God movement that swept France at the turn of the first millennium. The village is "one of [the country's] best medieval sites."

Cordoba, Spain
Conquered by Muslims in 711, this Andalusian city had become one of the world's largest, most ethnically diverse settlements by 1000, where Muslims, Jews, and Christians lived in relative harmony. La Mezquita (the Great Mosque) is an "extraordinary example of Moorish architecture" surrounded by the old Jewish and Moorish quarters.

Fez, Morocco
To navigate the convoluted passageways of Fez's ancient medina is to "wander through time," encountering scenes, sounds, and smells like those from ten centuries earlier. Founded in 808, the great Muslim cultural capital remains, to many, the Arab world's most complete medieval city.

Istanbul, Turkey

During its last great come-back in the late 10th and early 11th centuries, the Byzantine Empire stretched from the Mediterranean to the Middle East, centered in the city then known as Constantinople. The Hagia

Sophia mosque, built as a cathedral in the early sixth century, remains one of the world's "most stunning religious structures."

Jerusalem, Israel

"Navel of the world" for the Abrahamic religions (Islam, Christianity, and Judaism), Jerusalem drew a wave of millennial pilgrims from 1000 to 1033.

Mesa Verde National Park, Colorado

This national park, established in 1906, contains "remarkably well-preserved" cliff dwellings and mesa-top villages built by ancestral Pueblo between 550 and 1300—"an exceptional example of a people's ability to live in challenging circumstances."

Monte Alban, Mexico

Built by the Zapotecs around 500 B.C., this ceremonial center was past its prime by A.D. 1000 but remained occupied for 14 centuries. Its "inspiring" windswept setting atop a leveled mountain overlooks Oaxaca.

Santiago de Compostela, Spain

Through much of the Middle Ages, all roads led to this city in northwestern Spain. Up to half a million pilgrims journeyed here each year, and today, the magnificent 12th-century cathedral built to receive them dominates the town of about 93,000. "Be sure to watch, and smell, the giant incense burner that hangs from the cathedral ceiling."

Varanasi, India

The "Eternal City" on the banks of the Mother Ganges has been the spiritual capital of India, "a non-Christian Jerusalem," for more than 2,000 years. It's said that those who end their days in Varanasi are transported directly to heaven. The scenery may have changed dramatically, but a boat trip down the Ganges shows "people behaving in ways that haven't changed in centuries."

10 great places to find true Americana

In an increasingly techno world, there are still places and events that remain rooted in the heart and soul of the American past. Author Gary McKechnie searched for such Americana for the National Geographic book USA 101: A Guide to America's Iconic Places, Events and Festivals. *Here, he shares his favorites.*

Little League World Series, Williamsport, Pennsylvania
"Of all the things I've seen in America, few are as wonderful as the Little League World Series," says McKechnie, who compares the ballpark in Williamsport, headquarters of the Little League since the organization's founding in 1939, to the baseball classic *Field of Dreams. www.littleleague.org*

Mark Twain's America, Hannibal, Missouri
With its carefully preserved small-town living, the author's birthplace bills itself as America's Hometown. "Mark Twain created the American dream of childhood—whitewashed fences, exploring caves, swimming holes—the benchmark for the next 150 years." In Hannibal everything Twain is celebrated, from the author's boyhood home (now a museum) to the famous fictional fence, riverboat cruises, guided cave tours, theater groups, horse-drawn tours, and Twain and Tom Sawyer impersonators. *visithannibal.com*

All-American Soap Box Derby, Akron, Ohio
Soap box derbies peaked in popularity in the 1950s, yet kids from around the world still make their way to Akron each summer for the sport's main event. "It is absolutely one of my top favorites, bar none. You think it is just kids rolling down a hill, but it is so much more, so nostalgic. Jimmy Stewart postponed his honeymoon to

attend, Ronald Reagan went, Indy 500 drivers go." The annual weeklong event is held in late July and includes parties, parades, and races on Derby Downs, a 954-foot track. *aasbd.com*

Indianapolis 500, Indianapolis, Indiana

It is the "mother of all races," but many do not realize that the Indy 500, held the Sunday of Memorial Day weekend, is the culmination of the three-week 500 Festival, including the country's largest half marathon—run partly on the famous oval. Though NASCAR has surpassed open-wheel racing's popularity, "from a standpoint of pure Americana, the Indy 500 is well in the lead. It's like a small-town celebration—and the largest single-day sporting event in the world." *indianapolismotorspeedway.com*

Rock City, Lookout Mountain, Georgia

Since the 1950s, more than 900 barn roofs from Michigan to Texas have been painted with the cryptic words "See Rock City," and thousands of visitors do just that. What do they find? Rock City is "America's minimalist theme park. Kitschy, cool, and an American original, there are no fireworks, no thrill rides, no stage extravaganzas." The namesake feature is a natural "cityscape" of streets and avenues through the boulders, with rock and swinging bridges and a waterfall. Other highlights are extensive gardens and an overlook from which you can see seven states. It is also one of the nation's only such attractions that welcomes pets. *seerockcity.com*

Tournament of Roses, Pasadena, California

In 1890, the Tournament of Roses included the now-famous Rose Parade and sports such as ostrich racing and broncobusting—football was not added until 12 years later. Today there are more than 30 college football bowl games, but only the Rose Bowl is synonymous with New Year's Day. "This one has all the tradition. After Macy's Thanksgiving, it's the country's most famous parade." It's also the oldest bowl game, the first broadcast on radio, and the first on TV. *tournamentofroses.com*

Groundhog Day, Punxsutawney, Pennsylvania

"You won't find a town its size in America that is as famous for something." That "something" is Punxsutawney Phil, the weather-predicting groundhog. Groundhog Day is always February 2, but first comes Groundhog Day Eve, similar to a county fair, except in frigid temperatures. At night, the community center screens the Bill Murray comedy *Groundhog Day.* In the wee hours of the morning, visitors are bused to the top of Gobbler's Knob, where Phil makes his appearance at sunrise. *punxsutawney.com*

Albuquerque International Balloon Fiesta, Albuquerque, New Mexico

For nine days each October, the skies above Albuquerque are filled with balloons partaking in rides, races, and competitions in the largest event of its kind. The days start before dawn, and most wind down with fireworks. "It's not just something you watch; you can also participate. You get a lot of international pilots who come without a ground or chase crew, and you can register as a volunteer, work a few days, and get a flight thrown in." Paid flights are offered, tethered and nontethered alike. *balloonfiesta.com*

Grand Ole Opry, Nashville, Tennessee

The Mount Everest of country music, this is where virtually every star in the history of the genre has performed. It remains home to the nation's longest-running radio show and offers live ensemble performances several nights a week. "Every show, the talent is incredible. It's like if every basketball game you went to was the All-Star Game." The Opry Complex includes the Grand Ole Opry House, Acuff Theater, Opry Museum, and Opry Plaza. One of the Opry's original homes, the downtown Ryman Auditorium, is still used for smaller concerts. *opry.com*

Miss America Pageant, Las Vegas, Nevada

Beauty contests are an American staple, but this is the Super Bowl. There are three days of preliminaries before the finals in the pageant, and tickets are sold for each round. "One night they do talent, one night evening gowns, and so on, so it is pretty easy to buy tickets. Whatever they choose to do for the talent show they do very well, so the quality of the performance is as good as any show on the Vegas Strip." *missamerica.org*

States with the most Miss America wins*

California	6	Florida	2
Ohio	6	Hawaii	2
Oklahoma	6	New Jersey	2
Illinois	5	South Carolina	2
Michigan	5	Tennessee	2
Pennsylvania	5	Utah	2
Mississippi	4	Virginia	2
Alabama	3	Connecticut	1
Colorado	3	Georgia	1
Kansas	3	Indiana	1
Minnesota	3	Kentucky	1
New York	3	Missouri	1
Texas	3	North Carolina	1
Arizona	2	Oregon	1
Arkansas	2	Wisconsin	1
District of Columbia	2		

*As of January 2010

10 great places to absorb the reality of slavery

Celebrate freedom by reflecting on slavery. Molefi Kete Asante, author of African American History: A Journey of Liberation, *suggests historical sites in the United States.*

Museum of African American History, Boston, Massachusetts "The African Meeting House is one of four historical sites, two in Boston and two in Nantucket, that make up this museum. Built in 1806, the meeting house is the oldest standing African American church building in America. During the Civil War, it was the center of recruitment for Northern black regiments to enlist." The other Boston site, the Abiel Smith School next door, was the first public school in the United States for black children. *afroammuseum.org*

Frederick Douglass National Historic Site, Washington, D.C.
African American history is filled with great leaders, but "none stood so tall against slavery as Frederick Douglass." His 21-room Victorian mansion is a showcase of the abolitionist's good taste and successful career. The shed where he went for solitude was called "the growlery." *nps.gov/frdo*

Avery Research Center for African American History and Culture, Charleston, South Carolina
"This is one of the great troves of African American history. Many objects and documents from the era of enslavement are here." The collection includes slavery bills of sale, slave identification badges, and a small collection of slave-made furniture. *avery.cofc.edu*

Civil War and Underground Railroad Museum, Philadelphia, Pennsylvania
"One of the hidden treasures of the Underground Railroad and Civil War memorabilia." Many of the programs here are interpretive, based on the strong oral tradition of slavery. *cwurmuseum.org*

African American Civil War Memorial and Museum, Washington, D.C.
"A national museum dedicated to the African American participation in the Civil War" is how Asante describes this site. More than 200,000 names engraved on the Wall of Honor just inside this museum identify African Americans who fought in the war. Record books supplement the list to help visitors further trace their family names. *afroamcivilwar.org*

National Underground Railroad Freedom Center, Cincinnati, Ohio
A two-story slave pen, used to warehouse slaves until they were sold, brings the reality of slavery within arm's reach to visitors. This permanent exhibit, like many others here, is an intensely emotional

experience. The center "is a splendid repository of the struggles to undermine the slave system." *freedomcenter.org*

Andersonville National Historic Site, Andersonville, Georgia
"Andersonville Prison is a haunting place where hundreds of white Union troops were held. Many black troops who supported the Union were also held here. I have walked its length, intrigued that my ancestors enslaved in nearby Dooly County might have known about the huge camp." *nps.gov/ande*

Petersburg National Battlefield, Petersburg, Virginia
"Approximately 7,800 United States Colored Troops were engaged in the Siege of Petersburg, a 9½-month-long campaign." The troops also built batteries, dug trenches along the defense lines, and worked on the railroads at this important Confederate supply center, 25 miles from Richmond. *nps.gov/pete*

Vicksburg National Military Park, Vicksburg, Mississippi
"The Vicksburg National Military Park recognizes the importance of this site for control of the Mississippi River. Black troops fought valiantly in the campaign. When the Union won the battle at this fortress, the black troops celebrated as much as anyone." Be sure to see the monument that honors Mississippians of African American descent who served in the campaign. *nps.gov/vick*

Harriet Tubman Home, Auburn, New York
"This town in the rolling hills of upstate New York is where Tubman lived. After serving as a spy during the Civil War, she fought for a meager pension and kept many indigent Africans in her house. Come here to meditate on the brilliance of the woman who brought more than 300 Africans to freedom." *harriethouse.org*

History is the sum total of all the things that could have been avoided.

—Konrad Adenauer

10 great places to explore American Indian lore

The myriad Native American museums in the United States combine "past, present, and future while celebrating our nation's heritage," says W. Richard West Jr., Southern Cheyenne and founding director of the Smithsonian Institution's National Museum of the American Indian in Washington, D.C. Here, West shares some noteworthy collections.

Southwest Museum of the American Indian, Los Angeles, California

"This museum, the oldest in L.A. (founded in 1907) and part of the Autry National Center, is one of the country's great national collections," featuring exhibits that promote the "understanding and appreciation of Native American cultures from Alaska to South America." *southwestmuseum.org*

Eiteljorg Museum of American Indians and Western Art, Indianapolis, Indiana

"In addition to being one of the active national centers for contemporary native art," including works by Kay Walkingstick and Frederic Remington, the Mihtohseenionki (the People's Place) gallery offers exhibits about Indiana's first inhabitants—the Delaware, Miami, and Potawatomi Indians. *eiteljorg.org*

Alaska Native Heritage Center, Anchorage, Alaska

"A museum of living cultures that addresses all of the great diversity of Alaska, the center offers 'a unique environment to learn about ancient traditions while celebrating contemporary ones.'" There's even a "talking circle" where games are demonstrated. *alaskanative.net*

Ah-Tah-Thi-Ki Museum, Clewiston, Florida

"This museum, one of the earliest and finest examples of a community-based tribal museum," is situated on the Big Cypress Seminole Reservation. Exhibits chronicle how the Seminole Indians lived in the swamps here in the late 1800s. Boardwalk nature trails take visitors to a Seminole village. *ahtahthiki.com*

Institute of American Indian Arts Museum, Santa Fe, New Mexico

The museum "presents the very finest in contemporary native visual art" and hosts traveling exhibits as well as art by students at the institute and permanent collections. *iaia.edu/museum*

Mashantucket Pequot Museum, Mashantucket, Connecticut

"This is the largest community tribal museum in the country." It's also a research center that spotlights the history of the Mashantucket Pequot Tribal Nation "via walk-through dioramas, collections, and interactive programs." *pequotmuseum.org*

Museum at Warm Springs, Warm Springs, Oregon

Created by the Confederated Tribes of Warm Springs (the Warm Springs, Wasco, and Paiute, all of whom live on the Warm Springs Indian Reservation), the museum is "another fine example of a community-based tribal museum, featuring a great collection of Great Basin cultures and materials." *warmsprings.com*

People's Center, Pablo, Montana

The museum, educating visitors about the Salish, Kootenai, and Pend d'Oreille tribal nations on the Flathead Indian Reservation, "provides some of the best insight into native communities and objects (such as photographs, artifacts, stone tools, and dance outfits) of the northern Great Plains." *peoplescenter.net*

Museum of the Cherokee Indian, Cherokee, North Carolina

The museum's extensive exhibits and collections "completely redone recently in a highly educational and attractive fashion, tell the story of the Cherokee people." *cherokeemuseum.org*

Mille Lacs Indian Museum, Onamia, Minnesota

Dedicated to telling the story of the Mille Lacs Band of Ojibwe American Indians who settled here, the museum features interactive exhibits and a demonstration area for cooking, birch-bark basketry, and beadwork "relating to Great Lakes native cultures and communities." *mnhs.org/places/sites/mlim*

10 great places to follow felonious footsteps

Crime may not pay, but it sure does sell. The public's fascination with murder, mayhem, and assorted other illegalities gets the tourist treatment in Crime Scene USA: A Traveler's Guide to the Locations of Famous and Infamous Murders, Robberies, Kidnappings, and Other Unlawful Acts. *Here, the book's editor, David Borgenicht, leads you to some notable crime scenes.*

Ford's Theatre, Washington, D.C.
The theater at 511 Tenth Street NW—where actor and Confederate sympathizer John Wilkes Booth shot President Lincoln on April 14, 1865 (he died the next day)—remains a working theater. "You can still attend plays, and hopefully you'll enjoy the show more than [Lincoln] did." *fordstheatre.org*

The Dakota, New York, New York
Rock legend John Lennon was returning to his apartment building at 72nd Street and Central Park West on December 8, 1980, when Mark David Chapman stepped from the bushes and fired four shots, killing the former Beatle. Nearby in Central Park is Strawberry Fields, a memorial to Lennon.

Lizzie Borden's house, Fall River, Massachusetts
In 1892, "Lizzie Borden took an ax and gave her mother 40 whacks," or so says the familiar children's ditty. Borden was acquitted of the killings of her banker father and stepmother, but she remained under a cloud of suspicion. The house at 92 Second Street is now a bed-and-breakfast and museum, whose owner offers tours. *lizzie-borden.com*

Danny Hansford murder scene, Savannah, Georgia
In 1981, Danny Hansford was found shot to death at 429 Bull Street, the tastefully appointed Savannah home of his employer and sometime-lover, Jim Williams. Williams, an antiques dealer and man about Savannah, was tried four times and ultimately acquitted. But the incident inspired John Berendt's best-selling

book (and Clint Eastwood's less successful movie) *Midnight in the Garden of Good and Evil*—much to the consternation of many residents. *mercerhouse.com*

Al Capone's haunts, Chicago, Illinois

Chicago was Al Capone's kind of town. The notorious gangster operated there from 1919 until his arrest for tax evasion in 1931. The St. Valentine's Day Massacre, one of the best-remembered incidents of gangster carnage, occurred in a garage at 2122 North Clark Street in Chicago, a building that has since been torn down. But 40 miles west of the city, Al Capone's Hideaway and Steakhouse still stands at 35W337 Riverside Drive in St. Charles, Illinois. "A sign by the urinal reads, 'Big Al hung out here.' " *speakeasycigarco.com*

Alcatraz Island, San Francisco Bay, California

The federal prison was built in the San Francisco Bay to isolate the hardest of hard-core criminals. Of the 36 convicts who attempted escape, two are known to have completed the swim (they were captured), but authorities can't account for five escapees. "They could still be alive, or they could be at the bottom of the bay. But with a little detective work, maybe you could find out." Tour boats depart from Fisherman's Wharf. *alcatraz.us*

Bonnie and Clyde Museum, Gibsland, Louisiana

The "Romeo and Juliet of armed robbery" had their final encounter with the law in this northern Louisiana town, which hasn't forgotten them. There's the museum and a stone marker. And on the weekend closest to May 23, Gibsland stages a Bonnie and Clyde Festival. *bonnieandclydemuseum.com*

The Sixth Floor Museum, Dallas, Texas

The sixth-floor window of the Texas School Book Depository from which Lee Harvey Oswald assassinated President Kennedy is now part of this museum at 411 Elm Street. *jfk.org*

Montpelier Bank Building, Montpelier, Idaho
Butch Cassidy (born Robert Leroy Parker) robbed the local bank
at 833 Washington Street in 1896, but the residents of this town in
southeastern Idaho aren't holding grudges: They occasionally stage
a reenactment of the robbery.

Old Style Saloon No. 10, Deadwood, South Dakota
After his law-enforcement career ended, James Butler "Wild Bill"
Hickok toured with Buffalo Bill Cody's Wild West Show, then
repaired to Deadwood for a life of drinking and gambling. That life
ended August 2, 1876, when he was shot in the back by a disgrun-
tled laborer who, according to legend, had lost $110 to Hickok in a
poker game. *saloon10.com*

10 great places
to enjoy historic trees

*Every day is a good day to plant a sapling or just
appreciate those big beauties in your backyard.
Jeffrey Meyer, author of* America's Famous and Historic Trees:
From George Washington's Tulip Poplar to Elvis Presley's
Pin Oak, *has made it his mission to locate the country's
historic trees and cultivate their descendants for future
generations. He shares his picks for U.S. trees to visit.*

Amelia Earhart Sugar Maple, 223 North Terrace, Atchison, Kansas
"Growing up in a typical white house in Atchison (now the Amelia
Earhart Birthplace Museum), young Amelia and her sister shared a
bedroom that looks out onto this large sugar maple. One can imagine the propellerlike seeds spinning in the air, setting her young
imagination on fire." *ameliaearhartmuseum.org*

John F. Kennedy Post Oak, Arlington National Cemetery,
Arlington, Virginia
"Inspired by the tranquil spring beauty at Arlington, John F.
Kennedy once remarked, 'It's so beautiful, I could stay here forever.' Six months later, it was that remark that inspired the grave
site selection of the slain president, beneath this towering post oak
tree." *arlingtoncemetery.net/jfk.htm*

Moreton Bay Fig, off Rodeo Drive, Beverly Hills, California
"At the intersection of Wilshire Boulevard and Rodeo Drive is one of the most expensive and beautiful shopping centers in the world." Via Rodeo, a cobblestone pedestrian street, was the first new street built after Beverly Hills was incorporated in 1914. "It was designed to spare this huge tree—at least 14 to 15 feet in diameter."

Eisenhower Green Ash, 208 East Day Street, Denison, Texas
"Here, in a humble white clapboard house, Dwight D. Eisenhower was born. A large green ash tree would have been a substantial size at the time, and it stands tall to this day."

Gettysburg Address Honey Locust, Gettysburg National Military Park, Gettysburg, Pennsylvania
"Lincoln stood near this honey locust tree and delivered the stirring Gettysburg Address. The trees at Gettysburg witnessed the whole battle . . . so most of the trees you look at are fairly awesome. I like to think that these trees must have many memories." The honey locust suffered severe damage in an August 2008 storm, but it was not entirely destroyed.

Mark Twain Cave Bur Oak, Highway 79 South, Hannibal, Missouri
"As a boy, Samuel Clemens and friends had adventures in Simms Cave in Hannibal. The imaginary days would be recalled when he wrote, as Mark Twain, of the adventures of Tom Sawyer and Huck Finn. This tree is right outside the cave."

Jacksonville Treaty Live Oak, Jessie Ball duPont Park, Jacksonville, Florida
"Legend holds that European settlers met with native Timucuan tribes to discuss peaceful coexistence in the shade of this massive, 200-plus-year-old live oak. The tree was saved by Jesse Ball duPont and now is surrounded by a lovely park," located about five minutes from downtown Jacksonville.

Elvis Presley Pin Oak, Graceland, Memphis, Tennessee
"Lining the driveway to Graceland are towering pin oak trees. Elvis must have loved trees, because he used to stand under them, just enjoying them. He also used them as a natural buffer between

himself and his fans here at Graceland. The oak trees completely overpower the house." *elvis.com*

George Washington Tulip Poplar, Mount Vernon, Mount Vernon, Virginia
"George Washington, a prolific tree planter, incorporated tulip poplar trees on the eastern lawn of Mount Vernon, which faces the Potomac River. The bowling green was a long row of trees, a long alley, for walking under after a big meal." *mountvernon.org*

Lewis and Clark Cottonwood, near Washburn, North Dakota
"Returning from two years of westward exploration, Lewis and Clark camped beneath these cottonwood trees with Mandan Indians. When the tribesmen attempted to take horses in the night, a brief skirmish occurred." The cottonwood tree is located "70 miles from the closest road (south of the intersection of highways 83 and 200), and it takes some doing to get to it, but it is my favorite tree."

10 great places to see Lewis and Clark sites

Plan an adventurous trip by following the historic route of Lewis and Clark. "By exploring the trail, you get a sense of the landscape that Lewis and Clark saw more than 200 years ago," says Elizabeth Grossman, author of Adventuring Along the Lewis and Clark Trail. *She shares her favorite stops here.*

Katy Trail, Missouri
This 225-mile walking and biking trail runs on the bed of the old Missouri-Kansas-Texas Railroad. "The longest nonmotorized part of the Lewis and Clark Trail, the Katy Trail follows the banks of the Missouri River between St. Charles and Clinton. It passes limestone bluffs, creeks, and campsites the explorers described in their journals." *mostateparks.com/katytrail.htm*

Missouri River and Loess Hills, Iowa
Located on the Iowa-Nebraska border, the DeSoto National Wildlife Refuge is "a great place to see the Missouri River Valley as

Lewis and Clark did when they passed through this stretch of river in August 1804. Head north into Iowa along Little Sioux River to see the Loess Hills rise above the valley." *midwest.fws.gov/desoto*

Niobrara River, Nebraska
"Paddle a scenic stretch of the Niobrara (which Lewis and Clark called the Rapid River) through Smith Falls State Park, then check out prairie dogs, bison, and elk at the Fort Niobrara Wildlife Refuge." *fws.gov/fortniobrara/*

Fort Pierre National Grassland, South Dakota
Lewis and Clark saw immense herds of buffalo, elk, and antelope in the Great Plains near this natural area in September 1804. "The National Grassland contains one of the Great Plains' few remaining roadless areas. Spring brings prairie chickens and grouse performing extraordinary courtship dances." *fs.fed.us/grasslands/lonetree/fortpierre.shtml*

Knife River, North Dakota
Lewis and Clark arrived at the Knife River in October 1804 "and spent the winter nearby at Fort Mandan. Walking trails at the Knife River Indian Villages Historic Site and the remains of Mandan earthen homes give visitors a sense of what this Great Plains river country was like 200 years ago." *nps.gov/knri*

Missouri River Breaks, central/eastern Montana
This wild, scenic stretch of the Missouri River flows past the famous "White Cliffs of the Missouri" that Lewis and Clark marveled at in May 1805. "The Breaks are now a national monument. Visitors can paddle or float the river here by  canoe, kayak, or river raft, camping where Lewis and Clark did to admire the same view." *blm.gov/mt/st/en.html*

Lemhi Pass, Idaho and Montana
"Lewis and Clark crossed the Continental Divide at Lemhi Pass in August 1805 and gazed out at the peaks of Lemhi, Boulder-White Cloud, and Sawtooth mountains. The Pass is now a national historic landmark. The mountains are rugged and beautiful, offering opportunities for adventurous hiking."
nps.gov/nr/travel/LewisandClark/lem.htm

Lolo Pass and Lochsa River, Montana and Idaho
The Lochsa River flows through the deeply forested Bitterroot Mountains on the Montana-Idaho border. "The Nez Perce trail that Lewis and Clark followed still can be walked today. Rushing creeks, hot springs, and mountaintop views make this a much-beloved section of the Lewis and Clark Trail."
fs.fed.us/r1/clearwater

Columbia River Gorge, Oregon and Washington
Dozens of spectacular waterfalls plunge down the cliffs of the Columbia River Gorge, home to more than 500 kinds of wild-flowers. "Hiking trails follow streams, where salmon swim in the shadow of enormous fir trees. Climb to views of Mount Hood and the stretch of river that Lewis and Clark first saw in October 1805."
fs.fed.us/r6/columbia

Mouth of Columbia River and Pacific Ocean, Washington and Oregon
"Watch the pounding surf from Cape Disappointment and the North Head Lighthouse on the Washington side of the river, where the explorers first saw the Pacific. Visit Fort Clatsop, where they spent the winter of 1805–06, then follow Clark's coastal trail toward Tillamook Head." Watch for elk, sea lions, and migrating whales.
nps.gov/lewi

There is nothing new in the world
except the history you do not know.
—Harry S. Truman

Lewis and Clark Center
details Indian influence

When it comes to epic journeys, the cross-country expedition of Meriwether Lewis and William Clark that began in 1804 is unmatched in U.S. history. Yet the explorers were far from the first to see the splendors of the West. There were, of course, thousands of Native Americans already there.

This sometimes-overlooked fact is the central theme of the Lewis and Clark National Historic Trail Interpretive Center in Great Falls, Montana. Dominating the exhibits at the $6 million museum, built into a bluff overlooking the Missouri River, are a walk-in Mandan Lodge, a Shoshone tepee, a Nez Perce willow-frame fish trap, and other displays of the life and culture of the tribes Lewis and Clark encountered.

"At first glance, visitors might wonder whether the exhibits focus more on the Indian people than the explorers," says director Jane Weber. But "further investigation will reveal the balanced story line."

The tribes, she says, are key to understanding the three-year expedition from St. Louis, Missouri, to Astoria, Oregon, and back. "What we've done is try to portray the tribes and their lifestyles at the time Lewis and Clark were passing through so visitors [can understand] what their reactions were when they met."

Focusing on the duo's interaction with Native Americans is, she admits, a "change in the way we traditionally think of this expedition." But the old model of Lewis and Clark as daring explorers slashing through the wilderness is outdated. They were diplomats searching out the "people who were living on the land."

She says that what was dubbed the "Corps of Discovery" didn't discover anything that Native Americans hadn't already known. The explorers, moreover, owed much to the Indian people. The Shoshone gave them horses; the Mandan and Hidatsa prepared them for their trip through Montana; the Nez Perce fed them.

The two-story center, run by the National Forest Service, is located roughly midway along the 3,700-mile Lewis and Clark trail. It is the largest museum devoted to the duo, with about three times more exhibit space than that at Fort Clatsop in Astoria.

10 great places to feel the melting pot's warmth

The United States is distinguished by vibrant ethnic neighborhoods in both urban and rural settings. Guidebook publisher Lonely Planet's global travel editor, Don George, suggests a gumbo of destinations that celebrate America's long history of diversity.

Ybor City, Tampa, Florida
Miami's Little Havana neighborhood may have more name recognition, and this Cuban enclave—once dubbed the "Cigar Capital of the World"—is better known for its tattoo parlors and party-hearty nightlife than for hand-rolled stogies. But Tampa's gussied-up Latin Quarter also features authentic Spanish and Cuban restaurants, and you can still watch cigars being made at Ybor Square.

Little Kabul, Fremont, California
This unremarkable neighborhood, a two-block commercial stretch of Fremont Boulevard in a suburb southeast of San Francisco, is the leading gathering spot for Afghan expatriates—thousands of whom settled here after the 1979 Soviet invasion. The fragrant kebabs at local restaurants are a must-try delicacy.

Sea Islands, Georgia and South Carolina
This cluster of low-lying islands off the Atlantic Coast was once the center of the Gullah, a community of former West African slaves whose isolation sparked a distinct language and culture. Though development on Hilton Head Island and elsewhere has eroded much of that uniqueness, several local tour companies and festivals celebrate what remains—from evocative storytellers to woven baskets of island sweetgrass.

New York, New York
No other city offers visitors such a smorgasbord of ethnic experiences, from El Museo del Barrio to Harlem's Apollo Theater and everything in between.

San Antonio, Texas

Settled by Spanish missionaries in the early 1700s, this predominantly Hispanic south Texas town celebrates its heritage with everything from Spanish-language masses in historic missions to killer margaritas and Tex-Mex food at La Villita and Market Square, two downtown shopping areas that attract both locals and tourists.

Little Tokyo, Los Angeles, California

The centerpiece of this historic downtown neighborhood is the Japanese American National Museum, dedicated the day after the outbreak of the city's Rodney King riots. Nearby, the Japanese American Cultural and Community Center offers city-weary visitors quiet refuge in an award-winning garden.

Ukrainian Village, Chicago, Illinois

The Windy City's mosaic of neighborhoods is home to dozens of ethnic groups, including the largest Polish population outside Warsaw. Along Chicago Avenue, west of the Kennedy Expressway, visitors to Ukrainian Village will encounter an eclectic mix of hipster bars, some of Chicago's finest church architecture, and a smattering of Polish and Ukrainian businesses. Among them: Caesar's Polish Deli, famous for what Chicago columnist Mike Royko called the "Rolls Royce of pierogi."

Albuquerque, New Mexico

Sometimes overshadowed by nearby tourist magnets Santa Fe and Taos, the state's largest city reflects a unique blend of Native American, Mexican, Spanish, and Western influences. Each April, over 3,000 American Indians from more than 500 tribes converge for the Gathering of the Nations Powwow and Indian Traders Market.

Cajun Country, Louisiana

Laissez les bons temps rouler ("Let the good times roll!") is more than a phrase in the bayous and prairies north of New Orleans. It remains a fiercely protected way of life that's evident in everything from French-language radio stations to the infectious enthusiasm of Saturday morning music sessions at Fred's Lounge in Mamou.

The Big Island, Hawaii
While a revival of traditional native Hawaiian culture has permeated the state in recent years, one of the best places to see the aloha spirit in action is in Hilo during the annual Merrie Monarch Festival. The Olympics of hula dancing draws standing-room-only crowds to watch competitors from some two dozen *halaus* (dance schools), with both ancient and modern styles on display.

Budget Travel Tips from the **USA TODAY Archive**

LODGING

Get thee to a nunnery

- Travel in the off-season. But always ask for a discount. In Spain's smaller hotels, if you pay cash, you get a discount.

- The best budget lodgings in London are student dorms. King's College and the London School of Economics (to name a couple) open up their dorms when classes are out. They're centrally located, clean, and safe—but don't expect decor.

- In Rome, "holy hotels" are monasteries run by sisters, and they are unbelievably wonderful. But don't expect sophisticated reservations systems.

- In Paris, consider renting an apartment. While the overall price may seem high, when you amortize it over a week, it's a good deal.

—Sandra Gustafson, *Great Sleeps/Great Eats*

Walk right in

If you wait until 7 or 8 at night to [walk in and] get a room, that's when you can get a deal. The hotel room is a perishable commodity. If there's room, the later you arrive, the more you can negotiate the rate.

—Wendy Perrin, *Wendy Perrin's Secrets Every Smart Traveler Should Know*

HOLIDAYS

✳ ✳ ✳ ✳

NEW YEAR'S

10 great places around the globe to ring in the New Year

Whether wild or mild, unique New Year's Eve celebrations offer memorable ways to fete the future. Melissa Biggs Bradley, editor of Town & Country Travel *magazine, shares some special spots.*

Time Warner Center, New York, New York
"Jazz at Lincoln Center moved into an extraordinary space in this new complex (in 2005), and one of its music halls is an intimate jazz club called Dizzy's. At night on New Year's, the views of Central Park fireworks and the lighted Manhattan skyline form an unforgettable backdrop." *jazzatlincolncenter.org*

Bauer Hotel, Venice, Italy
Celebrate Old World style at "a gala dinner at the 19th-century Palazzo Bauer, a gloriously historic hotel on Venice's Grand Canal. Its elegant owner, Francesca Possatti, presides over the annual eight-course dinner held at the rooftop restaurant. Everyone dresses in black tie, and at midnight you can hear the cheering from nearby St. Mark's Square, where crowds have gathered on this night for centuries." *bauervenezia.com*

St. Barts, French West Indies
"On this French Caribbean island, the festivities begin with a Round the Island yacht race. Dozens of boats compete and many others flock to picturesque Gustavia Harbor, site of the start and finish lines. Later in the night, fireworks illuminate the harbor as all restaurants with good views, such as Maya's and Wall House, buzz with an international mix of people."

The Bund, Shanghai, China

"This booming metropolis already has twice the number of skyscrapers as New York, and the best spots from which to see them are the restaurants in the fabulously restored neocolonial buildings on the Bund," the city's landmark waterfront. "From their windows, gaze across the Huangpo River to Shanghai's financial center of Pudong. At midnight on New Year's Eve, thousands of people gather along the Bund to watch fireworks shot off river barges."

Post Ranch Inn, Big Sur, California

"Enjoy a quiet, romantic evening for two at Post Ranch, a 30-room ecoluxury inn on the cliffs of Big Sur. End a day of yoga or hiking along the dramatic coastline, or in the redwood forest, with a massage and dinner in one of the five wood-and-glass ocean cabins. Each has its own terrace jutting 1,200 feet over the Pacific. There are no televisions in any of the rooms, so midnight is marked by the sound of crashing waves." *postranchinn.com*

Wynn Las Vegas, Las Vegas, Nevada

"Located on the Vegas Strip, the Wynn is a 50-story bronze tower with 2,700 rooms, all of which have floor-to-ceiling glass windows with views of the Strip and the property's own golf course and mountain." Check out the tower's many restaurants, "from gourmet French to Chinese, as well as shows, shopping, lounges, and nightclubs—all designed so you can observe the New Year's Eve crowds down on the Strip without ever leaving the resort." *wynnlasvegas.com*

The Villa by Barton G., Miami, Florida

"Right in the heart of South Beach's Deco district is an elaborate 1930s Spanish-style mansion, previously owned by the late Gianni Versace. It's now a members-only club with ten suites that anyone can reserve as a temporary member. The building features a gor-

geous indoor mosaic swimming pool and a Moroccan-style roof deck, with views of the beach and the fireworks."
casacasuarina.com

Punta del Este, Uruguay
"Casinos and nightclubs exist in Punta proper, but for a casual, chic South American experience, head to the nearby fishing village of José Ignacio, where restaurants serve grilled food at long tables set right on the beach. Sit next to people from a dozen different countries as you eat Argentine steak and sip Chilean wine. It's so low-key that you might not even notice when midnight arrives. Toast it a few minutes late."

The Little Nell, Aspen, Colorado
"This legendary gathering spot is popular for celebrities who annually descend on the resort. After a day of skiing, mingle at the hotel's bar, a lively après-ski scene" featuring a New Year's Eve band and a good vantage point to watch the town's fireworks. Private parties also abound on the mountain, and often the hosts put on additional fireworks shows for the whole town to see."
thelittlenell.com

Tsar's Ball, St. Petersburg, Russia
"This gorgeous city of palaces celebrates New Year's with balls. The grandest is the Tsar's Ball, held at the French baroque Catherine Palace just outside St. Petersburg in Pavlovsk. Guests in black tie spend the evening moving from one opulent hall to another for cocktails and dinner, during which opera singers and ballerinas perform. Enjoy champagne, vodka, and beluga caviar as fireworks explode in the French gardens outside at midnight. Then a jazz band begins, and everyone dances." *tsarball.com*

Ring out the old, ring in the new, Ring, happy bells, across the snow: The year is going, let him go; Ring out the false, ring in the true.
—Lord Alfred Tennyson

10 great places to break
New Year's resolutions

As the former owners of a California-based tour company called Wild Women Adventures, Martha Lindt and Carol Rivendell are experts at finding places designed to subvert such traditional New Year's pledges as drinking less, losing weight, and saving money. Here, they share some top contenders.

Lausanne Palace and Spa, Lausanne, Switzerland
"This is not a good-girl spa." Think decadent desserts made with Swiss chocolate, shopping at "outrageously expensive stores," and late-night jam sessions at jazz clubs in nearby Montreux. A plus for nicotine addicts: "You can even smoke between courses." *www.lausanne-palace.com*

Harrods' winter sale, London, England
You'll score big savings on some of Europe's "most opulent shopping" by hitting legendary department store Harrods' annual sale. Stock up on fattening foie gras and Stilton cheese in the cavernous Food Hall, or chow down in one of more than 25 on-site restaurants.

New Orleans, Louisiana
"If you want to break a resolution, you won't have to think very hard or wander very far" in the French Quarter, where you can sip Hurricanes and do-si-do 'til dawn. Start the fun by checking into a "wonderfully decadent, very private" hotel, such as the Hotel Maison de Ville.

Pub crawl, Dublin, Ireland
Dublin's ultrahip Fitzwilliam Hotel, around the corner from Grafton Street, is the perfect starting point for a bleary-eyed evening. Wind up at Charlie's on the Quay for rock 'n' roll at a "fabulous pub that's been offering up spirits since 1768."

Chateau de Chissay, Chissay-en-Touraine, France
"For gluttony at its most high," it's tough to beat this 15th-century castle-turned-hotel in the Loire Valley. The Gothic dining room

specializes in regional fare; unathletic gourmands will appreciate being able to take an elevator to their rooms, where they can "nap and recover before plunging into the next gastronomic gorging gala."

Hedonism II and III, Jamaica
"The name says it all: If you can think of it, you can do it" at these no-holds-barred, all-inclusive Caribbean resorts, where toga parties have never gone out of style. *www.superclubs.com*

Carnival, Venice, Italy
Italy's most famous pre-Lenten celebration features "nonstop partying" amid throngs of uninhibited, elaborately costumed and masked revelers. Finding a suitable partner to erase a vow of moderation "shouldn't be too hard."

St.-Germain-des-Prés, Paris, France
In this Left Bank neighborhood, which once hosted such bons vivants as Pablo Picasso, Anaïs Nin, and Ernest Hemingway, you can still throw caution to the wind by slurping champagne and raw oysters at such "tourist-filled" but atmospheric stalwarts as Brasserie Lipp and Cafe de Flore.

Las Vegas, Nevada
While Las Vegas is known for its over-the-top ambience, Sin City and its ever-increasing gaggle of hotels remains the best place to indulge in gambling, drinking, and...well...general revelry.

The Castro, San Francisco, California
This lively neighborhood, with its colorful past and inclusive spirit, "is a great place to break all the rules, and do it with aplomb."

An optimist stays up until midnight to see the New Year in. A pessimist stays up to make sure the old year leaves.

—Bill Vaughan

VALENTINE'S DAY

10 great places for a romantic weekend

Here are cozy options for a get-close getaway, suggested by Bill Gleeson, author of the Weekends for Two *paperback series.*

Applewood Inn, Spa & Fine Restaurant, Guerneville, California
This 1922 Mission Revival–style mansion, set among aging redwoods in the Russian River wine country, has been remade into an intimate inn. Its 19 rooms and suites are decorated individually and feature four-poster beds, fireplaces, double showers or whirlpool tubs, and private sitting areas and balconies. "One of its main attractions is the candlelit dinners." *applewoodinn.com*

Andrie Rose Inn, Ludlow, Vermont
"The most romantic inn in Vermont," at the base of Okemo Mountain with several other ski resorts nearby, offers rooms and suites "from rustic to opulent" in three 19th-century buildings. "Beautiful wall coverings," double whirlpool tubs, fireplaces, and such details as pedestal sinks, luxe linens, and generous amenities complement the storybook scenery. *andrieroseinn.com*

The Inn at Little Washington, Washington, Virginia
Rated a rare five stars by Mobil and five diamonds by AAA for both dining and lodging, this celebrated inn 65 miles west of "big" Washington, D.C., has 14 rooms and suites "to die for.... All have interesting angles, yards and yards of the best fabric, multiple contrasting wallpapers." Sybarites, don't miss dinner: Renowned food writer Craig Claiborne declared he'd had the best meal of his life here. *theinnatlittlewashington.com*

Blue Lake Ranch, near Durango, Colorado
No highway sign announces this isolated "utopia for lovers" in the Four Corners area; guests find the driveway by watching the odometer. "People skinny-dip in Blue Lake, it's so private." The

230-acre, flower-strewn property offers lodgings from rooms in the main inn to separate cottages with kitchenettes. "My favorite is Cabin on the Lake," a refurbished three-bedroom, three-bath log cabin with two rock fireplaces. *bluelakeranch.com*

Inn at Langley, Langley, Washington
Though "it looks rather anonymous from the street, [this] honey-moon destination has exquisite views and accommodations." The quaint village is on Whidbey Island, and the inn is built on a bluff overlooking the water of the Saratoga Passage. Each of the 28 rooms features a 180-degree waterfront view, private porch, fireplace, and double whirlpool tub. *innatlangley.com*

Inn on La Loma Plaza, Taos, New Mexico
A walled Spanish hacienda in a parklike setting 2-1/2 blocks from the gallery and restaurant area, "this is the poshest and most romantic inn in town,... luxuriously appointed and decorated with

Budget Travel Tips from the **USA TODAY Archive**

TRANSPORTATION

Ask the hard-currency questions

If you're going to be driving through several European countries, think carefully where you rent a car. Who knew? Rental cars are really reasonable in Germany vs. Switzerland or Austria.

—Wendy Perrin, *Wendy Perrin's Secrets Every Smart Traveler Should Know*

Wait for Wednesday's windfall

The worst day of the week to make an airline reservation is Saturday or Sunday. The best time to make one is 12:01 A.M. EST on Wednesday morning. That's because airlines start fare wars Friday, other airlines match them Monday, and tickets held for 24 hours and not bought are dumped Tuesday night.

—Peter Greenberg, *The Travel Detective*

artistic curios and cowboy collectibles." Its ten guest rooms "ooze
Southwestern charm," with handcrafted furniture, richly colored
fabrics, and fresh flowers. All have fireplaces too. *vacationtaos.com*

Combsberry Inn, Oxford, Maryland
At the end of a private dirt road on Maryland's Eastern Shore, this
historic brick mansion nestles among magnolias and willows on the
banks of Island Creek. "There's even a boat dock guests can use," as
well as a library, formal gardens, and water views from each room
(some with fireplaces and whirlpool tubs). *combsberryinn.com*

Glendeven Inn, Little River, California
Right on scenic coastal Highway 1, this "charming compound
set on lush acreage near the water [is] a nice place to stay if
you want to visit tourist-laden Mendocino" two miles north.
Accommodations range from a Federalist-style 1867 farmhouse—
"where you can stay in a room under the eaves with dormer
windows" or a two-bedroom suite with kitchen—to a contemporary
rustic building with commanding views, private decks, and fireplaces. *glendeven.com*

Inn on Mt. Ada, Avalon, California
The 1921 Wrigley mansion, set on a promontory overlooking Santa
Catalina Island's main community, is "probably the most romantic
inn in the state—even (our) bathroom had a view of the ocean and
the mainland." Four of the six antique-filled guest rooms have fireplaces, and the rates include breakfast; lunch; and free champagne,
wine, and beer anytime. Because the island doesn't allow cars and
the inn is "a steep walk up" from the village, guests are given golf
carts for the five-minute ride into tiny Avalon. *innonmtadad.com*

The Mansion Inn, New Hope, Pennsylvania
This yellow-and-white "traffic stopper," an 1865 French Victorian
manor house, "is as nice inside as out." Rooms are furnished with
antiques and fine art; mounds of down pillows top each comforter-
clad featherbed. Modern niceties such as gas fireplaces and double
whirlpool tubs grace most quarters, and the grounds include an
English garden and gazebo. *themansioninn.com*

10 great places where love bloomed on screen

There's nothing better than a good romantic movie on Valentine's Day—unless, of course, you can make it to the place where the romantic movie was filmed. Paris Permenter, copublisher of lovetripper.com, offers her list of favorite locales.

Grand Hotel, Mackinac Island, Michigan
Christopher Reeve and Jane Seymour may have been billed as the leads in the 1980 cult classic *Somewhere in Time,* but Mackinac Island's Grand Hotel also played a starring role. A particularly good time to visit is the second weekend in October for a *Somewhere in Time* celebration that includes stops at places made famous in the film. "Anytime couples visit, though, they can take in the movie locations, from the 660-foot-long porch, where the film's hero spent his first night in 1912, to the spot where Richard Collier and Elise McKenna first met (marked with a plaque among the trees)." *grandhotel.com*

From Here to Eternity Beach, Oahu, Hawaii
Perhaps no movie kiss is more memorable than the one shared by Burt Lancaster and Deborah Kerr in the 1953 movie *From Here to Eternity.* "Their romp in the sand took place on what was called Halona Cove but has since become known as the From Here to Eternity Beach. Just as it was in 1953, the small beach is set on an intimate cove surrounded by craggy cliffs that discourage many tourists from making the fairly steep climb down to the sand." *gohawaii.com*

Round Hill Hotel & Villas, Montego Bay, Jamaica
A favorite with red-carpet travelers (Ralph Lauren owns one of the villas, and names like Paul McCartney and Harrison Ford pop up in the guest book), this elegant resort was the setting for the 1998

film *How Stella Got Her Groove Back.* "Ask for Villa 11 to create your own Angela Bassett–Taye Diggs moment." *roundhilljamaica.com*

The Tides Inn, Port Townsend, Washington
"Request a stay in the suite where romance ignited between U.S. Navy aviation officer candidate Zack Mayo and local girl Paula Pokrifki, and you'll receive the key to Room 10 at The Tides Inn." Its windows still frame the same view of Port Townsend Bay that actors Richard Gere and Debra Winger saw during the filming of the 1982 movie *An Officer and a Gentleman. tides-inn.com*

Trump Wollman Skating Rink, New York, New York
"Cold weather and romance go hand-in-hand." With a backdrop of the Manhattan skyline, one of the most romantic experiences in New York City is ice-skating at Wollman Skating Rink in Central Park, just as Ali McGraw and Ryan O'Neal did in 1970's *Love Story.* "For about the price of lunch, the two of you can rent skates and take to the ice, hold hands, and feel like the whole city is at your feet." *wollmanskatingrink.com*

Mountain Lake Hotel, Pembroke, Virginia
Dirty Dancing aficionados are still having the time of their lives at the Mountain Lake Resort. "This seasonal Appalachian property (doubling for the Catskills in the 1987 movie) played the role of Kellerman's Resort in the coming-of-age story." Come for one of the Dirty Dancing weekends, featuring a tour of film locations; a trivia contest; and, of course, dirty dancing. "Couples can ask for Room 232, where Patrick Swayze stayed during the film's production." *mtnlakehotel.com*

InterContinental Carlton Cannes, Cannes, France
In the 1955 Alfred Hitchcock film *To Catch a Thief,* this hotel, overlooking the Bay of Cannes, served as an elegant backdrop for Cary Grant as he set out to snag a jewel thief and for Grace Kelly as she attempted to catch a husband. "For the seductive view of the fireworks-lit bay that Kelly and Grant shared, ask for a corner suite (Room 623 for real sticklers)." *ichotelsgroup.com*

Fontainebleau Miami Beach, Miami Beach, Florida
"The 1992 movie *The Bodyguard* (starring Kevin Costner and Whitney Houston) showed the world the romantic side of the Fontainebleau Miami Beach, which had also been featured in other less lovey-dovey movies like *Goldfinger* and *Scarface.* You might find yourself humming 'I Will Always Love You' if you pop in the Grand Ballroom, where Whitney sang the hit in the movie."
fontainebleau.com

Candy is the dandiest Valentine's Day gift

For any guy who tires of opening his umpteenth Christmas necktie gift... for any woman who thinks any more holiday jewelry gifts will be too much of a good thing... for any child whose sweet tooth isn't satisfied with Santa's dolls or trains... Valentine's Day is a welcome relief.

Those Christmas gift items don't finish anywhere near the top for Valentine's gifting. According to the National Retail Federation, these three things top the gift list across the United States for Valentine's Day: candy (47%), flowers (36%), and an evening out (36%).

Valentine's Day has become a time for love exchanges, even though opinions still abound on who was the original Valentine. The most popular theory is that he was a clergyman who was executed for secretly marrying couples in ancient Rome in spite of Emperor Claudius II, who felt marriage weakened his soldiers.

In any event, in A.D. 496, Pope Gelasius I declared February 14 St. Valentine's Day. Through the centuries, it has become a time for grownups to exchange gifts, love messages, nights out, or even marriage vows. For kids, any and every kind of candy satisfies their Valentine's desires.

Chatsworth House, Derbyshire, Great Britain
"Moviegoers looked through the eyes of Jane Austen when Chatsworth House appeared on screen in the 2005 adaptation of *Pride & Prejudice*." Visit the Painted Hall, where Lizzie's tour of Pemberley begins in the movie, and the Sculpture Gallery, where Keira Knightley, as the heroine, comes face-to-face with a carved bust of her future suitor, Mr. Darcy. Chatsworth House is open to the public from mid-March through December, but the grounds, also featured in the film, can be toured year-round. *chatsworth.org*

The View Point Inn, Corbett, Oregon
"During its first incarnation in the 1920s, silent-screen legend Charlie Chaplin and President Franklin Roosevelt were visitors at this inn overlooking the Columbia River Gorge. After years of lying dormant, the Tudor Arts and Crafts–inspired property has been resurrected, and today fans who were spellbound by the 2008 movie *Twilight* can dine in the area where the students of Forks High School held their prom and spend the night in the Roosevelt Suite, where the last moments of the movie took place." *theviewpointinn.com*

10 great places to be on cloud 9 with your sweetie

Soar to new heights with your love on Valentine's Day. Carley Roney, editor in chief of thenest.com, a popular lifestyle Web site for couples, shares her list of favorite over-the-top destinations.

Ladera Resort, St. Lucia, West Indies
"Nothing, not even a wall, comes between you and the lush, bird's-eye views of the Pitons, the island's twin volcanic peaks, and the ocean." Rooms in this boutique hotel, which is perched like a luxury tree house on a forested ridge 1,100 feet above the Caribbean, have only three walls, bringing you exhilaratingly close to nature. Have a couples massage at the spa, then feast at Dasheene, the hotel's restaurant with Caribbean accents. *ladera.com*

Top of the World Restaurant, Las Vegas, Nevada
"You'll feel like you're walking on clouds together at this revolving restaurant on the 106th floor of the Stratosphere Casino & Hotel, more than 850 feet above the sparkling lights of the 'Wedding Capital of the World.' Toast being a twosome with a two-foot-tall Stratoblaster glass filled with champagne at the expansive casino downstairs." *topoftheworldlv.com*

Napa Valley Aloft, Yountville, California
"Napa Valley is ultraromantic—especially when you fly high over the vineyards in a hot-air-balloon ride. You and your date get picked up at your hotel at dawn for a drive to the launch site, V Marketplace at Vintage 1870 Wine Cellar. Upon your return from the dramatic sights above Napa and Sonoma, you'll be treated to a delicious breakfast and driven back to your inn in time to begin a day of traditional vineyard tours." *napavalleyaloft.com*

Fairmont Le Château Frontenac, Quebec City, Quebec, Canada
"Request a room on the exclusive Fairmont Gold Floor and get the royal treatment at this grand hotel with castle-style architecture towering on a bluff above the St. Lawrence River in the heart of Old Quebec." Dress up for dinner at Le Champlain, where hotel chef Jean Soulard's cuisine includes selections from the surrounding agricultural region. Later, ride the funicular down to walk arm-in-arm on the cobblestone streets and explore this historic city. *fairmont.com/frontenac*

Goliath Hypercoaster, Six Flags Magic Mountain, Valencia, California
"Looking for a romantic rush? Strap into a wild ride at 85 mph on one of the tallest, fastest roller coasters in the world. The anticipation-building ascent will give you time to recount all the things you love about each other before you take the white-knuckled plunge

together. It's a full-body rush and will get those endorphins going, which is an instant aphrodisiac." *sixflags.com/magicmountain*

Top of the Rock Observation Deck, New York, New York
"Ride a glass-ceiling elevator up 67 stories to this historic perch atop one of Manhattan's most recognizable Art Deco landmark sky-scrapers: 30 Rockefeller Plaza. This romantic destination has 360-degree views of the city that never sleeps." Snuggle together on either the 67th-, 69th-, or 70th-floor observation decks and identify the Empire State Building, the Chrysler Building, Central Park, and the Brooklyn Bridge, as well as enjoy views of the Hudson River and the East River. *topoftherocknyc.com*

London Eye Ferris Wheel, London, England
"Also known as the Millennium Wheel, this landmark on the South Bank of the Thames takes you up 443 feet to catch dramatic views of Buckingham Palace, St. James's Palace, the Houses of Parliament, and views of London in every direction. Splurge and upgrade to your own Cupid's Capsule, a romantic private capsule complete with a bottle of Laurent-Perrier Champagne and pink truffles served by your host." *londoneye.com*

Hotel Villa Caletas, near Jaco Beach, Costa Rica
"Take in the lush tropics and eye-catching sunsets of Costa Rica's central Pacific coast from 1,150 feet above the ocean at the Hotel Villa Caletas. Enjoy cocktails and dinner set to music as you watch the sun dip into the horizon from the resort's cliffside amphi-theater. Then return to your French Colonial suite (with its own infinity pool) for private time." *hotelvillacaletas.com*

Space Needle, Seattle, Washington
"Whisper sweet nothings while viewing snowcapped Mount Rainier, the Cascade Mountains, and the majestic Olympics, as well as the waters of Puget Sound, sparkling Lake Union, and Elliott Bay. Share one of the Observation Deck's complimentary Swarovski telescopes that are so powerful you could spot a friend in the stands at the baseball stadium a couple of miles away. Munch on a sumptuous meal at SkyCity, the needle's 360-degree-view restaurant." *spaceneedle.com*

Willis Tower Skydeck, Chicago, Illinois
"If you're looking for a natural high together, head to Chicago and the Willis (formerly Sears) Tower Skydeck. On a clear day, the walk-around view (from the 103rd floor) includes Michigan, Indiana, Illinois, and Wisconsin, as well as the city's remarkable architecture. The sights aren't just out the window. Interactive, museum-quality exhibits inside tell the stories of Chicago's past and present." Stay at the Sofitel Chicago Water Tower, where a romance concierge and special Valentine's Day chocolate martini will complement your day. *the-skydeck.com*

Bonus destination: Sofitel Chicago

"Home of America's first skyscraper, this Midwestern metropolis is dreamy for duos who love architecture—from classic to postmodern showstoppers—and are looking to tear up the city in style," says thenest.com's Carley Roney. "Since you're in Chicago to see its gems, why not stay in one? The soaring triangular Sofitel Chicago Water Tower is designed to sparkle, and it does."

10 great places to mend your broken heart

You've been dumped, and you're still wallowing in memories of a Valentine's Day spent with cheap bubbly and a batch of black-frosted, broken-heart cookies. Time to snap out of it and plan the perfect escape with Marybeth Bond, author of 50 Best Girlfriend Getaways *in North America.* Bond shares soothing spots to heal from a broken romance, whether you're a man or woman.

Quebec City, Quebec, Canada
"Quebecers like to say their capital city is like France without the jet lag or the attitude. What you'll love the most is aimlessly wandering the narrow (and safe) streets, passing *boulangeries,* old churches, and slate-roof granite houses whose balconies drip with flowers. Over a long weekend in August, the New France Festival

takes you back to when the French occupied the colony. More than 1,500 artists and performers don authentic costumes; you can rent one of your own and join in on the fun." *quebecregion.com*

Monterey Peninsula, California
A trip along Highway 1 between Monterey and San Simeon is "a therapeutic and liberating journey on one of the world's most scenic roads." Hike at Point Lobos State Reserve or Julia Pfeiffer Burns State Park, pamper yourself at Esalen Institute in hot tubs sitting right over the ocean, or book a massage at Ventana Inn and Spa. And "don't miss the Ambrosia burger at Nepenthe, a redwood-and-glass building suspended over the coast at Big Sur." *seemonterey.com*

Key West, Florida
The 113-mile, 42-bridge highway through the Keys "leads to the edge of the world symbolically and removes you from everything you need to leave behind." Mallory Square is famous for sunsets, but there's a better option: Late afternoons, schooners head into the open sea. "With a glass of wine in hand, take in the sound of the wind in the sails as you watch the sun's descent." *fla-keys.com/keywest*

Glacier National Park, Montana
"Perhaps nothing puts life into perspective and rebuilds your self-esteem more than hiking among these remote glaciers. The beauty manages to push life's obstacles to the side, and to be humbled by these fields of snow and ice is to be uplifted by them too." In summer, 700 miles of maintained trails lead into a high-alpine setting, past waterfalls and icy blue lakes. *nps.gov/glac*

San Miguel de Allende, Mexico
Artsy San Miguel de Allende, four hours north of Mexico City, "encourages you to take risks, learn something new, and reinvent yourself. Its narrow cobblestone streets; pink-and-terra-cotta-colored buildings; blooming gardens; and enormous, Gothic-inspired church are right out of a postcard from Spain—a couple of hundred years ago. It's hard to stay away from one of the many workshops and schools when everyone else is painting, writing a novel, or learning Spanish or digital photography." *visitmexico.com*

Kripalu Center for Yoga and Health, Lenox, Massachusetts
Set high above Lake Mahkeenac in the Berkshires of
western Massachusetts, the Kripalu Center nurses
guests back to physical and psychological health
with "a loving atmosphere, healthful food, and
the simplicity of country living." Year-round
Healing Retreat packages include meals
served cafeteria-style, daily healing-arts
sessions with such options as aromatherapy, footwork reflexology, yoga, a
sauna, and hiking trails with a meditative
labyrinth. *kripalu.org*

Door County, Wisconsin
Its dunes, historic lighthouses, and 300 miles of shoreline have
earned this peninsula the nickname "Cape Cod of the Midwest,"
but Door County is also a great destination for retail therapy.
Hundreds of shops and galleries showcase the work of local clothing designers, crafters, antique collectors, and painters; in Fish
Creek, "the Oilery's expansive tasting bar lets you sample freshly
pressed olive oils in a variety of flavors." *doorcounty.com*

Moab, Utah
This quirky town is the gateway to two national parks, Arches and
Canyonlands, and "lays claim to the best mountain biking in the
nation." From here, take a road trip on the Grand Circle linking
Utah's Bryce and Zion with Arizona's Monument Valley and Grand
Canyon and Colorado's Mesa Verde national parks. You'll see some
of the country's most extraordinary natural wonders, "and the wide-
open desert, the dry air blasting through the open car window,
and the heat of the sun on your arms and shoulders are cathartic."
discovermoab.com

Cajun country, Lafayette, Louisiana
Dance away your blues to toe-tapping music after filling up on
the region's red beans and rice, po' boys, jambalaya, chicken-and-
sausage gumbo, and boiled crawfish at rollicking restaurant-cum-
dance halls like Prejeans and Randol's. The "ancient cypress trees
covered with Spanish moss, fields of rice and sugarcane, rundown

shanties, alligators, and signs reading *ici, on parle français* (French spoken here) let you know you're in another world." *lafayettetravel.com*

Nashville, Tennessee
Country music is Nashville's lifeblood. But even those who "don't care a lick" about the genre "will be relieved to know Nashville is not all barbecue and locals in ten-gallon hats. Its eclectic music scene, cosmopolitan ways, and laid-back character appeal to everyone. On Lower Broadway, honky-tonk bars line the street, showcasing live bands and never charging a cover." Work your way through spots like Tootsies Orchid Lounge, Robert's Western World, and The Stage, "pairing up with new dance partners or just kicking back." *visitmusiccity.com*

10 great places to keep
the fires burning

"Travel is often about escape and romance," says Klara Glowczewska, editor in chief of Condé Nast Traveler. *"And that includes in-room fireplaces. Even in the most remote destinations, it's a pleasure to return to your room after a long day and relax fireside." Glowczewska shares some terrific hotels to keep your tootsies toasty by an open hearth.*

Lake Placid Lodge, Lake Placid, New York
"Juxtaposing rustic ambience with indulgent luxury, LPL lights the fireplaces just prior to a guest's arrival. Each evening, while you dine, the wood is replenished, and upon return to your room there's a newly started fire. Nearby is a wicker basket filled with essential fixings for a tasty midnight snack of s'mores." *lakeplacidlodge.com*

Amangani, Jackson Hole, Wyoming
"During a ski trip to this resort, situated in the midst of the Grand Tetons, the room I stayed in had a (gas) fireplace with a remote

control. What a wonderful, relaxing way to end a chilly day on the slopes." *amanresorts.com*

Las Ventanas al Paraiso, Los Cabos, Mexico

"The suites here all have white-stucco, adobe-style wood-burning fireplaces. Fires are started by the staff, who keep the mesquite wood coming—as much as you want. The staff also arranges to have a fire burning in your suite, surrounded by candles, when you return from dinner." *lasventanas.com*

Grasmere Lodge, South Island, New Zealand

"Here at Grasmere Lodge, tucked away in the heart of the Southern Alps of New Zealand, guests find luxury blending with natural splendor. The Grasmere Suite is the perfect retreat, with a 'sink into me' sofa and armchairs in front of the schist (a type of stone) fireplace." *grasmere.co.nz*

XV Beacon Hotel, Boston, Massachusetts

"This chic boutique hotel offers fireplaces in each of its rooms, which can be operated from the comfort of your four-poster bed via a nearby wall control." With the fireplace crackling, you won't even think about venturing out in Beantown, just cocooning in your room. *xvbeacon.com*

La Posada de Santa Fe, Santa Fe, New Mexico

"Many of the rooms in this boutique property offer wood-burning Kiva fireplaces that invite guests to get cozy. The resort supplies firewood cut to size, newspapers, matches, and written instructions that explain how to light a Santa Fe fire." *laposada.rockresorts.com*

Singita Game Reserve, northeastern South Africa

"Offering the absolute best of everything—rooms, food, wine, guides, service, you name it—Singita is set on former farmland and features suites housed in two stone lodges, Boulders and Ebony, both of which retain an *Out of Africa* feel. Fireplaces add a dramatic touch to these rooms while you watch wildlife from your window." *singita.com*

Fairmont Chateau Whistler, Whistler, British Columbia, Canada

Nestled at the foot of Blackcomb Mountain, this hotel is spectacular, just like its in-room fireplaces. "A simple switch fireside will light your gas fireplace, no fuss, no muss. For additional warmth, borrow the mohair blanket off the bed and curl up in one of the oversized armchairs—fireside, of course." *fairmont.com/whistler*

Hotel Grande Bretagne, Athens, Greece
"In this landmark building, situated in the heart of Athens, the best suites are The Presidential and The Royal, both offering in-room fireplaces. The great thing about the fireplace in The Presidential suite is that it's two-sided, so you can enjoy it from the living room and the bedroom." *grandebretagne.gr*

The Little Nell, Aspen, Colorado
"The Little Nell blends the intimacy of a country inn with the personalized service and amenities of a grand hotel. This unique hotel literally hugs the base of the mountain, so no two rooms or views are alike. After a day of shopping, people-watching, or skiing, the gas-burning fireplace in each room adds the perfect touch to snowy evenings." *thelittlenell.com*

Budget Travel Tips from the **USA TODAY Archive**

TRANSPORTATION

Find a fare, then compare

If you're booking travel via the Internet, always comparison shop. In our view, there are no one-stop-shopping sites. Play the Web sites off against each other and against a travel agent. If you're given a fare or rate by an independent site, such as Expedia or Travelocity, see if it can be beat by checking with the branded Web site of that airline, hotel, or car-rental firm.

If you use a travel agent, don't assume that he or she automatically has your best interests in mind. Many travel agencies receive "override" bonus commissions to incentivize them to sell certain travel products over others. In the interest of full disclosure, ask about such deals.

—William J. McGee, travel consultant, *Consumer Reports*

ST. PATRICK'S DAY

10 great places for a wee bit of Irish cheer

Why celebrate St. Paddy's Day in Dublin when you can shake your shillelagh in Savannah or San Diego? "America celebrates it like no other country, even Ireland," says Guinness master brewer Fergal Murray. "It's fantastic! If you're Irish, your chest puffs out a bit, especially if you're representing Ireland's greatest export." When this Dubliner promotes Guinness stateside, he finds that cities parade their Irish heritage with Old World authenticity and local flavor. He highlights top parades.

Seattle, Washington
Civic-minded Seattle begins with a Catholic Mass for peace that includes a Methodist speaker and Lutheran organist, followed by the mayors of Galway and Northern Ireland's Lisburn marching together. The parade includes anyone who is bursting to express Irish pride, including a contingent of Irish wolfhounds. Bringing up the rear: the Shamrock Shuttle, for seniors and others who are unable to march the distance. *irishclub.org*

Denver, Colorado
"Denverites immerse themselves in the event with great enthusiasm. They create new traditions every year." *denverstpatricksdayparade.org*

New York, New York
"As the United States' largest, oldest, and most international parade, it's been going three years longer than we've been brewing." Irish military men held the first in 1762. Around two million spectators line Fifth Avenue to see more than 150,000 marchers. *nyc-st-patrick-day-parade.org*

Chicago, Illinois
The Chicago River dyed emerald green (a trade secret) is quite a spectacle, the Irish community is tremendously spirited, and the

Irish pubs are fantastic in their variety. "I always have a longer day in Chicago than anywhere else. With the celebrations happening citywide, everyone's out with their family and friends." Tip: Get into downtown early and take public transportation. *chicagostpatsparade.com*

Atlanta, Georgia

Gone with the Wind author Margaret Mitchell wrote of her Irish forebears, and one million Atlantans claim the lineage. Murray calls this effort "incredibly flamboyant, with the biggest floats and great dancers." And, oh, he loves the accents: "They go so well with an Irish brew." The parade culminates with free family entertainment at the Underground Atlanta Festival. *stpatsparadeatlanta.com*

Boston, Massachusetts

"Southie's" parade ranks as the second biggest. "The Irish bands are raring to go, the Irish roots really come out, and Boston is transformed." Expect a 600,000-plus turnout in South Boston for three hours of marchers, floats, and bands from throughout the country.

San Diego, California

Taking a cruise off the sunny coast in 1980, a few locals by the name of Foley, Shannon, and the like pledged to acknowledge their countrymen's local influence. Forming the Irish Congress of Southern California, they held the city's first St. Patrick's Day parade in 1981. "The climate's perfect for outdoor celebrations and walking in the parade." The marchers terminate at a festival on the green lawns of Balboa Park. *stpatsparade.org*

Savannah, Georgia

Savannah's parade is the Southeast's biggest single-day celebration. "The sheer size of the crowd is spectacle enough (about 400,000), and they dye city fountains green; people camp out just to have a nice viewing spot." *savannahsaintpatricksday.com*

Kansas City, Missouri

"A fine Irish town, with this parade being only one of its annual Irish celebrations." Presiding in the early days as grand marshal was Captain Jeremiah Dowd, a celebrated veteran of the Civil War and former police chief. Rich in tradition, this city's biggest single-day event stands out nationwide for its giant balloon floats. Don't be surprised to see aloft a giant leprechaun or St. Patrick. *kcirishparade.com*

Phoenix, Arizona
"Many people I've met here hail from Chicago, and they bring their enthusiasm for the event with them. Each year, it grows in size and splendor." *phxirish.org*

10 great places to turn green with Irish pride

The wearin' o' the green doesn't tell the half of it. In celebration of St. Patrick's Day, flutist Noel Rice, director of the Academy of Irish Music and president of the Irish American Heritage Center in Chicago, recommends places to appreciate the formative influences and contributions that Irish Americans have had on U.S. culture and history.

Henry Ford Museum & Greenfield Village, Dearborn, Michigan
"Henry Ford's accomplishments, which stand on their own, include this museum dedicated to American ideas and inventions that changed our world." Ford, the son of an Irish immigrant, is, of course, best known as a giant in the auto industry and creator of the assembly line used in mass production. Visitors to the museum can sit on the Rosa Parks bus or see the presidential limo in which John F. Kennedy was riding when he was assassinated. In addition to the vast automotive displays, there are exhibitions honoring other innovative geniuses—Thomas Edison's Menlo Park (New Jersey) laboratory, for example, and the Wright brothers' home and bicycle shop. *hfmgv.org*

Irish Fest Center, Milwaukee, Wisconsin
"The Ward Irish Music Archives, the largest collection of Irish recorded music in the United States, is here. You'll find sheet music and Irish instruments too." The center also sponsors a spirited four-day Irish cultural event in August, with everything from

Irish food to curragh races (a *curragh* is a canoelike vessel). Order a corned beef reuben roll and your day will be complete. *irishfest.com*

Old St. Patrick's Church, Chicago, Illinois

"The Chicago fire came within two blocks of this marvelous building but didn't touch it. People flock from distant suburbs to join the well-attended parish. The freshly renovated interiors have intricate Celtic knots and other design motifs on the ceiling, walls, and stained-glass windows." The church hosts a big summer bash, called Old St. Pat's World's Largest Block Party. *oldstpats.org*

Irish Hunger Memorial, New York, New York

This quarter-acre property in Battery Park City, complete with potato furrows and a two-room Irish stone cottage, memorializes the potato famine that began in 1845 in Ireland. A large family once lived in the cottage, which was brought here stone by stone from County Mayo. "Sited within view of the Statue of Liberty and Ellis Island, this poignant memorial represents the pestilence that reduced Ireland's population by half; 180,000 died directly and the rest just fled."
batteryparkcity.org

The Hermitage, Nashville, Tennessee

"President Andrew Jackson had a different beginning than other presidents. He was a penniless orphan with a Scotch-Irish heritage that gave him a strong air of independence. His self-reliance was perfect for the frontier life he embraced here." If Jackson walked into his onetime home on this 1,120-acre farm today,

The wearing of the green in... Butte, Montana?

Boston, Chicago, New York—these cities are all associated with immigrants from the Emerald Isle. But Butte, Montana? "This is one of the most Irish towns in America," says Ray O'Hanlon, author of *The New Irish Americans*. "The Irish moved West like everyone else. They were the second-largest European ethnic group in the United States, after the Germans." Butte's Gaelic heritage is tied to Irish-born Marcus Daly, who owned "the famous, or infamous, Anaconda Mining Co."

he would still recognize it, from his war memorabilia in the parlor to the many original furnishings. *thehermitage.com*

Margaret Mitchell House & Museum, Atlanta, Georgia

There's an emotional pull that draws people to the apartment where Mitchell wrote *Gone with the Wind*. Visitors can see the front door of Tara and walk through Mitchell's old neighborhood on Peachtree Street. "She named the plantation Tara after the seat of the high kings of ancient Ireland." Mitchell's ancestry was much like the fictional O'Hara's in *Gone with the Wind*: Her ancestors were Irish and Scotch-Irish, and the family had many soldiers who fought in wars, revolutions, and uprisings over the years. *margaretmitchellhouse.com*

Butte–Silver Bow Public Archives, Butte, Montana

"A large number of Irish came to Butte to work in the mines. Many of the copper kings were Irish, and the great buildings in the large historic district reflect their vision." An extensive collection of historic photos and documents can be viewed in the archives. The World Museum of Mining also covers the Irish connection. *buttearchives.org; mainstreetbutte.org*

John F. Kennedy Presidential Library & Museum, Boston, Massachusetts

"Kennedy's achievements were a source of Irish pride on both sides of the ocean. For years, even in Ireland, there were two photos you'd commonly see hanging on the walls in homes: the pope and JFK. This museum illustrates connections to his Irish roots." An example of what you'll find at the museum is the Fitzgerald family Bible. Used by JFK to take the presidential oath of office, it was brought from Ireland and has a handwritten chronicle of his 1917 birth. *jfklibrary.org*

Georgia O'Keeffe Museum, Santa Fe, New Mexico

"Georgia O'Keeffe's work embodies the open spaces, open attitude, open everything in America that is such a stark contrast to the closed society her forebears left behind." This pueblo-style, adobe museum, billed as the first in the United States dedicated to a single female artist, often displays work of other modernist painters as well. *okeeffemuseum.org*

White House Visitor Center, Washington, D.C.
"Leinster House in Dublin, the duke's residence (and currently home to the Irish parliament), was architect James Hoban's inspiration for the White House. You can compare the buildings at an exhibit in the visitor center celebrating Hoban and the building of the White House." The visitor center also displays china, furnishings, and decorative objects from the White House, making it an easy alternative to the limited, post-9/11 access to the presidential mansion. *whitehousehistory.org*

10 great places to raise a glass on St. Paddy's Day

Belly up. Whatever your choice of ale, Gregg Glaser, an editor with Modern Brewery Age, All About Beer, *and* Yankee Brew News, *shares his list of favorite places to pour a pint on this side of the Atlantic.*

Nine Fine Irishmen, Las Vegas, Nevada
Build a pub in Ireland, ship it to the United States, then plunk it down on the Vegas Strip—what a concept! But that's exactly the story of Nine Fine Irishmen, a pub in Sin City's New York-New York Hotel and Casino. "It even has the distinction of selling more Guinness than any other bar in the entire country (171,500 pints in 2008)." *ninefineirishmen.com*

McGuire's Irish Pub,
Pensacola, Florida
This pub is also the place for grub.
"Noted for cooking up some of the best Irish fare in the Southeast, McGuire's has been awarded *Florida Trend* magazine's Golden Spoon Award. Be sure to try the Irish boxties (garlic mashed potatoes rolled in herbed bread crumbs and flash fried) on the appetizer menu—they're as good as any you'll find in Dublin. And the drinks aren't bad either." *mcguiresirishpub.com*

Irish Snug, Denver, Colorado

This is one of the few pubs in the nation that has what's called a "snug" inside. "A snug is a small, private room with direct access to the bar. While you might not want to seclude yourself on St. Patrick's Day, this will give you a true Irish pub experience." *irishsnug.com*

Stats, Atlanta, Georgia

"Most people might not typically consider a sports bar an ideal place to raise a pint on St. Paddy's Day, but Stats in Atlanta is the exception. The best part is their unique setup whereby a table for bar patrons houses taps so that you can pour your own pint instead of waiting for your bartender to do it." St. Patrick's Day is a bit more subdued here. "Their festivities won't be centered on loud music and shot girls but rather communion with good friends and family." *statsatl.com/home.php*

Tom Bergin's Tavern, Los Angeles, California

This place is perhaps best known for its Irish coffee (coffee and Irish whiskey topped with whipped cream). But there's plenty more. "Upon entering, you are immediately drawn to the famous Horse Shoe Bar, which is said to have been the inspiration for the TV show *Cheers.* Another inspiration for the show, according to lore, was the pub's 'regulars' vibe, which is brought to life through the thousands upon thousands of cutout shamrocks, each bearing the names of happy bar patrons who have flocked to this famous pub over the years." *tombergins.com*

The Snug, Hingham, Massachusetts

This pub just outside Boston, arguably the greatest Irish American city, pays homage to the roadside pubs that are found throughout Ireland. "Located in a building that dates back to the 1820s, The Snug is a hidden gem that, unlike its counterparts, serves as a retreat from the hustle and bustle of the city. However, don't be fooled by its quiet demeanor. This pub offers its customers an extensive wine and beer list, starting, of course, with their 'perfect pint.'" *snugpub.com*

Pour the Perfect Pint, New York, New York
This is one of two pubs of the same name in Manhattan—the first is the popular watering hole at Times Square. This four-floor pub is a few blocks away at 203 East 45th Street. "What's different is the decor. You'll feel like you're actually enjoying a beer in Dublin, thanks to the Irish bric-a-brac, authentic gas lamps, and thatched walls on the rooftop deck." *theperfectpintnyc.com*

Celtic Crossings, Chicago, Illinois
"Irish pride is evident in every aspect of this authentic Irish haunt in the River North neighborhood. A strict no-television policy ensures that pints and conversation flow without interruption." Enjoy one of 13 beers on tap as you sit by the working stone fireplace. "If you're homesick or looking to re-create a past trip to Ireland, this is the place for you."

The Kerry Irish Pub, New Orleans, Louisiana
A little bit of the Emerald Isle right in the French Quarter—and with a little bit of something for everyone. "What started off as a venue for Irish and country music artists has since developed into a musical gumbo, if you will, that blends mixed sounds ranging from Irish, folk, blues, rock, and country, among many others." *kerryirishpub.com*

The Ugly Moose, Philadelphia, Pennsylvania
Sorry, no Irish roots here, but the *craic* can't be beat. "*Craic* is a Gaelic term to describe good fun, banter, and ambience, and The Ugly Moose always has it. From the friendly bar staff to the patrons that fill the bar area, it's never hard to strike up a conversation." The Moose, as it's known locally, also offers an array of authentic Irish fare on St. Patrick's Day. *theuglymoose.com*

10 great places to uncover the authentic Emerald Isle

To find the true essence of Ireland, we turned to Maeve Binchy, Ireland's best-selling international author. "Everyone you meet will have a different idea of the real Ireland," she says. And while she respects everyone else's choices, Binchy is quite firm about her own. Here, she shares her views on the topic.

Houseboating on the Shannon
"A great way to see the heart of Ireland is by renting a motor cruiser on the River Shannon. You cruise slowly past castles and little cottages and stop in small riverside towns to buy more [provisions] for the boat, or if you are lazy, to get out and have a wonderful lunch or dinner."

Sunset on Galway Bay
"Yes, some clichés really do work." Indeed, the nightly show on Ireland's west coast can be spectacular. And while you're in Galway, don't miss the "magical" Kenny's Bookshop and McDonagh's next door—"a great, noisy, happy fish restaurant."

Dingle Bay in County Kerry
The bay sports a resident dolphin named Fungi. "People claim he has calmed their souls as they go out in small craft to see him or even to swim with him."

Binchy's hometown of Dalkey
Just nine miles from Dublin, Dalkey "used to be a real sleepy hollow with one fish-and-chip shop, a little town where everything closed down for an hour and a half so that folk could go to their lunch, and lights were out by 10:00 P.M. every night. Not so these days. Its main street is full of gourmet restaurants and wonderful bars that serve lunches, like my own favorite, the Sorrento Lounge."

Youthful hangouts
"Ireland is a very young country…half the population is under the age of 25. So look around and see what these young people are up

to. There are galleries full of their paintings, stages for their plays, and a host of venues for their music and song."

A seaside rental cottage

"Rent a comfortable cottage with every convenience and live like the locals. There are some very sought-after places by the sea in places like Schull, one of the loveliest little towns in West Cork. Frequently, the local people say that visitors actually cry when they have to say good-bye at the end of [their visit]."

Hunter's Hotel in County Wicklow

Binchy's favorite hideaway hotel is in the small town of Rathnew, about an hour from Dublin. "They have a wonderful notice in the garden saying, 'Ladies and gentlemen will not, and others must not pick the flowers.' " *hunters.ie*

Burren area of County Clare

The roughly 100-square-mile area on Ireland's west coast sports a beautiful, lunarlike landscape teeming with life. "You will find birds and flowers that grow no other place on earth."

Irish festivals

From storytelling to match-making, Ireland's festivals are an entrée to its culture, history, and people. "It doesn't matter if you know nothing about oysters, jazz, or traditional Irish music. You'll learn."

Dublin's mass transit system

Take the DART (Dublin Area Rapid Transit), a train that travels along the coast north and south of Dublin. "That's where you will meet real people and get drawn into their lives."

Coping with jet lag

Melatonin can ease jet lag by accelerating the body clock's shift into a different time zone. But savvy travelers must plan in advance, says Dr. Al Lewy of Oregon Health & Science University, Portland.

- Traveling east: Take 0.5 milligram at 2:00 P.M. the day before you leave and the day of travel.
- Traveling west: Take 0.5 milligram upon awakening the day before travel and the day you go.

EASTER AND PASSOVER

10 great places to mark Christianity's holiest day

Celebrate the sacred Christian holiday of Easter with a journey to a religious site where faith and history come alive. Kevin J. Wright, president of the World Religious Travel Association and author of The Christian Travel Planner, *shares his recommendations.*

St. Peter's Basilica, Vatican City
"One of the most iconic and recognizable Christian destinations worldwide is the Vatican. Serving as the spiritual headquarters for more than one billion Catholics, Vatican City welcomes more than four million pilgrims and tourists annually. Visitors can explore St. Peter's Basilica, the Vatican Museums, Sistine Chapel, the catacombs, and even attend a General Audience with the pope." *vatican.va; www.stpetersbasilica.org*

Bethany Beyond the Jordan, Jordan
"More than one million people come here every year to see where Jesus was baptized by John the Baptist. Many get baptized themselves for the first time or simply wade in the same waters of the Jordan River as Jesus did 2,000 years ago. The Baptism Archaeological Park is also home to the area where the prophet Elijah ascended into heaven." *baptismsite.com*

St. Katherine Monastery, Mount Sinai, Egypt
"The Old Testament comes alive in the southern Sinai Peninsula of Egypt. It is here on Mount Sinai where God appeared in a burning bush to Moses and delivered the Ten Commandments. Today, pilgrims can hike to the top of the summit (and witness the spectacular sunrise), explore St. Katherine Monastery at the mountain base, and visit the Chapel of the Burning Bush, built upon the site believed to be where God appeared to Moses." *st-katherine.net*

Great Theater, Ephesus, Turkey

One of the most popular Christian trips is following in the footsteps of the Apostle Paul through Greece and Turkey. "In Ephesus, one of the Seven Churches of Revelation in Scripture, pilgrims can stand in the very theater where the apostle delivered sermons to the local population. In addition, visitors can explore the House of the Virgin, the home where Mary, the mother of Jesus, is said to have spent her last days."
sacred-destinations.com/turkey/ephesus-theater.htm

Church of the Holy Sepulchre, Jerusalem, Israel

According to many Christian traditions, the Church of the Holy Sepulcher was the site of Jesus' crucifixion and the empty tomb. But there's far more for the Christian traveler to see in this holiest of cities. "The Mount of Olives, Garden of Gethsemane, Via Dolorosa, Western Wall, and Garden Tomb are among the other places here most often visited by the faithful." *holysepulchre.com*

Cave of the Apocalypse, Patmos Island, Greece

" 'Dear visitor, the place you have just entered is sacred.' These are the words that greet visitors at the entrance of the Cave of the Apocalypse. According to tradition, John the Evangelist wrote the Book of Revelation inside this grotto at the end of the first century. Today, the cave itself and the famed St. John the Divine monastery that lies atop the island are recognized as World Heritage Sites."
sacred-destinations.com/Greece/patmos-cave-of-apocalypse.htm

Grotto of Massabielle, Lourdes, France

"More than six million people from around the globe travel each year to the renowned pilgrimage destination of Lourdes. It is here where in 1858 the Virgin Mary appeared to St. Bernadette Soubirous on 18 occasions. Today, Lourdes is best known for its reported miracles and healing waters. Pilgrims can explore the grotto where Mary appeared, the two basilicas, Bernadette's home, and join the evening Rosary Procession." *lourdes-france.org*

All Saints Castle Church, Wittenberg, Germany

"Wittenberg is home to one of the best-known figures in Christianity—Martin Luther. It is here that the Reformer posted his 95 Theses on the door of All Saints Castle Church and forever changed Christian history. Travelers can visit the largest Reformation museum in the world, Luther's home; see the Reformer's tomb; and, of course, view the famous door." *wittenberg.de*

Basilica of Our Lady of Guadalupe, Mexico City, Mexico
"The Virgin Mary is said to have appeared here in 1531 to St. Juan Diego and left an imprint of her image on his cloak. Visitors can still view the portrait to this day, which is on display next door at the new, larger basilica that opened in 1976." *sancta.org/basilica.html*

Cathedral of Santiago de Compostela, Santiago de Compostela, Galicia, Spain
During the height of the Middle Ages, the Cathedral of Santiago de Compostela (aka the Cathedral of St. James) was a top pilgrimage destination, ranking with Jerusalem and Rome. The shrine is still a major attraction (it contains the remains of St. James the Apostle) but so too is the arduous path in northern Spain that pilgrims travel along to get there. "Known as the Way of St. James, the route attracts tens of thousands of people who spend days or weeks walking, biking, and even horseback riding to Santiago de Compostela—some for religious purposes, others for leisure, and many for both." *catedraldesantiago.es*

Air travel and hub cities

If your trip includes a stop at a hub city:

- Find out if you have to change planes and how long it takes to get from arrival gate to connecting flight. Do you need to change concourses or terminals?

- Choose a flight that gives you enough time to make a connection, even with a delay of 15 minutes.

- Try to avoid a busy hub like Chicago or Atlanta at 8:00 A.M. or 5:00 P.M. weekdays—among the busiest hours.

10 great places to experience Jewish culture

Jewish holidays, including Passover, are filled with reflection and meaning. "There is a little-known world of Jewish museums—more than 80 in the United States and a growing number in Europe, South America, Australia, and New Zealand"— offering insights into the history and rituals of the religion, says Joan Rosenbaum, director of The Jewish Museum in New York City. Here, she offers a list of notable Jewish museums.

The Israel Museum, Jerusalem, Jerusalem, Israel
Featuring "the world's foremost collection of archaeology of the Holy Land, the world's most comprehensive collection of Judaica, and the ethnology of the Jewish people around the world, this museum also features fine arts holdings." *www.imj.org.il*

The Jewish Museum, New York, New York
This institution "explores the intersection of 4,000 years of art and Jewish culture. At the heart of Museum Mile (the city also boasts Yeshiva University Museum and the Museum of Jewish Heritage: A Living Memorial to the Holocaust), this museum offers exhibitions and educational programs that inspire people of all backgrounds." *thejewishmuseum.org*

The Jewish Museum of Maryland, Baltimore, Maryland
The United States' "leading museum of regional Jewish history, culture, and community pays special attention to Jewish life in Maryland. It now includes two historic synagogues and a modern building housing changing exhibitions, collections, and education programs." *jhsm.org*

Jewish Historical Museum, Amsterdam, the Netherlands
"Housed in a complex of four historic synagogues," the museum has more than 13,000 pieces in its collection, which focuses on illustrating Jewish life in general as well as Dutch Jewish life in particular. *jhm.nl*

Jewish Museum Vienna, Vienna, Austria
Located "in a historic mansion, this museum boasts a permanent

exhibition on Austrian Jewish history and on the Jewish religion in addition to many temporary shows on Jewish culture and art." *jmw.at*

Musée d'art et d'histoire du Judaïsme, Paris, France
"Displays are based on key events from the settlement of Jewish communities in France and Europe to the expulsion of the Jews from Spain, from the political emancipation of the Jews under the French Revolution until World War II." *mahj.org*

Jewish Museum Berlin, Berlin, Germany
This "lively center for history and culture" presents two millennia of German Jewish history in a "spectacular building designed by Daniel Libeskind." *jmberlin.de*

The Jewish Museum of Australia, St. Kilda, Victoria, Australia
"As an innovative cultural center and community museum, this museum—recognized for its excellence in exhibitions and educational programs—explores the Jewish experience in Australia." *www.jewishmuseum.com.au*

Jewish Museum in Prague, Prague, Czech Republic
Founded in 1906, it offers tours and exhibitions featuring a "rich variety of ritual objects and textiles. Its renowned Judaica collection includes objects acquired from the Bohemian and Moravian Jewish communities" and synagogues liquidated by the Nazis. *jewishmuseum.cz*

Skirball Cultural Center, Los Angeles, California
"Exploring connections between 4,000 years of Jewish heritage and the vitality of American democratic ideals, the Skirball features a museum offering changing exhibitions" plus performing arts, film, family, and literary programs, "all in a stunning setting designed by Moshe Safdie." *skirball.org*

Talk to the Expert

TAKE THE ROAD CHEAPLY TRAVELED

Sandra Gustafson spends months at a time on the road searching out contenders for her *Cheap Eats/Sleeps* series. Here, she offers strategies for finding hotels and restaurants that are good and cheap.

Q: You personally visit all the hotels recommended in your books, but do you actually stay in them?

A: No. I tried that and all I was doing was moving from one hotel to another. I've gotten so I can size up hotels really fast.

Q: What are some of the indicators of a good hotel?

A: I size up the general look of the place. Does it need a paint job? Are the plants alive or dead? And then when I get inside, I glance around the lobby. Are the chairs sagging? Who's behind the desk? Are they watching TV and smoking and minding their business so they can't take care of mine? Then I ask to see rooms in all categories.

Q: Cheap is a subjective word. How do you define it?

A: There's no dollar limit on it. Travelers should ask themselves what is their bottom line of acceptance. It has to be a place where you feel comfortable and safe and not out of sorts.

Q: How do you select restaurants?

A: I try to stay away from the tourist places. I look around. Who's eating there? If it's full of locals, I'm onto something. If you read about it in a guide, you're 20 years too late.

Q: Do you have tips for the thrifty that transcend locales?

A: In restaurants, always order the prix fixe, or set, menu. You get three courses, and it can include bread, wine, tax, and service. I also recommend eating your main meal at noon because that food will cost you up to half what it will in the evening.

Q: Any other suggestions for getting a decent low-cost meal?

A: Stay within the limits of the kitchen. If you're in a fish-and-chip place, don't order a hamburger. Also, standing at the bar is always cheaper than sitting at a table and much cheaper than the terrace.

10 great places to top things off

"In your Easter bonnet, with all the frills upon it, you'll be the grandest lady in the Easter parade." So wrote Irving Berlin at a time when Easter hats were as de rigueur as today's denim. Other than church ladies, Ascot's horsey set, and the occasional iconoclast, "no one wears hats anymore," laments fashion designer Oleg Cassini, creator of Jacqueline Kennedy's famous pillbox. "Yesterday is yesterday," says Cassini, who claims a contemporary, pragmatic approach by offering clients jeweled baseball caps and handmade tiaras. Not quite Eastery enough? Here, he shares some heady hot spots for those in a millinery mood.

Lord & Taylor, Chicago, Illinois
With its stylish populace and cold lake winds, Chicago has always been a big hat city. Lord & Taylor, known for its sophisticated accessories, is located in the Windy City's tony Water Tower Place. "Look for pretty, springy, pastel straws." *lordandtaylor.com*

Bloomingdale's, New York, New York
Bloomies' spring hats range from fun and practical to stylish straws and felts to designer whimsy featuring fabric flowers and a few veils. *bloomingdales.com*

Rustans, Manila, the Philippines
"The No. 1 department store in the Philippines, known for luxury brands and a rich-and-famous clientele, boasts an extensive warm-weather collection of straws in addition to fabric and organza hats."

David's Bridal, various locations
Wear a tiara, be a queen. For special-occasion tiaras and evening hats, "David's features little wisps of fabric and veil or glittering creations" of crystals, pearls, and diamantés. *davidsbridal.com*

Sheplers, Wichita, Kansas
Cowgirls like to get gussied up too. Since its start in 1946, this all-things-Western conglomerate "offers a unique twist on Western hats—everything from simple pinch-front straw styles to traditional Stetsons, made fancy for her with rhinestones, red roses, and for Easter a pale pink felt with a feather-boa band." *sheplers.com*

Borsalino, Milan, Italy
"Known for luxury and high-quality made-to-order craftsmanship," Borsalino has a simple philosophy of "the art of hat: [The hat] has a very strong use and a clear, fashionable connotation." Choose from wool caps, classic fedoras, or straw Panamas for men and women and a charming line for children. Couture models are entirely handmade. *borsalino.com*

De Bijenkorf, Amsterdam, the Netherlands
A luxurious landmark destination and one of the Netherlands' leading stores for international fashionistas, De Bijenkorf is Amsterdam's answer to Bloomingdale's, "offering a wonderful array of pretty, classic hats and kicky, contemporary caps," all infused with a restrained touch of Dutch practicality. *debijenkorf.nl*

Galeries Lafayette, Paris, France
"Shopping is a French treat under this renowned department store's historic glass dome." With an entire department devoted to chic chapeaus, you'll be in Parisian hat heaven as you try on creations—styles range from sleek to fanciful—from Paris's premier designers such as Chanel, Dior, and Lacroix. *galerieslafayette.com*

Harrods, London, England
"London's well-known bastion of shopping boasts enough hats to satisfy the most discerning shopper of chapeaus, a tradition in the U.K." Browsers will find the classics plus a number of fanciful Easter confections. Before she was a princess, Lady Diana picked out a few hats and plunked down a few pounds here. *harrods.com*

El Palacio de Hierro, Mexico City, Mexico
"The Paris of North America is a dress-up city in a formal culture where hats are embraced and encouraged. Here, at Mexico's deluxe upscale department store, find a colorful-to-classic abundance of straws, fedoras, and caps." *elpalaciodehierro.com.mx/ph/*

10 great places for a leisurely holiday brunch

Holiday family meals are increasingly being eaten out, and brunch is "the one meal...without structure or time," says Ben Watson, author of Slow Food *and editor of the* Slow Food *city guides. The Slow Food movement's rationale, he says, is well suited to holidays such as Easter and Passover, with their traditional dishes like the paschal lamb. He suggests these places for a holiday brunch.*

Inn at Baldwin Creek, Bristol, Vermont
Nestled in a beautiful small town in the Green Mountains, the inn offers both Easter brunch and Easter dinner. Among the brunch offerings are planked salmon and stuffed French toast; the four-course prix fixe dinner features rack of lamb. "The owners, Linda Harmon and Doug Mack, have been committed to using local, seasonal ingredients in their cooking since before it was cool." *innatbaldwincreek.com*

North Pond, Chicago, Illinois
Brunch on the enclosed patio, whose nine-foot French windows offer grand vistas of the city's famed skyline and Lincoln Park. Its three-course Easter brunch features entrées from strawberry crepes with fromage blanc filling and pistachio gratinée to sautéed Dover sole with leek and Meyer lemon cream, crab tortellini, and beet puree. The circa 1912 building—originally a skaters' warming hut—edges the park's lagoon. *northpondrestaurant.com*

The Hungry Cat, Los Angeles, California
Terrific Bloody Marys are served here (including one with house-pickled veggies), along with Bellinis made with blood-orange juice. A "small, sleek, contemporary restaurant and bar," the Hungry Cat offers a Sunday brunch featuring raw-bar offerings and American sturgeon caviar, as well as egg dishes and desserts like vanilla beignets with a compote of local blackberries. *thehungrycat.com*

A 16, San Francisco, California
Named for the Italian highway that runs from Naples to Bari, A 16 specializes in dishes from Italy's Campania region. For the

Marina District restaurant's Easter brunch, Neapolitan pizza is typically on the menu, as is a mixed grill of Napa Valley–raised lamb. Traditional Easter dishes get the Southern Italian treatment: asparagus and spring onion sformato with prosciutto, for example. *a16sf.com*

Savoy, New York, New York
This SoHo standout offers a three-course Easter meal in the afternoon. The menu includes other spring favorites, such as soup with wild leeks (ramps), fava beans, and mint, and braised dandelion greens with new potatoes. Followed, of course, by holiday sweets, including the traditional Russian dish of sweetened fresh cheese with a delicate sauce. *savoynyc.com*

The Farm at South Mountain, Phoenix, Arizona
"Much of the produce served here comes from Maya's at the Farm, an onsite organic garden." Menu items include petite greens in a salad of baby Chioggia beets and heirloom tomatoes with bocconcini, marinated mozzarella, and basil. Those dishes join eggs with applewood-smoked bacon and turkey sausage, free-range chicken saltimbocca, and a garden frittata on the Easter brunch menu. *thefarmatsouthmountain.com*

Hominy Grill, Charleston, South Carolina
This down-home local institution offers classic Southern cooking seven days a week. The weekend brunch includes such "unpretentious and wonderful food" as a Low Country omelet with red rice and shrimp gravy, a fried-green-tomato BLT sandwich, and numerous specials featuring Low Country delicacies. "Everything is prepared from scratch," including the grits from a foodie favorite, Anson Mills. *hominygrill.com*

The Savvy Gourmet, New Orleans, Louisiana
Founded as a cooking school and gourmet retail store, Savvy opened its Magazine Street location just ten days before Hurricane Katrina. "After the storm, they realized that the first returning inhabitants needed a place to gather and eat, so they opened the restaurant." The brunch menu features dishes like Creole shrimp and creamy grits with fried eggs and cinnamon French toast with

roasted pears, pecans, and honey butter. The restaurant chef gets "nearly all his ingredients through the Crescent City Farmers' Market." *savvygourmet.com*

Devotay, Iowa City, Iowa
The special Easter brunch buffet offers plenty of pork, "this being Iowa," but there's plenty more, featuring many items from the regular menu at this locals' favorite. Among the spring highlights: a hot tapas plate of grilled fresh local asparagus with aioli; a cold tapas dish of applewood-smoked trout mousse made with trout from Rushing Waters, an organic fish farm in Wisconsin; and local, free-range organic chicken—and their eggs. *devotay.net*

Hattie's Hat, Seattle, Washington
Recently renovated, Hattie's Hat still honors its self-proclaimed "unique, 'dive' ambience." Although it's far from a fine-dining establishment, its classic diner food is "too good to leave out" of this list. Located in the heart of trendy Ballard, the city's Scandinavian neighborhood, Hattie's Hat makes its weekend brunch an all-day affair. The house-smoked-salmon chowder is made "right out back." *hattieshat.com*

10 great places to hit your sweet spot for Easter

Need help filling your Easter basket? Dylan Lauren, founder of the popular Dylan's Candy Bar, a whimsical candy emporium, is a self-described Easter enthusiast and candy addict. She lists her favorite places to shop for sweets.

Cottage of Sweets, Carmel, California
"This unique shop has a homey feel and is one of the town's most charming landmarks. It has a nice assortment of prepackaged and bulk candy." Licorice lovers will be in heaven to discover the many varieties, from sweet to salty, available here. There's also a great assortment of hard-to-get European candies and nostalgia mixes. *cottageofsweets.com*

Candylicious, Houston, Texas

"This bite-size-candy store has fun, retro candy. They also have 'candy cakes' made on site," custom creations that are made with foam core and studded with candy. The Easter Hut, a springtime version of these popular items, is as alluring as a Christmas gingerbread house and can be used as a centerpiece or in lieu of an Easter basket.

The Candy Lady, Albuquerque, New Mexico

"People often call me the candy lady. But in Albuquerque's historic Old Town, Debbie Ball is second-generation. She brings true Southwestern flavor, including red chili, to fudge and other sweets at this cozy shop created by her mother." She also uses piñons, the delicately sweet cone seeds from piñon pines, the state tree, to make nut clusters, toffee, caramels, brittle, and fudge. No hollow Easter bunnies here, only solid chocolate. *thecandylady.com*

Sugar Heaven, Boston, Massachusetts

"Their motto is 'We have something for everyone,' and it's definitely true. This store has a very cool collection of vintage tins and lunchboxes for the bulk and novelty candy. They let you mix and match items, which is perfect for a personal touch on an Easter basket." Boston Baked Beans, candied fruit slices, and Atomic Fireballs are among 15,000 items to choose from. *sugarheaven.us*

E.A.T. Gifts, New York, New York

"I am a rabid rabbit collector, and this store offers rabbit-themed plates, plush toys, stationery, even piñatas." It also carries rabbit-topped PEZ candy dispensers; plastic wind-up chickens that lay small candy eggs; chocolate-covered sunflower seeds in rabbit-themed containers; and Bunny Bait, a carrot-shaped container filled with orange jelly beans.

Savannah Sweets, Savannah, Georgia

"They have fresh taffy, fudge, and candy apples that are accessorized with sprinkles in springtime colors and shapes at this old-school candy shop." It also has Bunny rice crispy treats, as well as pralines, glazed pecans, homemade caramels, peanut clusters, sugar-and-spice pecans, praline pecans, peanut brittle, cashew brittle, divinity candy, and other Southern classics. Solid chocolate bunnies are hand-molded for Easter. *savannahsweets.com*

Rocky Mountain Chocolate Factory, Aspen, Colorado
"The chocolate-covered marshmallows here are my favorites," Lauren says of this store, one of more than 300 franchises in the United States, Canada, and United Arab Emirates. "The fresh-dipped strawberries and other items can be packaged into a beautiful box for delicious gifts." *rockymountainchocolatefactory.com*

Big Top, Austin, Texas
"This is a combination candy store and old-fashioned soda fountain where they still make classics like floats and malteds. It's a cute and quirky place, just like the city." The store has a wall of nostalgia candy, including rarities such as Valomilks and Black Jack gum. *myspace.com/bigtopcandyshop*

M&M's World, Las Vegas, Nevada
"The Colorworks section of this store offers an M&M's lover customizable packages in over 20 colors in any of the milk, peanut, and dark varieties." For future holidays and special occasions, you can personalize M&M's with photos and messages for a one-of-a-kind gift. *mymms.com*

Yippy I-O Candy Co., Jackson Hole, Wyoming
"The utterly Western vibe in this barrel-stocked store is not your typical Easter candy haunt, but you can find malted Easter eggs and bunny candy corn in pastel colors to create your own springtime assortment. They have tons of bulk candy. I love the vintage tin signs for my antique candy collection." The store also has sour bunnies, gummy bunnies, and Easter gift tins.

FOURTH OF JULY

10 great places to fly your patriotic colors on July 4th

There's nothing like a good old-fashioned Fourth of July parade to bring out the red, white, and blue in all of us. Steve Schmader, president and CEO of the International Festivals & Events Association, shares his favorite parade venues.

America's Independence Day Parade, Washington, D.C.

"For sheer scale and ambience, the annual parade in our nation's capital can't be beat. Marching bands, floats, giant balloons, military and equestrian units, and celebrity guests join the procession down Constitution Avenue past all of the storied national monuments."
july4thparade.com

Racine Fourth Fest Parade, Racine, Wisconsin

Located on the shores of Lake Michigan between Milwaukee and Chicago, Racine hosts one of the largest Fourth of July parades in the Midwest. "This parade began as a collaborative effort between corporations and labor unions to set aside 'one day of peace' between workers and management. With nearly 200 units— equestrian entries, clowns, jugglers, floats, bands, fire trucks, antique cars, dignitaries, and more—Racine's parade has grown to become a huge community- and family-oriented celebration."
racine.wi.net/4th.html

Southwest Airlines July 4th Parade, Philadelphia, Pennsylvania

"When it comes to celebrating patriotism, it's pretty hard to beat Philadelphia. This red, white, and blue procession of bands, floats, and balloons also features a variety of groups that reflect the cultural mosaic of our country." The parade makes its way down Benjamin Franklin Parkway and ends at the steps of the Philadelphia Museum of Art, immortalized in the movie *Rocky*.
americasbirthday.com

Gatlinburg Midnight Independence Day Parade, Gatlinburg, Tennessee

"For those who want to be among the first to celebrate Independence Day, Gatlinburg's parade provides that opportunity each year. Conceived in 1976 to commemorate America's bicentennial, the parade always begins at the stroke of midnight on the Fourth. Every unit is brightly lit, creating a spectacular procession through town." *gatlinburg.com*

Old Glory Boat Parade, Newport Harbor, Balboa Island, California

If your idea of a perfect Fourth of July involves boats and the water, this Southern California event may be the one for you. Begun in the 1950s, Balboa's festive parade on water includes some 100 entries, from tall clipper ships to yachts, sailboats, and dinghies. "Each craft is decorated in a patriotic theme—and participants try to outdo each other using combinations of music, costumes, live entertainment, and loads of patriotic spirit." *balboa-island.net/e4bp.htm*

Bristol Fourth of July Parade, Bristol, Rhode Island

Bristol's annual Fourth of July celebration is billed as the longest uninterrupted string of Independence Day parades in the nation. "Established in 1785, the Bristol parade has gone on through wars, the Great Depression, bad weather, and a host of other historical challenges. The event draws more than 100,000 attendees each year. Fireworks, a drum-and-bugle corps competition, and other activities are also part of the celebration." *july4thbristolri.com*

Greeley Stampede/9News Independence Day Parade, Greeley, Colorado

"For those looking to add a little Western flavor to their Fourth of July celebration, this annual parade in Greeley will likely fit the bill." Part of what's hailed as "The World's Largest Fourth of July Rodeo and Western Celebration," the parade starts with more than 100 head of

longhorn steers and a U.S. Air Force flyover. Greeley's procession also features bands, floats, and rodeo clowns. *greeleystampede.org*

"We the People" Fourth of July Parade, Belton, Texas
Located about 40 miles north of Austin, the town of Belton is known throughout Texas for its Fourth of July parade, which draws participants and spectators from across the state. Featuring floats, bands, decorated bicycles, classic cars, and rodeo riders, the procession—which dates from the mid-1800s—has been an annual event since 1919. "Belton's parade is a true celebration of patriotism and the family, with a Texas flavor. The parade's theme, 'Mom, Dad, and Apple Pie,' says it all." *rodeobelton.com/parade.htm*

Veiled Prophet Parade, St. Louis, Missouri
The Veiled Prophet Parade (inspired by the book *Lalla Rookh* by Irish poet Thomas Moore) has been a tradition since 1877. "Organized and supported by local civic leaders, this parade is a major annual event in St. Louis. Highlights include elaborate floats, giant balloons, marching bands, military units, and local sports celebrities. There's also plenty of live entertainment." *vpparade.org*

Pittsfield Fourth of July Parade, Pittsfield, Massachusetts
"Once billed as 'Your Hometown America Parade,' the Pittsfield Fourth of July Parade dates back to 1824, when the procession consisted of Revolutionary War veterans and politicians riding in horse-drawn carriages. Today's modern parade has floats, balloons, and marching bands but still retains the small-town, patriotic flavor of its roots." *pittsfieldparade.com*

Hazards cloud Independence Day

In 2008 an estimated 4,200 people were hurt in accidents with charcoal or gas grills, according to the Consumer Product Safety Commission. Fireworks killed 7 people and injured 7,000 that same year, the commission says. More than 4,700 boating accidents caused 709 deaths and injured nearly 3,300 in 2008, according to statistics from the Coast Guard. Both agencies say more such accidents and injuries occur over the July 4th weekend than any other.

10 great places to be
red, white, and true blue

Patriotism—that indefinable blend of pride, love of country, reverence, a sense of being connected, and an awareness of duty and responsibility. Patriotism, in one of its purest forms, can be evoked by a historic or symbolic place. "You go there," says William Bennett, former secretary of education under Ronald Reagan, "and you say, 'Once upon a time.' All of these places have a once-upon-a-time quality." The editor of such books as Our Sacred Honor, The Children's Book of America, *and* The Children's Book of Heroes, *Bennett offers symbolic places to feel patriotic.*

Marine Corps War Memorial, Washington, D.C.
The 32-foot statue of five Marines and a Navy corpsman raising the American flag atop Mount Suribachi during the battle for Iwo Jima is based on the famous 1945 photograph. "It's an incredible place, filled with memories and significance."

Pikes Peak, Colorado
With its commanding location in the Rocky Mountains' Front Range, 14,110-foot Pikes Peak offers a view that is said to be the inspiration for Katharine Lee Bates when she wrote "America the Beautiful" in 1893. "Part of our patriotism is a belief that we are specially blessed with the beauty of this country."

Independence Hall, Philadelphia, Pennsylvania
In the Assembly Room here, the Declaration of Independence was issued, our flag's design approved, and the Constitution drafted. "(Alexis) De Tocqueville said the American Revolution was established by thought and reflection, not by force. And this is where it happened."

Statue of Liberty, New York, New York
A gift from France to the United States and dedicated in 1886, the 152-foot figure that stands upon the 150-foot pedestal on Liberty Island is sheathed in copper. On the tablet, in Roman numerals, is the date: July 4, 1776. "It's a recognition by others of what America stands for."

The Alamo, San Antonio, Texas
The Texans preserve it as sacred ground: the stone mission where James Bowie, Davy Crockett, William Travis, and perhaps 180 others fought to the death against the Mexican army of General Antonio Lopez de Santa Anna on March 6, 1836. "American courage." An estimated 2.5 million visit every year.

North Bridge, Minute Man National Historical Park, Concord, Massachusetts
It was "the shot heard 'round the world." The first skirmish between rebellious Americans and British regulars was from opposite sides of this bridge, today an authentic reproduction of the original. The date was April 19, 1775, "and this was the beginning of our liberty." The site is part of a 900-acre park.

Lincoln Memorial, Washington, D.C.
Anchoring the west end of the National Mall, the templelike memorial, dedicated in 1922, faces the Washington Monument and, beyond that, the Capitol. Inside, to the right and left of the seated figure of Abraham Lincoln, are the words of his Gettysburg and Second Inaugural addresses. "I go there three or four times a week. It's a holy place of liberty and equality."

Mount Rushmore, Keystone, South Dakota
The 60-foot carved busts of presidents George Washington, Thomas Jefferson, Theodore Roosevelt, and Abraham Lincoln represent 150 years of American history and took well over a decade for artist/sculptor Gutzon Borglum to cut into the granite of South Dakota's Black Hills. "When I saw it, it just captured my heart."

U.S. Military Academy, West Point, New York
General George Washington established his headquarters here in 1779, and President Thomas Jefferson signed the law in 1802 that established it as an academy. "It's the oldest continuously occupied military post in America. Duty, honor, country. It stands for readiness."

Antietam National Battlefield, Sharpsburg, Maryland
Before 9/11, the Civil War battle fought here on September 17, 1862, was the bloodiest single day of violence in American history. Fought to a savage standstill before Robert E. Lee withdrew, it left 3,650 dead and more than 17,000 wounded. President Abraham Lincoln used it as a chance to issue the Emancipation Proclamation. "It concentrates the mind, as Lincoln said, thinking about the amount of death that went on in such a short period of time there."

AND ANOTHER THING...

PLACES TO GO "FOURTH" IN OUR NATION'S CAPITAL

What could be more patriotic than spending the Fourth of July in the nation's capital? Former mayor Anthony Williams shares some favorite spots, many of which are beyond the well-trod tourist path.

- Frederick Douglass Home—"After the Civil War, [Douglass] moved to Washington, where he purchased, in 1877, Cedar Hill in Southeast D.C., now a National Historic Site."

- Ben's Chili Bowl—"You don't find restaurants like this just anywhere in the United States—people from all walks of life sit shoulder-to-shoulder, enjoying the world's greatest hot dogs, burgers, and chili."

- U.S. National Arboretum—"Each visit to the Arboretum is unique. There is never a moment to rest while exploring the miles of nature's beauty."

- Chesapeake & Ohio Canal—"Once used as a major East Coast transportation route, the 183-mile C & O Canal (running through Georgetown) features historical locks, boathouses, and aqueducts."

- Meridian Hill Park—"A 12-acre park in the middle of the city, the grounds were first built to surround a mansion used by John Quincy Adams after he left the White House in 1829. In the early 1900s, the park was remodeled into spectacular public gardens with inspirational sculptures throughout."

10 great places to honor the home of the brave

Whether you hail from a small town or a metropolis, the Fourth of July always includes fireworks. But where are the best places to watch? Julie Heckman, executive director of the American Pyrotechnics Association, shares her patriotic picks.

Washington Monument grounds and the West Lawn of U.S. Capitol, Washington, D.C.
This event, with its picturesque backdrop of the U.S. Capitol and Washington Monument, presents "a vivid tribute to our great nation."

Macy's display, New York, New York
Ellis Island, the Statue of Liberty, and Manhattan's skyline contribute to this "dazzling pyro-musical production, featuring more than 28,000 aerial shells from around the world, fired digitally from five locations on the East River between 21st and 42nd streets." Fireworks fans experience the Patriotic Mile (columns of blue arch below red and white bursts cascading from above) and the famous Golden Mile, a shimmering golden wall from high in the sky to the water's edge.

Penn's Landing, Philadelphia, Pennsylvania
The town is painted in American flag colors as the nation's birthplace hosts the annual Sunoco Welcome America Festival. "The fireworks extravaganza [is] discharged from three barges along the Delaware River and [includes] a variety of specialty nautical shells, parachutes, aerial wheels, and aerial bursts."

Fisherman's Wharf, San Francisco, California
This sky concert is "the largest show in California, with over 10,000 shells, Roman candles, and special effects" discharged from two locations near Aquatic Park and Pier 39 in the Fisherman's Wharf area.

Freedom Fair, Ruston Way Waterfront, Tacoma, Washington
"Tacoma hosts one of the largest displays of patriotism during the

Freedom Fair. The picturesque mountains surrounding Puget Sound Bay [provide] a breathtaking view of the fireworks extravaganza. Kudos to the longshore union folks who help set up this amazing display."

Grant Park, Chicago, Illinois
"The city skyline provides a perfect backdrop for the volume of fireworks discharged in this premier waterfront event. This display is beautifully choreographed and [is] fired from barges on Lake Michigan."

Addison Airport strip, Addison, Texas
This small town (4.3 square miles) on the northern edge of Dallas offers a unique sky show visible for miles. "The 30-minute ground-launched fireworks, silver flashes, and glittering mums dance to simulcast music. For a tiny town, this is one big, beautiful fireworks display."

Waterfront, near Cape Fear, Southport, North Carolina
"As part of the North Carolina Fourth of July Festival, the fireworks spectacular [marries] the best of the reds, whites, and blues for an overwhelming tribute to the spirit of America."

Taste of Minnesota Festival, Harriet Island, St. Paul, Minnesota
The largest fireworks event in Minnesota on July 4th features a spectacular sky show along the Mississippi River. The St. Paul skyline in the background adds to the breathtaking view.

Arroyo de Deportes Park, Rio Rancho, New Mexico
Rio Rancho, a suburb of Albuquerque, hosts "the state's largest July 4th fireworks show. The display features unique red, white, and blue comets in layers of gold-to-red, gold-to-silver, and gold-to-blue plume patterns. A truly magical display not to miss."

One flag, one land, one heart, one hand,
One Nation, evermore!
—Oliver Wendell Holmes Sr.

HALLOWEEN

10 great places to get spooked by your surroundings

A resident ghost or two can be good for business, particularly during Halloween. Dennis William Hauck, author of Haunted Places: The National Directory, *says that to rate inclusion in his guide to 2,000 paranormal hot spots, the locale must have been investigated by a "reputable" organization. Still, while the author says he has experienced "ghostly manifestations" (cold spots, poltergeist effects, and the like), he has yet to see an actual apparition. Undeterred, here are Hauck's directions to some notable haunts.*

Shirley Plantation, Charles City, Virginia
The 18th-century plantation house is just one of a number of "well-documented" ghostly haunts in this James River city. Of note: a first-floor bedroom where a painting of early resident Martha Pratt reportedly raises a ruckus whenever it's moved from a spot facing the ancestral graveyard. "Whenever it was removed, the frame would shake and make popping sounds." *shirleyplantation.com*

Fort Warren, Boston, Massachusetts
The Civil War fort on George's Island in Boston Harbor reputedly is haunted by "The Lady in Black," a devoted wife who was hanged for attempting to break her husband out of the Confederate prison. Sightings have been numerous over the years, particularly when it's foggy. "There's a lot of atmosphere. It's a spooky site." *bostonislands.com*

White House, Washington, D.C.
The Executive Mansion is "one of the most haunted places in the United States." Ronald Reagan and Eleanor Roosevelt, among

others, have reported ghostly sightings. Among the apparitions: William Henry Harrison in the attic, Dolley Madison in the Rose Garden, and most frequently Abraham Lincoln in his namesake bedroom. "You can hardly name a president all the way back to Coolidge who hasn't felt [Lincoln's] presence."
whitehouse.gov/history/tours

Whaley House, San Diego, California
Even before Thomas Whaley completed his house in 1857, the execution by hanging of "Yankee" Jim Robinson on the site presumably primed future ghostly scenarios. Not only are Robinson's footfalls believed to be heard in the house, but a number of other ghosts are said to occupy the Old Town residence. "There are hundreds of reports from people who have felt cold spots." Voices have been recorded and electromagnetic energy detected.
whaleyhouse.org

Winchester Mystery House, San Jose, California
The house was built by Winchester rifle heiress Sarah Winchester with direction from designing spirits. Starting with an eight-room ranch house, Winchester added on continuously for 38 years, resulting in an unfinished 160-room Victorian mansion. At nightly séances, "good spirits" recommended building stairways to nowhere and halls with dead ends to thwart "bad spirits." The house may be a tourist attraction, but it's also a good place for paranormal study. "She was very much a spiritualist. Her writings indicated she wasn't crazy, but she did a lot of crazy things."
winchestermysteryhouse.com

Bachelor's Grove Cemetery, Midlothian, Illinois
The small cemetery of just over an acre in suburban Chicago hasn't had a burial since 1989, but it continues to be a source of "fairly well-documented" activity. Ghostly apparitions appear—and not just of people but also of animals and even buildings.

Waverly Hills Sanatorium, Louisville, Kentucky
Built in the 1920s, the former tuberculosis sanatorium "is abandoned and dangerous. There are still beds and equipment inside. It looks haunted." The place has spawned "lots of negative experiences with

ghosts, [including] poltergeist activity where things are thrown at people." Most of the activity is on the fifth floor.

Devil's Den, Gettysburg National Military Park, Gettysburg, Pennsylvania

This formation of giant granite boulders was the site of a fierce and bloody Civil War battle. "There's a lot of electromagnetic and voice phenomenon here. It's one place I go and really feel something. It's not scary, but it's unusual. There's lots of energy." It's just one of many haunted spots in Gettysburg. "Almost anyone there has a ghost story to tell." *nps.gov/gett*

17 Hundred 90 Inn, Savannah, Georgia

The inn, which bills itself as the city's oldest, is said to be haunted by a heartbroken woman who jumped from a third-floor balcony in the early 1800s as her lover's ship sailed out to sea. "I've talked to tourists who have seen her." The ghost has plenty of local company. "Almost any house in old Savannah has people talking about ghosts." *17hundred90.com*

Fire Station No. 2, New York, New York

The station on West Third Street in Greenwich Village is said to be home to the ghost of a fireman with salt-and-pepper hair who wears an old-fashioned helmet and a red shirt. "We call it a *lepke*—an apparition that looks so human you think it is, until it walks through a wall or something. People will go up and talk to him, and he disappears."

10 great places to go on a haunted hike

National parks are great for camping, biking, hiking … and things that go bump in the night. Andrea Lankford, a former park ranger, is the author of Haunted Hikes: Spine-Tingling Tales and Trails from North America's National Park System. *She shares some of her favorite getaways for ghosts, paranormal events, and the like.*

Chesapeake & Ohio Canal National Historic Park, Maryland

The Gold Mine Trail begins at the Great Falls Tavern Visitor Center near Potomac, Maryland, outside Washington, D.C., and passes by the site of an explosion that killed a miner in 1906. After the accident, spirits known as "Tommy Knockers" were said to haunt the dark recesses of the mine. The mine closed two years later, after a night watchman encountered "a ghostly-looking man with eyes of fire and a tail ten feet long" crawling out of the shaft. *nps.gov/choh*

Yosemite National Park, California

A wind with a weird name is the spooky thing here. The Miwok Indians believed Yosemite's spectacular waterfalls were haunted by an evil wind called Po-ho-no. The wind, they said, entices the unwary to the roaring brink of the falls and then pushes them off the edge. "Which explains why the National Park Service has fortified the falls overlooks with so many safety railings. The topside views have been as deadly as they are sublime." *nps.gov/yose*

New Jersey Pinelands National Reserve/Wharton State Forest, New Jersey

"Since 1735, hundreds have seen or heard a yellow-eyed creature with a bat's wings, a dragon's breath, and a kangaroo's tail that, according to legend, makes the Pine Barrens its home." To improve your chances of spotting this UBE (unidentified biological entity), hike a section of the Batona Trail, a 49-mile route connecting Batsto Village and Ong's Hat. "This path ventures deep into prime New Jersey Devil habitat." *nps.gov/pine*

Virgin Islands National Park, St. John, U.S. Virgin Islands

The idyllic Jumby Beach and many park trails are haunted by mischievous spirits the locals call "jumbies." Men, they say, have the most to fear while on the self-guided nature trail to Annaberg Sugar Mill Ruins. "This historic plantation site is stalked by a female jumby who is looking for love in all the wrong places." *nps.gov/viis*

Mammoth Cave National Park, Kentucky

With more than 150 documented paranormal events, Mammoth Cave is one of the spookiest natural wonders of the world. "On the Violet City Lantern Tour, park rangers guide you into the cave using old-fashioned kerosene lamps. And during such trips, rangers have reported seeing apparitions resembling the slave guides who led visitors into the cave before the Civil War." *nps.gov/maca*

Great Sand Dunes National Park and Preserve, Colorado

"Nature's giant sandbox is also a flying saucer hot spot." Since the 1950s, visitors claim to have seen black triangles, cigar-shaped red orbs, and multicolored lights hovering over the park. "For the best UFO-watching, climb to the top of 750-foot Star Dune on a moon-lit summer night." *nps.gov/grsa*

Oregon Caves National Monument, Oregon

Kids will especially enjoy the fright factor at this gem of a park. "Tour the cave to see 'moonmilk,' which is made by space aliens or cave gnomes, depending on whom you ask. Hike the Big Tree Trail where, in July 2000, a psychologist witnessed Bigfoot spying on his family. And spend the night at the cozy yet creepy Oregon Caves Chateau, where Elizabeth, the ghost of a jilted bride, startles guests." *nps.gov/orca*

Grand Canyon National Park, Arizona

Park employees have long told stories of the North Rim's "Wailing Woman. Wearing a white dress printed with blue flowers, she floats along the Transept Trail between the lodge and the campground on stormy nights . . . crying and moaning over the son and husband she lost to the canyon." *nps.gov/grca*

Blue Ridge Parkway, Virginia

In November 1891, four-year-old Ottie Powell vanished while collecting firewood in the forest. Five months later, a hunter found his body near Bluff Mountain, where a memorial for Ottie can still be found. "Backpackers say the toddler's ghost haunts the Appalachian Trail leading to Bluff Mountain and that his youthful spirit annoys those brave enough to spend a night inside the Punchbowl Shelter." *nps.gov/blri*

Big Bend National Park, Texas
"If you hear peculiar noises while camping in the Chisos Mountains, you're not alone." *Chisos* means "ghosts," and park rangers say hikers often report hearing "things" in the nightly winds. "Among the ghouls wandering this desert range are a betrayed Indian chief, a troop of long-dead Spanish warriors, and a ghost steer seeking revenge against the cowboys who branded him with the word *murder.*" *nps.gov/bibe*

Budget Travel Tips *from the* **USA TODAY Archive**

LODGING

Drop your pretensions

In choosing hotels, usually the difference between an expensive hotel and an inexpensive hotel is not in physical comfort but in psychology. Upscale hotels fill you with the feeling that you are enjoying a privileged existence, that you are living luxuriously. In actual fact, when you turn off the light and go to sleep, you cannot tell if you are in a luxurious hotel or a budget hotel. What matters then is whether the mattress is firm, whether the room smells good. Learn to overcome the psychological resistance to a simple, unpretentious hotel.

—Arthur Frommer, founder, Frommer's travel guides

SHOPPING

Get credit when credit is due

Always use a credit card because, if it doesn't work out, your credit-card company will go to bat for you.

Be careful if you have a taxi driver who says he knows a wonderful place where you can buy something. Typically, that driver will get a commission from the place, and you're going to be overcharged.

—Joel Widzer, *The Penny Pincher's Passport to Luxury Travel*

10 great places to act
out a scary movie scene

*Some of the most memorable horror movies were
filmed not on soundstages but in real places.
Don Sumner, creator of best-horror-movies.com,
shares his list of favorite locales.*

Union Cemetery, Burkittsville, Maryland
This graveyard in Burkittsville, about 40 miles west of Baltimore,
is where the student filmmakers of 1999's *The Blair Witch Project*
began their creepy documentary about the legendary Blair witch.
"The story, of course, is completely fabricated. But the town and
the cemetery really exist. If you pay a visit, you might also consider
a side trip to Seneca Creek State Park—the 'Black Hills' where the
students became lost and terror-stricken."

Michael Myers House, South Pasadena, California
In the 1978 horror movie classic *Halloween,* which stars Jamie Lee
Curtis in her first film role, psychotic killer Michael Myers returns
to his childhood home to wreak havoc on Halloween night. "The
abode of Michael's childhood and later shenanigans is a real South
Pasadena house, located at 1000 Mission Street. The house now
serves as a chiropractor's office, but it retains the unmistakable
aura of the infamous Myers house."

Monroeville Mall, Monroeville, Pennsylvania
About ten miles east of Pittsburgh, the Monroeville Mall served
as the principal location for 1978's *Dawn of the Dead,* written and
directed by zombie-meister George A. Romero. "This film—a
sequel to Romero's cult classic *Night of the Living Dead*—is a
continuation of the plight of humanity after an abrupt transforma-
tion of the dead into walking flesh-eaters. In the movie, survivors
barricade themselves in the shopping mall and fight for their lives."
monroevillemall.com

***The Exorcist* Stairs,** Washington, D.C.
"*The Exorcist* is considered by some to be the scariest and most
disturbing horror film of all time." Much of this 1973 movie was

shot in the D.C. neighborhood of Georgetown, including two grisly death scenes that take place on a set of sinister-looking stairs. "In reality, these 75 steps, located on the corner of Prospect Street and 36th Street NW, are often used by health enthusiasts seeking an aerobic workout."

Point Reyes Lighthouse, Inverness, California

The Fog, starring Adrienne Barbeau, is an eerie tale of mass haunting and revenge in a northern California fishing town called Antonio Bay. "Much of the action in this 1980 John Carpenter–directed film takes place at an isolated lighthouse, where Barbeau broadcasts an all-night radio program. Antonio Bay is actually Inverness, and the lighthouse is the historic Point Reyes Lighthouse, built in 1870." *ptreyeslight.com/lthouse.html*

Santa Cruz Beach Boardwalk, Santa Cruz, California

In the 1987 horror film *The Lost Boys,* a band of hooligan vampires (led by Kiefer Sutherland) roams the night looking for victims at a California beachside amusement park. "That amusement park exists and is still open for business in Santa Cruz. To this day, the park is almost exactly as depicted in the film." Presumably, sans vampires. *beachboardwalk.com*

Timberline Lodge, Mount Hood, Oregon

In the 1980 film *The Shining,* based on Stephen King's novel and directed by Stanley Kubrick, writer Jack Torrance (played by Jack Nicholson) takes a winter job as caretaker of a Colorado mountain lodge called the Overlook Hotel. "The isolation, along with ghostly apparitions, drives Jack insane, and he goes homicidal on his poor, unsuspecting family. The haunted Overlook is actually Timberline Lodge, located on the south side of Mount Hood, about 60 miles east of Portland." *timberlinelodge.com*

The Dakota, New York, New York

In the 1968 film *Rosemary's Baby,* Mia Farrow moves with her new husband into an upscale New York apartment building called The Bramford, where she soon becomes the target of a demonic conspiracy. "The Bramford is actually The Dakota, located on the northwest corner of 72nd Street and Central Park West." Built in the early 1880s, the ornate Dakota has housed a roster of famous residents, including Andrew Carnegie, Judy Garland, Lauren Bacall, and Leonard Bernstein. "The building has a history of rumored hauntings and bad luck." Ex-Beatle and Dakota resident John Lennon was shot and killed outside his apartment there in December 1980.

Junction House Restaurant, Kingsland, Texas
"In Tobe Hooper's 1974 horror classic *The Texas Chainsaw Massacre,* a group of teenagers driving through an isolated part of Texas is terrorized by the infamous Leatherface and his clan. The house that served as the demented family's home still stands." Today it's the Junction House restaurant, at 1010 King Street in Kingsland, about 35 miles northwest of Austin. *junction-house.com*

Tom's Market, Vivian, Louisiana
"The 2007 monster flick *The Mist* is based on a Stephen King short story in which the inhabitants of a small town hide from a creature-infested mist inside a grocery store. That grocery store is actually Tom's Market, located at 212 North Pine Street in the town of Vivian, about 20 miles north of Shreveport."

AND ANOTHER THING . . .

OTHER SILVER SCREEN SPINE-TINGLERS

- Bela Lugosi's grave, Culver City, California—The 1956 burial of Bela Lugosi at Holy Cross Cemetery is a thing of Hollywood legend because, as depicted in 1994 by Tim Burton's *Ed Wood*, he was put in a coffin while wearing his Count Dracula regalia—cape and all.

- *Friday the 13th*'s Camp Crystal Lake, Blairstown, New Jersey—Camp No-Be-Bo-Sco, a Boy Scout camp like no other, was the location for Sean Cunningham's 1979 seminal stalk-and-slash shocker. The Sand Pond became the movie's Crystal Lake.

THANKSGIVING

10 great places to give thanks

*These days, many time-pressed drumstick devotees
are making reservations instead of Thanksgiving dinner.
And not just at restaurants: The holiday weekend extends an
invitation to celebrate away from home. Barbara Peck,
executive editor of* Travel & Leisure *and* Travel & Leisure
Family, *shares some tempting getaway suggestions.*

Spring Creek Ranch, Jackson Hole, Wyoming
"They'll have snow" for Thanksgiving in the Tetons at this luxury
resort surrounded by Grand Teton and Yellowstone national parks,
and the ski slopes are open at Grand Targhee, just a short drive
away. Cross-country ski trails dot the 1,000-acre property; other
activities include a wide variety of sports, sleigh rides, and pre-
Thanksgiving cooking classes. *springcreekranch.com*

Sundance, Utah
This 6,000-acre mountain community, an hour's drive from Salt
Lake City, shows "a family holiday film" in the private screening
room of founder Robert Redford. The complex includes an artisans
center, "so there's always a strong arts component there," as well
as hiking and other activities. The Foundry Grill serves an all-day
Thanksgiving brunch. *sundanceresort.com*

Sun Mountain Lodge, Winthrop, Washington
"Really get away from it all" at this 3,000-acre resort, a five hours'
drive from Seattle in the North Cascades. Wilderness trails,
horseback riding, and mountain biking await, and the lodge has a
full-service spa. The rustic restaurant serves a Thanksgiving buffet.
www.sunmountainlodge.com

Sun Valley Lodge, Sun Valley, Idaho
"If you're ready to start skiing," try this traditional mountain lodge,
where the four-night Thanksgiving package includes lift tickets as
well as lodging and a buffet holiday dinner. Or stay in the condo village behind the lodge, "the best place for families." *sunvalley.com*

Red Lion Inn, Stockbridge, Massachusetts
Nestled in the Berkshires, this classic 1897 inn "makes a big deal of Thanksgiving. They serve locally pressed cider, and each guest gets a chocolate turkey to take home." Completing the picture: The Norman Rockwell Museum is just three miles away. *redlioninn.com*

Cheeca Lodge, Islamorada, Florida
"You'll get palm trees and ocean breezes" at this 27-acre resort in the self-proclaimed sport-fishing capital of the world. The Thanksgiving menu at Cheeca's acclaimed Atlantic's Edge restaurant includes roast bison and Florida shellfish stew as well as turkey. "It's a family resort," where the 6- to 12-year-old set can learn about the animals, plants, and waters of the Florida Keys at Camp Cheeca. *cheeca.com*

White Barn Inn & Spa, Kennebunkport, Maine
This luxurious resort, less than a half-hour's drive from Portland, offers "a wonderful Thanksgiving dinner in a reconstructed barn that's decorated with antique farm implements." *whitebarninn.com*

Carmel Valley Ranch, Carmel-by-the-Sea, California
Six miles out of town on 1,700 acres, the ranch has swimming and tennis on-site and will arrange horseback riding, biking, and hiking in the Santa Lucia Mountains. "Bring binoculars: You can see sea lions, sea otters, and a host of seabirds at nearby Point Lobos State Reserve." The ranch's restaurant, The Oaks, serves a traditional Thanksgiving dinner with such California touches as fresh local greens and roasted Sonoma quail. *carmelvalleyranch.com*

Hotel Santa Fe, Santa Fe, New Mexico
Basing its design on the terraced adobe pueblos first built 1,000 years ago, this family-oriented hotel features a 22-foot tepee in the yard and Native American dancers on Saturday nights. The Corn Dance Cafe's Thanksgiving feast to the Great Spirit includes such authentic touches as cranberry-piñon sauce for the turkey, a soufflé of cheese and green chilies, and Indian pudding. *hotelsantafe.com*

Mayflower Hotel on the Park, New York, New York
"You can see Macy's Thanksgiving Day Parade from your window"
as it passes the hotel. It's also just a few blocks from where the
huge helium balloons are inflated, "so you can go there the night
before and watch them do it."

10 great places to put the "giving" in Thanksgiving

*This Thanksgiving season—and all year—why not
show your thanks by putting the emphasis on giving?
Sheryl Kayne, author of* Immersion Travel USA: The Best &
Most Meaningful Volunteering, Living & Learning Excursions,
shares her favorite volunteering vacations.

Heifer Ranch, Perryville, Arkansas
"Heifer International works to end world hunger by providing sustainable gifts of livestock and agricultural training to impoverished
people around the world." Many of the animals the organization
donates are raised on a 1,200-acre ranch in rural Arkansas. "The
ranch welcomes volunteers, who participate in caring for livestock,
supporting administrative operations, and putting together educational programs for the public." *heifer.org*

Fur Seal Rookery, St. George Island, Alaska
Part of a five-island volcanic archipelago in the Bering Sea,
St. George Island is the principal breeding ground for northern fur
seals. Earthwatch Institute, a nonprofit group that funds and con-
ducts environmental research, offers a ten-day vacation to monitor
and study this threatened species. "Participants hike to the rookery
and spend four hours each day observing the seals and recording
numbers."

Hole in the Wall Gang Camp, Ashford, Connecticut
"Founded in 1987 by Paul Newman, this wonderful facility provides a recreational and therapeutic camping experience for
children with serious medical conditions." Open from early June
through late August, it welcomes volunteers to serve as camp coun-
selors. *holeinthewallgang.org*

Navajo Nation, Tuba City, Arizona
"For a volunteering opportunity that is also a cultural experience, you can spend a week at the Navajo Nation in Tuba City." Amizade, a worldwide community service organization, enlists volunteers to tutor Navajo schoolchildren, organize recreational activities, and assist with cultural programs. "Volunteers also participate in Navajo traditions to learn about and experience the culture." *amizade.org*

Continental Divide Trail, Rocky Mountain Region
The 1,600-mile Continental Divide Trail, which traverses the spine of the Rocky Mountains from Canada to Mexico, was designated a National Scenic Trail in 1978. "Each year from May through early October, the nonprofit Continental Divide Trail Alliance recruits volunteers to help repair, maintain, and expand various segments of the trail. This is a wonderful opportunity to enjoy the great outdoors while helping to preserve a national treasure for future generations." *cdtrail.org/getinvolved*

Big Dipper Eco Farm, Kingsley, Michigan
Want to learn how to farm organically from people who've been doing it successfully for more than 20 years? Volunteers at Big Dipper Eco Farm can work a few days, a week, or longer in exchange for room and board. "Tasks include weeding, hoeing, picking, and packing crops for market. Family-style meals are prepared and eaten together." Big Dipper is a member of WWOOF-USA, an organization that links volunteers with organic farmers around the country. *wwoofusa.org/farms/1189*

Historic "Shotgun Houses," Cairo, Illinois
As part of a redevelopment effort in this historic river town situated at the confluence of the Ohio and Mississippi rivers, volunteers can spend a week helping to renovate abandoned shotgun-style houses. "These are unique post-Civil-War-era dwellings built on narrow lots—one-room wide and with all the doors aligned. Volunteers work with building-conservation specialists to rehabilitate the homes with the goal of providing quality, affordable housing." The program is organized by Heritage Conservation

Network in partnership with Southern Illinois University and local residents. *heritageconservation.net/ws-cairo.htm*

Elephant Sanctuary, Hohenwald, Tennessee
The Elephant Sanctuary is the nation's largest natural-habitat refuge for elephants that have been retired from circuses and zoos. "Set on over 2,700 acres, the sanctuary has separate environments for Asian and African elephants, with pastures, forests, spring-fed ponds, and heated barns." Volunteers help with chores such as painting, fencing, facility renovation, or construction of new habitat areas. *elephants.com*

Heron Lake State Park, Los Ojos, New Mexico
Many state parks nationwide need assistance with special events. At New Mexico's Heron Lake State Park, volunteers can help with the Osprey Festival, held each July to spotlight one of North America's largest birds of prey, which nests in the park. "Festival volunteers are trained and employed as needed for activities including pontoon-boat tours, assisting naturalists with live raptor exhibits, and helping visitors view osprey nests with spotting scopes." *emnrd.state.nm.us/prd/heron.htm*

Louisiana Children's Museum, New Orleans, Louisiana
Under a program run by Relief Spark, a community-based organization that coordinates volunteer efforts in the New Orleans area, volunteers can help rebuild children's hope and self-confidence at the Louisiana Children's Museum. "Volunteers participate in hands-on art and science projects, interactive learning games, and storytelling for visiting school groups." *lcm.org*

I awoke this morning with devout thanksgiving for my friends, the old and the new.

—Ralph Waldo Emerson

CHRISTMAS, HANUKKAH & KWANZAA

10 great places to have a historical holiday

Historic mansions are attractive holiday destinations for families seeking a peek into past traditions, says Richard Moe, president of the National Trust for Historic Preservation. "There's no better way to celebrate this time of year than to experience the customs of those who established the diverse holiday traditions in America." Here, he shares historic halls decked with holly—and holiday spirit.

Filoli, Woodside, California
This grand Georgian mansion is "one of America's greatest treasures. Visitors can view... the gold-leafed ballroom adorned with sparkling 18-foot-high Christmas trees, swags of evergreens, and exquisite floral displays." *filoli.org*

Brucemore, Cedar Rapids, Iowa
"Seasonal greenery, dried-flower arrangements, bright poinsettias, twinkling lights, and exquisitely decorated trees adorn the late-19th-century mansion and community center. Events include evening tours, festive music, and several visits from Santa." *brucemore.org*

Shadows-on-the-Teche, New Iberia, Louisiana
"Victorian-style garlands and wreaths made of local greenery, fruit, and ribbons decorate this grand 19th-century plantation house, located just off the Bayou Teche. Tours of the mansion focus on the historic holiday celebrations of the antebellum period." *www.shadowsontheteche.org*

Molly Brown House Museum, Denver, Colorado
"Recounting the life of Margaret Tobin Brown, the 'unsinkable lady' known for surviving the *Titanic* disaster, the MB House creates an elaborate Victorian Christmas display with candlelight tours, festive wreaths, mistletoe, ribbon, and special events recounting the holidays as Brown experienced them." *mollybrown.org*

Graceland, Memphis, Tennessee
Elvis Presley famously decorated for the holidays. Today, "the staff continues Elvis's traditions by placing Christmas trees in several rooms. Look outside for Elvis's life-size Nativity scene, the lighted aluminum trees, and the winding driveway outlined with hundreds of blue lights." *elvis.com*

Lyndhurst, Tarrytown, New York
Rooms in the Gothic Revival mansion on the Hudson River represent different fairy tales. "Included in the decorations are the glittering ornaments donated to Lyndhurst by Scarsdale native Christopher Radko." *lyndhurst.org*

African Meeting House, Boston, Massachusetts
"Celebrate an Abolitionists' Christmas at the oldest extant black church building in the United States built by free African American artisans. Enjoy the holiday presentation of the Greater Boston Youth Symphony Orchestra, workshops featuring ornament making, or West African drum rhythms in a hands-on interactive session" that teaches the principles of Kwanzaa. *afroammuseum.org*

Pabst Mansion, Milwaukee, Wisconsin
More than 100 Christmases ago, sea captain and beer baron Captain Frederick Pabst built his Flemish Renaissance Revival mansion. "Intricately decorated trees and seasonal decor are in every room on the first two floors." *pabstmansion.com*

Colonial Williamsburg, Williamsburg, Virginia
"Nothing quite matches the excitement, sights, sounds, and grandeur of the Christmas season in Williamsburg. Watch the Grand Illumination with candles and a huge display of fireworks. Seasonal

programs include children's theater, seminars on Williamsburg's decorations, 18th-century musical performances, and tours of private homes decorated for the season." *history.org*

Biltmore Estate, Asheville, North Carolina
Since George Vanderbilt and his family first celebrated Christmas here in 1895, "America's largest home continues the tradition with a larger-than-life celebration that includes holiday music, candlelight tours; hundreds of poinsettias; dozens of Christmas trees; and a Fraser fir adorned with lights, brass ornaments, and gifts." *biltmore.com*

Gathering holiday gifts

Whether you're buying gifts for Hanukkah, Christmas, or Kwanzaa, finding the perfect presents for everyone on your list can make a grinch out of even the most festive. Following are some special stores far from the maddening mall crowds.

- **ABC Carpet & Home, New York, New York**—Whimsy and luxury permeate this ten-floor home emporium in the historic Flatiron District, where finds from Venetian chandeliers to Victorian calling cards overflow. Furnishings, antiques, imported bed linens, eclectic collectibles—everything in the store is for sale. "One of the ten best stores in the world," says super-shopper Suzy Gershman, author of Frommer's *Born to Shop* book series.

- **Amen Wardy, Las Vegas, Nevada**—According to Gershman, this branch of the Aspen-based shop carries "one-of-a-kind, playful gifts" like hand-painted birdhouses, picture frames, and picnic sets—"things to amuse the person who has everything."

- **Bell'occhio, San Francisco, California**—With its vintage and hand-dyed ribbons, French silk roses, velvet violets, and other decorative items, this eccentric little shop with "a sense of humor…

is sort of a Martha Stewart supply room," says Gershman. For the holiday season, there are novelty boxes shaped like lumps of coal, Yule logs, snowballs, and pinecones. And Bell'occhio's gift-wrapping is as imaginative and pretty as its wares.

- **Brownes & Co., Miami Beach, Florida**—In the Lincoln Road pedestrian mall, where models whiz by on skates, this face and body care shop is "perfect for a town that's so body-conscious," says Gershman. Its soaps and soaks; creams and lotions for hair, face, and body; makeup; and related items come in "a great array of international brands that you don't find in department stores."

- **Bush Antiques, New Orleans, Louisiana**—This charming "trove of secret places and hidden parts" is packed with "small objects, religious items, and furniture and accessories, artfully laid out so you want all of it," says Gershman.

- **Gorsuch, Aspen, Colorado**—Schussing shoppers can ski right into this purveyor of "Wild West chic" at the base of Aspen Mountain. "It's not tacky stuff," says Gershman, and the store, next to the exclusive Little Nell, also carries cashmere sweaters, ski togs, and boots.

- **REI, Seattle, Washington**—REI (Recreational Equipment Inc.) has expanded to other cities, but this is the flagship of the co-op, full of gear "for any sport you can imagine [and] outdoor everything," says Gershman. You can find gifts for anyone at any price range, and "it's a great playground" for active shoppers.

Christmas is not a time nor a season, but a state of mind. To cherish peace and goodwill, to be plenteous in mercy, is to have the real spirit of Christmas.

—Calvin Coolidge

10 great places to catch up with Santa

Santa is not only coming to town during the holiday season, he's coming to parks, parades, and museums nationwide. Teresa Plowright, mother of three and editor of about.com's Family Vacations, talks about her favorite places to visit jolly ol' St. Nick.

The Polar Express (Grand Canyon Railway), Williams, Arizona

"This brings the classic children's book *The Polar Express* to life. Santa gives each child a sleigh bell, just like in the book." Kids wearing their pajamas and fuzzy slippers have hot chocolate and cookies while listening to the audiobook on the northbound train trip. No one gets off at the North Pole, but you can glimpse Santa's village from the window as he boards the train with a special gift. *thetrain.com/polarexpress*

Gaylord Opryland Resort, Nashville, Tennessee

The Radio City Christmas Spectacular with 40 dancing Santas is among dozens of shows and attractions at Gaylord Opryland's "A Country Christmas." See Santa in the Winter Wonderland area, which also features ICE!, an annual display that uses "two million pounds of sculptured ice. Guests get parkas when they enter." *christmasatgaylordopryland.com*

Christmas Town, Bethlehem, Connecticut

"Kids can go to the local post office here and cancel their holiday cards with a 'Bethlehem' postmark." Visit Santa on the Village Green and sing along with carolers strolling Main Street at the lantern-lit Christmas Town Festival in this small country town. And don't miss the Gregorian chants of the Benedictine nuns at the Abbey of Regina Laundis. The nuns also sell wreaths and Christmas trees. *christmastownfestival.com*

Celebration in the Oaks, New Orleans, Louisiana
"Schools have tree-decorating competitions for this big celebration in City Park, and Santa visits every night until Christmas." The park also has a train and one of the oldest operating carousels in the nation. The original "Mr. Bingle," a little snowman from a 1950s Maison Blanche department store window display, is now part of the park's holiday decorations. *celebrationintheoaks.com*

Legoland California Resort, Carlsbad, California
"Kids are welcome to climb on this bigger-than-life-size Lego Santa." They can also join him in his sleigh, drawn by Lego reindeer, to take photos. Other holiday touches in the park throughout December include smaller Lego Santas in Mini-land, a stilt-walking toy soldier, and strolling carolers. *legoland.com*

Santa on the Chimney!, Chimney Rock Park, North Carolina
"Santa takes a 26-story elevator to the top of Chimney Rock, then rappels down. After visiting with the crowd, he goes back up again." Santa is available for photo ops at the Sky Lounge and when he reaches the parking lot. Enjoy hot chocolate, spiced cider, and cookies while listening to holiday music. *chimneyrockpark.com*

An Old-Fashioned Christmas, West Chester, Pennsylvania
"Visit with Santa after the parade, when he lights up the Community Tree in front of the courthouse in this hip, historic town near Philadelphia." Join St. Nick for breakfast at the Chester County Historical Society, and don't miss the dollhouse exhibit there. The downtown, which looks much as it did a century ago, offers plenty of shopping opportunities.

Santa's Village, Jefferson, New Hampshire
"You'll see Santa with real woodland caribou, better known as reindeer, and lights strung everywhere at this outdoor theme park. Make sure you bundle up and wear your boots and hats." Ride the monorail, called The Skyway Sleigh, and the Christmas Carousel, where reindeer substitute for horses; then view the White Mountains from the top of the Ferris wheel. Decorate your own cookies at the Gingerbread Bakery, or order a dozen to take home and decorate later. *santasvillage.com*

Stone Mountain Park, near Atlanta, Georgia
"Two million lights twinkle throughout the village where this holiday event takes place. There is a Christmas parade with Santa and Mrs. Claus riding in their sleigh." Meet Santa later at his workshop. Then look skyward as the snow angel flies overhead, bringing snowfall and fireworks. *stonemountainpark.com*

Celebration Crossing, Indianapolis, Indiana
"This exhibit at the Indiana State Museum is part of the '12 Free Days of Indy Christmas' celebration, during which admission is free on each day at specific Indianapolis museums and other attractions." The museum's walk-in Santa house is modeled after a traditional holiday display at L. S. Ayres, a former department store in Indianapolis. Children too shy to visit Santa can peer in the windows of this imaginary town or ride the child-scale train around a small track. *indianamuseum.org*

10 great places to shop
for stuff for stockings

Giving is its own reward, and when you find the right store, so is the shopping. Travel and lifestyle editor Yolanda Edwards shares her list of favorite places to shop for stocking stuffers.

Sons + Daughters, New York, New York
"The owner of this East Village children's boutique has an amazing eye. She finds things all over the world, from knee-high socks made in Germany to Dutch-sequined crowns. Check out the art-supply table for affordable and cheery gifts." Targeted for children up to age eight, the shop offers gifts for as little as $10.

Genius Jones, Miami, Florida
"Before Miami was thought of as a design destination, Genius Jones, with its clean, minimalist interiors, was already there. Everything they carry…is carefully chosen." The staff will help find hair accessories, stamp sets, and other stocking stuffers. *geniusjones.com*

Grasshopper Store, Portland, Oregon

"In Portland, there's a huge demand for all things organic and locally made. People flock to this shop for the boutique's thoughtful edit of handmade knit animals; pull-along wooden toys; and, yes, organic onesies." Wild Carrots, the in-house clothing line designed by the owner, is timeless not trendy. *grasshopperstore.com*

TOMODACHI, Roseville, Minnesota

"Somehow, the Japanese toys and packaging here are as much fun to buy and give as they are to get. This store (just outside the Twin Cities) has a vast selection of imported toys." Robots, stationery, gadgets, and designer toys are among the unusual items offered. Japanese snacks and Ramune, a popular Japanese carbonated soft drink, also are sold here. *tomodachi.us*

Hands of the World, Seattle, Washington

"In the Pike Place Market, one of the most exciting places to find yourself in Seattle, is this global store." The store, in business for more than 25 years, does extensive work with women's co-ops. A wide range of fair-trade accessories, as well as authentic African folk art, also are sold here. *handsoftheworld.com*

Black Ink, Boston, Massachusetts

"This overstocked store, just bursting at the seams, is especially appealing during the holidays. You can check everything off your list at once and have a great time doing it." In addition to toys and baby gifts, the Beacon Hill store carries housewares and greeting cards. *blackinkboston.com*

Richard's Variety Store, Atlanta, Georgia

"This family-owned store (in the Buckhead section), which began as a five-and-dime, has been in business for [more than] 50 years. They have everything from Lincoln Logs to jacks to harmonicas. There's even a mechanical horse ride in the middle of the store that kids can enjoy for 10 cents." A wide selection of noncomputer toys, novelties, and cheery cards can also be found there. *richardsvarietystore.com*

Chinatown Kite Shop, San Francisco, California

"Just walking down Grant Street in Chinatown will turn up a

gazillion stocking options, but one of the most colorful shops to put on your list is this one. There are plenty of kites that fold up small. They come in bright colors and crazy shapes." *chinatownkite.com*

Monkeyhouse Toys, Los Angeles, California
"How rare is it that handmade by locals turns out right and not ready for the church bazaar? The owner has connections with local artists and commissions them to do, among other things, fantastic stuffed animals, paintings, and piggy banks." *monkeyhousetoys.com*

Tugooh Toys, Washington, D.C.
"All the toys are crafted from materials like untreated wood and food-grade (nontoxic) paint. Plus, they carry organic products for pregnant and new moms." Concerned about the safety of merchandise, owner Grace Marupa makes a point of knowing what the products are made of and where they come from.

Bypassing holiday hassles

Heading out for the holidays? Join the crowd. And get ready for hassles. We asked experts for advice on how to steer clear of, or at least minimize, the stress level of travel.

- Prepare mentally. Tom Turkey and St. Nick aren't the only sure signs of the season. Every bit as prominent, albeit less welcome: delayed airline flights, long lines, and whiny kids. But don't totally blow your cool. Just get in the right frame of mind. Psychologist Dr. Ronald Nathan of Albany, New York, suggests rapid relaxation techniques.

  "Take a deep breath—it's an instant stress reliever," he says. Use your imagination as a stress break. "Imagine you're at your destination already or mentally re-create the wonder of Christmas past. Remember: you can't control travel problems, but you can control your response to the stress they create."

- Planning, in this case, is everything. "Give yourself plenty of time to find your way around the airport or train station, extra time to buy magazines or food," says Denver-based clinical psychologist Thomas Olkowski. "Make sure the kids are well-rested, bring snacks and toys to keep them busy." If the kids are old enough, explain what airports are about, tell them how to find the gate and understand departure schedules. That will help keep them occupied too.

To further cut down on hassles, Carlton Van Doren, retired professor of tourism sciences at Texas A&M University, suggests calling ahead to make sure your flight is on time. And if possible, get someone to drive you to the airport so you won't have to deal with fighting for a space in full parking lots.

- Avoid peak travel times. Generally, the two days prior to Thanksgiving and Christmas are the most crowded—whether you're at the airport or on the highway. So pick another time, if possible. Planes, for example, are far less crowded if you leave on Thanksgiving or Christmas morning or return home on the Saturday following the holiday.

For motorists, try to avoid the road on holiday weekend Sundays—easily the most crowded, says Jerry Cheske, former spokesman for the American Automobile Association. And, of course, plan around late-afternoon rush hours in urban areas.

If you decide to rent a car, be aware that heavily booked days are expected to be the Wednesday before Thanksgiving and the Friday and Saturday before Christmas week.

- Lighten the gift load. Don't get bogged down carrying gifts and packages. Mail ahead. Or, if you'll be at your destination with time to spare, wait until you get there to shop.

The U.S. Post Office recommends mailing packages before December 16 for parcel post and December 21 for first-class mail to avoid delays. Book rate and parcel post are generally the cheapest. If you insist on carrying packages aboard an airliner (and millions will), the standard rule is one or two items of carry-on baggage, which must fit in the overhead compartment or under your seat.

- Short trip? Drive instead. Driving may be the best way around holiday hassles—if the destination is within 200 to 500 miles.

- Stay home. Instead of leaving town, ask friends and family to your place. Just don't let them move in. Suggest a hotel. Remember: This is a slow time for many chains in major cities, so they often offer good deals to beef up business. Just ask when you call for reservations.

10 great places to visit by flickering lights

Enjoy Christmas by candlelight as historic homes and towns offer glimpses of yesteryear. "Candlelight tours are a wonderful way to experience the heritage of America's many diverse communities," says Richard Moe, president of the National Trust for Historic Preservation. Here, he shares historic spots aglow in holiday light.

Biltmore Estate, Asheville, North Carolina
"America's largest private home offers Candlelight Christmas Evenings through December 31. Luminarias lead the way to the front door as firelight and candlelight fill the house and accent dozens of Christmas trees, hundreds of poinsettias, thousands of ornaments, miles of evergreen garland, and a 35-foot live Fraser fir. Musicians perform holiday favorites daily." *biltmore.com*

Dana-Thomas House, Springfield, Illinois
"For Luminaria Evening, 1,000 candles in paper sacks line the sidewalks and ledges of this sprawling, Prairie-style structure designed by Frank Lloyd Wright. Conducted tours on this night are silent except for the live music being played in the house, filled with more than 100 pieces of Wright-designed furniture and over 450 art-glass windows and fixtures." *dana-thomas.org*

The American Club, Kohler, Wisconsin
"Experience a magical candlelit evening, including caroling and readings of favorite holiday tales. The events are held in candlelight to replicate life for the immigrant factory workers employed at the Kohler Co. in the early 1900s. A candlelight outdoor garden tour, followed by a candlelit gathering in the greenhouse, also is available." *destinationkohler.com*

The Farmers' Museum, Cooperstown, New York
"A much-anticipated holiday tradition, Candlelight Evening celebrates 'friendship, family, and community with caroling, sleigh

rides, winter games, and wassail.' The museum is decorated in beautiful greenery and lighted by hundreds of candles as St. Nicholas, dressed in 1840s costume, reads ''Twas the Night Before Christmas.' " *farmersmuseum.org*

Strawbery Banke Museum, Portsmouth, New Hampshire
"This ten-acre museum, depicting how Portsmouth has lived over the past 400 years, presents an annual Candlelight Stroll. Enjoy festively decorated historic homes in the glow of hundreds of luminarias nestled in snow. Family activities include horse-drawn-carriage rides, Old St. Nicholas, hot cider, and seasonal music." *strawberybanke.org*

Stowe at Night, Stowe, Vermont
"Carry a candlelit lantern on a one-hour walking tour (with indoor stops) as you view the town's historic buildings and listen to stories of the resident ghosts of Stowe." *gostowe.com*

Molly Brown House Museum, Denver, Colorado
During Christmas Candlelight Tours, a rare opportunity to see the museum at night, "festive music accompanies costumed guides as they lead guests on a flickering tour…followed by a reading of ''Twas the Night Before Christmas.' " *mollybrown.org*

Mary Todd Lincoln House/Hunt-Morgan House, Lexington, Kentucky
"Witness Christmas magic in candlelight at two of Lexington's historic homes. Guides in period costumes lead tours through both houses, lavishly decorated for the holidays. Refreshments are served, and visitors may take a carriage ride from one house to the other." *bluegrasstrust.org*

Farolito Walk, Santa Fe, New Mexico
"Starting at sunset, join the Christmas Eve stroll up Canyon Road. The evening is a feast of lights as bonfires and *farolitos* (candles in paper bags) adorn the walk. Enjoy caroling around the fires as

residents and gallery owners offer *bizcochitos* (the anise-flavored shortbread is the state cookie), hot chocolate, and cider."

Napa County Landmarks, Napa County, California
"Enjoy the unique history of early Napa as docents take visitors through six candlelit homes and a historic bed-and-breakfast in the St. John's Historic District. Wine, hot and cold beverages, desserts, and musical entertainment all are available at this festive event." *napacountylandmarks.org*

10 great places to be enthralled by heavenly music

The holidays just wouldn't be the same without the distinct and powerful sound of holiday-themed organ music. Tony Thurman, director of development and communications for the American Guild of Organists, shares his picks for notable sight-and-sound experiences.

Mormon Tabernacle, Salt Lake City, Utah
The Mormon Tabernacle, world famous for its choir, also has an excellent organ-music program. "The Tabernacle organ is one of the world's largest and most intricate, with more than 11,000 functioning pipes. The organ has been enlarged and renovated several times, but some of its pipe work dates from the original 1867 instrument." *mormontabernaclechoir.org*

Grace Cathedral, San Francisco, California
Grace Cathedral sits on Nob Hill, affording striking views of the city and San Francisco Bay. "The building itself, of Gothic design, is breathtaking, and the organ, which dates from the 1930s, is gorgeous. Grace has a tremendous music series, with over 400 services and concerts scheduled each year. Some of it is rather unique because they embrace what's called organ improvisation—a highly specialized art form in organ playing." *gracecathedral.org*

Riverside Church, New York, New York
Modeled after the 13th-century Gothic cathedral in Chartres, France, Riverside Church is located on Manhattan's Upper West

Side near Columbia University. Its pipe organ, built in 1930 and expanded over the years, is one of the largest in the country. "The organ was played for years by the late Virgil Fox, a very famous and flamboyant organ virtuoso. He really put Riverside on the map, and it remains a premier venue for organ music. The building's acoustics are fantastic." *theriversidechurchny.org*

Fourth Presbyterian Church, Chicago, Illinois
Fourth Presbyterian, in downtown Chicago on Michigan Avenue's Magnificent Mile, boasts the largest organ in the city and one of the largest in the Midwest. "It's a very elaborate instrument with a wonderfully rich and complex sound. The church has an outstanding program of organ recitals and choral singing, particularly during the holiday season." *fourthchurch.org*

Trinity Church, Boston, Massachusetts
In the center of Boston at Copley Square, Trinity Church is truly an American landmark. "The building dates to 1877, and its organ is a magnificent instrument. The church offers free organ programs on Fridays, featuring recitalists from throughout the United States and abroad. The holiday atmosphere is always very festive, with the Copley Square Christmas tree right outside." *trinitychurchboston.org*

National Cathedral, Washington, D.C.
The National Cathedral, in northwest Washington, D.C., is truly the "nation's cathedral. It's a beautiful building of arresting architecture that belongs to all of us. The cathedral's historic pipe organ is a remarkable instrument. Built in 1938, it's been enlarged several times and now has 10,650 pipes." *cathedral.org*

Morton H. Meyerson Symphony Center, Dallas, Texas
Designed by renowned architect I. M. Pei, the Meyerson Symphony Center is known as the "crown jewel" of Dallas. "The Meyerson is visually striking inside and out, and it has one of the largest organs ever built for a concert hall." *dallasculture.org/meyersonSymphonyCenter/*

Wanamaker Organ at Macy's, Philadelphia, Pennsylvania
The Wanamaker Organ—the largest functioning musical instrument

in the world—was designated as a National Historic Landmark in 1980. "It was installed in the Wanamaker Department Store (now Macy's) in 1911 and dedicated by then-president William H. Taft. Visitors are welcome to tour the console area and meet the staff after the concerts." *wanamakerorgan.com*

Peachtree Road United Methodist Church, Atlanta, Georgia
Peachtree, in the heart of Atlanta's historic Buckhead Community, has a superior music program and excellent acoustics. "They also have one of the finest newer organs in the country. Installed in 2002, it has an exceptionally responsive keyboard. This gives the player more control of the organ's voice, which makes for a very rich listening experience." *prumc.org*

First Congregational Church, Los Angeles, California
Founded in 1867, First Congregational is the oldest Protestant church in Los Angeles. "They claim to have the largest church organ in the world. That's really a moving target, because the biggest church organs are continually being refurbished and upgraded. But they certainly have one of the most impressive instruments I know of." *fccla.org*

Budget Travel Tips from the **USA TODAY Archive**

DINING

Don't take it sitting down

Throughout Europe, when you go to a bar, stand, don't sit. The price doubles or more if you sit down.

In London and Paris, the best values are at lunch. At wonderful one- and two-star restaurants, you can have a two-course menu with a glass of wine, including service, for a third of the cost of dinner. In Spain, you can make a whole meal on tapas.

—Sandra Gustafson, author, *Great Sleeps/Great Eats* series

THE GREAT OUTDOORS

✳ ✳ ✳ ✳

PARKS

10 great places to spring out of a winter rut

Once spring has officially sprung, there's no better time to head outside for some natural activity. Keith Bellows, editor in chief of National Geographic Traveler *and author of* National Geographic's Guide to the National Parks, *gives his foolproof destinations to enjoy the best of the new season.*

Great Sand Dunes National Park, Colorado
"Backed by the 13,000-foot peaks of the Sangre de Cristo Mountains, this vast ocean of dunes are a trekker's delight, especially in spring before sand temperatures skyrocket." The park is home to America's tallest dunes, some towering up to 750 feet.

Visitors can explore the dunes by hiking through them, sliding down them, and riding along them with the help of a "dunes wheelchair." *nps.gov/grsa*

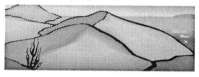

Great Smoky Mountains National Park,
Tennessee and North Carolina
Bellows prefers visiting this southern spot in spring. "Now's the time to visit America's busiest park—before the summer hordes arrive and the fall leaf peepers crowd the roads. For my money, the smells and scenics of spring display the park at its prime." *nps.gov/grsm*

Glacier Bay National Park, Alaska
As the name indicates, glaciers are prevalent in the bay as ice from the surrounding mountains slides down to the water. But it's not

always freezing here. "In May, the days are at their sunniest, and you can cruise by no fewer than nine calving glaciers in the bay, home to humpback whales, moose, and black and brown bears." *nps.gov/glba*

Shenandoah National Park, Virginia
"Spring arrives first in the park valleys and then moves upward— the result is an ever-expanding carpet of wildflowers." Check out the 105-mile Skyline Drive to take in the scenery, or rent a canoe and raft through the mountains down the Shenandoah River. *nps.gov/shen*

Virgin Islands National Park, U.S. Virgin Islands
Catch the Caribbean between high and hurricane season as prices drop in mid-April. The island of St. John has hills, valleys, and beaches, but the best is under water: The park includes more than 5,000 acres of coral seascapes. "There are travel bargains galore in this haven of powdery sand, coral reefs, and more than 800 sub-tropical plant species." *nps.gov/viis*

Redwood National Park, California
"In spring, the towering redwoods—the world's tallest living things—overlook musky groves that blaze with flowering rhodo-dendrons and bristle with migrating birds." Roosevelt elk freely roam the prairies, and the endangered marbled murrelets fly across the treetops. *nps.gov/redw*

Haleakala National Park, Hawaii
Desolate volcanic landscapes, subtropical rainforests, and seemingly endless miles of hiking trails provide visitors with a unique tour of Hawaii's ecosystems. "Take the 38-mile drive from sea level to the 10,000-foot summit of Maui's volcanic Haleakala." The route "boasts among the world's steepest gradients and offers stunning views of ocean and lush rain forests." *nps.gov/hale*

Capitol Reef National Park, Utah
Don't let the name of this landlocked park fool you. The name
represents how the "hundreds of miles of ridges surf the desert."
Geologists go gaga over this park, and it's no secret why: a nearly
100-mile-long warp in the earth's crust, called the Waterpocket
Fold. Visit in late afternoon for "a spectacular show of light and
dark as the sun wanes. It's so remote that the nearest stoplight is
78 miles away." *nps.gov/care*

Power to the people's park

When vacationers cruise past the welcome signs to Great Smoky
Mountains National Park, they naturally start looking for the booth
where they'll cough up the entry fee, just like at every other top-tier
national park. Only here, there are no booths. No tackily khakied toll-
takers. No admission charge.

In one of the country's most visited national parks, all 521,085 acres,
384 miles of roads, and 100,000 life forms are free for the
exploring.

Free as the air you'll suck into your lungs when you climb to the
observation tower atop 6,643-foot Clingmans Dome.

All 100 varieties of trees and 66 types of mammals, including
1,500 bears—free as the wispy blue fog that gives the peaks their
name.

Nearly everything in this rich, majestic nature preserve is as free as
the birds—240 species of them, including the black-capped chicka-
dees that flit around Newfound Gap.

Even once you're in the park, it's hard to spend a dime. There's just
one lodge (LeConte Lodge), no restaurants, no gas stations. You
need only pull out your wallet at a couple of camp and souvenir
stores, the snack bars, the low-cost campgrounds, and the bicycle
and horseback-riding concessions.

About the only thing that can be spent here is time, as in the two
or three hours it might take during peak seasons to creep along
the 11-mile-loop road through the park's most popular section,
Cades Cove.

Carlsbad Caverns, New Mexico
Visitors trek through the Chihuahuan Desert and the Guadalupe
Mountains to get to the 113 caves hidden in this park. "Will Rogers
called it the 'Grand Canyon with a roof on it.' " Once inside the
park, visitors can opt to take the self-guided tour or one of the
guided tours. These vary in difficulty from very open areas to
crawling through narrow passageways, and "the bats take wing in
April." You've been warned. *nps.gov/cave*

Voyageurs National Park, Minnesota
"More than 30 lakes and 900 islands pepper this Minnesota water-
scape. Kayaks and canoes are preferred transportation once the
winter ice breaks in spring." In the forests surrounding the water,
visitors can see some of the oldest rock on earth on the shoreline.
Stay alert, though, as wolves and black bears call this park home.
nps.gov/voya

10 great places to take
the kids on a bike ride

*A family bike ride is a great way to get in some
exercise and fresh air while spending quality time
together. Michael Frank, executive editor of*
Mountain Bike *magazine, shares his recommendations
for car-free, scenic, and kid-friendly trails.*

Forest Park, Portland, Oregon
Forest Park is true to its
name—and at 5,161 acres,
it's the largest fully forested,
natural inner-city park in the
United States. "Enter and
you'd swear you're very far
from civilization. The niftiest
way to see the park is via Leif

Erikson Drive, an 11.2-mile, relatively flat dirt road that bisects the
greenbelt and is shared by joggers, hikers, and cyclists."
portlandonline.com/parks/

Burke-Gilman Trail, Seattle, Washington
"The 27-mile Burke-Gilman Trail goes along scenic Lake Washington—and rolls by wineries (Columbia, Chateau Ste. Michelle) and excellent restaurants such as the Herbfarm in Woodinville—ultimately linking up to the East Lake Sammamish River Trail." *cityofseattle.net/parks/BurkeGilman/bgtrail.htm*

Griffith Park, Los Angeles, California
This urban park in the heart of the city, home to the Los Angeles Zoo and the Griffith Observatory, is also rugged enough to harbor wildlife like foxes and deer. "While this isn't a cyclist's paradise, it's a great place for families to ride from attraction to attraction, including several playgrounds, a bird sanctuary, and a merry-go-round. The best loop runs along Crystal Springs Drive and Zoo Drive, then rolls back along the Los Angeles River and ends on Los Feliz Boulevard near the main entrance." *laparks.org/dos/parks/griffithPK/attractions.htm*

Lost Prospector Trail, Park City, Utah
Known as a skier's paradise and home of the Sundance Film Festival, Park City is also a mountain biker's nirvana. "On the seven-mile route called Lost Prospector, you can spy natural attractions, including lovely stands of aspen and frequent views of the epic Wasatch Crest peaks and a bird's-eye view of Park City." Want completely flat? Hit the less taxing 28-mile Union Pacific Rail Trail. *mountaintrails.org*

Charles River Bike Path, Boston, Massachusetts
"Beantown's bike scene is vibrant, and its path network is huge. One of the friendliest places to ride is along the 17-mile paved Charles River Bike Path, rolling by Harvard, the Museum of Science, and the Charles River Esplanade. Watch crew teams practicing, sailors racing, and kayakers enjoying the water." Rent a boat and join the fun, or stop for a family picnic by the riverside and watch. *mass.gov/dcr/recreate/biking.htm*

Summit County Recreational Path, Colorado
Summit County is interconnected with a 55-mile network of asphalt—nonmotorized pathways that link towns and resorts such as

Breckenridge, Dillon, and Copper. "Most climb and descend gently, and the Breckenridge area has an entire network of family-friendly, single-track dirt trails that use preexisting mining paths that date to the Colorado gold rush." *gobreck.com*

Mohonk Preserve, New Paltz, New York
This 6,500-acre nature preserve in the Shawangunk Mountains is about 90 miles north of New York City. "Miles of rolling carriage roads weave throughout the beautiful woodland and link to those at the adjacent Minnewaska State Park Preserve. Enjoy the mountain air and cliff views, and if you head out at dawn or dusk, you might be lucky enough to spot wildlife, including porcupines and owls." *mohonkpreserve.org/index.php?bike*

Florida Keys Overseas Heritage Trail, Key Largo, Florida
Old railways make perfect bicycle routes because they never climb or descend too steeply. "In Florida, which already is relatively flat, Henry Flagler's rail line, which linked the Keys to the mainland at the end of the 19th century, is being converted into a 106-mile path connecting the islands. Some of the existing sections go through Key Largo, Tavernier, Long Key Big Pine, and Stock Island, and side trips on county road shoulders make for beautiful riding." *dep.state.fl.us/gwt/state/keystrail/default.htm*

Battle Creek Regional Park, St. Paul, Minnesota
This large county park, with nearly eight miles of single track, arcs along its namesake tributary of the Mississippi River. "The riding can be challenging, but there are also mellower, wide dirt paths, and you can even ride from downtown St. Paul along a paved bike path that runs directly to the park." *co.ramsey.mn.us/parks*

Cape Fear River Trail, Fayetteville, North Carolina
One of the largest of all bike paths in the nation will be the East Coast Greenway, a 3,000-mile, car-free route that will stretch from northern Maine to southern Florida when it's completed. About 20 percent of the city-to-city system has been opened, and perhaps no segment is more typical than the Cape Fear River Trail. The 3.7-mile paved path features wooden walkways and bluebird houses. *fcpr.us/cape_fear_river_trail.aspx*

10 great leafy getaways
tucked away in the big city

*Getting back to nature doesn't necessarily mean
getting out of town. Nancy Somerville, executive
vice president and CEO of the American Society of Landscape
Architects, shares her list of favorite urban parks.*

Golden Gate Park, San Francisco, California
"There's not a bad time of year to visit this unique urban park."
There are so many trails, enclaves, gardens, and groves of exotic
trees that you can keep rediscovering on each visit. Among the
great finds are a glass-domed Victorian greenhouse, free Sunday
concerts performed by the park's own band, a small herd of bison,
and vintage Dutch windmills to pump irrigation water.
golden-gate-park.com

Teardrop Park, New York, New York
Teardrop Park is one of several green spaces that make up Battery
Park City. This community along the Hudson River in lower
Manhattan was created in part with earth and rocks excavated
for construction of the ill-fated and nearby World Trade Center
complex, which was destroyed in the 9/11 attacks. Teardrop is a
"wonderful gem of an urban oasis that might be overlooked by visitors to New York. Designed by award-winning landscape architect
Michael Van Valkenburgh, it includes a wonderful play area."
bpcparks.org

Millennium Park, Chicago, Illinois
Just north of the Art Institute, this downtown
gathering place blossoms into spring color
with tulips, daffodils, and crocuses. "The
24.5-acre park, which replaced an under-
utilized rail yard and parking garage, now
covers an underground parking lot and may
be one of the world's largest at-grade green
roofs. The park incorporates the work of well-
known designers and artists, including landscape architect

Gustafson Guthrie Nichol Ltd." Visitors spread out on the Great Lawn for free classical, jazz, and world music concerts throughout the summer. *millenniumpark.org*

Zilker Metropolitan Park, Austin, Texas
"Cypress trees and other riparian species surround the ornamental Lady Bird Lake with its active kayaking and sculling scene. Lady Bird Johnson helped create the ten-mile trail system that lines the lake named for her." Take a dip in the natural limestone-bottom swimming pool open year-round. Fed by a spring that gushes 69-degree water, generations of locals learned to swim in this iconic swimming hole. *www.ci.austin.tx.us/zilker*

Balboa Park, San Diego, California
"The many lush lawns and gardens here are like a trip around the world, from the Desert Garden and the two-acre Rose Garden to the Japanese Friendship Garden and Alcazar, designed after the gardens of Alcazar Castle in Spain." Known for its ornate Spanish Revival buildings constructed for the 1915 Exposition, the park also includes the San Diego Zoo and 15 museums. *balboapark.org*

Boston Common, Boston, Massachusetts
"Pick up a map and stroll along the grassy pathways shaded by gorgeous old trees to find the many Revolutionary and Civil War memorials throughout America's oldest park," which dates from 1634. The only frogs near the park's Frog Pond are the big brass sculpted ones that welcome you to skate there in winter; cool off under the 50-foot plume of water that shoots into the shallow pool in the summer; or contemplate near the reflection pool between seasons. *cityofboston.gov/parks*

Constitution Gardens, Washington, D.C.
"Located on Constitution Avenue, just north of the World War II memorial, this six-acre oasis from the bustle of the District is often overlooked by tourists and residents alike." Visit the pond with an island memorial to the signers of the Declaration of Independence. The surrounding park benches are a great place for enjoying a bag lunch while watching ducks and geese paddle in the garden pool. *nps.gov/coga*

Gas Works Park, Seattle, Washington

"A truly original park born out of a brown field—a former coal gas-ification plant—that artistically incorporates remnants of the site's industrial past. Landscape architect Richard Haag has won multiple awards for the design." The former boiler house is now a picnic shelter, and the exhauster-compressor building has been converted to a children's play barn in this unusual park with spectacular views of downtown Seattle. The park also is a favorite place to fly kites. *seattle.gov/parks*

Loring Park, Minneapolis, Minnesota

"Across the street from the Walker Art Center, this park was designed by landscape architect Horace Cleveland in the late 1800s. Known for its summer movie nights and arts festivals, it is also great for walking, biking, or just enjoying fresh air and foliage." *minneapolisparks.org*

George Washington Memorial Park, Jackson, Wyoming

"The elk-antler arches scream Wyoming, and a pause here makes for great relaxation before heading off into the wilderness and national parks that surround Jackson Hole." George Washington

Budget Travel Tips from the **USA TODAY Archive**

DINING

Dine in Ladies' Lingerie

For reasonably priced meals, try the restaurants or cafeterias of department stores.

—Jens Jurgen, founder, *Travel Companion Exchange*

Save space for dinner

Stay at a hotel or B&B that serves a continental breakfast. Opt to buy sandwiches at a local store for lunch. That way you'll have more to spend on a nicer dinner.

—Lysa Allman-Baldwin, senior travel writer, SoulOfAmerica.com

Memorial Park, aka the town square, was built in 1932, but the antler arches, commissioned by the Rotary Club, were added later from antlers dropped at a nearby elk refuge.
tetonwyo.org/agencyhome.asp?dept_id=parks

10 great national parks
that will engage your kids

*Planning a family vacation? There are few better
to ask for advice than Trefoni Rizzi, author of*
Teddy's Travels: America's National Parks, *a guide
for families. Here, he shares his list of favorite sites.*

Statue of Liberty National Monument &
Ellis Island Immigration Museum,
New York Harbor, New York/New Jersey

"Inside the statue base is a museum with an actual-size replica of Lady Liberty's foot. It's a great way to show children how large she really is. Board the ferry in Lower Manhattan or across the Hudson River in Jersey City. Point out Ellis Island on your boat trip and involve the children by asking them to imagine being a child on this huge journey across the ocean, coming to live in a strange country." *nps.gov/stli*

Cape Hatteras National Seashore, North Carolina
"This park is filled with the history of pirates, shipwrecks, and lighthouses. Check out the many 'Especially for Kids' programs at the visitors center to learn more. Kids will love taking the ferry from Hatteras Island to Ocracoke Island, and, best of all, it's free." *nps.gov/caha*

Great Smoky Mountains National Park,
Tennessee and North Carolina
"This is the Salamander Capital of the World: At least 30 species of salamanders are found here. Go on a hike and see the wildlife, including bears. Bring your camera and capture one of the many waterfalls. Great programs for kids include the ranger-led

interpretive talks, historical buildings, museums, and two working gristmills." Drive along the Blue Ridge Mountain Parkway for a wide-angle view. Take a picnic and stop at one of the scenic lookouts. *nps.gov/grsm*

Mount Rushmore National Memorial, South Dakota

"The sheer size of the sculptures can put a child's world in perspective. Join a ranger-led tour to the base of the sculpture to learn why the presidents on the mountain were chosen. Attend the Evening Lighting Ceremony for breathtaking views and drama." *nps.gov/moru*

Yellowstone National Park, Wyoming/Montana/Idaho

"You must visit Old Faithful and the geyser basin, but one of my favorite places in Yellowstone is the Mud Volcano/Sulphur Caldron area and the bubbling mud pots. As you drive through the park, watch for Continental Divide signs and count how often you cross it." *nps.gov/yell*

Yosemite National Park, California

"Hikes to the base of the waterfalls are fairly easy and pretty exciting too. Tuolumne Meadows offers more great hiking, incredible views, and meadows filled with wildflowers. Don't miss driving up to Glacier Point to look over the valley from above Curry Village. Bicycling is a great way to get to the features of the valley floor." *nps.gov/yose*

Olympic National Park, Washington state

"If you are in Seattle, half the adventure of a visit to Olympic is taking the ferry to get there. Olympic is like three parks in one: the mountains, the rain forest, and the ocean. Hikes in all three areas of the park will give your children the chance to experience the varied habitats and perhaps catch a glimpse of each area's wildlife. While on the trails in the rain forest, watch out for giant slugs." *nps.gov/olym*

Jefferson National Expansion Memorial, St. Louis, Missouri

No trip here would be complete without taking the tram ride to the top of the famed Gateway Arch. But there's much more. "This is a great place to learn about Lewis and Clark. The Museum of Westward Expansion, underneath the arch, takes you on a journey through the history of the American West." *nps.gov/jeff*

Carlsbad Caverns National Park, New Mexico
"Don't miss the Evening Bat Flight Program that runs from mid-May through October." Take a guided tour or do it on your own. While this park is about what's underground, wonderful hikes are above ground too. *nps.gov/cave*

Hawaii Volcanoes National Park, Big Island of Hawaii
"Take the Crater Rim Drive to see steam vents; recent lava flows; and the giant, fuming summit crater of Kilauea Volcano. For a fun nature walk, stop at Nahuku and walk through the tree fern forest and the lava tube." Check out the Pu'uloa Petroglyphs, located a short hike off the Chain of Craters Road. Stop by the Jaggar Museum to touch types of lava and make your own earthquake on the seismograph. *nps.gov/havo*

10 great places to slumber under the stars

The warm weather of summer makes it the perfect season for sleeping outdoors, and there is no more relaxing vacation than stretching out under a dark sky filled with bright stars and planets. Stephanie Pearson, senior editor of Outside *magazine, shares some of her favorite places for camping under clear skies— and possibly enjoying an otherworldly experience.*

Assateague Island National Seashore, Maryland/Virginia
This long sliver of an island, famous for its bands of wild horses, has Chincoteague Bay on one side, the Atlantic surf on the other, and endless miles of hiking trails between. "There's no potable water, so bring your own, and you'll have the stars to yourself." *nps.gov/asis*

Canyonlands National Park, Moab, Utah

"This unsung park does not get as crowded as neighboring Arches National Park. As night begins to fall, watch the sun blaze crimson until the 200-foot red-rock canyons frame the stars." *nps.gov/cany*

Big Bend National Park, Texas

"Right around Labor Day, things start cooling off in southwest Texas. The guaranteed coolest part of the park, with the biggest views to Mexico and the stars above, are the Chisos Mountains. Camp out in the Class A campground or stay at one of six stone cottages at Chisos Mountains Lodge." *nps.gov/bibe*

Sequoia High Sierra Camp,
Giant Sequoia National Monument, California

"The Sequoia High Sierra Camp, a 36-tent retreat nestled in the majesty of the Sequoia and Kings Canyon National Parks, comes equipped with down comforters and serves gourmet dinners—a welcome alternative to tight mummy bags and freeze-dried ice cream. Plus, at 8,282 feet, there's very little to obstruct your view of the heavens." *sequoiahighsierracamp.com*

Loreto Bay, Baja California, Mexico

"There are no private beaches in Mexico, so anyone can spend the night on a sandy stretch on the pristine Sea of Cortez, along the eastern shore of the Baja Californian peninsula." Campers can even pick a spot right behind a hotel. Since there is rarely cloud cover, in summer or winter, the view of the stars is nearly always assured. *gotoloreto.com*

Nelson's Dockyard, Antigua, West Indies

"When it comes to unadulterated stargazing, a sailboat makes a welcome change from a beach. On this driest of the British West Indies' Leeward Islands, clouds and rain will be scarce. Charter a boat at one of the island's marinas (Nelson's Dockyard is the most historic), and find your favorite vantage point in the Caribbean." Or simply stay aboard in the harbor and be rocked gently to sleep. *www.antigua-barbuda.org*

Denali National Park, Alaska

There are stars aplenty in the skies of the Last Frontier, plus a possible bonus: the aurora borealis, aka the Northern Lights, the ultimate nighttime heavenly spectacle. The show goes on all year-round but can be faint during summer in the United States; visibility is better as the nights grow longer and darker. Campers in Denali National Park should check with rangers for the best spots to avoid brown bears. Or, Pearson suggests, "consider bedding down at a place like Susitna River Lodge, a family-friendly resort on the banks of the Susitna River." The lodge is just outside Talkeetna, south of the national park. *nps.gov/dena*

Chaco Culture National Historical Park, New Mexico

"In the Land of Enchantment, nothing interferes with the night sky. Perhaps the best spot in the state for sleeping under the stars—not to mention exploring an impressively intact ancient ruin—is Chaco Canyon, 100 miles northwest of Albuquerque. This lonely valley sees only nine inches of rain a year, which makes for sublime camping, especially when the intense summer heat has passed. Stay at one of the park's 48 designated campsites." *nps.gov/chcu*

Lake Superior, Minnesota

"Even in the summertime, the Lake Superior air is crisp, making the Minnesota sky seem even sharper. Camp at one of the many state parks that line the lake's northern shore or along the Superior Hiking Trail, which features some glorious granite peaks that make you feel as close to the sky as you'll get in the relatively flat Midwest." *www.dnr.state.mn.us/index.htm; shta.org*

Singita Lebombo Lodge, Kruger National Park, South Africa

The Singita Game Reserve in the Lebombo concession of Kruger National Park is home to the Singita Lebombo Lodge, which provides guests with beds on their balconies for an incredible experience—and picture-perfect views of a deep sky reaching to other galaxies. "Because this is the Southern Hemisphere, the Southern Cross is visible in all its glory. Just remember that the seasons of the year are reversed." *singita.com/lebombo.html*

10 great places to pitch in at a park

Lend a hand for the common good by volunteering at one of the nation's state parks. Will Rogers, president of the Trust for Public Land, a nonprofit organization for land conservation, offers his list of parks to enjoy and enrich.

Andrew Molera State Park, California

"This beach-access park, with open meadows and redwood forests, is one of the crown jewels of the Big Sur coast. Camp hosts—volunteers who live in the park for several months without charge—are needed here. They usually stay in their RVs, although one host tent site is available during the summer." Duties range from greeting hikers and campers to doing trail work. The park is a worldwide birding destination and offers great marine life and animal viewing. *parks.ca.gov/?page_id=582*

Tomoka State Park, Florida

"This amazing place is a historic treasure trove. There's a tribal village, sugar mills, and one of the largest oak trees in the South—all in a highly urbanized county" near Daytona Beach. Campground hosts, who help guests feel welcome, are always needed, especially in the summer, when many snowbird volunteers return home. After work, volunteers kick back, play cards, or have potluck dinners. *floridastateparks.org/tomoka*

Mesilla Valley Bosque State Park, New Mexico

"The gorgeous park…is part of a system of state parks strung along the Rio Grande. Many volunteers teach in the Outdoor Classroom here." Docents, many of them former teachers or teacher hopefuls, help bring to life stations on wildlife tracking, water quality, plants, and birding habitats. *emnrd.state.nm.us/prd/mesillavalley.htm*

Minnewaska State Park Preserve, New York
"Volunteer hikers, mountain bikers, rock climbers, and skiers assist in patrols and maintenance in this 21,000-acre park with lakes and waterfalls in the Shawangunk Mountains," an area in the Hudson Valley region known to climbers around the world.

Voices from the wilderness

Here's a sampling of national park memories from USA TODAY readers.

Grizzled camper bests a bear

When our four children were young, visiting the closest national parks was an affordable way to vacation. The kids slept in a tent, while my husband and I slept in a converted truck bed.

One night in Yosemite, I woke up to find the truck-bed camper rocking back and forth. I knew it was a bear. My grumpy husband got up, leaned forward, and opened the hatch.

"You're right," he said, sticking his head back in. "It's a bear."

My heart was racing. I was afraid for my children in the nearby tent. But my husband stuck his head back outside, waved his arms, and growled.

The bear scampered away.

—Beverly D., North Las Vegas, Nevada

Beauty is a common language

Twenty years ago, we camped at the Grand Canyon. On the third afternoon, we hiked out to the rim to catch the sunset. We found a great spot, along with 30 to 35 other people from different countries, speaking French, Japanese, German.

The colors and shadows of the sunset in the canyon were so inspiring, so incredible, that as the sun crossed the horizon all of us present could only exchange smiles. Spontaneously, everyone stood and applauded!

My family will never forget that simple experience we shared with each other and the other travelers, with whom we found a way to communicate.

—Bob W., Ballwin, Missouri

Mountain bikers patrol 35 miles of old carriage roads, assist with enforcement of helmet laws, and radio for staff in emergencies; climber volunteers work on climbing access roads; and ski patrol volunteers sweep skiers out of the park before nightfall in the winter. *nysparks.state.ny.us/parks*

Kiptopeke State Park, Virginia

"This water-oriented park, at the very southern tip of Virginia's Eastern Shore, provides access to the Chesapeake Bay and its waterways. You can fish from the pier, crab from the beach, swim, or go out on a boat." Volunteers can work in the flower garden and butterfly gardens or help with special projects as needed. Bring a kayak and go island-hopping in the bay or visit a vineyard. *dcr.virginia.gov/state_parks/kip.shtml*

William B. Umstead State Park, North Carolina

"Acres of old-growth oak, beech, and hickory shade this urban oasis just minutes from Raleigh and Cary. It is a great escape into the wilderness, with lots of creeks and streams, horse-back riding, bicycling, and hiking trails." A wide range of volunteer opportunities, including litter cleanup, vine removal, and maintenance of the many 1930s-era timber buildings, are available, along with camping options.
ncparks.gov/Visit/parks/wium/main.php

Pinnacle Mountain State Park, Arkansas

"The interconnectivity of this dramatic mountain park, going from wilderness to downtown Little Rock—including the William J. Clinton Presidential Center—makes it a great place to visit or volunteer." Volunteer opportunities in this day-use park vary from repairing signs to assisting trail guides with their interpretive program. *arkansasstateparks.com/pinnaclemountain*

Palo Duro Canyon State Park, Texas

"This park, called the Grand Canyon of Texas, is dazzling, especially the bright, banded cliffs. Volunteers serve as camp hosts in exchange for an RV site. They also get the pleasure of being in this ecological and historic treasure." In addition, the park in the Texas Panhandle has 1,500 acres of equestrian trails in the horse-camping area, where volunteers can help. *palodurocanyon.com*

Punderson State Park, Ohio
"If you want to take photos of moraines, kames, and eskers, this park needs you. These glacial remnants, and resulting lakes called kettle lakes, dominate the park. You'll see wetlands and bogs, teeming with wildlife too." *dnr.state.oh.us/parks*

Ebey's Landing National Historical Reserve, Washington state
"A 17,400-acre reserve encompasses the historic seaport town of Coupeville on Whidbey Island in the Puget Sound. It is also home to two historic state parks—Fort Ebey and Fort Case, complete with armories and canons used for WWII coastal defense." Volunteers help with prairie revegetation, office assistance, event planning, and docent work. Rocky beaches and steep bluffs with views of mountains, working farmland, and Puget Sound are part of the remarkable setting. *nps.gov/ebla*

PLANTS AND ANIMALS

10 great places to catch a whale of a sighting

There's good whale watching somewhere in the world during most any season. Trevor Day, author of Whale Watcher: A Global Guide to Watching Whales, Dolphins, and Porpoises in the Wild, *tells where to spot the behemoths.*

The Azores, Portugal
Visitors to this Portuguese archipelago in the Atlantic Ocean, about 1,000 miles from Lisbon, view whales and dolphins from lookout towers called *vigias.* Small whale-watching vessels also operate tours. "From May to October, see sperm whales, the largest of all toothed whales at up to 59 feet long and weighing up to 55 tons."

Look too for several species of beaked whale rarely seen elsewhere. *destinazores.com/whalewatching.php*

Dominica, West Indies

The deep waters off the west coast of this Caribbean island attract the blunt-headed sperm whales year-round. "Winter, though, is the best time to see these sperm whales, along with humpback whales that come to Dominica's bays to breed and reward visitors with acrobatic displays." *dominica.dm/site/whalewatching.cfm*

Hermanus, South Africa

"Hermanus offers some of the best land-based whale watching in the world. Several hundred Southern right whales migrate past its shores between July and November." Playful and sometimes curious, the 50-foot adults court and mate while pregnant mothers calve. *hermanus.co.za*

Glacier Bay, Alaska

Glacier Bay is where whale experts first studied humpback whales "bubble-netting"—blowing bubbles to herd fish into a tight ball before swallowing them. "If visitors are really lucky, they can see up to a dozen whales engaged in this remarkable hunting technique." Groups of orcas (killer whales) patrol the entrance to the bay, while porpoises and dolphins are commonly seen inside the bay. Best time to visit: June to early September. *whale-watching-alaska.com*

Hervey Bay, Queensland, Australia

Between July and November (winter and early spring Down Under), humpback whales hurl themselves clear out of the water in exuberant displays in the quiet, protected waters of Hervey Bay. "Humpbacks grow to more than 50 feet long and can weigh nearly 50 tons. Yet these gentle creatures are curious, and some will approach boats." *herveybaywhales.com*

Monterey Bay, California
Visitors can see whales, dolphins, and porpoises in the vicinity
of Monterey Bay year-round. "In mid-December to April, see
migrating gray whales. In summer and fall, humpback whales and
the world's largest whale, the blue whale, migrate here to feed."
Pods of orcas are farther out. *seemonterey.com/tourist-activities/
enjoying-the-outdoors/animals-and-wildlife*

Stellwagen Bank, Massachusetts
Southern New England hosts over 30 companies offering whale-
watching tours from more than 15 seaside communities. "A focus is
Stellwagen Bank, a submerged sandbank that runs from the tip of
Cape Cod to Boston's north shore at Cape Ann. April to May is the
best time to see the highly endangered Northern right whale (only
a few hundred survive). Between April and October, spectacular
humpback whales are a common sight."
stellwagen.noaa.gov/visit/welcome.html

Peninsula Valdes, Patagonia, Argentina
Peninsula Valdes is a hot spot for Southern right whales and orcas.
"Southern right whales arrive in July and stay to November, but the
best time to see them is September to October. A remarkable spectacle is watching them 'sail' on the wind, with their flukes raised

Whale moves

Watch closely while whale watching, and you'll probably spot the
whales performing a few classic moves. Puffs of wet air, for instance,
might spout 10 to 15 feet from the behe-
moths' blowholes. Or you might see
"fluking," when the whales' powerful
split tails rise from the water in
preparation for a dive. If a whale
pops only its head above water
for a look around, that's "spy hop-
ping." And it can also "breach" by launching its entire body out of the
water for a dramatic but ungainly belly flop.

in the air to catch the breeze. Orcas are present year-round, but from mid-February to mid-April, they hunt sea-lion pups and on selected beaches will ride onto the shore to snatch pups."

Vancouver and Vancouver Island, British Columbia, Canada
More than 400 orcas swim in the waters around Vancouver. "Between May and September, visitors can see the whales by ferry, cruise ship, whale-watch boat, and even from the land." In summer, about 40 to 50 gray whales also feed in the waters off Vancouver Island. In March and April, many more pass through on their northward migration. *britishcolumbia.com/WhaleWatch*

Sea of Cortez, Baja California, Mexico
"The Gulf of California (Sea of Cortez) just south of Baja, or 'lower' California, is arguably the best place to see the world's largest whales, blue whales. These 75-foot giants, weighing more than 100 tons, are regularly seen between January [and] April along with several other baleen (filter-feeding) whales, such as the humpback and fin." In the same season, gray whales, with their barnacled and scarred bodies, court and calve in the lagoons. *bajaexpo.com/whales.htm*

10 great places to be awed by a rain forest

After more than 20 years of photographing rain forests, Thomas Marent, whose work appears in the coffee-table book Rainforest, *remains fascinated by their "incredibly high biodiversity, all the bright colors, and extraordinary weird shapes." Marent shares his choices of the world's best rain forests.*

Fiordland National Park, New Zealand
"This is the most beautiful landscape of rain forests because everything is covered by moss, lichen, and ferns," Marent says of this temperate rain forest in the south of New Zealand's South Island. "But it is poor in biodiversity because of its cold climate." *doc.govt.nz/ parks-and-recreation/national-parks/fiordland/*

Danum Valley, Sabah, Malaysia

"Scientists say that the Danum Valley in Sabah (on Borneo) is the hot spot of the rain forest in Asia. There are lots of carnivorous pitcher plants and the largest flower in the world, rafflesia," which can weigh 15 pounds or more. Danum Valley also is home to more than 275 bird species and more than 100 species of mammals, including giant flying squirrels, gibbons, bearded wild boars, flying frogs, Asian elephants, and Sumatran rhinoceroses. "Unfortunately, [the area] is highly dangerous because of ruthless logging."

Southern New Guinea Lowland Rain Forests, New Guinea

"The rain forests in New Guinea have the paradise birds, the largest butterflies in the world, and some other weird insects. It is hard to get there, and there are almost no tourists—just scientists and missionaries."

Gondwana Rain Forests, Australia

In this region on Australia's east coast, "there are some interesting endemic species, like the bower birds and cassowary. And it has good access for visiting the forests." *whc.unesco.org/en/list/368*

East Coast of Madagascar, Madagascar

The rain forests on this island off the east coast of Africa are disappearing because of farming and timber harvesting. What remains is a "paradise for chameleons; weird geckos; and, of course, the lemurs, which are very threatened." *rainforestfoundationuk.org/Madagascar*

Congo Rain Forest, Congo

In this African rain forest, one of the most threatened in the world, "you can find some of the most fascinating animals, like the gorillas and the chimps. But political problems make it difficult to access." *rainforests.mongabay.com/congo*

Atlantic Rain Forest, Brazil

See it before it's gone. "This is probably the rain forest that has suffered the most destruction." High population growth has obliterated all but about 4 percent of the original rain forest. "There are amazing species like the golden lion tamarin (monkey) that are in danger."

The Amazon, Brazil
"What I like about the Amazon is the high diversity." The world's largest rain forest covers about 3.4 million square miles; the bulk of it is in Brazil, but it also encompasses parts of nine South American countries. The rain forest "starts along the east of the Andes, where you find cloud forests with different species; then in the lowland forest, you can see lots of animals and plants closer because the trees are not as tall." Thousands of species of trees and plants coexist with a like number of insects and birds. Among critters encountered: jaguars, tapirs, vampire bats, anaconda snakes, and leaf-cutter ants. *amazon-rainforest.org*

Choco Rain Forest, Ecuador and Colombia
The Choco, which runs along the Pacific Coast of Ecuador and Colombia, "is even wetter than the Amazon and not well researched yet." Two reasons for its largely undiscovered status: drug smugglers and Colombian guerrillas, who make the area dangerous. Some species, such as the Colombian black spider monkey, live nowhere else.

Corcovado National Park, Costa Rica
"The rain forests in Costa Rica are probably the best-visited rain forests by tourists and scientists in the world. You can visit different kinds, like cloud forests and lowland forests on the Pacific Coast." Look for scarlet macaws, red-eyed tree frogs, and squirrel monkeys among hundreds of species of birds, amphibians, reptiles, and mammals that inhabit Corcovado.
centralamerica.com/cr/parks/mocorcovado.htm

10 great places to experience spring on the wing

You know it must be springtime when you wake up to the sound of singing birds instead of snow blowers. John Flicker, president of the National Audubon Society, shares his list of favorite spring bird-watching sites.

Kern River Preserve, Weldon, California
"Southern California's Kern River Valley sits at the juncture of six major ecoregions, providing a microcosm of California's rich bird diversity all in one place. During the spring months, visitors can spot more than 200 species of birds here." The Kern River Valley Spring Nature Festival, held annually at the preserve, offers guided bird walks, exhibits, and other activities for birding enthusiasts. *kern.audubon.org*

Francis Beidler Forest Sanctuary, Harleyville, South Carolina
Located in the heart of South Carolina's Lowcountry between Columbia and Charleston, this sanctuary sprawls over 15,000 acres of swamp forest, some of which is old growth that's more than 1,000 years old. "A 1.75-mile boardwalk takes visitors into a virtual cathedral of ancient cypress trees, a truly  spectacular setting. Birds are everywhere in the spring, with tiny warblers singing their insistent songs and owls calling out even in midday." *sc.audubon.org/centers_fbf.html*

Rowe Sanctuary, Gibbon, Nebraska
Each spring along Nebraska's Platte River, more than half a million sandhill cranes stop off to rest and refuel during their northward migration. This annual long-haul flight takes the cranes from their winter home along the Texas Gulf Coast to summer breeding grounds in Alaska and Eastern Siberia. "The viewing blinds at Rowe Sanctuary are the place to be predawn, as these magnificent

birds wake up and then fly out for breakfast. Viewers are treated to an amazing spectacle of sound and flight." *rowesanctuary.org*

Waunita Lek, Gunnison, Colorado
"One of the rarest birds in the world, the Gunnison Sage-grouse also has one of the most dramatic mating displays, with males performing an elaborate dance ritual to attract females." Each spring, birding enthusiasts can observe this bizarre show at Waunita Lek, a breeding ground about 20 miles east of Gunnison. "Make sure you're in place before sunrise." *siskadee.org*

High Island, Texas
"From late March through early May, millions of birds fly up to the Texas Gulf Coast from Mexico, looking for food and safety on their way north." One of the best places to view the spring migration is High Island, about 45 miles south of Beaumont, where the Houston Audubon Society has four sanctuaries. "If

Budget Travel Tips *from the* **USA TODAY Archive**

TRANSPORTATION

Think small
When renting a car, specify a subcompact or the smallest car size of which you are aware. In many cases, you are automatically upgraded, often because they don't stock up on subcompacts. You will automatically get a bigger car without spending an extra penny.
—Arthur Frommer, founder, Frommer's travel guides

Then think big
Ask for the lowest rate, the most economical car. Then ask how much it would be to upgrade to the next level. Most often, it is about $1 to $5 per day extra.
—Joel Widzer, *The Penny Pincher's Passport to Luxury Travel*

you're lucky, you may get to experience a 'fallout,' when warblers, thrushes, buntings, orioles, and other migratory songbirds seem to fall out of the skies all at once." *birdinghighisland.com*

Eastern Egg Rock, Muscongus Bay, Maine
"Some of the richest bird habitats occur where the land meets the sea. Coastal Maine is such a place, and some of the best birding occurs from the boats that tour the nesting seabird islands like Eastern Egg Rock." Puffins, razorbills, terns, gulls, and many other seabirds take advantage of the rich coastal waters here. "Puffins are very social birds and are especially fun to watch." *projectpuffin.org*

Ottawa National Wildlife Refuge, Oak Harbor, Ohio
This popular bird-viewing refuge is a living remnant of the Great Black Swamp, a marshland that once encompassed 300,000 acres on the southern edge of Lake Erie. Today, 9,000 acres of this habitat are preserved in the refuge, a stop-off point for several species of migratory birds. "Warblers, willets, teal, waterfowl, and various shore birds accumulate here each spring in great numbers." *fws.gov/midwest/ottawa*

Central Park, New York, New York
"Most people think of bird-watching as a rural pastime. But year after year, Central Park in midtown Manhattan hosts one of the most enjoyable spring migration parades in the country. The urban surroundings require the birds to move to the best natural habitat in the neighborhood—and for thousands of songbirds every spring, that means Central Park. It's a huge green spot that draws migrating birds in like a magnet." *centralpark.com*

Souris Loop National Wildlife Refuges, Minot, North Dakota
Minot, in the northwestern part of North Dakota, is surrounded by the Souris Loop National Wildlife Refuges, which comprise three protected habitats that feature restored marshes, lakes, native grassland, lowland meadows, and sandhills. "By late May,

the refuges are teeming with waterbirds, including five species of grebes, sharp-tailed grouse, Sprague's pipits, and several rare species of sparrows." *ndparks.com/nature/birding.htm*

Tara Wildlife, Vicksburg, Mississippi
Huge numbers of birds fly north up the Mississippi River every spring. One of the best places to see the migration is Tara Wildlife, a privately owned, 17,000-acre reserve about 30 minutes northwest of Vicksburg. "A unique bird to look for here is the painted bunting, a bird-watcher's favorite. It's a beautiful, multicolored bird that looks like it was designed by committee." *tarawildlife.com*

10 great places to go on safari—in the USA

Lions and tigers and rhinos, oh my! And right here in the United States, no less. Nancy Schretter, managing editor of the Family Travel Network, has been scouting safari sites nationwide since seeing wild ponies at Assateague Island as a child. Here, she shares her favorites.

Moose Alley, northern New Hampshire
"Route 3 running from Pittsburg, New Hampshire, north to the Canadian border, affectionately dubbed Moose Alley, is a great place to take a moose safari. The best times to see these huge, majestic creatures are in the early morning and at dusk. Designated a 'Watchable Wildlife Corridor,' there is a viewing station on Route 26 in Dixville Notch." *northcountrychamber.org*

Cumberland Island National Seashore, St. Marys, Georgia
Accessible only by ferry, Georgia's southernmost barrier island is an unspoiled beach destination. "It's home to nesting sea turtles as well as manatees, wild horses, white-tailed deer, bobcats, armadillos, raccoons, otters, and more than 300 species of birds.

You'll find mansions and ruins located throughout this wilderness island, originally home to the Carnegies and other prominent families. Come over for the day, camp overnight, or stay at the historic Greyfield Inn." *nps.gov/cuis*

Everglades National Park, Homestead, Florida
"This 1.4-million-acre park is teeming with wildlife. Take a safari through the lush sea of grasses of Florida Bay or through the backcountry Wilderness Waterway to see manatees, crocodiles, deer, wild hogs, alligators, roseate spoonbills, great blue herons, hawks, eagles, and a wide variety of other birds that varies by season. There are privately run boat tours with park-trained naturalists who provide an interpretation of the resources at both the Flamingo and Everglades City entrances into Everglades National Park." *nps.gov/ever*

The Living Desert, Palm Desert, California
"There are many family-friendly activities here. From January through May, you can sleep in tents on overnight Starry Safaris that feature a special Wildlife Wonders Presentation, dinner, and a guided nighttime walk through the park." Look too for cheetahs, sand cats, badgers, and baby foxes at this zoological park. *livingdesert.org*

Spring Creek Ranch, Jackson Hole, Wyoming
"Spring Creek Ranch, located near Grand Teton National Park and Yellowstone National Park, offers a variety of wildlife safaris in the parks for its guests. The safaris are led by the staff naturalist. Wildlife viewing may include herds of bison, moose, elk, mule deer, pronghorn antelope, coyotes, and birds of prey." *springcreekranch.com*

Fossil Rim Wildlife Center, Glen Rose, Texas
"If you can't take the family to Africa this year, Fossil Rim is the next best thing. More than 1,100 animals representing 60 species

AND ANOTHER THING . . .

UNLOCK NATURE'S STRONGHOLDS AROUND THE WORLD

If you'd like to explore the wildlife reserves of other countries, check out this list from husband-and-wife writing team and naturalists William and Laura Riley.

- Serengeti National Park, Tanzania—Every spring, "1.5 million wildebeest, the world's largest migratory group, trek in search of fresh water and grass to give birth to their young—thousands on a single morning. Watching for stragglers: lions, leopards, cheetahs."

- Bandhavgarh National Park, India—"Once a maharaja's private hunting preserve for his friends to kill countless Bengal tigers, this reserve is now the protected home for these magnificent striped predators." Not to miss: "rare jungle cats, elephants, hyenas, chital deer, and more than 200 avian species."

- Danube Delta, Romania—"This 2,417-square-mile delta, the largest wetland in Europe, features thousands of white pelicans that fill the sky with a pinkish glow. Other tenants include 2,500 pairs of pygmy cormorants, thousands of little bitterns, iridescent multicolored bee-eaters, and violet rollers."

- South Georgia, Antarctica—"This sub-Antarctic island is the wildlife high spot, with more than two million fur seals, five million macaroni penguins, and large colonies of majestic king penguins. Blue whales, the largest of all mammals, swim by occasionally."

- Danum Valley Conservation Area, Borneo, South Pacific—"Here are 162 square miles of primary rain forest buffered by another 3,860 square miles of similar habitat with orangutans, Sumatran rhinos, Asian elephants, shy sun bears, leaf monkeys, and more."

- Great Barrier Reef, Australia—"It's the marine equivalent of a terrestrial rain forest and one of the most species-rich environments on earth."

- Pantanal, Brazil—"Seasonally a wetland half the size of France, this is home to giant anteaters, rare maned wolves, 300-pound jaguars, spotted ocelots, and giant river otters."

roam freely on 1,800 acres—including giraffes, Thomson's gazelles, cheetahs, zebras, wildebeests, rhinos, oryxes, and seven other varieties of antelope. For that true safari feeling, stay overnight in a tented cabin at the Foothills Safari Camp overlooking one of Fossil Rim's most popular wildlife watering holes." *fossilrim.com*

Isle Royale National Park, Michigan
"Isle Royale is a remote island located in the northwest quadrant of Lake Superior. This wilderness national park, the site of the world's longest-running wolf/moose predator/prey study, is a sanctuary for these two magnificent animals. They are two of the main attractions here, but visitors can also spot beaver, red fox, lynx, snowshoe hare, mink, osprey, and bald eagles. Access is by ferry or float plane only." *nps.gov/isro*

Chincoteague National Wildlife Refuge, Assateague Island, Virginia
"Come to this 37-mile-long barrier island to see herds of the famous wild ponies at the refuge, as well as tiny Sika elk, fox squirrels, muskrats, white-tailed deer, raccoons, and more than 300 varieties of birds—and stay for the beautiful beaches, fishing, hiking, and biking." Camping is permitted on the Maryland side of the island. *chinco.fws.gov*

National Bison Range, Moiese, Montana
"Hundreds of buffalo, along with elk, bighorn sheep, black bear, white-tailed and mule deer, pronghorn antelope, and coyotes roam 18,766 acres here. More than 200 species of birds can also be found in this area. The best time to visit is mid-May through mid-September." *bisonrange.fws.gov*

Denali National Park, Denali Park, Alaska
"Alaska is like the domestic equivalent of Kenya or Tanzania. There are so many fabulous places to see wildlife that it's difficult to pick just one. In south-central Alaska, for example, one can journey to Denali, where 39 species of mammals dwell,

and view grizzly bears, sheep, and moose." Cruise companies offer packages that include Denali land excursions. *nps.gov/dena*

10 great places to see animals on their home turf

Next time you're in need of an animal fix, veer away from the zoos and check out a more natural animal habitat. David Mizejewski, a naturalist with the National Wildlife Federation and correspondent for the Animal Planet series SpringWatch USA, *offers his suggestions.*

Rocky Mountain Arsenal National Wildlife Refuge, Commerce City, Colorado
Just 11 miles from downtown Denver, the Rocky Mountain Arsenal National Wildlife Refuge is home to a diverse group of critters that includes coyotes, red foxes, raccoons, badgers, deer, black-tailed prairie dogs, birds of prey, seven species of snakes, and a herd of bison. "Visitors who come to this neck of the woods can take part in nature programs [or] go on nature trails." *fws.gov/rockymountainarsenal*

Indian Boundary Prairies, Markham, Illinois
This area, just south of Chicago, is known as a biological "ark" for the future, with more than 350 insect species as well as an array of birds, gray foxes, amphibians, and reptiles. "The prairies are in full bloom in April, and it's a great time to plan a trip to experience nature, bird-watch, and learn more about prairie life." *ibprairies.org*

Kiawah Island, South Carolina
Just off the coast of South Carolina outside Charleston, this family-friendly resort island is simply majestic for wildlife watching. "You can catch a glimpse of the gray fox, the white-tailed deer, alligators, bobcats, and diamondback terrapins. And during spring, all are in the prime of birthing and egg-laying season." *kiawahresort.com*

Lewes, Delaware

"A smorgasbord of natural wonders" describes this coastal region of Delaware. "During the spring, it's all about the horseshoe crab, which spawn and lay millions of eggs—many of which, in turn, become dining delicacies for migrating birds." Some of the notable fowl that can be spotted include the red knot, snow geese on their way to the Arctic, and long-tailed ducks. And in the water near the end of spring—mid- to late May—the cow-nosed ray makes an appearance in the sandy, soft bottom waters. *www.destateparks.com/chsp/chsp.htm*

Rowe Sanctuary, Gibbon, Nebraska

Starting in March and continuing into April, visitors to the Platte River Valley in south-central Nebraska can see the world's largest congregation of sandhill cranes, known for their harmonious sounds and dancing rituals. "More than a half million of the wading birds use wetlands as a 'layover' on their migratory journey." *rowesanctuary.org*

Monterey, California

Monterey, on the Pacific coast south of San Francisco, is one of the top destinations to witness sea otters, gray whales, and other marine creatures. One of the major springtime attractions: gray whales making their way north. *seemonterey.com*

Yellowstone National Park, Idaho/Wyoming/Montana

"Yellowstone National Park is a springtime hot spot, if you truly want to be at one with the natural world and have a fabulous time doing so. The park is blooming. You see a variety of wildlife, including amphibians, mountain lions, moose, coyotes, and unique birds, as well as just-born bison, one of the most popular spring attractions." *nps.gov/yell*

Moosehead Lake Region, Greenville, Maine

Spring is perfect for spotting the famous moose of this lake region in north-central Maine. "The best times to watch are in the early morning or around dusk—and the moose prefer shady, wet areas. Only males grow antlers, which they shed in early winter and regrow during the year and display during the fall mating season." Each spring, the region hosts Moose Mania, featuring such family-friendly activities as a canoe race and crafts fair. *mooseheadlake.org*

Congress Avenue Bridge, Austin, Texas
March marks the return of 1.5 million Mexican free-tailed bats that migrate to and from Mexico each winter. They hang around until Halloween or thereabouts. "The massive colony—the world's largest urban bat colony—lives under the Congress Avenue Bridge and makes for spectacular viewing during the spring and summer." *austincityguide.com/content/congress-bridge-bats-austin.asp*

Arizona-Sonora Desert Museum, Tucson, Arizona
Various cacti, ocotillo, mesquite, palo verde, and numerous desert wildflowers "bloom in mad profusion in spring." With nearly two miles of hiking trails and more than 21 acres of desert, the museum combines the best of a nature center, a zoo, and a botanic garden. "Rattlesnakes, mule deer, and gray foxes will all be there. So will Gambel's quail, roadrunners, cactus wrens, and Gila woodpeckers, all of which will be nesting. Javelina (a wild-boar-like animal) will be having babies in the spring. Regal horned lizards and Gila monsters will be laying eggs, as will king-snakes." *desertmuseum.org*

10 great places to look up to a tree

"Only God can make a tree," poet Joyce Kilmer wrote. But it's people who plant them—and save them. Deborah Gangloff, executive director of American Forests, describes some of the champion trees listed on the National Register of Big Trees.

General Sherman giant sequoia, Sequoia National Park, California
The national champion giant sequoia—the world's biggest tree and largest living thing—reigns over this park almost midway between

Taking great scenic photos can be a snap

Whether you travel with a point-and-shoot or enough high-tech gear to qualify for a *National Geographic* assignment, these tips can help ensure your photos are top quality.

- **Pack an alarm clock.** Rising before dawn may not be most travelers' idea of a relaxing vacation, admits longtime travel photographer Bob Krist, a columnist for *National Geographic Traveler*. But the "magic light" during the hour and a half after sunrise and before sunset is ideal for photographs, he says. As a bonus, "you'll find far fewer crowds than in the middle of the day."

- **Look for unusual angles.** "People don't trust their own vision and playfulness enough," says Jeff Wignall, author of *The Kodak Guide to Shooting Great Travel Pictures*. "If you see the Eiffel Tower through a café window, it will probably be a much better shot than one taken head-on from two blocks away."

- **Getting above it all can help too.** City street scenes and markets that seem chaotic from ground level often look orderly from a second-floor balcony, Krist says.

- **Include local faces.** "Photographing people isn't for the shy of heart," acknowledges photographer and lecturer Nevada Wier, author of *Adventure Travel Photography*. "You have to be friendly and forthright and have a lot of panache to approach strangers."

- **Use a flash for outdoor portraits.** Despite the fact that most cameras include an automatic fill flash, many outdoor photographers forget to use it when shooting people against a bright background. The result: deeply shadowed silhouettes.

- **Think small.** Focusing on details can often establish a more meaningful sense of place than an overview, advises Wignall. A favorite example: a series of photos exploring doorknockers on European cathedrals.

- **Do your homework.** Even if you limit your research to scoping out the postcard rack in your hotel lobby, it's helpful to know what kinds of local scenes have caught other photographers' fancies, Wignall says. And pretrip reading can alert you to out-of-the-way places you'd otherwise miss.

San Francisco and Los Angeles. "It's as tall as a 27-story building and would take 15 people to encircle it." One of three remaining champions from the first Big Tree list (1945), it's between 1,500 and 3,500 years old. *nps.gov/seki/snrm/gf/new/sherman.htm*

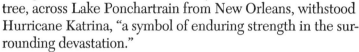

Seven Sisters live oak, Lewisburg, Louisiana
Its sprawling, low limbs and shady crown allow the live oak to withstand hurricane-strength wind and rain. This 1,200-year-old tree, across Lake Ponchartrain from New Orleans, withstood Hurricane Katrina, "a symbol of enduring strength in the surrounding devastation." *louisianagardenclubs.org/live_oak_society/about.html*

Jujube, U.S. Capitol grounds, Washington, D.C.
The 61-foot-high national champion Jujube—one of many jujube trees on the Capitol grounds—is the only national champion in the District of Columbia "but far from the only national treasure."

Honey mesquite, Hill Country, Texas
One of the primary features of the picturesque landscape in the part of the Texas Hill Country that meets the South Texas Brushlands is the dozen or so monumental trees in Real and Uvalde counties, including bald cypress, honey mesquite, and Texas live oak. The national champion honey mesquite "is just inside the fence of an old family ranch" in Real County "on one of the state's most scenic farm-to-market roads." *texasforestservice.tamu.edu/main/default.aspx*

Hawthorns, Morton Arboretum, Lisle, Illinois
The arboretum's 1,700 acres (25 miles west of Chicago) contain more than 3,700 types of plants and trees, among them three national champion hawthorns—a fireberry, a broadleaf, and a Kansas (found in northern Illinois). All hawthorns are low-growing, but they develop a lot of character: Older ones often have "twisting branches that grow up to the sky and then back down toward the ground." *mortonarb.org/explore.html*

Yellow tulip poplar, Bedford, Virginia
The largest tulip poplar tree in the world
and the largest tree in Virginia, this
national champion is in Bedford's 1-1/2-
acre public Poplar Park on Grand Arbre
Drive. At 146 feet tall, the tree is worth
a few minutes' drive from Poplar Forest,
Thomas Jefferson's summer home, which
he named "for the beautiful tulip poplars
in the region." *visitbedford.com*

Sitka spruce and Western red cedar, Olympic National Park,
Washington
"If you are interested in seeing some big trees and taking a bit
of a hike to get there, the eight national champions in Olympic
National Park are perfect." The park's big trees include the sub-
alpine fir, Western hemlock, Western red cedar, Sitka spruce, and
mountain hemlock. The fourth-biggest champion tree in the country is the cochampion Sitka spruce; the Western red cedar, "like
the General Sherman giant sequoia in California," is one of the few
original champions. *nps.gov/olym*

Coast Douglas fir and Coast redwoods, Jedediah Smith Redwoods
State Park, California
"A trip to the Jedediah Smith Redwoods State Park in northern
California will put you in the presence of some jaw-dropping
mega-trees." The champion Coast Douglas fir "is one of the few
remaining of its kind." And the national cochampion Coast redwoods, named the Lost Monarch and the Del Norte Titan, are second only to the General Sherman in size. These redwoods and the
forest surrounding them are "an impressive sight, making you feel
tiny beneath their boughs." *parks.ca.gov/default.asp?page_id=413*

Eastern hemlock, Great Smoky Mountains National Park,
North Carolina and Tennessee
This park holds the record for big tree champions in a national
park: 16. "Unlike some other locations, [here] it is hard work finding champions . . . most are on trails spread throughout the park. So
if you plan on visiting . . . bring your tent and sleeping bag." Most

notable is the 165-foot-tall Eastern hemlock, but the park's tallest peak, Clingmans Dome, offers "plenty of ridgeline views along the way to the park's champion trees."
nps.gov/grsm/pphtml/subnaturalfeatures32.html

Soldierwood and red stopper, Key Largo, Florida
The Florida Keys are home to nearly 50 national champion trees, about 20 of them on Key Largo. They're much smaller than the West Coast giants, "but bigger isn't always better." The champion red stopper, in Key Largo Hammock Botanical Park, looks almost Caribbean with its peach-colored bark. In addition, two of Key Largo's three champion soldierwoods are in the John Pennekamp Coral Reef State Park. *floridastateparks.org/keylargohammock/default.cfm; pennekamppark.com*

10 great places to go wild over zoo animals

Newt Gingrich, former speaker of the House of Representatives, says his first act of public service was a childhood visit to a city council meeting in his hometown of Harrisburg, Pennsylvania, where he gave an impassioned speech on why the city needed a zoo. "We didn't get the zoo, but since then I've had the pleasure of touring dozens of zoos around the world," says Gingrich, who wrote an introduction for the book America's Best Zoos. *Here, he shares his favorites.*

San Diego Zoo and Wild Animal Park, San Diego, California
One of the largest and most progressive zoos in the world, the San Diego Zoo pioneered the concept of open-air, "cageless" exhibits that re-create natural animal habitats. The zoo also operates the Wild Animal Park, which displays animals in a more expansive environment toured by tram. "These two great facilities combine to form the best zoo in the world, with an amazing array of quality exhibits." *sandiegozoo.org*

Zoo Atlanta, Atlanta, Georgia
"Zoo Atlanta has a world-class gorilla exhibit, and the reptile house has a superb collection that includes two Komodo dragons." The

zoo also boasts impressive naturalistic habitats for elephants, black rhinos, Sumatran tigers, and a pair of giant pandas. *zooatlanta.org*

Disney's Animal Kingdom, Walt Disney World, Orlando, Florida
"More than just a zoo, the Animal Kingdom is an extraordinary experience of animals, rides, and performances. The exhibits have the scale and creativity you associate with Disney. The African safari ride is terrific and worth riding several times." The park also features an interactive animal conservation exhibit for kids and a troop of rare silverback gorillas. *disneyworld.com*

Central Park Zoo, New York, New York
"The Central Park Zoo is a little gem in the middle of the city. Its penguin exhibit is terrific, and the seals are a permanent center of attraction for children." The zoo's history dates back to the 1860s, when animals were first displayed at the southeast corner of Central Park. Completely revamped in the mid-1980s, the facility also added a children's zoo in 1997 that lets kids interact with gentle creatures up close. *centralparkzoo.com*

Audubon Zoo, New Orleans, Louisiana
"The Audubon Zoo is just a few blocks from Tulane University. They have done a brilliant job here creating a modern zoo in a historic park setting. The Louisiana swamp exhibit—which includes unique white alligators—is truly spectacular." Another popular attraction is a re-created Mayan archaeological dig set in a jungle rain forest amid monkeys and jaguars. *auduboninstitute.org*

National Zoo, Washington, D.C.
Formally known as the Smithsonian National Zoological Park, this zoo is best known for its three giant pandas—one of which

was born at the zoo. "The cheetah exhibit here is first-rate, and the reptile house is fascinating. There is also a wonderful orangutan exhibit where the orangs can climb from one area to another over the heads of visitors." *nationalzoo.si.edu*

Cincinnati Zoo, Cincinnati, Ohio
Opened in 1875, this facility on 65 acres in the central city is
the second-oldest zoo in the United States. "Cincinnati has one
of the most diverse animal collections in the world, with more
than 500 species represented. They also have a really good insect
exhibit." The zoo's giraffe habitat allows visitors to encounter the
animals at eye level. *cincinnatizoo.org*

Arizona-Sonora Desert Museum, Tucson, Arizona
"This innovative and highly specialized facility is a zoo, museum,
and botanical garden all in one." Walking along two miles of paths
that meander through a preserved desert landscape, visitors can
view interpretive displays of animals and plants native to the
Sonoran Desert, an arid region encompassing parts of Arizona,
California, and northern Mexico. Among the animals on display are
mountain lions, Gila monsters, and the rare Mexican wolf.
desertmuseum.org

Palm Beach Zoo, Palm Beach, Florida
The Palm Beach Zoo houses more than 1,500 animals within
23 acres of lush tropical habitat. "The lake in the middle
of the zoo attracts a remarkable array of local birds, and
for Northerners it is a great introduc-
tion to the beauty of Florida
fauna. The zoo also has a
world-class jaguar exhibit,
wonderful giant anteaters,
and rare Malayan tigers."
palmbeachzoo.org

ZooAmerica, Hershey, Pennsylvania
"This is the place where I spent many wonderful childhood afternoons, wandering around and imagining that someday I could
become a zookeeper. It's built around a stream and has beautiful
winding walkways—just a delightful place to take children that
allows them to see animals up close and enjoy them."
zooamerica.com

10 great places to peep at the peak foliage

Think fall colors, and the back roads of Vermont and New Hampshire immediately come to mind. But plenty of other locales for exploring seasonal foliage are often overlooked—even in New England. Scotty Johnston, a fall-foliage guide with Tauck World Discovery, suggests some less familiar places to see autumn's artistry.

Brooklyn Botanic Garden, Brooklyn, New York
"When you think of fall's colors in New York, you're thinking the Adirondacks and places upstate. It's surprising to find a place to look at foliage in an urban area." Brooklyn Botanic features 52 acres of gardens filled with 10,000 kinds of trees and plants from around the world. When to visit: late October and early November. *bbg.org*

Porcupine Mountains, Michigan
In the northern section of Michigan's Upper Peninsula is an area of about 60,000 acres along the shores of Lake Superior. "The area has an amazing contrast of colors. Several hikes offer a panoramic view of the red, orange, and yellow mountains with the blue of Lake Superior. There's also an evergreen tree called hemlock, which offers more contrast." When to visit: late September. *porcupinemountains.com*

Color alerts

Planning a tour to see the turning leaves? The U.S. Forest Service (fs.fed.us) and the Tauck Tours Foliage Hot Line (800-214-8209) offer recorded updates on the status of fall foliage around the United States.

Crested Butte-Gunnison, Colorado

"The foliage is a different kind from what we find in the East. You get three distinct shades along the long slopes. At higher altitudes is the western larch that turns a beige color. At the mid-slope is the aspen tree, which turns a beautiful gold color. When you get down low along the river valley, you have the soft yellow shade of cottonwood." Drive between Crested Butte and Gunnison through the Kebler Pass and along the Gunnison River almost anytime in September for great views. *gunnisoncrestedbutte.com*

Litchfield County, Connecticut

"The area is virtually overshadowed by Vermont and New Hampshire, but it's part of the Appalachian chain and has beautiful foliage. There are also antique shops, craft fairs, pumpkin picking, and unique items like the covered bridge in Cornwall." When to visit: the third and fourth weeks of October. *litchfieldcty.com*

United States National Arboretum, Washington, D.C.

"China and Japan have amazing foli-age." And much of it can be found right here at the National Arboretum: "You'll see things more common in Asia." Drive, bicycle, or walk the 446-acre site. When to visit: late October and early November. *usna.usda.gov*

The Pig Trail, Arkansas

The Pig Trail, officially known as Highway 23, cuts 19 miles through the Ozark Mountains between the towns of Ozark and Brashears in northwestern Arkansas. "It's a wiggly old highway that reminded people of a pig's tail. There are abundant good views, and the canopy of the trees form a verdant archway." When to visit: late October and early November.
arkansas.com/things-to-do/scenic-drives/pig-trail.asp

Acadia National Park, Maine

"People don't think of the coast as a good foliage spot, but it's just as beautiful. It's just as beautiful as the scarlets and golds contrast with the blue of the Atlantic. And the colors appear later and last longer because the ocean has a moderating influence." For a spectacular vista, head to the summit of the park's Cadillac Mountain, the highest point along the Atlantic. Peak season usually starts in mid-October. *nps.gov/acad*

Shenandoah National Park, Virginia

There are amazing places to see autumn's colors all along the Blue Ridge Parkway, a 469-mile national scenic byway that runs from Virginia into North Carolina. During the third week of October, head to Shenandoah National Park, north of the parkway in Virginia. "The fall wildflowers add even more color to autumn's spectacle. There are astor, goldenrod, and harebells." *nps.gov/shen*

Santa Fe, New Mexico

The Western larch, aspen, and cottonwood are the highlights of the foliage near the Sangre de Cristo Mountains outside Santa Fe. Ski Santa Fe offers chairlift rides with panoramic views. Fall color is usually at its peak the first two weeks of October. *santafe.org*

Lake Louise, Alberta, Canada

The trees are similar to what you'll find in Colorado, but the area offers a stunning contrast of colors. "The lake is a beautiful azure blue. The fall foliage and the glacier on the other end make it a picture-taker's delight. There's hiking and canoeing. And you might hear the male elk. It's a profound sound when you hear it as you come through the mountains." When to visit: mid- to late September. *banfflakelouise.com*

People travel for the same reason as they collect works of art: because the best people do it.

—Aldous Huxley

BEACHES
10 great tickets to a warm, sunny island paradise

It's never too soon to start planning for a warm-weather island getaway. Steve Davey, author of Unforgettable Islands to Escape to Before You Die, *shares his picks.*

Bali, Indonesia
This Indonesian island features palm-tree-fringed beaches, bustling villages, exotic crafts, and much more. "You can be hiking through rice terraces in the morning and lying on a beautiful beach in the afternoon. It's a cultural haven of temples and temple festivals. Every day seems to be a festival day, and the food is glorious."
bali-tourism-board.com

Huahine, French Polynesia
The French Polynesian islands all feature beautiful landscapes of dramatic peaks and turquoise lagoons. And this idyllic getaway is no exception, though it's much less renowned than nearby Tahiti. "The lesser known Huahine maintains a vibrant sense of community, where you can still hang out in local bars and restaurants, as well as relax on an idyllic beach paradise. The lagoon is full of all manner of tropical fish, and you can even snorkel with rays and reef sharks."
go-to-tahiti.com/islands/huahine/huahine.asp

St. Lucia, West Indies
This volcanic island in the Caribbean is more mountainous than most islands there. "It is a laid-back yet stylish island, dominated by the twin peaks of the Pitons." In addition to snorkeling, diving, and other water-based activities, there are various trails through the rain-forest-covered mountains. The island also features a now-

329

dormant volcano, which visitors can drive into and see the steamy sulfur springs. *stlucia.org*

Yasawa Islands, Fiji
"Usually you have to spend serious money to enjoy the best beach-side properties, but in the Yasawa Islands you will find a range of midrange and even backpacker places right on the waterfront." These islands in the South Pacific "are craggy and verdant green. Right at the end of the chain is the fabled Blue Lagoon from the film of the same name." *fijime.com*

Islands of Phang Nga Bay, Thailand
Most of the islands in Phang Nga Bay, off the west coast of Thailand, are uninhabited but reachable by boat. "Some of the islands are tiny, and others are towering crags of scoured lime-

---

Budget Travel Tips *from the* USA TODAY Archive

LODGING

Don't be taken to the cleaners

Everything in the hotel is a profit center. I would not use the laundry in the hotel anytime. There probably are dry cleaners with 24-hour service ten minutes away. Pizza places deliver.

—Peter Greenberg, *The Travel Detective*

Be direct about it

Call direct instead of booking over the Internet. You cannot negotiate with a computer. You can use the Internet to find out what is available; it gives you a good benchmark for the prices available.

When you're talking to the reservationist, ask them to put a note in your record requesting an upgrade or a nicer room. This applies much more overseas. People overseas tend to be more rules-structured, and if they see [a note] in there when you check in, they tend to feel like they must do it. Every time I've asked them to do that in Europe, I've been upgraded.

—Joel Widzer, *The Penny Pincher's Passport to Luxury Travel*

stone, resembling those melted wax candlesticks popular in '70s bistros. Take a boat and explore these islands, and you can lounge on a beach on your own all day, kayak into a lagoon, or meet local sea gypsies, who farm tiny birds' nests for the Chinese soup market." Also worth a stop: James Bond Island, featured in the film *The Man with the Golden Gun. phuket.com/island/phangnga.htm*

Aitutaki, the Cook Islands

"The pearl of the Cook Islands has to be Aitutaki, which has the most perfect lagoon in the world." The entire South Pacific island is set within a lagoon, enclosed by a barrier reef. Come for the snorkeling, swimming, or just relaxing by the clear waters. "The iridescent turquoise waters are dotted with tiny, sand-fringed islets. This is a place that redefines paradise." *cookislands.travel*

Cousine Island, the Seychelles

This private island in the Indian Ocean off the east coast of Africa is a nature reserve known for its birds, marine life, and severe restrictions on tourism. "Cousine is a boutique resort of four chalets on a tiny, ecologically unique island in the Seychelles. All of the profits are put into the preservation of the island and research by the resident naturalists. The only time you will  have to share the perfect curve of beach is when the turtles come out of the sea to lay their eggs." *cousineisland.com/3-cousine.php*

Eleuthera, the Bahamas

"Less developed than much of the Bahamas, Eleuthera boasts some of the best beaches in the Caribbean and a quiet, rustic charm." The island, the first permanent settlement in the Bahamas, also offers snorkeling and diving among the coral reefs and shipwrecks. "And it is home to one of the most perfect beach-bar restaurants you will find anywhere. Tippy's has a small wooden veranda overlooking the beach and a predictably good choice of rum." *www.bahamas.com*

Lord Howe Island, Australia
This dot off the east coast of Australia "is a quiet, laid-back ecological paradise, with many endemic plant species, deserted beaches, and fine walks." The crescent-shaped island protects a coral reef and lagoon, while the island itself features subtropical forests and two mountains made from the remnants of lava flow *lordhoweisland.info*

Vanuatu, South Pacific
"People are tremendously important to an unforgettable island, and Vanuatu is reputed to be the most friendly place in the world, inhabited by the happiest people." This island nation in the South Pacific was a model for James Michener's storied Bali Hai in his work *Tales of the South Pacific.* "There is fantastic diving here. And naghol, or land-diving. This forerunner of the modern bungee jump involves locals throwing themselves from towers, held only by vines around their ankles." *southpacific.org/guide/vanuatu.html*

10 great places to go coastal with your kids

Know before you go on a family beach week that not all stretches of sand and ocean are created equal, says Stephen Leatherman (aka Dr. Beach), professor and director of the International Hurricane Research Center & Laboratory for Coastal Research at Florida International University in Miami. "Taking the kids to the beach can be a great experience, if you choose the right one." Author of Beach Vacation Travel Journal, Dr. Beach's Survival Guide, *and* America's Best Beaches, *he offers a list of sandy fun-in-the-sun family destinations.*

North Beach (Fort De Soto Park), St. Petersburg, Florida
"A great place to do all things beachy, such as swimming in the warm, clear waters; fishing in the channels between the five islands; bird-watching; barbecuing at one of the many grills; camping in the park; exploring a Civil War fort; fishing off one of two long piers; taking a ferry over to an island in the mouth of Tampa Bay; bringing your bike or renting one to roam the miles of paved trails." *pinellascounty.org/park/05_Ft_DeSoto.htm*

Rehoboth Beach, Delaware
"This small-town beach is known for its mile-long wooden board-walk, great for strolling or watching fresh french fries and saltwater taffy being made. There is a fun amusement park at the south end with great bumper cars. Make sure to bring your boogie board, because there's good surf on most days." *cityofrehoboth.com*

Myrtle Beach, South Carolina
"This popular beach is part of the Grand Strand that extends some 60 miles. Although it gets a bit crowded, the kids will have fun swimming and shelling on this very-fine-sand beach. Look for small, elongated coquina clams, which wash up between waves. Nearby, there are water parks galore." *visitmyrtlebeach.com*

East Beach, Santa Barbara, California
"This popular beach, which faces southward, has better weather (more sunny days) than most beaches in Southern California, courtesy of the mountain. Beach sports include Frisbee and volley-ball, kayaking, parasailing, or biking and in-line skating on the paved trail. This small town, a fun place to explore, has some great seafood restaurants." *santabarbara.com/activities/beaches*

Cannon Beach, Oregon
"While the water is chilly, even in summer, children still love to run and splash in it here. The sand is remarkably fine and the beach flat; at low tide, it's hundreds of feet wide, so it's great for build-ing sand castles. (There's an annual sand-castle-sculpting contest in June.) Just offshore sits the 235-foot-high Haystack Rock, an impressive backdrop to this beautiful beach, where exploring the intertidal pools yields starfish, sea urchins, and other interesting creatures." *cannonbeach.org*

Coronado Beach, San Diego, California
"This 1½-mile-long beach is an oasis within the San Diego area but a world away on an offshore island accessible by bridge. The

This beach is right on deck

And the latest gee-whiz thing on a cruise ship is . . . a beach.

Royal Caribbean's *Oasis of the Seas*—the largest ship ever built—is the first in the industry with a "beach pool" that re-creates the vibe of a shoreside resort. Built with a beachlike sloping entry (with faux sand) where passengers can wade into rolling waters and surrounded by beach chairs, the pool is part of a four-pool complex known as the Pool and Sports Zone—the largest decktop area ever designed for a ship.

The Pool and Sports Zone also has a main pool, a sports pool for such activities as water polo, and one of the line's signature H_2O Zone water play pools. The area also has two FlowRider surfing simulators and private decktop cabanas.

The more than 220,000-ton *Oasis of the Seas* can hold a record 5,400 passengers at double occupancy—a once-unthinkable number in the cruise business. It's so big that it can dock in only a handful of ports, including Cozumel, Mexico, and Charlotte Amalie, St. Thomas.

water is warm and calm, great for swimming, and the beach is flat and glimmering because of tiny flakes of mica in the sand. The San Diego Zoo and Sea World are nearby."
a-zsandiegobeaches.com/coronadocitybeach.htm

Cooper Beach, Southampton, New York
"Here at these world-famous Hampton beaches, Cooper is a wide sandy area backed by large grassy sand dunes. The beach face can be fairly steep—some kids like to run and jump into the surf—and there are good rolling breakers for board

surfing or bodysurfing. An added extra: The beach pavilion has tasty food and ice cream." *southamptonchamber.com*

Holden Beach, North Carolina

"This 11-mile-long barrier island has been developed as a family beach. You can swim in the warm, safe waters; beachcomb for shells; fish from the surf; or go boating on the ocean or the Intracoastal Waterway. At night, chase the ghost crabs with a flashlight—they dart quickly across the beach and have serious pinchers, which means you don't really want to catch them." *hbtownhall.com*

Panama City Beach, Florida

"Bring the sunglasses when you visit this stunning stretch of beach boasting the finest, whitest sand in the world. The shallow, clean, emerald-green water normally has no waves, which makes this a great beach for swimming and snorkeling. Other activities include arcades, amusement parks, and miniature golf." *pcbeach.org*

Coast Guard Beach, Cape Cod, Massachusetts

"Outer Cape Cod is one of the world's special places. The old white Coast Guard Station sits on a sea cliff, and down below you see Nauset Spit and the salt marshes. In Colonial days, lobsters were so numerous, they were caught by hand in the tidal channels; today, you have to dive offshore or go to a nearby restaurant. While the water is nippy, a short dip is always refreshing. Bring your kite, as the wind always seems to be blowing on this island, known for 'free air conditioning.' " *capecodchamber.org*

Leisure is the mother of Philosophy.
—Thomas Hobbes

10 great places to leave the swimsuit at home

Don't look now, but nude recreation is more widespread than you think: 40 million Americans have skinny-dipped in mixed company, according to a Roper poll, and a YPB&R/Yankelovich Partners travel survey revealed that vacationers rated access to nude recreation higher than golf or tennis in choosing a destination. American Association for Nude Recreation president John Kinman recommends top clothing-optional beaches.

Little Beach, Maui, Hawaii
"Makena State Park, on the island of Maui, can lay claim to two stunning beaches: Big Beach and clothing-optional Little Beach. The nude beach continues to thrive because the local community recognizes the positive economic impact of naturist travelers from the mainland U.S. and Europe."
littlebeachmaui.com

Wreck Beach, Vancouver, British Columbia, Canada
"Wreck Beach, Canada's first and largest legal clothing-optional beach, is so spectacularly beautiful that it is a mecca for tourists from all over the world. The confluence of the Fraser River with the Straits of Georgia and English Bay, under white cliffs and an emerald-green forest, attracts more than 500,000 visitors annually."

Cap d'Agde, France
Cap d'Agde, on the Vermeille coast of south-central France, has earned the sobriquet of the World's Capital of Nudism. In the "naturist quarter" of this resort town on the Mediterranean Sea, nudity is legal not only on the beach but also in banks, restaurants, and shops. Too much of a good thing? Just head down the road. "Nearly every beach in southern France is topless."
www.capdagde.com

Hawksbill Bay, Antigua
The Caribbean island of Antigua is said to have 365 beaches, one for every day in the year. "For a nudist beach, check out the crescent-shaped coves of scenic Hawksbill Bay, one of which is clothing-optional. Some of the secluded Ffryes Bay beaches are unofficially clothing-optional."

Haulover Beach, Miami Beach, Florida
The northern end of Haulover Beach is a clothing-optional "good-citizen" success story: A nudist-lobbying campaign reclaimed a park infested with drug dealers. "As a city facility, Haulover has great amenities, including barbecue grills, refreshment stands, and lifeguards." Not to mention one million visitors a year.

Gunnison Beach, Sandy Hook, New Jersey
Gunnison Beach is one of several beaches in northern New Jersey's Gateway National Recreation Area, on the Sandy Hook peninsula. Boasting a panoramic view of New York Harbor and Lower Manhattan, Gunnison is legally recognized as clothing optional, with official signs, a lifeguard, and police protection. "As the largest clothing-optional beach on the Atlantic coast of the United States, Gunnison draws more than 5,000 visitors a day on sunny summer weekends." *gunnisonbeach.org*

Collins Beach/Rooster Rock, Columbia River, Oregon
The "Mighty Columbia" near Portland is host to two clothing-optional beaches, both of which can fill up on sunny days: Rooster Rock State Park, the country's first officially designated clothing-optional beach, and Collins Beach on Sauvie Island, where some 75 percent of the users go nude or topless, while the rest choose to wear suits. "The crowd of friendly people here creates a true community atmosphere." *oregonstateparks.org/park_175.php*

Orient Bay, St. Martin, West Indies
Orient Bay, on the French side of the island of St. Martin–St. Maarten, is a popular destination for naturist vacationers, thanks to

its proximity to Grand Case, considered by many to be the gourmet capital of the Caribbean for its mingling of French, Dutch, and West Indian cuisines. "Although the clothing-optional beach is right in front of the Club Orient Resort, one need not be a guest of the hotel to bathe there."

Samurai Beach, Port Stephens, Australia
Within the bounds of Tomaree National Park, about 120 miles north of Sydney, lies ruggedly unspoiled Samurai Beach, one of the first legal nude beaches Down Under. "Samurai Beach is famous in the naturist world for hosting the annual Nude Olympics every November, with events like the Nude Torch Relay."

Black's Beach, San Diego, California
"Black's Beach is a breathtaking one-mile stretch of state-controlled coastline, where nude and suited sunbathers can enjoy views of porpoises riding distant breakers and hang gliders soaring from cliffs above. Black's Beach has never officially been designated as clothing-optional, but authorities acknowledge that nude bathers will not be hassled." Caution: Physical access to the beach is daunting because of the steep grade. *blacksbeach.org*

10 great places to have some fun on a boardwalk

"People love boardwalks for the same reason they wax nostalgic about the small-town Main Street of yesteryear," says Steve Millburg, senior editor at Coastal Living *magazine. "It's a community gathering place where you can meet friends and make new ones. Boardwalks literally elevate you out of the ordinary." Here, Millburg shares some favorites.*

Kemah, Texas
"The Kemah Boardwalk draws four million visitors a year to this once-sleepy town on Galveston Bay near Houston. In addition to

showcasing overpriced, tourist-oriented restaurants, the boardwalk also includes amusement rides, shops, an unpredictably programmed water-jet fountain (a definite kid favorite), and a surprisingly nice boutique hotel called the Boardwalk Inn." *kemahboardwalk.com*

Old Orchard Beach, Maine

"This pier and small boardwalk is big on old-fashioned charm. Kids still play Skee-Ball at a beachfront arcade across from the Palace Playland amusement park. As with all great boardwalks, there's a certain amount of what some might call tackiness here, although I prefer to think of it as American vernacular." *oldorchardbeachmaine.com*

Long Beach, Washington

"The aptly named Long Beach Peninsula, 28 miles of sand, stretches like a beckoning finger along the Pacific Ocean at Washington's southwest corner. You won't find games or taffy stands on the Long Beach Boardwalk, just interpretive displays about the dunes, water, and wildlife. But this low-key planked pathway parallels the beach, where kite fliers congregate year-round." *funbeach.com*

Ocean City, Maryland

"More than any other, this boardwalk brings back that exhilarating teenage sense of summer-vacation freedom and possibility. Throbbing with energy day and night, fueled by Thrasher's fries soaked in vinegar (a true delicacy), the 'walk' features cool reversible benches that flip back and forth, depending on whether you want to gaze at the Atlantic Ocean or the passing parade along the boardwalk itself." *ococean.com*

Santa Cruz, California

"I love this boardwalk, even if it is one of the 'boardless' varieties. Actually, Santa Cruz Beach Boardwalk refers to both the seaside amusement park and the concrete path that runs through it. Here, find everything from

a classic wooden roller coaster, a 1911 carousel, arcade and video games, and an extra-wide beach with volleyball nets to free concerts, great surfing and windsurfing, and a half-mile-long pier lined with seafood restaurants. Coastal nirvana." *beachboardwalk.com*

Hollywood, Florida
"They call it 'the Broadwalk' here—a 2-1/2-mile paved promenade along the sand in this low-key community between Miami and Fort Lauderdale. Concerts, dances, and theater productions liven the beach as cafés, shops, and modest motels line the other side of the Broadwalk. The whole scene is reminiscent of a small town that happens to sit on a palm-studded beach, complete with locals who stake out their favorite shady spots." *visithollywoodfl.org*

Virginia Beach, Virginia
"A boardwalk in spirit if not in composition—it's concrete—this path runs three miles past beachfront hotels, restaurants, stores, museums, bike-rental shops, and street performers. Three stages present free summer entertainment, and two small museums belly up to the boardwalk." *vabeach.com*

Ocean City, New Jersey
"OC offers as much fun, energy, and great food as you'll find anywhere in an amazingly clean, family-friendly atmosphere. This old Methodist-camp-meeting town has banned alcohol since 1879, so those looking to party congregate elsewhere." *oceancity-nj.com*

Venice, California
"Venice Beach offers the best people-watching on the planet. Street performers, sand sculptors, body builders, panhandlers, and

those best categorized as 'other' hang out all along the concrete boardwalk, aka Ocean Front Walk. Restaurants, flea markets, and boutiques line the nonbeach side, interspersed with some chic homes. Not recommended after dark, but everyone should visit here at least once." *laparks.org/venice/enter.htm*

Ketchikan, Alaska

"Shops, galleries, and museums occupy a haphazard collection of stilt-legged structures along a boardwalk that forms an actual street, Creek Street, which borders Ketchikan Creek. Perfectly respectable, the area nevertheless retains a certain raffishness left over from its past as the town's red-light district. And because this is Alaska, look in any direction for a vista of breathtaking natural beauty." *ketchikanchamber.com*

10 great places to rule an island

The fantasy is common: to escape to a deserted isle, far from the madding crowd. To loll on a beach with only seagulls (and someone special) for company. To reign over a private piece of paradise. Living out the fantasy is increasingly easy at one of the countless privately owned islands for rent around the world. Melissa Biggs Bradley, founder of Indagare Travel, picks ten islands—from sublimely hedonistic to naturally rustic—to call your own.

Little St. Simons Island, Georgia

"One of the last privately owned barrier islands, this 10,000-acre nature preserve is fabulous for its wildlife: deer, sea turtles, 280 species of birds." Set amid moss-draped forests, creeks, and beaches, the main lodge (built in 1917) and three cottages accommodate just 32 guests. "With its big family-style meals, it's perfect for family reunions." *littlestsimonsisland.com.*

Little Palm Island, Florida

A former fishing camp for presidents Roosevelt, Truman, Kennedy, and Nixon, this five-acre honeymoon haven in the Keys is "so exotic it doesn't seem to be in the United States. Mangoes, palms, and bougainvillea surround the very pretty beach and 14 thatched huts." A star chef turns out winning meals in a thatched open-air dining room lighted by torches. *littlepalmisland.com*

Gooseberry Island, Nova Scotia

Stay at the three-bedroom house on the island's rocky coast and you're likely to "wear fisherman-knit sweaters, take long coastal walks, curl up with a book by the fireplace, and listen to the wind howl outside. A great retreat for a writer."

Necker Island, British Virgin Islands

"A Balinese transplant in the middle of the Caribbean, this 74-acre isle offers the ultimate setting for a posh house-party weekend." Owned by Virgin Atlantic's Richard Branson, who was married there, it has accommodated the likes of Oprah Winfrey, Mel Gibson, and Princess Diana in its three lavish open-air villas. A staff of 26 pampers just 28 lucky souls. *neckerisland.com*.

Little Whale Cay, Bahamas

Imagine a 93-acre isle with peacocks and flamingos in the gardens; shells and bougainvillea in the three guesthouses; and its own landing strip, tennis court, and chapel (for intimate weddings). Robinson Crusoe never had it this good. *littlewhalecay.com*

Pine Cay, Turks and Caicos, British West Indies

"You arrive by boat, take off your shoes, wade ashore, and don't put your shoes back on until you leave." With its two-mile-long dazzling white beach, clear turquoise water, and 12 simple rooms, this resort is "the ultimate place to drop out and recharge your batteries." *pine-cay.com*

Bedarra Island, Australia

"The most exclusive of the island resorts off the Great Barrier Reef, it has 16 treehouse-style rooms tucked into the edge of a rain forest. A fabulous chef and incredible diving and snorkeling" make it special. No wonder the Duchess of York rented the whole island for herself and her entourage. *bedarra.com.au*

Turtle Island, Fiji

The quintessential "castaway South Pacific island was the location for the film *The Blue Lagoon.*" Lush tropical foliage envelops 14 thatched beachside bungalows clustered around the lagoon. "A boat will take you to one of 14 secluded beaches and pick you up again—perfect for honeymooners." *turtlefiji.com.*

Frégate Island, Seychelles

"Home to rare animals and plants, this is a mini version of the Galapagos Islands but in the Indian Ocean. Seven beaches, a tropical

---

Budget Travel Tips *from the* USA TODAY Archive

SHOPPING

Look for specialty items

Don't shop for things you can buy at home, like clothes (except in Paris and London). Look for what [the locals] do best.

—Sandra Gustafson, *Great Sleeps/Great Eats* series

Ship it and ship out

Do a little research prior to your trip to find out what products or services a location is known for and, if possible, learn what differentiates quality from trash. For large, delicate, or expensive items, consider the advantages of having it shipped directly to your home after you return. The items may also be insurable—which they are not if they are carried in your luggage on a plane. You might also save on duties or taxes by having your souvenirs shipped.

—Lysa Allman-Baldwin, senior travel writer, SoulOfAmerica.com

jungle, fruit and vegetable plantations, and incredible bird-watching draw sophisticated environmentalists, who stay in 16 villas with Thai silk, rare antiques, and Asian artwork." *fregate.com*

Mnemba Island, Zanzibar

Gilligan's island couldn't have been more idyllic than this Indian Ocean atoll, where "dolphins are the welcoming committee, and the dining is barefoot and fabulous." Ten hand-woven palm cottages peek through the foliage at the beach and coral reef that ring the isle. "A simple, chic place popular with Europeans." *mnemba-island.com*

10 great places for summer's last sand

It's always so hard to face the end of summer—and the end of beach season, a fate worse than rain for dedicated strand fans. Can't bear to put away your beach bag? Joan Tapper, contributing editor to Caribbean Travel & Life, *suggests these shore-thing places to forestall fall.*

Kauai, Hawaii

At the remote Barking Sands beach in Polihale State Park, "you hear this sharp, yipping sound" from the 100-foot dunes when wind or movement agitates the sand. Beware the riptides though. "More benign choices include Mahaulepu, kind of a locals' beach that's not really developed" on the south side, "and on the north side, beautiful Kee Beach, which has great snorkeling." *kauai-hawaii.com*

Santa Barbara, California

"The water is at its warmest in September, after it's had the summer to heat up. Go to Arroyo Burro Beach, which the locals call Hendry's Beach. You can see the dolphins from shore or look over to the Channel Islands. I recommend long sunset walks." *santabarbaraca.com*

Ilha Grande, Brazil
Besides mountainous jungles and ruins, the "Big Island" not far south of Rio de Janeiro is "full of beautiful beaches yet out of the hustle and bustle of Rio." The colonial port of Vila Abraão is "a nice little town" on the north side, where "the beaches are calmer; those on the southeast coast are better for diving." *ilhagrande.com.ar*

Shelter Island, New York
Nestled between the North and South Forks of Long Island, this island-within-an-island harbors a nature preserve that takes up nearly a third of its 8,000 acres. "September can be pretty warm," and the peaceful, rural island offers miles of breezy beaches, as well as nature and bird-watching trails, "good bicycling," and three deep-water harbors with marinas. *shelter-island.org*

Île de Ré, France
A long bridge connects the town of La Rochelle, on the west coast, with this sandy isle. The long, flat beaches have "incredible tides that go way in and way out. They make for wonderful gathering" of winkles, clams, and other mollusks. "The light is gorgeous, and the

island is known for its artists and galleries." A popular getaway, it's still warm in September when the August crowds are gone. *holidays-iledere.co.uk*

Whidbey Island, Washington
The longest of the San Juan Islands, this 45-mile strip has several state parks, and most of them include sandy beaches. "Head for Deception Pass State Park, especially for a low-tide walk on the beach or kayaking." It's on the northern end of the island and has "that Northwest look": forested hills, rocky headlands, and lakes for swimming and fishing. *whidbeycamanoislands.com*

The Outer Banks, North Carolina

"These barrier islands form long ridges of sand, [creating] incredible dunescapes." The protected Cape Hatteras National Seashore offers "an expanse of towns and [beach] with no houses or commercial development." The historic Cape Hatteras Lighthouse, long endangered by hurricane-driven land erosion of the fragile coastline, has been moved inland. *outerbanks.org*

Aeolian Islands, Italy

This set of seven volcanic islands off Sicily is "a top holiday spot for Italians." Vulcano Island "has mud baths and springs. You can also find volcanic springs right in the water—it's a strange sensation." The largest island, Lipari, offers "lovely white-sand beaches and hills of pumice you can slide down." On Stromboli Island, you can climb the active volcano—the exit of Jules Verne's heroes in *Journey to the Center of the Earth*—and stroll the black-sand beaches. "For chic sands, go to Panarea Island, which has villas and nice little beaches with restaurants." *thesicilianexperience.co.uk/aeolian.html*

Fraser Island, Queensland, Australia

Sparsely populated, dotted with a large number of lakes and great varieties of trees, plants, and wildlife, the 75-by-9-mile Fraser Island is simply the world's largest sandbar. "Ride along the beach in a rented four-wheel-drive"—just don't get stuck when the tide rolls in. Sharks and undertow make the sea a no-go, so swim in the lakes, "tea-colored from the tannin" in the island's lush vegetation. *seefraserisland.com*

Aruba and the Southern Caribbean

Though hurricane season looms over the Caribbean from June through November, "I wouldn't rule it out" at the end of summer, especially for a last-minute getaway. "Watch The Weather Channel and last-minute airfares. This is low season, so you can get

bargains." Besides, the islands off South America "are outside the hurricane belt." Aruba, for instance, is flat, with long, wide beaches like breezy Palm Beach, known for windsurfing. *aruba.com*

Spiffed-up Aruba

Aruba is known as a place to party and honeymoon, but it is not famed for chic hotels. Now, however, the island's lodging scene has been spiffed up, and here's a sampling of what you'll find:

- Bucuti Beach Resort, long a favorite with visitors in part because of its beachside Tara Suites, has spiffed up more and even added a hip outdoor lounge to its formerly dowdy beachfront space. *bucuti.com*

- Hyatt Regency Aruba Resort & Casino, a glitzy people-watching mecca, has undergone a major face-lift. *aruba.hyatt.com*

- Radisson Aruba Resort, Casino & Spa has a sumptuous new spa. *radisson.com/aruba*

- Westin Resort, Aruba, underwent a $22 million renovation. *westinaruba.com*

- In the all-inclusive category, the new Hotel Riu Palace Aruba is said to be a happening place with a great pool scene. *riu.com/en-us/Paises/aruba/palmbeach/*

Surely there is something in the unruffled calm of nature that overawes our little anxieties and doubts: the sight of the deep-blue sky, and the clustering stars above, seem to impart a quiet to the mind.

—Jonathan Edwards

RIVERS, LAKES & ALL THINGS WATER

10 great places to go float your houseboat

A houseboat offers a great way to get together with family and friends—or just get away. North America's most popular houseboating waters are Lake Powell in southern Utah and Lake Cumberland in Kentucky. Consider these other spots from Houseboat *magazine's managing editor, Brady Kay.*

Lake Ouachita, near Hot Springs, Arkansas
Set in the midst of the Ouachita (WAH-cheh-taw) National Forest, this beautifully clean lake has 975 miles of shoreline. "Most lakes today have a lot of homes around them, so its lack of homes and overall beauty make it unique. It's always getting awards for the clearest water, and it makes a lot of ten-best lists for largemouth bass fishing." *arkansasstateparks.com/lakeouachita*

Don Pedro Lake, near Modesto, California
"A lot of people will scratch their heads when they hear this one, because it is really off the beaten path. But the large mountains and its quiet setting make it a great houseboating destination." It's in the foothills of the Sierra Nevada, not far from the better-known Lake McClure, and only an hour's drive from Yosemite National Park. "The locals protect the lake and don't tell many people about it, so it doesn't get too crowded." *donpedrolake.com*

Smith Mountain Lake, southwestern Virginia
Nestled in the Blue Ridge Mountains with 500 miles of shoreline, the lake was made by damming the Blackwater and Roanoke rivers to generate electricity. The closest cities are Roanoke (west of the lake) and Lynchburg (east). "For houseboating, it's calm, and there are lots of places to rent boats." *smith-mountain-lake.com*

Dale Hollow Lake, on Kentucky/Tennessee border

Overshadowed by the nearby, popular Cumberland Lake, Dale Hollow Lake is "huge and great for cruising or entertaining. There are plenty of places to rent a houseboat, and they usually have the latest models" because most houseboats are manufactured in these two states. Fishing rods lure crappie and smallmouth bass. "It might be the best lake in (this area) that no one has ever heard of." *dalehollowlake.com*

Lake Sidney Lanier, near Atlanta, Georgia

Part of this lake's popularity is a result of its location, just north of Atlanta. Lake Lanier, as it is called, boasts "the largest floating dock in the United States. The houseboat slips are at Holiday Marina, and there are plenty of both private and rental houseboats." This large highland reservoir (1,071 feet above sea level) "would take years to fully explore." *lanier.sam.usace.army.mil*

Lake Mead, near Las Vegas, Nevada

"When you think about Western lakes, you always think of Lake Powell, but [there's also] Mead, which is part of the Colorado River system. You can see the Hoover Dam, though not as up close as before 9/11. There are great rock walls and canyons whose channels you can cruise through, or tie off your boat in a cove and hike." *riverlakes.com*

Table Rock Lake, near Branson, Missouri

"Lake of the Ozarks gets all the attention" in this area on the Arkansas border, "but that's where all the big powerboats are. Table Rock is a lot nicer for houseboaters." You can explore the many hidden coves, go to the beach, go shopping, or "get lost for the weekend. Because it's close to Branson, the area attracts a lot of people, but the people who flock to Branson for  concerts don't know the lake is there," and vice versa. *tablerocklake.us*

Shuswap Lake, British Columbia, Canada
Canada's largest body of water for houseboating, Shuswap (SHOO-shwop) has "about 300 boats" available to rent. It's surrounded by "a beautiful, dense forest in the mountains." Its calm water makes it "ideal for houseboating...in the Northwest." *shuswap.bc.ca*

Green River, southeastern Utah
Because the state has many "great places to houseboat," this one beneath the Wasatch Mountains, where the Green River merges with the Colorado River, is often overlooked, "but it's one of my favorite to visit. It's more a lake than a river," and the area has "a lot of personality and friendly, laid-back" locals. Some of the coves are well-known party spots, and "there's a big rock wall that people spray-paint." *go-utah.com/green-river*

Center Hill Lake, near Nashville, Tennessee
Of all the many places to houseboat in Tennessee, "this lake is your best option." Especially lovely in fall when the leaves change colors, the lake offers "a variety of scenery," and mostly undeveloped shoreline. *smithvilletn.com/lake*

Budget Travel Tips from the **USA TODAY Archive**

TRANSPORTATION
Go for the extra mileage
Don't blindly book the lowest airfare without considering the details: Can the return flight be changed or can you fly on an earlier day's flight on standby? Some foreign carriers don't give mileage for promotional fares in economy class, even though they are partners to major frequent-flier programs. Using two cents per mile as a rule of thumb, the lost mileage credit on a typical round trip to Europe could be worth about $160.

—Jens Jurgen, founder, *Travel Companion Exchange*

10 great places to have a dam good time

Pity the country's grand old dams. These gargantuan water guardians, once celebrated as monumental technological feats, "often today are portrayed as detrimental to the environment and especially to spawning fish," says dam historian Donald C. Jackson, author of Building the Ultimate Dam: John S. Eastwood and the Control of Water in the American West. *"Dams still play vital roles in municipal water supply, hydroelectric-power production, flood control, river navigation, irrigation, and lake-oriented recreation."*
Here, he lists some of the greatest.

Great Stone Dam, Massachusetts
"Spanning the Merrimack River in Lawrence, north of Boston, this 943-foot-long, 32-foot-high masonry dam was completed in 1848, when the dam fed water to some of the world's largest 19th-century textile mills. Today, it diverts water into a hydroelectric power plant, and, to restore the once-prolific fisheries, migrating fish are transported around the imposing barrier."

New Croton Dam, New York
"This 297-foot-high masonry structure, located across Croton River in Westchester County, helps regulate New York City's water supply system." Visitors take note: Access to the Croton Reservoir is restricted in order to protect water quality. *crotononhudson-ny.gov*

Holtwood Dam, Pennsylvania
"Spanning the Susquehanna River, ten miles southeast of Lancaster, Holtwood came on line in 1910 as the river's first major hydroelectric power plant. In the 1940s, the company owning the dam was headed by Prescott Bush, grandfather of George W. Bush. Recently, the dam has been fitted out with 'fish lifts' for shad restoration." *pplweb.com/holtwood/*

Hoover (Boulder) Dam, Nevada/Arizona
"This 726-foot-high dam is located across the Colorado River

between Nevada and Arizona, but California lobbied loudest for its construction. During construction in the early 1930s, the concrete structure was named for then-president Herbert Hoover, but after the election of FDR, it was called Boulder Dam. Fourteen years later, the name was changed back to Hoover Dam." Cars can cross the dam, and tours of the visitor center are available.
usbr.gov/lc/hooverdam

Norris Dam, Tennessee
"Constructed in 1936 over the Clinch River in eastern Tennessee near the town of Norris, this dam was the first structure built by the Tennessee Valley Authority created as part of President Roosevelt's New Deal."
www.state.tn.us/environment/parks/NorrisDam/

Bagnell Dam, Missouri
"Built in 1931, across the Osage River in the Ozark Mountains of Missouri, the 148-foot-high dam [provides] power to St. Louis (140 miles east). The dam's reservoir, bordered by Lake of the Ozarks State Park, covers 57,000 acres and features a shoreline 1,375 miles long" where recreational activities abound.
lakeozark.com/bagnell.html

Mansfield Dam, Texas
"Just ten miles from Austin, Lake Travis (created by Mansfield Dam) provides flood control, hydroelectric power, and recreation. Efforts to win federal approval for the mile-long dam across the Colorado River at Marshall Ford played a momentous role in the early political career of Lyndon B. Johnson."
www.co.travis.tx.us/tnr/parks/mansfield_dam.asp

Cheeseman Dam, Colorado
"For more than 100 years, Denver has relied upon a mountain-water supply stored behind the 232-foot-high Cheeseman Dam, built in 1904. Interestingly, the stretch of the South Platte River below the dam is prized by local anglers" in the hunt for rainbow trout.

Fort Peck Dam, Montana
"Completed in 1940, the massive 250-foot-high earth-fill dam across the Missouri River, east of Glasgow, was built for power and to foster navigation along the lower portion of the river." *fortpeckdam.com*

Grand Coulee Dam, Washington
"Rising more than 500 feet above its foundations, Grand Coulee—completed in 1942 across the Columbia River in the eastern part of the state—is the first masonry structure to use more material than the Great Pyramid of Cheops (Khufu) in Egypt. With a reservoir stretching north for 150 miles to the Canadian border, this dam [is] the largest hydroelectric plant in the country." *grandcouleedam.org*

10 great places to take an old-timey plunge

If you tire of yet another summer at the pool, break away from the mainstream, says Dianna Delling, senior editor at Outside *magazine, for an invigorating dip in a clear, cool, Tom Sawyer–like swimming hole. "Across the country, there are many fabulous destination swimming holes. Most take some planning and hiking to get to, but that's all part of the fun." Delling shares her top natural freshwater rewards.*

Buffalo National River, north-central Arkansas
Along this beautiful river (a unit of the National Park system) that flows eastward through the Ozarks' limestone bluffs, "there are countless swimming holes. One of the best is a kid-friendly pool right at the bend of Steel Creek campground that boasts warm, shallow water and a great gravel beach." *nps.gov/buff*

Big Bend, Petersburg, West Virginia
"Go for a dip anywhere as you inner-tube float on this mean-
dering hour-long river loop located on the south branch of
the Potomac River." This part of the river is near Big Bend
Campground, in the Smoke Hole Canyon portion of the
Monongahela National Forest, about ten miles southwest of
Petersburg. River loop campsites are available.
fs.fed.us/r9/mnf/rec/rog_campgrounds/bigbend_campground.htm

Rock Bluff Springs, Bell, Florida
Although the land around it is privately owned, "this large, shallow,
three-foot-deep pool (about five
miles northwest of Bell) is accessible
by canoe or boat." Stately cypress
trees rim the spring-fed pool,
which connects to several underwater caverns (recommended for
strong swimmers only) and ultimately to the Suwannee River.

thiswaytothe.net/springs/pages/rock-bluff-springs-gilchrist.html

Bass Lake, Point Reyes National Seashore, California
Only an hour from the San Francisco Bay Area, Point Reyes' Bass
Lake is "one beautiful swimming spot. The three-mile hike follows
the scenic Coast Trail to the freshwater lake where visitors can
picnic, swim, and just enjoy the exquisite scenery."
nps.gov/pore/planyourvisit/hiking_guide.htm

Havasu Falls, Supai, Arizona
"The hike (several miles) into these very well-known falls," located
in the Grand Canyon's remote Havasu Canyon on the Havasupai
Indian Reservation, "is worth the trip just to get to this spectacular
pool with blue-green water that stays at 72 degrees all year."

Jerry Johnson Hot Springs, east of Lewiston, Idaho
Named after a 19th-century prospector, the springs are actually
groups of rock-lined, clear-water, sand-bottom pools situated
along a creek in a forest of fir and cedar trees. "During the short

Pets on jets: Tips to reduce anxiety

Cats and dogs are flying more than ever. In 2006, about 29 million Americans took at least one overnight trip with their pets. Three years earlier, half as many pets traveled, reports the American Pet Products Manufacturers Association.

Pack them and go? No way. Air travel with pets can be confusing. Some airlines permit pets in the cabin but not in the cargo hold or vice versa. Some charge to bring pets in the cabin, some don't. Some airlines restrict the size and breed of an animal that they allow on board.

Which leads to our first tip, from Kim Noetzel, spokeswoman for the Arizona Humane Society: "Don't fly without checking the airline's policies." The second most important suggestion is to ensure that your pet's carrier fits dimension specifications of the airline.

Here are additional tips:

- Update pet immunizations and get a certificate of your pet's health within two weeks of traveling.

- Be ready to leave the pet in the carrier and to take the pet out. Some security officials allow pets to stay in their carriers while going through security, but others demand that pets be walked through the metal detector with their owners.

- Bring out the carrier a few days before the trip to allow your pet to become reacquainted with it. On the day of the flight, limit food but offer water, and go for a long walk. Make sure the pet has relieved itself before the flight takes off.

- Don't try to tranquilize your pet. Check with your veterinarian. "Never try to self-prescribe," says Noetzel.

- Make sure the carrier displays the owner's contact information.

- Pack a three-day supply of the animal's regular food when traveling in case of unforeseen travel delays.

- Pack wet wipes in carry-on luggage so messes can be cleaned up. Also, bring a plastic bag in which to dispose the wipes.

- Owners should pack a T-shirt, pillowcase, or something else that smells like them in the pet's carrier.

- Pets can pick up on their owner's anxiety, so remain calm when flying.

hike to the springs, located near Warm Springs Pack Bridge about 20 miles west of the Montana border on U.S. 12, you'll see an abundance of elk, deer, and moose."
idahohotsprings.com/destinations/jerry_johnson/index.htm

Barton Springs, Austin, Texas
"Brace yourself for a chilly dip (average summer temperature is 68 degrees) in this spring-fed, 900-foot-long natural pool in Austin's Zilker Park." The city's popular swimming hole, created when Barton Creek was dammed, varies in depth, so there are diving boards, ladders, and steps to get in and out.
www.ci.austin.tx.us/parks/bartonsprings.htm

Walden Pond, Concord, Massachusetts
"Even though it's a little touristy, Henry David Thoreau's own swimming hole is a clear, 102-foot-deep pond. It's surprisingly small, but this scenic, historic place, now known as Walden Pond State Reservation," draws visitors who also want to fish, canoe, or just sit on the beach, as Thoreau did, and contemplate life.
mass.gov/dcr/parks/Walden

Greeter Falls, Grundy County, Tennessee
In South Cumberland State Park, which encompasses Savage Gulf Natural Area, a picturesque 15,590 acres covering a portion of the Cumberland Plateau, "Greeter Falls, about a mile hike from inside the park, plunges more than 50 feet into a cold and deep pool perfect for swimming." *friendsofscsra.org/aboutthepark.htm#greeter*

Pikes Falls, northwest of Jamaica, Vermont
"This community swimming hole is a favorite for locals" and features ice-cold water in two pools that collect from the rock-flow falls. Located off a wooded path along Pikes Falls Road, the hole is tricky to find, but once you do, "it's cool here even in the middle of summer." *www.swimholes.com/holes/vermont/main/pikes.htm*

10 great places to see a cascade of water

When it's toasty outside, sprinklers and pools pale in comparison with Mother Earth's exhilarating natural show. "Waterfalls are spectacular, powerful phenomena that are really appreciated up close and in person," says Leslie Weeden, travel director at Outside *magazine. Here, she shares some cool spots to watch the water fall.*

Niagara Falls, Niagara Falls State Park, New York

"Known as a mecca for honeymooners and suicidal barrel runs, Niagara Falls straddles the U.S. and Canadian border, with the American Falls on the New York side and the larger, 188-foot Horseshoe Falls balanced between New York and Ontario. Currently, visitors can expect a torrent of 100,000 cubic feet of water per second shooting down the falls. Take a boat or view this colossus on foot. Either way you're sure to get drenched." *niagarafallsstatepark.com*

Bridalveil Fall, Yosemite National Park, California
"One of the subtler falls in Yosemite Valley, this waterfall drops 620 feet and is one of the few year-round falls in the park. Native Americans once called the fall 'Pohono,' after an evil spirit, but it was later renamed Bridalveil for its wispy likeness to a matrimonial headdress. Visitors can access several walking and hiking trails from the parking area just off Route 41." *nps.gov/yose*

Alamere Falls, Point Reyes National Seashore, California
"It's easy to miss the falls. Tucked into the southern end of the recreation area, the 40-foot-high falls run directly onto the beach and can only be reached by huffing it along the seashore. From the Palomarin Trailhead, hikers can take a 3.5-mile walk to the top of the falls." *nps.gov/pore*

Whitewater Falls, Cashiers, North Carolina
"Whitewater Falls crosses the border between North and South Carolina as North Carolina's Upper Fall tumbles 411 feet, making it the highest waterfall east of the Rockies. Three miles down river, South Carolina's Lower Fall spills another 400 feet. The Foothill Trail, running past the Whitewater Falls recreation area, is the best way to see both falls."
cs.unca.edu/nfsnc/recreation/wncwaterfalls/whitewaterfalls.htm

Gooseberry Falls, Gooseberry Falls State Park, Minnesota
"Only 40 miles northeast of Duluth, this series of five waterfalls runs along a mile stretch of the Gooseberry River on the north shore of Lake Superior. Cascading in 30-foot tiers, the falls are accessible by trails starting from the park's visitor center. Bring hiking boots for the poplar- and spruce-lined promenades to the Lower Fall and Fifth Fall."
www.dnr.state.mn.us/state_parks/gooseberry_falls/index.html

Calf Creek Falls, Grand Staircase–Escalante National Monument, Utah
"En route to the 126-foot Lower Calf Creek Falls, hikers pass pine trees, ancient rock art, and Native American cliff dwellings before reaching the more popular of the two falls and its crystal-clear pond. Lower Calf Creek spills over a sheer, mineral-rich sandstone, resulting in a rainbowlike stain."
brycecanyoncountry.com/escalante.htm

Havasu Falls, Supai, Arizona
"Known for its brilliant Southwest colors, the 100-foot falls, southwest of Grand Canyon National Park, requires advance reservation (up to three months). From the Hualapai Hilltop parking lot, hike in ten miles through Havasu Canyon. Havasu bursts forth at 28,000 gallons per minute, over red-rock walls, into a turquoise pool open for swimming." *waterfallswest.com/az-havasu-falls.html*

Multnomah Falls, Columbia River Gorge National Scenic Area, Oregon
"The 620-foot Multnomah Falls is one of Oregon's top tourist attractions. Visitors from Portland head 40 minutes east along

Interstate 84, which skirts the Columbia River, to reach what explorer Meriwether Lewis called 'the most remarkable of the cascade falls,' of which there are several nearby." *fs.fed.us/r6/columbia*

Hi'ilawe Falls, Waipio Valley, Hawaii
"One of the tallest [waterfalls] in the world is the more-than-1,000-foot freefall Hi'ilawe on the Big Island's rugged northern side. Though an honored home to ancient Hawaiian gods and goddesses, Hi'ilawe wasn't always a gusher; in 1989, a sugar company diverted headwaters toward the falls for irrigation purposes. The added rush lures hearty visitors [with a view of] a sky-high faucet rushing over plant-covered black lava rock." *world-waterfalls.com/waterfall.php?num=64*

Whiteoak Canyon Falls, Shenandoah National Park, Virginia
"Six waterfalls make up Whiteoak Canyon Falls, but the most visited is called, appropriately, No. 1. Water sluices 86 feet through a narrow canyon, past hemlock trees and large boulders. Despite its charge, it's one of the park's most tranquil areas." *nps.gov/shen*

Budget Travel Tips from the **USA TODAY Archive**

DINING

In Europe, sup with mom and pop

My favorite European restaurants are eight-table, mom-and-pop affairs. With lower taxes and cheaper labor, these eateries offer a better value.

—Rick Steves, host, *Rick Steves' Europe*

Schmooze with the maître d'

What is a restaurant reservation if not an implied contract? And restaurants violate them every day. Establish a relationship before you get there. Tell them you are coming in and looking forward to the experience. People need to relationship-build when they travel.

—Peter Greenberg, *The Travel Detective*

SPORTS

❋ ❋ ❋ ❋

BASEBALL

10 great places to touch base with the best

Batter up! Need more than going to a game to satisfy your baseball obsession? "Baseball's history is what separates it from other sports," says Chris Epting, author of Roadside Baseball: A Guide to Baseball Shrines Across America. *"For fans, making pilgrimages to historic baseball sites is like a rite of passage, a chance to pay homage to the great gods of the game." The traditional trek to Cooperstown is a must, but it's not the only game in town. Here, Epting shares more of baseball's special spots.*

Roger Maris Museum, Fargo, North Dakota
"This hometown tribute to Yankee slugger Roger Maris, accessible to all and free at his request, is an exhibit of videos, photos, bats, balls, trophies, and artifacts located in the West Acres Shopping Center. Maris, who shattered Babe Ruth's single-season home run record in 1961, was born in Hibbing, Minnesota, but grew up here." *rogermarismuseum.com*

Babe Ruth Birthplace and Museum, Baltimore, Maryland
"The Sultan of Swat was born February 6, 1895, in this brick row house that belonged to Ruth's grandparents. Today it's an excellent museum featuring rare photos, films, radio broadcasts, and other Ruth-related treasures. Located near Camden Yards, this is also the Baltimore Orioles' museum." *baberuthmuseum.com*

Rickwood Field, Birmingham, Alabama
"The oldest stadium in America, built in 1910 for the Birmingham Barons baseball team, also became home to the Birmingham Black

Barons in 1924. Satchel Paige and Willie Mays thrilled fans here while playing in the American Negro Leagues. Babe Ruth, Ty Cobb, and other legends also visited this field, now on the National Register of Historic Places." *rickwood.com*

Negro Leagues Baseball Museum, Kansas City, Missouri
"This museum recounts the formation and history of the Negro Baseball League prior to 1945, when the Brooklyn Dodgers signed Jackie Robinson. Displays include rare Negro League pennants, autographed baseballs, photos, and a video about the league's history narrated by Bernard Shaw." *nlbm.com*

Elysian Fields (former site), Hoboken, New Jersey
"In 1842 Alexander Cartwright and Daniel 'Doc' Adams drafted rules for a game called baseball. On June 19, 1846, the Knickerbocker Baseball Club played the first organized game against the New York Nine at Elysian Fields at the corner of 11th and Washington streets. A plaque marks the spot where the field was."

Louisville Slugger Museum & Factory, Louisville, Kentucky
Bats, bats are everywhere, from the 120-foot behemoth in front of the museum to the miniature Slugger each tour visitor takes home. "In 1884 the Hillerich & Bradsby Co. started making Louisville Sluggers, and today 2,000 wooden bats are produced daily. Visitors can tour the factory or stroll through the baseball history museum." *sluggermuseum.org*

Nolan Ryan Exhibit Center, Alvin, Texas
"The center, built by the Ryan Foundation and donated to the Alvin Community College in 1996, chronicles the life and baseball career of Alvin's favorite son in many state-of-the-art exhibits, including an interactive one in which the visitor 'feels' a Ryan fastball in a catcher's mitt." *nolanryanfoundation.org/museum.htm*

Field of Dreams, Dyersville, Iowa
" 'If you build it, he will come.' The movie may have been referring to a baseball legend, but it's tourists who now flock to the site where Kevin Costner's 1989 movie was filmed. Fans can run the bases, play catch, bat, or just sit in the bleachers and dream. The

house and cornfield also are open to visitors; the field is open daily from April to November." *fieldofdreamsmoviesite.com*

Forbes Field (former site), Pittsburgh, Pennsylvania
"From 1909 to 1970, Forbes was home to the Pittsburgh Pirates and the scene of one of baseball's most dramatic moments: Bill Mazeroski's Game Seven home run in the 1960 World Series to beat the Yankees (a sidewalk plaque marks the spot). Though the field is gone, remnants remain on the grounds of the University of Pittsburgh, including part of the outfield wall and the flagpole." *forbesfieldforever.com*

Ted Williams Museum & Hitters Hall of Fame, Tropicana Field, St. Petersburg, Florida
"The museum, just a few blocks from where Williams lived, is laid out like a baseball diamond: Each base represents a different chapter in The Splendid Splinter's legendary career. In addition to displays and memorabilia, video monitors run classic clips of Williams and other legends." *twmuseum.com*

Bonus destination: Cooperstown

A mecca for baseball lovers, this charming village in New York State has the National Baseball Hall of Fame and Museum, brimming with memorabilia, from Babe Ruth's bat to Hank Aaron's uniform. Don't miss the Cooperstown Bat Company to see bats being made. Go early in the season, since hotel rooms in Cooperstown are hard to come by in July and August.

Serious sport has nothing to do with fair play. It is bound up with hatred, jealousy, boastfulness, disregard of all rules, and sadistic pleasure in witnessing violence: in other words it is war minus the shooting.
—George Orwell

10 great places to relish fine stadium fare

"Buy me some peanuts and Cracker Jacks" goes the line from baseball anthem "Take Me Out to the Ball Game." But nowadays, the menu at the ol' ballpark goes way beyond that: fish tacos, pierogi—even sushi. Kevin Reichard, founder of ballparkdigest.com, suggests the best places for food fare and all the fixins at stadiums nationwide.

AT&T Park, San Francisco, California

AT&T Park, home of the San Francisco Giants, is a "foodie's delight," especially the stadium's Gilroy Garlic Fries and Cha Cha Bowl. "Gilroy (California) proclaims itself the garlic capital of the world, and that garlic is used to smother a plateful of fries." The Cha Cha Bowl, served at Orlando's BBQ on the centerfield promenade level, features blackened chicken, pineapple salsa, rice, and beans. "We could steer you to another half dozen notable food items at AT&T Park—Ghirardelli hot fudge sundaes, a 40-clove garlic chicken sandwich from the Stinking Rose, ahi tuna sandwiches, portobello mushroom burgers, anything at the Say Hey! Willie Mays Sausage stands, brisket sandwiches—and you'd come away impressed." *giants.mlb.com*

Kauffman Stadium, Kansas City, Missouri

"Barbecue is an increasingly common item at ballparks, and the best that we've run across is the Gates BBQ served at Kauffman Stadium, the home of the Kansas City Royals. Try one of the beef, turkey, or pork sandwiches; go for the side of BBQ beans; and wash it down with a locally brewed Boulevard beer." *royals.mlb.com*

Dodger Stadium, Los Angeles, California

Oh, that staple of any ballpark—the hot dog. It's tough to pick the best, but a particularly notable frank is the foot-long Dodger Dog, specially formulated by Farmer John for the Los Angeles Dodgers and found at most Dodger Stadium concession stands. "Eat one with relish and mustard. They were good enough for Cary Grant, they're good enough for you." *dodgers.mlb.com*

Petco Park, San Diego, California
The fish tacos at Petco Park, home of the San Diego Padres, come
from renowned local chain Rubio's. "Top them off with fresh
handmade guacamole and salsa. They're served in only three
La Comida stands, so they can be a little difficult to locate—but
they're worth the work." *padres.mlb.com*

Safeco Field, Seattle, Washington
Sushi may not be the first thing that comes to mind when you
head for a ballpark concession stand, but the Japanese delicacy
has become more popular at stadiums nationwide and is not the
novelty it once was. At Safeco Field, home of the Seattle Mariners,
"a dedicated stand serves all manner of sushi rolls, including the
Ichi-roll (a spicy tuna roll), named for star Ichiro Suzuki." Beyond
sushi, Safeco also features a wide variety of other highly regarded
offerings, including Ivar Dogs (fried fish served on a hot dog bun,
slathered with tartar sauce) from Ivar's Acres of Clams, as well as
"the best burgers in the majors"—the Kidd Valley burgers from the
locally acclaimed chain of hamburger joints. *mariners.mlb.com*

PNC Park, Pittsburgh, Pennsylvania
"Heart attack on a bun" is one way to describe the steak sandwich
served at the Primanti Brothers stand at PNC Park, home of the
Pittsburgh Pirates. "Featuring steak, coleslaw, cheese, and french
fries, it's designed as a total meal in a single sandwich." Perfect
with a locally brewed Iron City beer. *pirates.mlb.com*

Citizens Bank Park, Philadelphia, Pennsylvania
Similarly guaranteed to clog your arteries: the Schmitter, sold at
the home of the Philadelphia Phillies. "Yes, you could opt for a
cheesesteak from Geno's Steaks or Tony Luke's at the ballpark, but
why bother when you can have a cheesesteak on steroids?" Indeed,
the Schmitter has it all: fried salami, steak, three slices of cheese,
fried onions, tomatoes, and a special sauce. *phillies.mlb.com*

Progressive Field, Cleveland, Ohio
Buy me some peanuts and pierogi? Only in Cleveland. Pierogi are
potato- and cheese-filled dumplings of Eastern European origin—
and worth a trip to the concession stand at Progressive Field, home

AND ANOTHER THING . . .

TOP SPOTS TO SEE 'EM SWING FOR THE FENCES

"There's something about a ballgame that's good for the soul," says Jay Ahuja, author of *Fields of Dreams: A Guide to Visiting and Enjoying All 30 Major League Ballparks*. Ahuja, who has visited every major-league stadium, shares some of his favorite ballparks.

- **PNC Park, Pittsburgh, Pennsylvania**—The two-tier, baseball-only stadium seats only 38,362, but "its classic feel and riverside location make it an instant classic." pirates.com

- **Rangers Ballpark in Arlington, Arlington, Texas**—"A fan-friendly park, the home of the Rangers offers a great sense of nostalgia and all the amenities, including the Bullpen Grill, a bar/restaurant overlooking the field." texasrangers.com

- **Fenway Park, Boston, Massachusetts**—Red Sox park boasts "seats atop the Green Monster (Fenway's famous left-field wall)—yet another reason to go before this old yard meets the wrecking ball. It's a timeless, intimate park with great fan support." redsox.com

- **Oriole Park at Camden Yards, Baltimore, Maryland**—"The original retro ballpark accomplishes a combination of nostalgia and state-of-the-art fan amenities unlike any park before or since." orioles.com

- **AT&T Park, San Francisco, California**—The Giants' home seats 41,503, with a limited number of standing-room-only tickets for sold-out games. "Highlights include a great food selection, a giant old-fashioned fielder's glove in left field, and a wonderful waterfront location." sfgiants.com

- **Wrigley Field, Chicago, Illinois**—Wrigley is the home of the Cubs and legions of their die-hard fans. "The ivy-covered walls, classic center-field scoreboard, and Wrigleyville's atmosphere, before and after a game, make for a great day of baseball." cubs.com

- **Comerica Park, Detroit, Michigan**—"The carnival atmosphere, a nifty left-field Ferris wheel, the ornate carousel behind home plate, and stainless-steel statues of great Tiger players beyond the center-field fence, create a one-of-a-kind ballpark." tigers.com

of the Indians. "In a ballpark that sometimes resembles more a food court than a sporting facility, pierogi are the most notable items in the [Progressive] Field food lineup." *indians.mlb.com*

Coors Field, Denver, Colorado
Okay, this one may be a little hard to swallow, but Rocky Mountain oysters are the food item to search out at Coors Field, home of the Colorado Rockies. Oysters not in the traditional sense, mind you. Hereabouts, they're calf testicles, cut in half and deep-fried. "They're not as horrid as you might think—a little lighter and less dense than most fans would anticipate." *rockies.mlb.com*

Miller Park, Milwaukee, Wisconsin
Sausages of all sorts rule at Miller Park, home of the Brewers. "You could opt for mustard as a condiment, but do as the locals do:
Slather that sausage in Secret Stadium Sauce. We're not quite sure what it's made from—it tastes like a mix of clam juice and sweetened tomato sauce—but it's best served warm. Wash it down with a Miller High Life or one of the uniformly great microbrews from Wisconsin's own New Glarus Brewing Co." *brewers.mlb.com*

BASKETBALL

10 great places to get pumped for NCAA action

You don't have to be a huge basketball fan to get excited about college hoops. Here, author, sports commentator, and basketball aficionado John Feinstein gives his list of favorite venues for watching NCAA games.

Allen Fieldhouse, University of Kansas, Lawrence, Kansas
With the arena named for legendary Kansas coach Phog Allen and the court named for the game's inventor, James Naismith, Allen Fieldhouse is steeped in basketball history. The Rock Chalk chant before each game is one of the signature cheers in all of college

sports. "You haven't lived until you've heard 'Rock Chalk Jayhawk' in Allen Fieldhouse on a cold winter night." *kuathletics.com*

Rose Hill Gym, Fordham University, New York
"Rose Hill, home of the Fordham Rams, is the oldest facility in the country being used for Division I basketball, and it feels that way inside. The gym has been in continuous use since it opened in 1925. It's tiny—seating just 3,470—but has a wonderful ambience. If you're a college hoops fan, it's definitely worth the trip." *fordham.edu/athletics*

University Arena, University of New Mexico, Albuquerque
Home to the University of New Mexico Lobos, University Arena—affectionately known as The Pit—was opened in 1966. The nickname is a reference to the facility's unique subterranean construction—the floor sits 37 feet below ground level. The steeply tiered arena seats more than 18,000. "It's a truly unique place with a highly charged atmosphere. When the players walk on to the court in The Pit, it's like watching Roman gladiators emerging into a wall of sound." *golobos.com*

Hart Recreation Center, College of the Holy Cross, Worcester, Massachusetts
"This is another tiny gem, seating just 3,600. When it's packed, it really rocks—the student section is called The Hart Attack, which tells you all you need to know. Hanging from the rafters are championship banners from 1947 and 1954, a reminder that this is the school where Bob Cousy and Tom Heinsohn played before going on to the Celtics and the Hall of Fame." *holycross.edu/athletics/*

Mackey Arena, Purdue University, West Lafayette, Indiana
"Mackey is one of the last of the old Big Ten arenas. The team benches are actually situated below the court—the coaches have to jump up to give their players instructions." The arena's domed aluminum roof makes the crowd noise reverberate to mega-decibel level. "When the Boilermakers are on a run, you literally can't hear the guy next to you talking." *purduesports.com*

Cassell Coliseum, Virginia Tech University, Blacksburg, Virginia
Opened in 1962, Cassell Coliseum is now one of the oldest arenas

in the Atlantic Coast Conference. Although relatively large, seating more than 10,000, the arena is an intimate basketball showplace. "From the floor, the stands appear to go straight up to the ceiling. Walking into Cassell on a cold night, surrounded by Hokie fans, you'll feel like you're exactly where you should be." *hokietickets.com*

O'Connell Center, University of Florida, Gainesville, Florida
Known on campus as the "O-Dome," the O'Connell Center was built in 1980 and renovated in 1998. "It's the newest building on my list of favorites, but it doesn't feel that new. The student section—dubbed the Rowdy Reptiles—really lives up to its name." *oconnellcenter.ufl.edu*

The Palestra, University of Pennsylvania, Philadelphia, Pennsylvania
Opened in 1927, the Palestra has hosted more NCAA basketball games than any other facility in the nation. The small arena is famed for its intimate atmosphere, with the bleachers extending right up to the court. "The Palestra just oozes basketball tradition.

AND ANOTHER THING . . .

OTHER GREAT PLACES TO GET INTO THE COLLEGE GAME

Following are even more favorite spots for tapping into the spirit and history of college hoops.

- Hinkle Fieldhouse at Butler University, Indianapolis, Indiana
- Naismith Memorial Basketball Hall of Fame, Springfield, Massachusetts
- St. Elmo Steak House, Indianapolis, Indiana
- A Williams College–Amherst College basketball game at Williamstown or Amherst, Massachusetts
- Grimaldi's Ristorante, Syracuse, New York
- Holiday college games in Hawaii, Maui, and Oahu

Walk in the front door and read the plaque—'To play the game is great; to win the game is greater; but to love the game is the greatest of all'—and you get chills." *pennathletics.com*

Cameron Indoor Stadium, Duke University, Durham, North Carolina
Home of the Duke Blue Devils, a perennial college basketball powerhouse, Cameron has a reputation for being one of the toughest places for a visiting team to play. One reason is the highly vocal student section, affectionately called the Cameron Crazies. "The students are loud and raucous, and they create a great atmosphere. When you walk in, it almost feels like you're entering a high school gym." *goduke.com*

Pauley Pavilion, UCLA, Los Angeles, California
Although it may lack the character and charm of other premier college basketball venues, UCLA's Pauley Pavilion does not lack for history or tradition. "Just count the 11 NCAA Championship banners hanging from the rafters. Listen to the band play the famous Bruin fight song, and look for legendary coach John Wooden, who still attends most games. That's all you really need." *uclabruins.com*

10 great places to watch high school basketball

Need to feed your hoops obsession? Then there's nothing like a high school game to rejuvenate your spirit. The following gyms were selected by more than 2,600 USA TODAY *readers surveyed.*

The Fieldhouse, New Castle, Indiana
You want size and serious hoops obsession? Then your died-and-gone-to-heaven destination is New Castle, Indiana, where the likes of Kent Benson and Steve Alford have played in front of more than 10,000 in The Fieldhouse.

The Wigwam, Anderson High School, Anderson, Indiana
The original gym for Anderson's basketball team was destroyed by fire in 1958. The new Wigwam, which opened in 1961, is the second-largest high school gym in the United States. Anderson High moved to a new location in 1997, but the Wigwam is still

used for games. Despite recent struggles with poverty, under-performing schools, and high unemployment, Anderson has kept the iconic gym open.

Barre Municipal Auditorium, Barre, Vermont
Completed in 1939 as a WPA project during the last throes of the Depression, Barre Auditorium has grown into the state's mecca for high school basketball. Each winter the boys and girls semifinals and finals in the state's three smallest classifications are held at the auditorium. Thousands of Vermont youngsters have grown up dreaming of "making it to the Aud" and playing in the squat build-ing atop Seminary Hill.

Reed Conder Gymnasium, Marshall County High School, Benton, Kentucky
Reed Conder is nicknamed "Little Rupp Arena" after the University of Kentucky arena, and there is a waiting list for the 964 chair seats close to the floor. Those seats have been sold out for every game since the gym opened in 1980.

Sandra Meadows Memorial Arena, Duncanville High School, Duncanville, Texas
Duncanville has a state-of-the-art home court that compares favorably to many college venues. Features include a lofty ceiling, carpeted locker rooms, a press box, and a control booth. The arena is named for the legendary girls coach who won 906 games and four state titles. Meadows, who died of cancer in 1994, is enshrined in the Women's Basketball Hall of Fame.

Ralph Tasker Arena, Hobbs High School, Hobbs, New Mexico
Crowds here average nearly 3,500 a game, and season tickets are willed, or people wait up to a decade for the prized lower-tier seats. Thirteen Hobbs alumni have been drafted by NBA teams.

Willie E. West Jr. Pavilion, Crenshaw High School, Los Angeles, California
"I know coaches in L.A. who still tell me they can't catch a break at Crenshaw," says former Crenshaw star Marques Johnson. "The refs see the championship banners, see the crowd, and get intimidated."

Corn Palace, Mitchell High School, Mitchell, South Dakota
The prairie town, with a population of about 15,000, is renowned
for its monument to agricultural production. Tourists come to see
the Corn Palace's murals made from corn and other locally grown
grasses and grains that decorate the building's exterior. The art
changes every year. In the mid-'80s, Mitchell won 61 consecutive
games in the Palace.

Dan Buckley Gym, La Salle Academy, New York, New York
Attempting a three-pointer from the corners here is difficult,
because there's little room to spare. The facility, located on East
Third Street in the East Village of Manhattan, was constructed
from 1935 to 1938. Notable La Salle alumni include Ron Artest of
the Los Angeles Lakers and Hall of Fame guard Dick McGuire.
"It gets loud; that's why I liked playing in there," says Artest.

Central Gymnasium, Shelbyville Central High School,
Shelbyville, Tennessee
Shelbyville home games average 1,600 attendees, and fans aren't
allowed in the gym until an hour before tip-off. All seats are unre-
served, but many senior citizens arrive around 3 P.M. to place their
seat cushions on the bleachers.

FOOTBALL

10 great places to get a kick out of football

*Some pro-football fans treat football Sundays like a sacred event,
worshipping at modern-day cathedrals known as stadiums. ESPN's
Chris Berman, remembering Jets games at Shea Stadium with his
dad, shares favorite places to watch gridiron grit.*

Qualcomm Stadium, San Diego, California
Home to the San Diego Chargers, Qualcomm is in the heart
of Mission Valley. With a football seating capacity of 71,500,
the stadium boasts 52 concession stands, three restaurants, and
113 executive suites. It has hosted the Super Bowl twice (three

times if you count 1988, when it was the Jack
Murphy Stadium). *sandiego.gov/qualcomm/*

Lambeau Field, Green Bay, Wisconsin
In cheesehead country, you'll find warm brats
paired with cold beer and even colder temps.
"This is true Packers football, from Don Hutson to Vince
Lombardi to Brett Favre." With a $295 million renovation, the
stadium's capacity has increased to 72,928. Good thing: The season-
ticket waiting list contains 81,000 names, and the average wait time
is 30 years. *lambeaufield.com*

Raymond James Stadium, Tampa, Florida
This stadium, home to the Tampa Bay Buccaneers, features end-
zone terraces, cupholders on all seats, and 88 restrooms. It also was
named best playing field in 1998 and second-best surface in 2009
by the NFL Players Association. *raymondjames.com/stadium*

Gillette Stadium, Foxborough, Massachusetts
Gillette Stadium opened in 2002 in suburban Boston at a cost
of $325 million. New England Patriots fans can choose from
68,756 seats (6,600 of those are club seats) and 500 New England–
themed concession stands. *gillettestadium.com*

Lincoln Financial Field, Philadelphia, Pennsylvania
You can't go wrong with "Philly cheesesteaks and 'flubber' (half
grass, half rubber) on the field." The football-only facility cost
$512 million and is located next to the site of the former Veterans
Stadium, the Eagles' home for more than 30 years. Nearly two-
thirds of the seats are on the sidelines and 60 feet from the field.
lincolnfinancialfield.com

Soldier Field, Chicago, Illinois
Opened in 1924 as a memorial to soldiers of World War I, the
Chicago Bears' stadium was rebuilt in 2003 and now features
61,500 seats, with 133 suites and 8,600 club seats. *soldierfield.net*

Qwest Field, Seattle, Washington
Located south of downtown Seattle, the Seahawks' $360 million
home "is a great stadium." Tours of the 72,000-capacity facility

reveal extra-wide concourses, 112 executive suites, and 7,000 club seats. *qwestfield.com*

INVESCO Field at Mile High, Denver, Colorado
The Broncos' stadium—a whopping 1.8-million-square-foot facility—sits adjacent to the old Mile High Stadium parking lot. It boasts 76,125 seats, three video display boards, and $2 million bronze horse sculptures. Of course, the old white horse still sits atop the south scoreboard. *invescofield.com*

Candlestick Park, San Francisco, California
Home of the San Francisco 49ers since 1971, Candlestick Park holds 70,207 spectators and cost only $24.6 million to build. *49ers.com/stadium/index.html*

Ralph Wilson Stadium, Orchard Park, New York
Built in 1973 and renovated in 1999, Ralph Wilson Stadium's playing field is 50 feet below ground level, eliminating long walks for Buffalo Bills fans to the three decks of blue and red seats. *buffalobills.com/tickets/stadium/index.html*

10 great places to score a football feast

Attending a football game involves cherished rituals, and tailgate parties are as familiar as the national anthem. Shirley Fong-Torres (aka the Wok Wiz) has added "sports nut" to her résumé. Here, with help from her writing partner, Jim Duncan, she runs down top sites for football stadium fare.

Aloha Stadium, Oahu, Hawaii
The state's largest outdoor arena—home to the University of Hawaii's Warriors—is best known as the site of the NFL Pro Bowl and the Sheraton Aloha Bowl. "Refreshment stands sell poi (a paste of crushed taro root) and poke wraps (wraps of cubed raw fish seasoned with onions, soy, and seaweed)." Menu must: sashimi (sliced raw fish). *alohastadium.hawaii.gov*

Rose Bowl, Pasadena, California
The site of the famed New Year's Day game is home turf for both

the UCLA Bruins and the Los Angeles Galaxy, whose soccer games are "now a day-long Latin American fiesta, with music and cooking and impromptu games." Menu must: spit-roasted pork tacos. *rosebowlstadium.com*

Husky Stadium, Seattle, Washington
"The tailgate scene [has] an amphibious ambience," with fans arriving by boat as well as car. "The north upper deck offers sweeping views of Mount Rainier, the Olympic Mountains, and downtown Seattle.... The University of Washington crew team provides shuttle service." Menu musts: Coho salmon and Dungeness crab salad. *gohuskies.com*

Lambeau Field, Green Bay, Wisconsin
"The whole town [turns] into a tailgate party when the Packers play.... [Tailgaters share a] love of outdoor cooking, polka music," and German American food. Menu musts: "Duh, sausage and beer." *lambeaufield.com*

Falcon Stadium, Colorado Springs, Colorado
On the campus of the U.S. Air Force Academy, stadiumgoers park free, and many leave belongings in their cars, "knowing that military patrols protect the parking lot while the Falcons play." Menu must: pan-fried Rocky Mountain trout. *goairforcefalcons.com*

Darrel K. Royal–Texas Memorial Stadium, Austin, Texas
"Austin is the epicenter of the best beef barbecue in the world. Lazy tailgaters stop at ... small-town Q's and buy beef brisket by the pound." Menu must: beef brisket and sauce. *texassports.com*

Tiger Stadium, Baton Rouge, Louisiana
"Stages and barbecues completely circle [the arena]. It is not unusual—when Alabama is the opponent—for the RV parking lots to fill up on Wednesday for a Saturday game." Menu musts: As Hank Williams's "Jambalaya (On the Bayou)" instructs, "jambalaya, crawfish pie, filé gumbo." *lsusports.net*

Kenan Memorial Stadium, Chapel Hill, North Carolina
"Tar Heel tailgaters bring pulled pork from barbecue oases like Lexington, Shelby, and Goldsboro." Wash it down at UNC's Old

Well. Modeled on the Temple of Love at Versailles, the well "is said to be a source of good luck for all who drink" from it. Menu must: pulled pork and vinegar-based dip. *tarheelblue.com*

M&T Bank Stadium, Baltimore, Maryland
When the Army–Navy game is played here, "it becomes an epic tailgate event," fueled by the service academies' pageantry and the "culinary wonders of the Chesapeake Bay." When the NFL's Ravens play, they "give designated drivers free soft drinks." Menu musts: oysters and duck. *baltimoreravens.com*

Harvard Stadium, Boston, Massachusetts
"Good tailgating in Boston is easier than saying 'I parked my car in Harvard Yard.' " Menu must: clam chowder. *gocrimson.com*

Ben Hill Griffin Stadium, Gainesville, Florida
"Affectionately nicknamed The Swamp," this stadium provides free parking on the University of Florida campus "amid the gorgeous cypresses and magnolias. . . . Barbecue is prevalent but so are table-cloths and corkscrews, as Gator fans take outdoor dining upscale." Menu musts: frozen drinks and cold soups. *gatorzone.com*

10 great places to drink in the Super Bowl action

A couple of TVs, beer on tap, and microwaved munchies used to define a "sports bar." Not anymore. Today's premier sports bars not only have multiple high-definition screens for watching the action, but they also offer premium brews, boutique wines, and a killer menu. Tanya Steel, editor in chief of epicurious.com, talks about places to watch the Super Bowl.

Spitfire, Seattle, Washington
With 22 LCD TVs and two large-screen projectors, Spitfire attracts ardent sports fans every day of the week. "This airy, loftlike establishment also brings them in because of its authentic and full-flavored Mexican fare. Fish tacos, chorizo-and-cheese-stuffed mushrooms, and roasted pork tamales are just a few of the offerings—complemented by 18 types of margaritas." *spitfireseattle.com*

The Bulldog Northeast, Minneapolis, Minnesota
The Bulldog Northeast doesn't look like your standard sports bar.
It has light brick walls, floor-to-ceiling
windows, and a very whimsical modern
bar. But sports-viewing is at its core,
with flat screens visible from every seat.
"Patrons also come for the Bulldog's
creative take on traditional sports bar
fare. The menu boasts a dozen 'designer
burgers'—including a togarashi burger with Japanese coleslaw and
wasabi mayo." *thebulldognortheast.com*

Thomas Street Tavern, Charlotte, North Carolina
Open 365 days a year, this popular, family-owned, neighborhood
tavern features an outdoor patio in front and a beer garden in back.
"Both are pet-friendly, so you can bring your pooch and still check
out the game. The menu tends toward the natural and organic,
with most ingredients bought from local farmers markets and
bakeries. There are 60 different bottled beers to complement the
excellent cuisine."

Waterfront Cafe, Boston, Massachusetts
Located in Boston's historic North End district, the Waterfront
Cafe bills itself as an "Italian Pub"—and is apt to be crowded with
rabid Patriots fans each Sunday. The menu is extensive, with homemade ravioli and pastas predominating. "But they're also known
for their seafood and juicy Black Angus burgers." An extensive
wine list includes labels from all the regions of Italy. "If you tire of
watching sports on the 15 televisions, there's also a great view of
Boston Harbor." *waterfront-cafe.com*

Jake Melnick's Corner Tap, Chicago, Illinois
The motto splashed across the wall at Jake Melnick's says it all:
"Why go home? You're here." This homey Chicago establishment
offers 80 beers and a selection of authentic regional hot dogs to
choose from. "You can also attempt the eight-pound monster
burger or the savory 17-Hour Slow Smoked Barbecue Beef Brisket
Sandwich." There are also 17 flat-screen TVs strategically placed
for sports fans. *jakemelnicks.com*

Frankie's Sports Bar and Grill, Dallas, Texas
Located deep in the heart of Dallas, Frankie's is nirvana for Texas sports fans. Patrons can view games on any of 26 high-definition plasma TVs, including two 10-foot-wide projection screens. "Frankie's offers a classic sports bar menu—but it's a menu on steroids. The nachos, for example, are topped with big strips of steak." *frankiesbar.com*

The Blue Seats, New York, New York
Tucked away in the heart of New York's Lower East Side, The Blue Seats is a sports bar with edge and attitude. "It has more flat-screen televisions (62 at last count) than beers, martinis served ten different ways, and a menu that includes items like bacon-wrapped scallops and a grilled vegetable and goat cheese quesadilla." *theblueseatsnyc.com*

Average Joe's Sports Pub and Grub, Indianapolis, Indiana
This popular Indianapolis hangout has dedicated itself to what it calls "the weekend warrior—the average 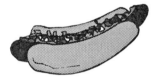 beer-drinking, hot-dog-eating sports fanatic." These same amateur sportsmen and sportswomen—whose photos cover the walls—can watch the pros on the pub's 14 televisions (including two in the bathrooms). "Joe's offers chicken wings served 13 different ways, with a slate of premium beers to wash them down with. *www.averagejoes.ws*

Barney's Beanery, West Hollywood, California
When the first Barney's Beanery opened in 1920 on historic Route 66, travelers could trade in their license plates for a free beer. In the 1960s, the place was a hangout for rock icons such as Janis Joplin, Jim Morrison, and Jimi Hendrix. "Today, patrons come not just to soak in the atmosphere and history but to catch games on the 40 TVs. With over 130 beers and hundreds of items on its menu, Barney's has become one of L.A.'s top spots for sports fanatics." *barneysbeanery.com*

Dino's Sports Lounge, Latrobe, Pennsylvania
"Pittsburgh sports fans drive out to this beloved Latrobe bar for

the atmosphere and to chow down on Dino's most popular fare—the Wings of Joy." Sports memorabilia adorn the walls, much of it dedicated to the Steelers, who train in Latrobe, about 35 miles or so from downtown Pittsburgh. "One side of Dino's is a family-friendly restaurant, and the other side a traditional sports bar. No matter which one you choose, you're sure to have a great seat for the game." *dinoslatrobe.com*

10 great places for
a parade of football

You've watched your alma mater put up a fight on the field all season, and now the bragging rights come down to one game. But which bowl games are worth the trek? ESPN/ABC analyst Craig James shares his list of top bowl locales.

Rose Bowl presented by Citi, Pasadena, California
The Rose Bowl is rooted in history, and pigskin aficionados come from far and wide. "Tradition, great games, scenery, excitement. I love being in Pasadena, California, on New Year's Day. The weather is awesome, and Game Day is a special event." The game follows the world-famous Tournament of Roses parade. *tournamentofroses.com/rosebowlgame/*

FedEx Orange Bowl, Miami, Florida
It's easy to get caught up in *la vida loca* in Miami with its endless bars and nightclubs. "I was reminded how beautiful Miami is after announcing a game there this season—even more so in January, when you're surrounded by sun, water, beaches, and people with free spirits. Dining in South Beach is off-the-charts good. It's a city with the entire package: scenery, food, and atmosphere." *orangebowl.org*

MAACO Bowl Las Vegas, Las Vegas, Nevada
Sin City's MAACO Bowl is for fans who like to work hard in the stands, then play hard after the game. "The city has a consistent energy. Not to be confused with a town full of tailgating crazies all painted up, but at game time, there is a full stadium with a nice

atmosphere." It goes almost without saying that entertainment options after the game are endless. *lvbowl.com*

AT&T Cotton Bowl, Dallas, Texas
Out-of-towners and locals alike flock to the urban-chic West End for museums and nightlife. "Big D has Victory Park near downtown for social events." *attcottonbowl.com*

Pacific Life Holiday Bowl, San Diego, California
One of James's favorite cities, San Diego hosts the Pacific Life Holiday Bowl each December. Among major draws: nightlife in the Gaslamp Quarter and visiting a world-class zoo in the daytime. "Lunch in La Jolla is the best. The Holiday Bowl is always packed with fans and usually one of the better games of the season." *holidaybowl.com*

Champs Sports Bowl, Orlando, Florida
Orlando boasts theme parks galore, including Walt Disney World and Sea World, so parents and kids can have fun in the sun together. "The city brings out the kid in you, and it's an easy place to get to." *fcsports.com*

Tostitos Fiesta Bowl, Glendale, Arizona
"It's obvious why so many people winter in this area. It's a green oasis in the middle of the desert. The Fiesta Bowl committee knows how to put on a first-class event." The area is renowned for spas and meditation resorts, so try to sneak in some time to ease those game-day nerves. *fiestabowl.org*

Gaylord Hotels Music City Bowl, Nashville, Tennessee
Grab your cowboy hat and head to Nashville, country music capital of the world. "You can walk the streets of downtown and go door-to-door, and each restaurant and bar has live music." Also, don't miss the Country Music Hall of Fame and Museum. *musiccitybowl.com*

Valero Alamo Bowl, San Antonio, Texas
"There's nothing more historical in football-rich Texas than the Alamo. Ride in a boat along the river, with the Christmas lights hanging in the trees. It's fiesta time." *valeroalamobowl.com*

Sheraton Hawaii Bowl, Honolulu, Hawaii
For the ultimate bowl-game vacation, head to Hawaii. "I've
announced two of these games, and it's almost silly to put in for
a paycheck for working. Shopping, the beaches, you name it. It's
Hawaii!" *sheratonhawaiibowl.com*

Bowled over with sponsors

There once was the Sugar Bowl in New Orleans, the Orange Bowl in
Miami, the Cotton Bowl in Dallas. Straightforward. Clean. Simple.

No longer.

The Sugar Bowl is now the Allstate Sugar Bowl, the Orange Bowl
is the FedEx Orange Bowl, and the Cotton Bowl is the AT&T Cotton
Bowl.

What next?

Well, there's also the Tostitos Fiesta Bowl, the AdvoCare V100
Independence Bowl, Roady's Humanitarian Bowl, the AutoZone Liberty
Bowl, the Chick-fil-A Bowl, and the Little Caesars Pizza Bowl. And the
sponsorships show no sign of stopping.

---

10 great places to watch
a high school football game

*The magic is in the names: Paul Brown Tiger Stadium...the
Wolvarena. The magic is in the traditions: tailgating at West
Monroe, Louisiana...the smell of fried chicken and catfish at Belle
Glade, Florida. The magic is in the night: each fall Friday, when
the populations of entire towns and cities are the congregations
and high school football stadiums their places of worship. With
help from reader input, USA Today came up with this list of places
where the sights and sounds of high school football are most vivid.*

The Pit, Elder High School, Cincinnati, Ohio
A sign on the press box sums it up: The Pit, Elder's 12th Man.
Opened in 1947, with a 10,000-seat capacity, the stadium's side-
lines are five yards from the concrete stands, creating an intimate

and intimidating setting. Students of the Catholic boys school stand during the entire game, their cheers drowning out the opposing quarterback. Arrive early or you'll park as much as a mile away.

Dr. Effie Grear Stadium, Glades Central Community High School, Belle Glade, Florida
During the games, the grill smoke of chicken wings, ribs, Jamaican jerk meats, seafood, catfish, and baked beans wafts above the stadium. There are a limited number of season tickets sold as part of a reserved-seat section at the 50-yard line, where the lucky few devour shrimp, crab, and other treats. And that's just the food. Glades Central has sent 31 players to the pros, including four first-round draft choices, and the school reports that nearly 100 former players are playing some level of college football.

Turtle Creek Stadium, aka the Wolvarena, Woodland Hills High School, Pittsburgh, Pennsylvania
Built in 1942, the stadium got its name from the school's nickname, the Wolverines. The field has no track, and the 12,500 seats begin less than ten yards from the sidelines. If you really want an earful of gossip on game day, head over to Smitty's, a legendary establishment 100 yards from the stadium entrance. Fans can dine on Eastern European favorites at the stadium such as stuffed cabbage, kielbasa, and sauerkraut.

Cleveland Field at Bazemore-Hyder Stadium, Valdosta High School, Valdosta, Georgia
There is a tunnel leading out of the locker room to the stadium, which was built in 1922. On their way out, the players, usually 90 or more, hit the underside of the tin roof with their helmets. The noise can be intimidating, especially when a microphone is placed next to the tunnel and fed to a full stadium.

Ratliff Stadium, Permian High School, Odessa, Texas
Permian High School was the subject of the popular book, movie, and TV program *Friday Night Lights*, which detailed the personality of the town and program. When the wave of black-clad players

comes on the field, the cheering erupts. The parking lots around the stadium can have a college feel, because fans drive their RVs to the stadium and set up grills for tailgating. The Permian band has 300 members, and it can stir the crowd with its rendition of the *Hawaii 5-0* theme song.

Paul Brown Tiger Stadium, Washington High School, Massillon, Ohio

Games at Paul Brown Tiger Stadium have a long-standing tradition of community fan involvement originated by former coach and Pro Football Hall of Famer Paul Brown in the 1930s. Game day includes bonfires, parades, and an average of almost 10,000 fans. Townsfolk show their spirit by adorning shop windows with orange-and-black decorations; even the fire hydrants have tiger stripes. But that's nothing compared to this: Every male child born in the township has a tiny Massillon rubber football placed in his cradle.

Duchon Field, Glenbard West High School, Glen Ellyn, Illinois

This affluent community in the western suburbs of Chicago lays claim to one of the most scenic football settings around. The school is built in the style of a castle, complete with roof turrets, atop what was called Honeysuckle Hill in 1922. The Hilltoppers' home field is a short downhill walk away. The field's backdrop is Lake Ellyn Park, a manmade lake surrounded by copious trees. Spectators in the bleachers of the home side are treated to a colorful display of foliage on autumn Saturday afternoons.

Arthur County High School, Arthur, Nebraska

Arthur County is nestled between the Great Plains and the foot-hills of the Rockies—the Nebraska sand hills, a series of rolling, grassy rises. Tucked behind the schoolhouse in a grove of trees and surrounded on all sides by the rolling hills is the football field. It doesn't have a name or lights, but on Friday afternoons in fall, the courthouse closes early, and most of the county's 400 residents can be found at the game. Fans drive right up and find seats on the benches or, in the case of most of the dads, follow the ball up and down the sidelines.

Dunlavy Stadium, Sonora High School, Sonora, California

Dunlavy Stadium's cement bleachers are embedded into the foothills of the Sierra Nevadas. During the fall, the foliage is spectacular, and you can hear the roar of the crowd and band in downtown Sonora, a half mile away. Arrive early on game night for the Future Farmers of America Barbecue, featuring beef ribs, tri-tips, Polish sausage, and chili beans.

> ## And they're not even pros
>
> The $30 million film *Friday Night Lights*, starring Billy Bob Thornton, about the Permian High School football team earned $61 million in theaters in 2004.

Rebel Stadium, West Monroe High School, West Monroe, Louisiana
West Monroe offers a college atmosphere with great tailgating food, specializing in red beans and rice and jambalaya. Home games are sold out, with the crowd ringing cowbells throughout. A national-award-winning band along with cheerleaders and a pep squad keep the air reverberating with spirit.

10 great places to stand and cheer college football

You don't have to be part of the alumni to enjoy college pigskin play. For those looking to catch a live game, check out ESPN/ABC's Ed Cunningham's picks for preferred playing fields.

Neyland Stadium, Knoxville, Tennessee
"The Southeastern Conference deserves several on this list, because the game truly is followed more passionately in the Southeast than any other part of the country. You would be well served to learn 'Rocky Top' before getting to Neyland Stadium, so you can join in with the 102,000-plus University of Tennessee fans who will be singing it at the top of their lungs if the Vols deliver a big win that afternoon." That is, if the fans still have their voices left after the infamous pregame tailgates. *utsports.com*

Darrell K. Royal–Texas Memorial Stadium, Austin, Texas
If you're hoping to have a ball in Austin, plan accordingly. "With its mix of politics; hippie culture; and the large, world-class University of Texas with its Darrell K. Royal-Texas Memorial Stadium, you'll

need at least three days to take in a great college football atmosphere. Add in the music scene on Sixth Street and the Tex-Mex food, and this is always a favorite stop." *texassports.com*

Husky Stadium, Seattle, Washington
By land or by sea, the University of Washington's home field offers seats with a view. "Find a friend of a friend who can offer a boat ride on Lake Washington to Husky Stadium for the game to tailgate in a whole new way. If the sky is clear, venture up to the northwest upper deck and take in a spectacular view of Mount Rainier and the game." *gohuskies.com*

Folsom Field, Boulder, Colorado
"Situated in one of the most beautiful towns in all of America, you can catch yourself looking at the views more than the action at Folsom Field, home of the University of Colorado Buffaloes. If you happen to be lucky enough to be on the field for the game itself, always keep your eyes peeled for the running of Ralphie the Buffalo, the school's mascot. His handlers are not really directing him as much as hanging on for dear life." *cubuffs.com*

Memorial Stadium, Clemson, South Carolina
The cheers and jeers of Clemson University fans in Memorial Stadium can be deafening, earning it the nickname "Death Valley." "Pack your earplugs for when the Tigers rub 'Howard's Rock' before taking the field, as college football's coolest team entrance gets the loyalists' vocal cords good and ready for the action. If you happen to go the weekend the hated Gamecocks of the University of South Carolina visit, plan an extra two to three hours to get to your seat, as more people come to hang outside of the stadium than go into it on that particular November Saturday." *clemsontigers.com*

Beaver Stadium, State College, Pennsylvania
Penn State fans take to the bleachers as much for the coach as they do for the players. "Go before Coach (Joe) Paterno stops roaming the sidelines of Beaver Stadium, which is one of the few venues in the sport that looks bigger in person than on your flat screen. Be in the building in time to see 'JoePa' greet the student section during warm-ups, and make sure

to stop by the Berkey Creamery to get a scoop of Peachy Paterno while on campus." *gopsusports.com*

Lane Stadium, Blacksburg, Virginia

Virginia Tech's game-goers make a sport out of being a fan. "Make sure to take your 'college-football-is-so-much-better-than-the-pros' buddy to a Thursday night game at Lane Stadium and experience how the Hokies helped make that the Monday Night Football for the college game. Book far enough in advance to stay in Blacksburg, and you'll enjoy a great small college town during your downtime." *hokiesports.com*

Vaught-Hemingway Stadium, Oxford, Mississippi

If a Heisman were awarded for top tailgater, the winner would surely come from Ole Miss. "Pack a picnic and hit the Grove on campus early on game day, as the regulars often stake claim to their territory the night before. The day-long party is one of the great scenes in all of college football, and it will hit a fevered pitch when the Rebels walk through on their way to Vaught-Hemingway Stadium." *vaughthemingway.com*

Memorial Stadium, Lincoln, Nebraska

"The all-red-clad patrons of Memorial Stadium make this a memorable place regardless of the outcome. Lincoln is one of those college towns that give the term 'college town' such special meaning." *huskers.com*

Camp Randall Stadium, Madison, Wisconsin

A few Hail Mary passes from the State Capitol, it's often the postgame festivities that fans love most at the University of Wisconsin. "If you don't know where State Street is for the after-game festivities, just follow the masses. Make sure deep-fried cheddar balls are on the menu before fighting for a table." *uwbadgers.com*

Football is not a contact sport; it's a collision sport. Dancing is a good example of a contact sport.
—Hugh "Duffy" Daugherty

Pro mascots play with danger

While professional athletes go out and tear up the playing field, the team mascot may be on the sidelines tearing up his knees, ripping tendons, or suffering heatstroke inside those heavy, furred, or feathered costumes.

Edward McFarland, director of adult orthopedics and an associate professor for orthopedics at Johns Hopkins University, found in a 2001 study of 48 professional team mascots that 58 percent had suffered heat-related injury, 44 percent reported chronic lower back pain, and 17 percent suffered knee injuries while on the job.

Questionnaires completed by the mascots, who represent pro football, baseball, and basketball teams, reported an average of 2.7 injuries for every 1,000 appearances. In all, 179 injuries were reported by the mascots, and 22 required surgery.

"Overall, they're relatively safe," McFarland says, "but some of the injuries were pretty bizarre."

One mascot was pushed off a wall by a fan, another tore his knee doing a somersault, one was hit by a camera truck, and several were injured by fans, "which reflects the fact that sometimes we don't think that there's a person inside that costume," McFarland says.

Former Orioles mascot Bromley Lowe once lost the tip of a finger on his right hand in a freak accident caused by limits on peripheral vision imposed by the giant bird costume. He was in a basement area before going onto the field. "I put my hand against what I thought was a wall, but it was the opening of a steel door that automatically closed and cut off part of my finger," he says.

He also suffered heat exhaustion, requiring emergency intravenous fluid replenishment, and says he regularly lost ten pounds during a baseball game inside a suit that was "black fur from the top of my head to the bottom of my feet." Lowe says the job was physically demanding and exhausting. "If it wasn't fun," he says, "this would be the most miserable job on earth."

GOLF

10 great places to tee off
on a course to die for

*Unlike summer-only games, golf can be played—in some places—
all year-round. Chris Santella, author of* Fifty Places to Play
Golf Before You Die: Golf Experts Share the World's Greatest
Destinations, *shares some special courses favored by the experts.*

Banff Springs, Banff, Alberta, Canada
"Situated a mile high in the Canadian Rockies, Banff Springs
is one of the most spectacular golf-course settings in the world.
Legendary architect Stanley Thompson sculpted the course on a
broad scale to maximize the impact of the vistas. A hole called the
'Devil's Cauldron' is framed by Mount Rundle and considered one
of the game's most compelling par-3s." *fairmont.com/banffsprings*

Pebble Beach Golf Links, Pebble Beach, California
"Located on the incomparable Monterey Peninsula, Pebble was
created by Jack Neville. Masters and British Open winner Mark
O'Meara says he puts Pebble at the top of his list, and the
par-5 18th hole defines Pebble for many television viewers:
O'Meara has walked that fairway as a champion five times."
pebblebeach.com

Highlands Links, Ingonish Beach, Cape Breton, Nova Scotia,
Canada
"Cape Breton is one of the world's most beautiful islands, boasting
this world-class golf course. Stanley Thompson, commissioned by
the Canadian National Park Service to design Highlands, fashioned
a great seaside and mountain course—check out the par-5 15th
hole with its wildly rolling fairway." *golfcapebreton.com*

Old Works Golf Course, Anaconda, Montana
"Designed by Jack Nicklaus, the course was built on the site of an
old copper smelter and incorporates smelters and other elements
of the defunct mining operation into the backdrop. Most notable

are the intimidating black slag bunkers" and prevailing winds. *oldworks.org*

Waialua Municipal Golf Course, Kauai, Hawaii

"Kauai is home to many wish-list golf venues such as Princeville and Kauai Lagoons, but locals, such as former LPGA pro Mary Bea Porter King, favor Waialua Municipal. Tucked on the eastern coast of Kauai, Waialua winds through groves of coconut, Norfolk pine, and ironwood trees, with four holes adjoining Waialua Bay and Waialua Golf Course Beach."

Sugarloaf/USA Golf Club, Carrabassett Valley, Maine

"Hewn from the Maine woods on mountainous terrain filled with wildlife, Sugarloaf affords panoramic views of the Carrabassett Valley; noted course architect Robert Trent Jones claims it as 'one of the most spectacular courses I've ever been associated with.' Holes 10 through 15, dubbed the String of Pearls by Jones, run adjacent and over the Carrabassett River." *sugarloaf.com/summer.html*

Genoa Lakes Golf Club, Carson City, Nevada

"Resting on the dry eastern side of the Sierra Nevada, Genoa Lakes boasts expansive views of the mountains to the west and Nevada's great open spaces to the east. The course, codesigned by PGA champion Peter Jacobsen, winds along the Carson River and accompanying wetlands, bringing water into play on 13 holes." *genoalakes.com*

Casa de Campo Resort, La Romana, Dominican Republic

"One of legendary architect Pete Dye's most celebrated courses, [Casa de Campo's] Teeth of the Dog is named for a local term describing the island's jagged-edged coral reefs. The Caribbean-bordering par-3s are the Dog's main draw, and down on the fifth and the seventh holes, you're so close to the water that you can feel the spray." *casadecampo.com.do*

The Sagamore, Bolton Landing, New York

"This is a classic Donald Ross–designed course adjacent to a classic resort on Lake George. Routed through a thick pine forest and accented with occasional plots of heather (a nod to Ross's youth in Scotland), the routing offers glimpses of the lake and the Adirondack foothills, plus Ross's trademark small and subtly contoured greens." *thesagamore.com*

Pacific Dunes, Bandon, Oregon
"When Bandon Dunes opened in 1999, it took the golf world by storm, but when Pacific Dunes opened in 2001, it wrested the attention from Bandon. Architect Tom Doak exploits the site's rugged terrain, tremendous vistas, and giant sand dunes to sublime effect. Thick fields of gorse punish errant shots," and undulating fairways challenge the best. *bandondunesgolf.com*

10 great places to go for the green—and be green

It's undeniably hip to be green nowadays—and nowhere is that more true than on golf courses, many of which are taking a leadership role in environmental stewardship. Joe Passov, senior editor for travel and course rankings at GOLF Magazine, shares his picks for top ecofriendly resort courses.

Amelia Island Plantation, Amelia Island, Florida
Bracketed by the Atlantic Ocean and the Intracoastal Waterway, this island resort sits just 30 miles north of Jacksonville. A master plan that dates to the resort's opening in 1971 includes protections for tidal marshes, oceanfront dunes, native grasslands, and savannahs. "Amelia Island's four courses aren't long, but they're incredibly scenic. Aside from the great golf, guided environmental tours with staff naturalists are available to guests." *aipfl.com*

Barton Creek Resort & Spa, Austin, Texas
This 4,000-acre spread rests in the heart of Texas Hill Country. Thanks to the resort's efforts to protect native wildlife and vegetation, all four Barton Creek golf courses are Certified Audubon Sanctuaries. "Barton Creek's back-to-nature appeal stems from a plethora of stout live oaks, tall cedars, waterfalls, and rock outcroppings. The par-5 18th hole at the Fazio Foothills course, which plays over and around a natural limestone cave, is unforgettable." *bartoncreek.com*

The Broadmoor, Colorado Springs, Colorado
Located one hour south of Denver, with a head-on view of the
Rocky Mountains, the Broadmoor is one of the grandest resort
properties in the United States. In addition to a resortwide recycling program, the Broadmoor uses innovative water-use reduction
methods for its three golf courses, including drip irrigation and a
high-tech rain monitoring system. "The resort has also converted
50 acres of golf turfgrass to native grasslands and wildflower areas."
broadmoor.com

Kapalua Resort, Kapalua, Maui, Hawaii
In the native Hawaiian language, *kapalua* means "arms embracing
the sea." These days, the Kapalua resort embraces environmental protection. "The resort's two golf courses are both Certified
Audubon Sanctuaries, preserving native plants and protecting rare
species of birds and animals that are found nowhere else in the
world. And where else can a golfer spy a breaching whale while
teeing off?" *cms.kapalua.com*

Pebble Beach Resorts, Pebble Beach, California
Since 1919, two of the most magical words for traveling golfers
have been "pebble" and "beach." Put them together and you have
one of the world's most exalted golf
resorts. You also have one of the
most environmentally sensitive.
"Wastewater reclamation, protecting harbor seal nursery areas, and
preserving waterfowl habitat are
among Pebble Beach's positive
efforts. The golf here is legendary,
but it's the small, quiet moments

that linger—like a quartet of deer grazing contentedly ten feet
from where you're teeing off." *pebblebeach.com*

Kiawah Island Golf Resort, Kiawah Island, South Carolina
Situated on a protected barrier island 20 miles south of Charleston,
this low-key resort is the only facility on a ten-mile stretch of
beach. "Kiawah has five golf courses, all of which seamlessly
blend into the natural Lowcountry environment. If you tire of the

great golf, there is twilight kayaking on the Kiawah River, canoeing through the resort's labyrinth of tidal creeks, and bicycling on 30 miles of trails." *kiawahresort.com*

Mauna Lani Resort, Big Island, Hawaii
"This lava-strewn retreat has worked since its 1981 inception to protect the unique natural and historic features that grace the area. The architects did an admirable job of incorporating and preserving trails, spring-fed fish ponds, rock carvings, and ancient lava-tube dwellings throughout the resort's two golf courses. A three-acre photovoltaic system also allows Mauna Lani to generate the most solar electric power of any luxury resort in the world." *maunalani.com*

Pinehurst Resort, Pinehurst, North Carolina
This historic property in the North Carolina Sandhills has been called "the St. Andrews of American Golf." From U.S. Opens to the Ryder Cup, Pinehurst has hosted just about every big event in the sport. "The purity of the golf experience here is unsurpassed. But the resort is also known for being a pioneer in the 'green golf'

Bonus destination: Myrtle Beach

Greater Myrtle Beach, South Carolina, has more than 100 golf courses and is synonymous with bargain-priced golf (not to mention mini golf). But the area's low cost of living is not limited to hotels and greens fees: It is also a very reasonably priced second-home destination, as many buyers have discovered.

Home of the "shag" dance, Myrtle Beach already was booming as a beach resort by the 1950s. Today the city is the anchor of several adjoining municipalities that make up the Grand Strand, a 60-mile crescent-shaped section of coastal beaches, restaurants, bars, live entertainment venues, malls, and other tourist attractions.

Golf is omnipresent in Myrtle Beach, and while priced low, the quality of play is high: About half the courses are rated four stars or better by *Golf Digest*. Most courses have condos or houses, and most residential developments in the area have at least one golf course—or several.

movement. Among other initiatives, Pinehurst established a Safe Harbor program in 1995 to protect and enhance habitat for endangered birds." *pinehurst.com*

Reynolds Plantation, Greensboro, Georgia
Situated an hour east of Atlanta, Reynolds Plantation's four public-access courses are all Certified Audubon Sanctuaries. "The Plantation also recently earned an Outstanding Business Leadership Award from Rivers Alive, a Georgia environmental-outreach program that centers on keeping waterways clean. Reynolds's backdrop of 19,000-acre Lake Oconee is truly compelling. Residents and golfers alike share space with eagles, owls, wild turkeys, and a host of other wildlife." *reynoldsplantation.com*

Turning Stone Resort & Casino, Verona, New York
Northern New York and great golf resorts are seldom mentioned in the same sentence, but this facility 30 miles east of Syracuse has proved to be a remarkable exception. "The Oneida Indian Nation—which built and owns Turning Stone—has long been known for treating its ancestral lands with the utmost care and respect. The resort's five beautiful golf courses all embody this strong commitment to protect the environment." *turningstone.com*

Regarding the practice of no other sport perhaps on the face of the earth is there so much difference of opinion as in that of golf. The confusion and multiplicity of styles that prevail among players are proof enough of this.
—H. B. Farnie

In so many English sports, something flying or running has to be killed or injured; golf calls for no drop of blood from any living creature.
—Henry Leach

TENNIS

10 great places to get a backhand compliment

*Tennis, anyone? "A lot of sports, over the years, become a game,"
says legendary tennis star Billie Jean King, ranked No. 1 in the
world five times between 1966 and 1972, listed in the top ten for
17 years, and a four-time winner of the U.S. Open. Today, she is an
active promoter of public access to and public programs in tennis.
"I'm a product of the public parks system, and if I had not had my
first free group lesson at Houghton Park in Long Beach, I may not
have become a tennis player." Here, she shares some favorite public
spots to "keep tennis alive in hometowns" and elsewhere.*

Barnes Tennis Center, San Diego, California
"Few public facilities cater to and focus on junior players, but this
one is a mecca for juniors, who all play free. As a junior, I remember we begged for court time or waited around for a pickup match
with an adult. Things are different at Barnes; it's why the WTT
Junior National is held here each August." *barnestenniscenter.com*

Tualatin Hills Park and Recreation District, Beaverton, Oregon
"The 14 hard courts at this public tennis center are a real gem
in the Pacific Northwest. One of the better-run facilities in the
country, they offer several leagues and scheduled events. You
also can just drop in and pick up a game."
thprd.org/facilities/hmttennis/home.cfm

University of Nevada at Las Vegas, Las Vegas, Nevada
"An excellent place to play or watch tennis is right here at UNLV,
located just off the Strip. When the women's and men's collegiate
seasons are in play, there is some great action to catch at this
well-run facility, with 12 lighted courts and a great stadium setup."
unlvrebels.com/index-main.html

East Beach Tennis Center, Kiawah Island, South Carolina
At the Kiawah Island Golf Resort, "there is an abundance of
choices if you are combining tennis with vacation." Hall of Fame

tennis pro Roy Barth oversees clinics, drills, and lessons on clay and hard courts for players of all skill levels. *kiawahresort.com/tennis*

Jimmy Evert Tennis Center, Fort Lauderdale, Florida

Billed as "one of the nation's finest public tennis facilities," the center, located in tropical Holiday Park, "was started by Chris Evert's father (Chris Evert played and practiced here) and also was home court to Jennifer Capriati. It features 18 lighted clay courts and three hard courts, plus instruction for all levels and ages." And don't forget to visit the center's own Hall of Fame. *ci.ftlaud.fl.us/tennis/jetc.htm*

Tennis Complex at Golden Gate Park, San Francisco, California

"This facility, home court to the great Alice Marble, Rosie Casals, William 'Little Bill' Johnston, and others, has something for everyone." The complex features 21 courts in addition to "a number of lessons and special programs, especially for young players—and there is so much history in this great park setting." *sfgate.com/neighborhoods/sf/goldengatepark*

El Paso Youth Tennis Center, El Paso, Texas

"This public facility has hosted several national tournaments, from juniors to professional-level events. The staff is committed to taking care of the area youth and assists with college scholarships for program participants." *epytc.org*

USTA National Tennis Center, Flushing, New York

"The home of the U.S. Open is the largest public tennis facility in the world and operates almost year-round. It has 45 courts, including a great indoor setup, and all of the famed outdoor courts where the current greats of the game do battle. The center runs a number of programs for players of all ages and playing levels—it's great to drop in and pick up a game." *usta.com*

Dwight Davis Memorial Tennis Center, St. Louis, Missouri

"Missouri is home to several of the finest public tennis facilities in the nation. This one, named for the founder of the famed Davis

Cup, is located in Forest Park, the second-largest public park in the country." *dwightdavistennis.com*

Blackburn Tennis Center, Atlanta, Georgia
In Atlanta, "they really enjoy their tennis, and there is an abundance of excellent tennis facilities, such as the Bitsy Grant Tennis Center, Stone Mountain, and Blackburn, an outstanding county facility that features 18 lighted hard courts and instruction for all levels." *blackburntenniscenter.net*

10 great places to indulge your love for tennis

Even if you haven't quite mastered your ace serve, you can still enjoy playing for fun—and watching professional players take it to the net. Bud Collins, who has covered tennis worldwide for more than 40 years, shares his favorite venues.

Indian Wells Tennis Garden, Indian Wells, California
This state-of-the-art facility, which hosts the BNP Paribas Open, boasts the second-largest tennis stadium in the world (seating capacity 16,000) and a full-service tennis club. "It's a beautifully designed venue, situated right at the base of the Santa Rosa Mountains. The tournament draws many of the world's elite players, the weather is ideal, and the atmosphere friendly and festive." The nearby golf courses, shops, and restaurants of Palm Springs offer plenty of diversions. *iwtg.net; bnpparibasopen.org*

Tennis Center at Crandon Park, Key Biscayne, Florida
The Sony Ericsson Open has grown to become one of the world's premier pro tournaments, drawing dozens of top players to South Florida each spring. "The setting is wonderful, just a stone's throw from the Atlantic Ocean. The atmosphere here has a touch of Latin culture to it, with terrific food and music." *sonyericssonopen.com*

Foro Italico, Rome, Italy
Built in the 1930s, Foro Italico encompasses several historic sports venues, including the Stadio Olympico, which hosted the 1960 Olympic Games. Today Foro Italico hosts the Internazionali

BNL d'Italia each spring. "The tennis center sits at the foot of Monte Mario, the highest hill in Rome. The back courts here are particularly appealing—they're surrounded by tall pines and terraced lawns, allowing fans to sit on the grass in the shade and watch the matches." Another unique aspect to this clay-court event: Men and women compete in successive weeks (men play first). *internazionalibnlditalia.it*

Stade de Roland Garros, Paris, France
The French Open, the historic clay-court tourney dating back to 1891, was the first of the four Grand Slams to go "open" in 1968. The main stadium here—which seats 14,800—is named after

If the sporting life's for you, these tours are too

More and more travel companies are specializing in sports vacations. A sampling of tours:

Pick a sport, any sport

Canadian-based Roadtrips offers professional hockey, basketball, football, golf, baseball, and auto racing vacations. *roadtrips.com*

A vacation to love

Love tennis? Grand Slam Tennis Tours specializes in major tournaments. Tours include accommodations and transfers to the event. *tennistrips.com*

Gentlemen, start your trip

Grand Prix Tours, based in Newport Beach, California, focuses on auto racing packages. Travelers can choose from Formula One, NASCAR, Le Mans, and Vintage races worldwide. Packages include accommodations, breakfast, and airport and track transfers. Tickets are sold separately. *gptours.com*

Back in the saddle

Equestrain Vacations puts travelers in the saddle with equestrian tours around the world. Most packages include accommodations but not air or taxes. *equestrianvacations.com*

Roland Garros, an early French aviator and World War I fighter pilot. "The French Open has become a huge Parisian event. The atmosphere is highly charged. The fans are knowledgeable and quick to show emotion." When you've had enough tennis, the cafés, shops, museums, and vibrant streets of Paris await. *rolandgarros.com*

Monte-Carlo Country Club, Monte Carlo, Monaco
The annual Monte-Carlo Rolex Masters boasts one of the most beautiful settings on the men's ATP Tour. "The club, which dates to the 1920s, is built on a series of 'shelves' overlooking the Mediterranean Sea. The grounds are beautifully landscaped, with palm trees, vibrant colors, and spectacular views." This is a clay-court tournament, which makes for hard-fought rallies and ferocious play. Après tennis, fans can enjoy the sophisticated shops, elegant hotels, and posh restaurants of this compact principality. *smett.mc*

International Tennis Hall of Fame & Museum,
Newport, Rhode Island
In 1881, Newport hosted the first U.S. National Lawn Tennis Championships, which ultimately became the U.S. Open. "The event now held here each summer (the Campbell's Hall of Fame Tennis Championship) is the last remaining professional tennis tournament played on grass in North America. The annual Hall of Fame induction ceremonies take place during the final weekend, adding quite a bonus for the fans." Near the grounds, several of the lavish "Newport Cottage" mansions are open for public tours. *tennisfame.com*

All England Club, Wimbledon, England
Since the first "Championships" were held here in 1877, Wimbledon has grown from its roots as a garden-party gathering into a Grand Slam tournament with a following of millions around the world. "Yet, Wimbledon has managed to retain both its charm and its unique traditions. Ivy and flowers still cover the grounds, strawberries and cream are still offered, and the matches are still played on 'God's own sod'—grass." One welcome change: The famed Centre Court now sports a retractable roof. *wimbledon.org*

Connecticut Tennis Center at Yale,
New Haven, Connecticut
Billed as "New England's Ultimate Tennis Experience," the Pilot Pen Tennis Championships are held on the historic and beautiful campus of Yale University each August. The "Ivy League Casual" atmosphere is appealing to fans and players alike. "This tournament has an intimate feel that lets fans see the tennis action up close. Within walking distance of campus is downtown New Haven, which offers a host of shops, art galleries, and exquisite restaurants." *pilotpentennis.com*

USTA Billie Jean King National Tennis Center,
New York, New York
The year's fourth and final Grand Slam, the U.S. Open is a distinctively American tennis event. "Sitting in Arthur Ashe Stadium—which holds 23,000—is a bit like going to a ballgame at Yankee Stadium. The crowds are always loud and boisterous." The smaller outside courts give tennis fans a chance to see the players up close in the early rounds of play. "The grounds here are spacious, with musical entertainment and a host of other diversions." *usopen.org*

Melbourne Park, Melbourne, Australia
The annual Australian Open is the calendar year's first Grand Slam tournament. "It's nicknamed the 'Happy Slam' by the pros, and for good reason. The tournament is held during Australia's midsummer; many people are on vacation; and the atmosphere is friendly, relaxed, and partylike." The stadium's retractable roof protects players and fans against what can be blistering hot temperatures. *australianopen.com*

Sports do not build character.
They reveal it.
> —Heywood Broun

BOATING AND FISHING

10 great places to inspire Dad to post "Gone Fishing"

Not much can top the time-honored tradition of a father-child fishing trip for sports-enthusiast dads. Michael Cooley, president and CEO of The Sportsman Channel, suggests spots that will make Dad fall hook, line, and sinker.

Clear Lake, California
California's largest natural freshwater lake is known for its stock of largemouth bass. Take Dad here and try to break the world record by reeling in a big one. Clear Lake is "not your traditional tourist trap. It's a rustic place to enjoy the scenery and go camping and fishing." Its location, not far from San Francisco and near Mendocino, Sonoma, and Napa counties, also makes it ideal to combine with a wine-tasting trip. *parks.ca.gov/?page_id=473*

Lake Guntersville, Alabama
"On a good day you can boat 20 to 40 two- to six-pound bass" at Alabama's largest lake. The area has plenty of good guides and lodging for a father-child getaway. Save time to go eagle-watching or play a round at the championship 18-hole golf course on the grounds of Lake Guntersville State Park. *alapark.com/parks/park.cfm?parkid=5*

Apalachicola, Florida
Soak up the sun on the Apalachicola River, along the Gulf of Mexico, which has everything from redfish to speckled trout, grouper to snapper. The area, southwest of Tallahassee, has miles of uncrowded beaches and some of the finest seafood along the bay. Spend some time strolling through the small town's more than 200 historic buildings, or rent a kayak to explore the isolated marshes and swamps located upriver. *apalachicolabay.org*

Sitka, Alaska
"This seaside community offers king and steelhead salmon and halibut fishing at its best." Set against the dramatic scenery of

snowcapped mountains to the east and the Pacific Ocean to the west, this is a top spot to fish, whether on a boat or wading into shallow waters. Take a boat trip to see whales, sea otters, and sea lions. The area, which lies at the heart of the world's largest temperate rain forest, is also perfect for hiking. *sitka.org*

Venice, Louisiana
This city was nearly destroyed by Hurricane Katrina, but reconstruction is progressing. "Locals will agree that the redfish and speckled-trout fishing is the best it's been in years." Venice Marina offers charter boats. *venicemarina.com*

White River, Arkansas
For some quiet and peaceful wilderness time, fish near the clear, cold, and fast waters of the White River near Bull Shoals Lake. Fish with Dad, then enjoy fresh-cooked trout right on the shore. *bullshoals.org*

Montauk, New York
This fishing port at the eastern end of Long Island offers striped bass, bluefish, sea bass, and flounder. Charter a boat for offshore fishing and try to reel in tuna, shark, and marlin. *onmontauk.com*

Eagle River, Wisconsin
"For freshwater fishing at its best, bring your dad here." The Eagle River Three Lakes Chain consists of 28 interconnecting lakes and is the largest inland chain in the world. Cast out for trout, musky, walleye, panfish, and both smallmouth and largemouth bass. *eagleriver.org*

Cape Cod, Massachusetts
Plan a late-summer trip to Cape Cod to watch the striped bass or "striper" migration. "It is a breathtaking experience that will last a lifetime." The area is a haven for lovers of the outdoors, with charter boats for deep-sea fishing and whale watching, and some of the most popular beaches in New England spread along more than 500 miles of coastline. *capecodchamber.org*

North Platte River Valley, Wyoming
Fly-fish against the dramatic mountain backdrop along the North Platte River Valley in Wyoming. This under-the-radar fishing area

is the perfect place to bond while catching brook trout, rainbow trout, brown trout, and a Colorado River cutthroat trout. The area also has the Casper Whitewater Park, a manufactured whitewater facility for kayaking and rafting.

10 great places to take a brand-new tack

Summertime invites boaters to sail away, but you don't have to be regatta-ready to enjoy the wind at your back. Chris Santella, author of Fifty Places to Sail Before You Die, *shares favorite spots to raise the sails.*

Annapolis, Maryland
Citizens of Newport have been known to dispute Annapolis's moniker as "America's Sailing Capital," but the city is undeniably the hub of the mid-Atlantic sailing community. "While it is home for some high-profile races—and the U.S. Naval Academy—a favorite nautical amusement for many Annapolites are the Wednesday night races, sponsored by the Annapolis Yacht Club, where 150 boats or more may compete." *visitannapolis.org*

Marblehead, Massachusetts
"Quaint Marblehead is custom-made for sailing, with water on three sides and a deep natural harbor. Historically, it was where Bostonians came to moor or race their sailboats." The port is a popular spot for starts and finishes of numerous races. "If there's one week to soak in the ambience of Marblehead, it would be the Marblehead Race Week, held each year at the end of July." *visitmarblehead.com*

Newport, Rhode Island
Home to America's Cup races, this historic vacation spot for the well-heeled is a sailor's mecca. "Newport has it all: a deep-water harbor, a large navigable bay, easy access to the ocean, and a great funneling sea breeze. Making landfall in Newport via the East Passage with the wind behind you is one of sailing's great moments." *gonewport.com*

Biscayne Bay, Florida

"Biscayne Bay boasts beautiful turquoise waters, extending some 35 miles south from Miami to Key Largo. One highlight of the racing season is the Rolex Miami Olympic Classes Regatta, an Olympic-qualifying event that draws 600 of the most talented sailors in the world." *nps.gov/bisc*

Resurrection Bay, Alaska

"Alaska has more than 47,300 miles of shoreline, but sailors can get a good sense of the 49th state's sailing opportunities on Resurrection Bay, adjoining the town of Seward. You can sail south and anchor in a fjord in Kenai Fjords National Park and take in the glaciers; cast a line for a fresh coho salmon; and watch sea lions, porpoises, and orcas, as well as gray, humpback, and minke whales swim by." It's not all aquatic wonders you'll spy on this bay. "Moose and grizzly and black bears may also make an appearance onshore to complete your Alaska nature experience." *travelalaska.com*

Channel Islands, California

In this archipelago of islands off California's southern coast, no two are alike. "San Miguel is exposed to harsh open-ocean conditions, where 50-mile-per-hour winds are common." Calmer Catalina "sees more than one million visitors annually, thanks to its 20-odd-mile proximity to Los Angeles." *nps.gov/chis*

San Juan Islands, Washington state

The San Juan Archipelago boasts 700 islands and appeals to the full spectrum of sailors. "There's the scenic beauty of distant snow-capped mountains and pine-studded shorelines, abundant anchorages whichever way the wind is blowing, and the variety of the islands themselves. You can rub elbows with blue-blooded sailors at Roche Harbor, hang out at fun and funky Friday Harbor, or get away from it all on secluded Sucia Island. If you're lucky, you'll spy some of the 90 orcas that call the San Juans home in the summer." *visitsanjuans.com*

Lake Michigan, Illinois

With a nickname like "The Windy City," it's not surprising Chicago sustains a strong sailing community. "The city skyline is brilliant from the deck of a sailboat, especially as night falls. Sailing fever spikes in late July, when the Chicago to Mackinac race is held. The 333-mile race to a small island just beyond Lake Michigan's boundaries dates back to 1898. *choosechicago.com*

Boothbay, Maine

"With more than 3,500 miles of coastline—including hundreds of inviting deep coves and harbors—Maine is a sailor's delight." Start your sail in Boothbay, and head north along the coast. "Further north is Southwest Harbor and the pristine waters surrounding Acadia National Park; all along the way there's the opportunity to enjoy fresh lobster at dockside eateries." *boothbayharbor.com*

San Francisco Bay, California

"Many local sailors use three words to define San Francisco Bay: intense, exciting, and exhilarating. Strong winds, powerful tides and currents, and abundant commercial traffic make for challenging navigation. But racers who come out on top here know they've attained a high level of expertise." Views of the cityscape don't hurt either. *onlyinsanfrancisco.com*

10 great places to compete— hook, line, and sinker

Fishing is a sport—and a competitive one at that, even if you're just fishing with your buddies. David Kinney, author of The Big One, *shares his list of best places to competitively bait a hook.*

$150,000 Ice Fishing Extravaganza, Brainerd, Minnesota

For a reason unfathomable to summer anglers, Minnesotans love their winter ice fishing. The Brainerd Jaycees say that 20,000 holes are drilled in the ice for their annual three-hour contest at Gull Lake. "This claims to be the largest ice-fishing tournament anywhere in the world, and no one disputes that. More than 9,000 bundled-up anglers brave the freezing weather each year for a shot at a pickup truck and other prizes." *icefishing.org*

Bisbee's Black & Blue Marlin Tournament, Cabo San Lucas, Mexico
"This one is billed as the richest fishing tournament in the world. A single crew took home a check for almost $4 million one year. It's a wild scene too, with colorful contestants, super-expensive boats, and lavish parties." *bisbees.com*

Big Rock Blue Marlin Tournament, Morehead City, North Carolina
There are several big-money ocean fishing tournaments on the East Coast, but this event is one of the most notable. More than 150 boats convene on the "Crystal Coast" of North Carolina to try for $1.8 million in prizes. "Even if you don't fish, it's worth cruising down to the waterfront in Morehead City to see the boats come in and watch the fish get weighed to the crowd's applause." *thebigrock.com*

S. Tokunaga Store Ulua Challenge, Hilo, Hawaii
The Ulua Challenge has one especially unique feature among ocean-fishing tournaments: All participants must fish from shore. "There are three other reasons I'd like to fish this one someday: It takes place in Hawaii, the weigh-in and award ceremony goes down in a lively joint called Aunty Sally Kaleohano's Lu'au Hale, and the quarry is the *ulua*—aka the giant trevally—which can top 100 pounds." *tokunagastore.com*

Okie Noodling Tournament, Pauls Valley, Oklahoma
Entrants in this contest don't need any fishing gear at all. "Noodling" is a local term for bare-handed catfishing. Participants prowl the lakeshores and riverbanks in search of catfish holes, then reach in and try to pull the fish out. "The hand-to-gill combat guarantees that fishermen will end up scratched and scraped. But there's also the risk of something worse: There could be a giant catfish in that hole—or even a snapping turtle." *okienoodling.com*

Alabama Deep Sea Fishing Rodeo, Mobile, Alabama
"This one is worth the trip just because it's probably the oldest ongoing fishing tournament in the country. The contest was started back in 1929 by a Mobile businessman trying to drum up tourism. Today more than 3,000 contestants fish it every July,

chasing tarpon, king mackerel, amberjack, and two dozen other kinds of sport fish." At stake: $400,000 in prizes. *adsfr.com*

Martha's Vineyard Striped Bass & Bluefish Derby, Martha's Vineyard, Massachusetts

Held during the region's annual fall fish migration, this month-long fishing tourney is a near-religious experience for its devotees. "Fishing enthusiasts get to spend five weeks chasing stripers and bluefish while competing for more than $250,000 in cash and prizes. To a Vineyarder, winning the derby is like slipping on the green jacket at the Masters." *mvderby.com*

Operation: Catch Fish, Baghdad, Iraq

"This contest grew out of the Baghdad Anglers Club and School of Fly Fishing, founded in 2005 by Navy officer Joel Stewart to spread his love of the sport." The site of the annual tournament is "Z Lake," next to one of Saddam Hussein's former palaces. "The quarry is asp, carp, or whatever else turns up." *baghdadflyfishing.com*

Don Hawley Invitational Tarpon Fly Tournament, Islamorada, Florida

"Catching a tarpon on the fly is a breathtakingly awesome experience. That's one reason this annual five-day tourney has attracted such notable contestants, including the late Ted Williams. It isn't cheap…and there's a long waiting list to join the 25-angler field. But once you make the cut, you'll be part of a truly legendary event." *donhawleyfoundation.org*

FLW Forrest Wood Cup, Pittsburgh, Pennsylvania

The Bassmaster Classic is the original and, thanks to ESPN, the best-known freshwater bass-fishing championship. But the winner of the Walmart FLW Tour Forrest Wood Cup will claim the sport's richest haul: $1 million. "The Cup is the crown jewel of a nationwide bass-fishing series held each year. But it's not limited to the pros you see on TV. Just as a good amateur golfer can qualify for the U.S. Open, weekend anglers can work their way toward the Cup by advancing through local feeder competitions." *flwoutdoors.com/forrestwoodcup*

RUNNING

10 great places to have fun afoot

As an avid jogger and well-traveled executive of a California telecom firm, Warwick Ford could write a book on great places to run in big cities across the United States. And he has: Titled Fun on Foot in America's Cities, *it outlines 50 top running (or walking) routes in 14 metro areas nationwide. Here, he offers some favorite park routes. Distances are four to ten miles.*

Chain of Lakes, Minneapolis, Minnesota
"Minneapolis has the nation's best on-foot trail system, and its heart is the Chain of Lakes. Dedicated pedestrian paths, minimal vehicular traffic, and pleasant surroundings characterize this area." Starting downtown, take Loring Greenway to Loring Park, go through the sculpture garden, and work your way to Lake of the Isles. Circumnavigate one, two, or three lakes. *minneapolisparks.org/grandrounds/*

Charles River Reservation, Boston, Massachusetts
The banks of the Charles are Boston's major "on-foot playground. From the Longfellow Bridge to Harvard, there are attractive paved paths on both sides, skirting the MIT and Boston University campuses." Quieter trails continue upstream as far as Waltham. Walk from downtown or Back Bay hotels or take the "T" (Boston's subway) to Longfellow Bridge. *mass.gov/dcr/parks/charlesRiver/*

Golden Gate Park, San Francisco, California
Golden Gate Park has much to offer, including a jog-friendly botanic garden, attractive lakes, a Japanese Tea Garden, a field of bison, and two waterfalls. "With some advance planning, you can find on-foot routes that minimize automobile encounters." Drive there or take the Muni Metro from downtown. *sfgov.org/site/recpark*

Riverside Park, New York, New York
"While Central Park is great for runners, Riverside Park, along the Hudson River on the Upper West Side, is better." Its virtues:

scenic views, wide trails, and fewer crowds. "You can make a nice circuit by running Central Park to its northwest corner and then connecting to the Hudson via Morningside Park. Go south through Riverside Park, exiting at 79th Street for the Upper West Side's restaurant and bar precinct." *nycgovparks.org/parks/riversidepark*

Balboa Park, San Diego, California
"Balboa Park is big, green, pleasant, and close to downtown San Diego." Run or walk from downtown hotels or take the trolley to Sixth Avenue. "You then have a choice of underfoot terrain, ranging from flat, paved trails to sunny, hilly paths through fields of wildflowers to steep wilderness trails in the canyons." *balboapark.org*

City Park, Denver, Colorado
Denver's largest urban park is popular with pedestrians of all types and is well known for its scenic overlook (near the Museum of Nature & Science) of the park's lakes; the city skyline; and, in the distance, the Rocky Mountains. "You can craft a nice route to the park via the Cherry Creek Greenway and Cheesman Park." Afterward, wind down in nearby Restaurant Row. *denvergov.org/parks*

Fairmount Park, Philadelphia, Pennsylvania
The 9,200-acre Fairmount Park claims to be the nation's largest urban park. Start at the Museum of Art and follow the Schuylkill River upstream. "There are great underfoot conditions, lovely scenery, and many points of interest on the way—charming Boathouse Row, for instance." Continue upstream to Midvale Avenue or Manayunk before catching an R train back downtown. *fairmountpark.org*

Washington Park Arboretum, Seattle, Washington
"Here there are beautiful trails, a variety of plant life, no cars, and interesting trail segments to tack on." Start at the Montlake Bridge and follow the Arboretum Waterfront Trail before entering the arboretum proper. Exit the arboretum at its southern end and follow sidewalks to the Lake Washington shore. Continue to your choice of lakeshore parks. Downtown buses service the start and finish. *depts.washington.edu/wpa*

Rock Creek Park, Washington, D.C.
Rock Creek Park is enormous, comprising 1,775 acres and consuming 4.5 percent of the land area of the nation's capital. "Its wilderness is remarkable.... It's often hard to believe you're in the middle of D.C. You can start from the Van Ness/UDC Metro (subway) station and trek hidden Soapstone Valley or follow streets to Rock Creek." *nps.gov/rocr*

Lincoln Park, Chicago, Illinois
The run along the northern lakeshore, embracing Lincoln Park, is Chicago's best. Start from Navy Pier and head north to Addison or beyond before turning inland to the legendary Wrigley Field vicinity for a food or beverage stop, then catch the Red Line back downtown. "The Lincoln Park trails are excellent underfoot, facilities are abundant, and the lakeshore environment is always exhilarating." *chicagoparkdistrict.com*

10 great places for runners to hit the road

Lace up your sneakers and do a little sightseeing while racing through town. Bart Yasso, chief running officer at Runner's World, *shares his list of great road races in which runners can tour the city.*

Boston Marathon, Boston, Massachusetts
"This is the granddaddy of all marathons. It's the most prestigious and historic." The race—the oldest annual marathon in the country—takes place on Patriots' Day, a Massachusetts holiday on the third Monday of April that commemorates the start of the Revolutionary War. The entire city gets behind the runners, including the Boston Red Sox. The team always plays a home game at 10 A.M. so fans can cheer runners on as they run past Fenway Park before finishing the race in front of the John Hancock Building. *bostonmarathon.org*

Twin Cities Marathon, Minneapolis/St. Paul, Minnesota
The race, which also offers a ten-mile option, starts in downtown Minneapolis before leading runners along several lakes and the

banks of the Mississippi, then through St. Paul before ending in front of the Capitol. "It's run in October during peak foliage. And every time you look up, you're near a lake. You get the combination of a really scenic course and a tour of the city. It's spectacular." *mtcmarathon.org*

Monument Avenue 10K, Richmond, Virginia
This 6.21-mile race takes runners down treelined Monument Avenue, which is dotted with historic statues and surrounded by beautiful Southern homes. "You get the sense that Richmond really was the capital of the south. There are bands that play along the course and a costume contest. It's a big party." *sportsbackers.org*

San Francisco Marathon, San Francisco, California
The marathon, which includes a half-marathon option, loops runners through the city's funky neighborhoods, then out and back on the Golden Gate Bridge. "On a clear day, you get the best views of the city. Every once in a while, it's completely fogged in. You hear

Going the distance

Each year, thousands of people will try to go the distance in U.S. marathons, from the St. George (Utah), Portland (Oregon), and Twin Cities marathons to the country's largest, the New York Marathon. Veteran runners say marathon training groups and the acceptance of walking help make the 26.2-mile challenge attainable to a new tier of people.

"Running has matured to the point where it embraces all abilities," says Ryan Lamppa, a researcher for Running USA, a national nonprofit for distance running that's based in Colorado Springs, Colorado. Approximately 465,000 marathon finishing times were recorded in the United States in 2009—about a 10 percent increase from 2008. Median times were a bit faster for 2008 and 2009 compared to '06 and '07, and about 59 percent of finishers in 2009 were male, while 41 percent were female.

the foghorns on the ships below you, but you can't see anything. It's so surreal. That's also part of the mystique of San Francisco." *runsfm.com*

Miami Marathon, Miami, Florida
This race starts before sunrise to take advantage of the cooler temperatures and takes runners across a causeway into South Beach. "All the Art Deco lights are lit up, and the clubbers are just heading home. It's funny to see these Paris Hilton look-alikes cheering for you. It really shows off what the city is about." The race, which has a half-marathon option, also takes runners through Miami's neighborhoods and past where all the cruise ships are docked. *www.ingmiamimarathon.com*

Vermont City Marathon, Burlington, Vermont
Burlington is "a hippie enclave and college town." The race, which takes runners along Lake Champlain and through the city's neighborhoods, lets you experience Burlington's free spirit. "Most people cheering for you are wearing tie-dye and playing the Grateful Dead. At mile 15, there's a hill and they have this ensemble of drummers playing at the base to get the runners pumped. It all speaks to the artsy vibe of the city." *runvermont.org*

Philadelphia Marathon, Philadelphia, Pennsylvania
"As a tourist, it would take a couple of days to see everything you see when running this race." The marathon, which includes a half-marathon option, starts and finishes at the Philadelphia Art Museum with its "*Rocky* steps." In between, runners see City Hall, the Liberty Bell, and Independence Hall before winding along the Schuylkill River and Boathouse Row. *philadelphiamarathon.com*

Rock 'n' Roll Arizona Marathon, Phoenix, Arizona
This race takes runners through Phoenix, Scottsdale, and Tempe. "You're surrounded by mountains, but you're on the valley floor. You get to see the mountains, but you're not running them." Participants also pass beautiful hotels and spas like the Arizona ⁺more Resort & Spa. "After the race, runners spoil themselves ⁿ treatments. There's nothing better than a mud bath and a ⁻er a marathon." *arizona.competitor.com*

Chicago Marathon, Chicago, Illinois
Runners get a real tour of the city during the Chicago Marathon, which starts and finishes at Grant Park and weaves through almost 30 neighborhoods and along Lake Michigan. In each neighborhood, crowds come out. "It's a very spectator-friendly race. All the people who live there come out in droves and cheer. You feel like you have an intimate look at the city because you really see the people that make up Chicago." *www.chicagomarathon.com*

Cooper River Bridge Run, Charleston, South Carolina
This 10K race starts outside the city and takes runners across the Arthur Ravenel Jr. Bridge, the longest cable-strung bridge in the United States. "You get amazing views of Charleston as you cross over the bridge." The race then takes you into the historic section of the city to Marion Square. "It's one of the prettiest towns, and the race gives you both a skyline view from the bridge and a more intimate look at the city." *bridgerun.com*

SKIING AND SNOWBOARDING

10 great places to learn to ski

Let's face it: Skiing isn't exactly easy. With all that exertion, the cold temperatures, and the inevitable equipment hassles, only about 15 percent of people who give skiing a try stick with it. Andrew Bigford, editor and publisher of PEAKS magazine, says resorts are attempting to make things better, offering instructional programs to lure newcomers. Most will have you skiing on your own in about three days. Here are Bigford's top picks for learning the slopes.

Sunday River, Maine
An entire part of the mountain, the South Ridge learning area, is dedicated to beginners. It offers wide-open slopes and well-defined trails, a rarity at novice areas. Sunday River also is home to the Perfect Turn Ski & Snowboard School, a one-stop shop where first-timers meet instructors, pick up rental equipment, and learn the basics. *sundayriver.com*

Killington, Vermont
The sprawling ski mecca offers
350-plus acres of beginner terrain.
But quality is as important as quantity. As at Sunday River, the resort
has a ski and snowboarding school
that takes adults and kids as young
as two. *killington.com*

Mount Snow, Vermont
This southern Vermont area may
have the best learning program of any resort. Offerings include a
three-story learning center where registration, rentals, and lessons
are all under the same roof. The building also is home to ski camps
for three-year-olds and for four- to six-year-olds, and the resort has
beginner terrain areas for adults and kids. *mountsnow.com*

Jiminy Peak, Massachusetts
This is one resort where you are guaranteed to have fun learning how to ski. Literally. Bigford lauds the resort's offer of a free
lesson to skiers who don't learn the first time—or don't at least
have fun trying. It's part of the resort's Guaranteed Easy Turn,
or GETSkiing, method, which puts students on short skis (about
two-thirds normal size) and rotates them among teaching stations.
jiminypeak.com

Winter Park, Colorado
Perhaps Colorado's best-kept secret, this low-key ski area near
Denver "has been the city's learn-to-ski mecca for years." Catering
mostly to families, it offers 29 beginner trails (more than 266 acres)
and is home to one of the industry's first children's centers. But
perhaps the biggest innovation is at the resort's 30-acre beginners
area, Discovery Park, which has a version of each major type of
chairlift (a double, triple, and quad), so first-timers can practice
getting on and off. *skiwinterpark.com*

Spirit Mountain, Minnesota
This premier Midwestern resort proves that learning to ski can be
affordable. While tiny by Western standards, the resort's 700-foot

vertical drop gives it some of the longest runs in the heartland. And it offers an array of packages for beginners. *spiritmt.com*

Paoli Peaks, Indiana

This might be the most unusual learn-to-ski experience in the nation. To make the most of its short season, the resort stays open (and offers lessons) 18 hours a day on weekends mid-December through early March. Instructors are often seen swooshing around in shorts—"a scene not to be missed." Shenanigans aside, the resort, located in south-central Indiana, takes teaching seriously and is a great place to pick up the basics. *paolipeaks.com*

Big Bear Lake, California

Many a southern Californian has taken those first turns at this modest-sized resort in the San Bernardino Mountains. Just 100 miles from Los Angeles, Big Bear Lake offers one of the

---

Skiing: Not without its risks

According to the National Ski Areas Association, skiing and snow-boarding are no more dangerous than other "high-energy participation sports" such as swimming and bicycling. However, these sports are physically challenging and involve some inherent risk.

"The best skiers are tuned in to the need to be in shape weeks, even months in advance," says Dr. Richard Hawkins, an orthopedist with the Steadman Hawkins Clinics of the Carolinas. "Those who don't prepare come up here, get on skis, and get out on unfamiliar turf or into challenges they can't handle, like a mogul run or a surprise patch of deep powder, pretty quickly."

To avoid injury, start running, biking, swimming, or other aerobic exercises weeks ahead of time. Add weight-resistance exercises for strength. And play some change-of-direction sports, such as tennis, soccer, or basketball, which promote quickness and coordination, says Hawkins, a former consultant to the U.S. Ski Team.

What if you have a minor fall, say a little twist to the knee or some bruises? "Think RICE—rest, ice, compression, and elevation. Don't soak in the hot tub. That's better for general tiredness and muscle aches."

largest, most sophisticated snowmaking operations in the West. *bigbear.com*

Kirkwood, California

This Sierra Nevada resort overlooking Lake Tahoe offers wide bowls and gentle slopes that are perfect for beginners. The resort guarantees that you'll learn the ropes on your first day or you can keep coming back until you do. Not that it'll come to that. "The instructors are very experienced." *kirkwood.com*

Summit at Snoqualmie, Washington

Much like resorts in Europe, Snoqualmie has more than a dozen small ski schools competing for students, something "absolutely unique" in the United States. But the choices don't end there. The resort bills itself as an all-around winter recreation area. In addition to downhill and cross-country ski lessons, Snoqualmie offers programs in snowshoeing, snow biking, and snow scooting (they look like snowboards with handlebars). The mountain is in the Cascade Range, tucked in the Wenatchee National Forest, just 50 miles from Seattle. *summitatsnoqualmie.com*

10 great places to do the old snowshoe

"Snowshoes are sort of like a backstage pass to winter," says David Howard, senior editor at Backpacker *magazine. "Follow groomed trails or go where no cross-country skier or snowmobiler can. That means deep, silent woods to yourself, cruising over obstacles like toppled trees, dense brush, or rock debris." Howard shares some hot snow spots to 'shoe.*

Yosemite National Park, California

"The wildly popular Loop Road is clogged with traffic in summer, but it's not plowed in winter and thus mostly untouched. Snowshoe the eight-mile loop through the Mariposa Grove of giant sequoias, including one that's 2,700 years old. The red bark is stunning against the white backdrop." *nps.gov/yose*

Camel's Hump State Park, near South Burlington, Vermont

"Two options for this idyllic swath of the northern Green

Mountains: Tackle the eponymous 4,083-foot summit via the Burrows Trail (4.8 miles), or bring the kids and take the Camel's Hump View Trail (about 1 mile). The former is above treeline and exposed to winds that lash one of the state's most prominent features, so know the forecast." *vtstateparks.com/htm/camels*

Olympic National Park, Port Angeles, Washington
"The six-mile hike to Hurricane Ridge is probably the premier Olympic snowshoe experience: It features massive alpine meadows with undulating snowdrifts, ice-coated evergreens, and classic Mount Olympus panoramas. Not everyone will reach the hilltop, because the six-mile route follows the crest of a sometimes icy ridge, but the views are great throughout." *nps.gov/olym*

Timms Hill Park, Price County, Wisconsin
"Reaching the state's high point (1,951 feet) isn't quite as daunting as it sounds, since the trek from the parking area is only a couple hundred feet in elevation gain. Follow the Green Trail, and then follow the steep switchbacks up to the observation tower for sweeping vistas." *pricecountywi.net*

White Grass Touring Center, Davis, West Virginia
"Surprisingly, this little chunk of the High Alleghenies averages 150 inches of snow a year. Cross-country skiers are limited to groomed trails, but snowshoers can plunge off in any direction, up to the nearest elevated ridgeline or over to the nearby Canaan Valley." *whitegrass.com*

The Adirondacks, Upstate New York
"The High Peaks region offers some of the most eye-popping scenery in the East. Head for the 4,580-foot summit of Wright Peak, a reasonably challenging but doable 6.5-mile snowshoe trek that delivers powerful views of the range's bigger peaks, including Algonquin. Bring crampons for the last section before the summit, which can get a bit icy." *dec.ny.gov/62.html*

San Francisco Peaks, Coconino National Forest, Arizona
"Yep, Arizona. Park at Arizona Snowbowl, the Flagstaff ski area, and follow the Kachina Trail, which follows beautiful rolling terrain through several small meadows and stands of aspen and ponderosa,

with sweet views of red-rock desert on the horizon. The trail goes five miles out, but you can walk as far as you feel like before turning back." *arizonasnowbowl.com*

Mount Greylock, North Berkshire County, Massachusetts
"The Berkshires are loaded with day trips, and Greylock is the alpha—it takes about eight miles to get up there and back via the Hopper Trail to the Appalachian Trail. The view is epic; see into five states from the 3,491-foot peak."
mass.gov/dcr/parks/mtGreylock/

Black Canyon of the Gunnison National Park, Gunnison, Colorado
"Think Ansel Adams in this black-and-white landscape that evokes his classic images. Snowshoe three miles out to Devil's Lookout, a spectacular rim perched atop 2,000-foot-high walls of volcanic schist." *nps.gov/blca*

Boundary Waters Canoe Area Wilderness, Superior National Forest, Minnesota
"When the lakes freeze up, this wilderness is largely devoid of human life, which allows snowshoers to follow wildlife tracks through otherwise untouched backcountry. The Big Foot Trail unfurls across Flour Lake, through stands of balsam and spruce and over glacial remnants." *bwca.cc*

10 great places to let the others go downhill

If hittin' the slopes isn't your thing, you can still catch some excitement off skis at top North American destinations. Marc Peruzzi, editor in chief of Skiing *magazine, offers his list of great mountain resorts for nonskiers.*

Whistler Blackcomb Ski Resort, Whistler, British Columbia, Canada
"Whistler has two great mountains with a huge variety of expert terrain. The nightlife is almost as diverse. You can check out lots of good music and dine at top-tier seafood and sushi restaurants." The whole family can enjoy the no-skill thrill of tubing at the Coca-Cola Tube Park. Choose from eight lanes of varying difficulty. A

conveyor will breeze you back up Blackcomb Mountain for more. *whistlerblackcomb.com*

Jackson Hole Mountain Resort, Teton Village, Wyoming
"Outdoorsy nonskiers can snowmobile into Yellowstone National Park and see Old Faithful as well as moose and bison." Enjoy the snowy serenity of the nearby National Elk Refuge, home of 7,500 wintering elk. Sample "new Western" cuisine, which includes local game, at the Teton Mountain Lodge. *jacksonhole.com*

Bridger Bowl Ski Area, Bozeman, Montana
"Home of Montana State University, this college town has a lively arts, music, and shopping scene. A blue light in town alerts locals to powder days at Bridger Bowl." Everyone else can head to Southside Park and practice their figure eights at the municipal

Still a ski town, but with so much more

Steamboat Springs, Colorado, has cultivated an image as a ski-bum paradise, where slopes meet the wooden sidewalks of the Old West. But now, with a billion-dollar urban renewal project and more than $30 million in ski area improvements, it's attracting more second-home buyers.

Steamboat, which bears the trademarked name "Ski Town USA," has several things that set it apart from other Colorado ski towns.

First, there's the snow, which is among the driest and deepest in the country. Situated in north-central Colorado, the town's mountain catches the state's blizzards as well as those that hit Utah and Wyoming. It averaged more than 400 inches of snow in 2007 and 2008.

The resort also is a family-friendly destination, recently ranked best in North America by *SKI* magazine. In addition to the major Steamboat resort, with its acclaimed children's instruction programs, the municipally owned Howelsen Hill has long been a training ground for local kids and future Olympians. Both offer specials aimed at children.

The final attraction is the town itself, just more than two miles from the ski resort. Lincoln Avenue is the main drag, and it has a traditional Main Street setup.

ice-skating rink. Other fun excursions off the mountain include the Museum of the Rockies, the Gallatin Pioneer Museum, and the American Computer Museum. *bridgerbowl.com*

Stowe Mountain Resort, Stowe, Vermont
"Boasting the longest average trail length in New England (3,603 feet), Stowe is one of the best resorts in the East. And there's a lot to do off the slopes too." The luxurious spa at Stoweflake will lift your spirits as high as the Green Mountains. Head into Montpelier for the architecture and diverse food of this charming town, or go to Waterbury for the Willy Wonka-esque Ben & Jerry's factory tour. *stowe.com*

Park City Mountain Resort, Park City, Utah
"With three top ski areas and all the amenities of a large city within a 45-minute drive, it's easy to ignore Park City proper. Don't. The place really heats up during Sundance Film Festival, but celeb-watching is a year-round activity. Book a dinner at the Canyons Ski Resort's Viking Yurt restaurant and take a moonlit sleigh ride to midmountain, where a gourmet meal is served in a wood-stove-warmed yurt." *parkcitymountain.com*

Vail Mountain Resort, Vail, Colorado
"Vail offers more than just superior back bowls and acres upon acres of incredible skiing. Ice climbing and snowmobile trips leave from town"; saddle up for winter horseback riding through the Colorado back-country; or hike to the huts, part of the Tenth Mountain Division Hut system, in White River National Forest. *vail.com*

Steamboat Ski Resort, Steamboat Springs, Colorado
"Ascend in a hot-air balloon ride over the snow-covered Yampa Valley, or winter fly-fish for trout and northern pike down below." There are still active cattle ranches in the area. You might even meet a real cowboy at the Ore House at Pine Grove, known for its

steak and prime rib and cinnamon rolls in the breadbasket. *steamboat.com*

Heavenly Mountain Resort, South Lake Tahoe, California
"The town has several casinos and a sort of Vegas-circa-1970 thing going for it. That's not a bad thing. The Mont Bleu Casino lets you feel a bit like James Bond." Take a cruise on Lake Tahoe and marvel at the Sierra Nevada range surrounding it on all sides. *skiheavenly.com*

Angel Fire Resort, Angel Fire, New Mexico
"Less than half an hour from the galleries and Indian crafts shops in Taos, this resort is great for all levels of skiing and [has] ice fishing for rainbow trout at nearby Eagle Nest Lake." Save time to go dashing through the snow on a horse-drawn sleigh ride across the wide-open, high-alpine Moreno Valley. *angelfireresort.com*

Mont-Tremblant Resort, Quebec, Montreal, Canada
At the highest peak in the Laurentians, get high on nature with Acrobranche, located between the resort's ski trails. At the scary but safe aerial obstacle course, harnessed participants zip from tree to tree through a series of games. Headlamps are provided for the more challenging nighttime course. *tremblant.ca*

Dining high on the slopes

Chili and burgers still may be standard fare at ski resorts, but those crowded cafeterias reeking with the scent of wet wool have been joined by dozens of mountain restaurants where food quality—and prices—compete with the lofty views. Here are just a few, found on and off the slopes.

- Mount Washington Hotel, Bretton Woods, New Hampshire (mtwashington.com)

- Alpenglow Stube, Keystone, Colorado (keystoneresort.com)

- The Inn at Sawmill Farm, Dover, Vermont (theinnatsawmillfarm.com)

- Snow Park Lodge, Deer Valley, Utah (deervalley.com)

SPORTS OF ALL SORTS

10 great places for a hot-ticket view of sports

Sports aficionados around the country fantasize about those primo vantage points that seem to belong by birthright to the scions of season subscribers, celebs, and political or business bigwigs. Premium tickets, they're called, and ticketsnow.com can snare some guaranteed-authentic ones for you, even if you are not a high roller. Here, ticketsnow.com's CEO Mike Domek describes these unforgettable perches.

Finish Line Suite at the Indianapolis 500, Indianapolis Motor Speedway, Indianapolis, Indiana
There you are, in an audience of "200,000 people, [but] you're in an air-conditioned suite, enjoying catered food and drinks, [yet] you still feel in the thick of it." The suite is "close to the action. It's equivalent to the second level; you can see into the stands behind you and into the pits," where the cars are refueled and their tires changed. "They have radios, so you can listen to the drivers and crews." *indy500.com*

"Green Monster" section, Fenway Park, Boston, Massachusetts
In 2003, the park installed seats atop its famed home-run wall, just 310 feet from home plate. From the front seats, you can lean over and see the dents that players made with powerful line drives. Sitting up there, where it feels as if you're playing left field or backing up the shortstop, is "a once-in-a-lifetime experience." *redsox.com*

13th green, "Amen corner" at the Masters, Augusta National Golf Club, Augusta, Georgia
This par-5 hole, the last of the three that constitute the so-called "Amen corner," is the place to see and be seen at the Masters. *Sports Illustrated* coined the term in 1958 when tournament winner Jack Nicklaus, after a hard rain the previous night, "got a ruling he could pick up his ball in the grass and sank an 18-foot putt for an eagle at the 12th hole." *masters.org*

Bleachers for a game vs. the rival White Sox, Wrigley Field, Chicago, Illinois

Experience being one of the beloved Cubs' Bleacher Bums, the most avid (and long-suffering) fans in the country. It's "the great melting pot of all Cubs fans," a true working-class hangout. "You don't see the suits and ties—even the

execs are in their shorts drinking beers." *cubs.com*

50-yard line at the Texas–Oklahoma game, Cotton Bowl, Dallas, Texas

The Texas State Fair hosts this annual October game, one of the top traditional rivalries in the sports world. "They call it the Red River Shootout. The Cotton Bowl was chosen in 1929 to be a 'neutral' meeting ground for the two teams, and it's still going strong." *cottonbowlstadium.com*

Courtside seats at a Lakers playoff game, Staples Center, Los Angeles, California

What could be better than a seat beside Jack Nicholson or Spike Lee while Kobe shoots and scores? The basketball great could even wind up in your lap on national TV. The NBA postseason games are top-notch entertainment. *staplescenter.com*

Clubhouse Suite at the Kentucky Derby, Churchill Downs, Louisville, Kentucky

"It's amazing that so much can be built around a two-minute race." This suite "at the finish line, with its upscale decor and gourmet food and beverages . . . is a hot place for Hollywood now." Celebs and royalty from around the world sip their mint juleps in the so-called Millionaire's Row, and all 140,000-plus spectators at the track sing "My Old Kentucky Home." *churchilldowns.com*

Midcourt for a Duke–North Carolina game, Cameron Indoor Stadium, Durham, North Carolina

College basketball rules at the home of Duke's Blue Devils, where the Cameron Crazies, the student superfans, are as much a part of the attraction as the epic contest with the Tar Heels of North

Carolina. The two schools are only eight miles apart, and "it's an enormous rivalry" between "the two biggest teams" in the Atlantic Coast Conference. *goduke.com*

50-yard line at a Packers–Bears game, Lambeau Field, Green Bay, Wisconsin
Vince Lombardi's lair still lures perhaps the most emotional of all football fans, and the highlight of the Packers' season is their face-off with the Chicago Bears—another one of the fiercest rivalries in sports. "Even as a Bears fan, I had to experience Lambeau," where you can "mingle with the Packer faithful or get away from the chaos in one of the skyboxes." *packers.com*

Corner box at the U.S. Open, Arthur Ashe Stadium, Flushing Meadows, New York
The famed tennis tournament, showcasing the top stars in the world over two weeks of matches, is said to have the highest ticketed attendance in all of sports. The best box seats are in the corner on the lower level, "so your head doesn't ping-pong back and forth." *usopen.org*

10 great places to have a swell time

That perfect wave is out there, and if you're a surfer, you'll do anything to catch it. Rob Barber, long-time surfer, surfing coach, and an editor for Carve Surfing Magazine, *got off his board long enough to share the top wave spots.*

Oahu's North Shore, Hawaii
Two of the most famous waves in the world—the North Shore's Banzai Pipeline and Waimea Bay—bring experienced surfers and photographers alike to Oahu. Surfing was already well established in Hawaii by the time British explorer Captain James Cook first observed it in the late 1770s. Oahu's swells are "definitely the most powerful waves I've experienced. Surfer's reputations are made and lost" here, especially in winter when waves are at their highest. *aloha-hawaii.com/activities/north+shore+surfing*

Black's Beach, San Diego, California
Beloved by locals and foreign surfers alike, Black's Beach is "one of the best reef breaks" and receives an abundance of wave swell. But "this is a nudist beach—so be prepared." In the winter, when nearby Big Bear and Mammoth mountains are snowy, it's possible to surf and snowboard on the same day.
sandiego.gov/lifeguards/beaches

Teahupo'o, Tahiti
The waves in Teahupo'o (pronounced "cho-poo") are "the most talked about and feared." They're home each May to one of surfing's most challenging contests, the Billabong Pro Tahiti. Though the reef breaks around the island of Tahiti and nearby Moorea are for "expert surfers only," less-experienced board-riding visitors will find astonishing sea life in the "Colgate blue" waters.
surfline.com/surfing-a-to-z/teahupoo-history_925/

Bali, Indonesia
Indonesia's still-active volcanic archipelago is "my personal favorite because it offers toasty-warm water, the most incredible reef breaks, and a never-ending supply of swell." After exploring Bali's waves, take in the island's Hindu and Buddhist culture and stunning scenery, then island-hop  to neighboring Nusa Lembongan, Lombok, or Sumbawa. It's easy to "find your own uncrowded paradise." *baliwaves.com*

Margaret River, western Australia
Though in awe of the "ferocious" Indian Ocean wave known as "The Box" (which "needs to be seen to be believed"), Barber is less than taken with the "barren landscape, relentless wind, and annoying sand flies." But these annoyances keep crowds small. This consistently challenging spot with its "diverse big wave forum" remains one of his favorites. *margaretriver.com/pages/surfing*

Coolangatta, Queensland, Australia
Running from Snapper Rocks to Kirra, the "Superbank"—a long underwater sandbank that the waves break across—can "offer tube

rides more than ten seconds long." Locals here "eat, sleep, and speak surfing 24/7," so it's no surprise that Australia's Gold Coast has spawned some of the world's greatest surfers.
coolangatta.net/coolangatta/surfbreaks.html

Cape Town, South Africa
The aptly named "Dungeons" off the coast are "doubly dangerous." These big waves are among the most feared in the world and also "by far the sharkiest," thanks in part to the large seal colony next door. Visitors looking for more *Jaws*-free paddling can head north to the netted beaches of Durban for "fun waves and warm water."
wavescape.co.za/top_bar/spots/capetown.html

Praia da Vila, Brazil
Though much of Brazil's long coast offers an "amazing selection of breaks," Barber's favorite is here, south of Florianopolis. The beaches here don't just feature "crystal-clear water and white-sand beaches"; they're also great for people-watching, because some of "the most beautiful women in the world are basking on them."
surf-forecast.com/breaks/PraiadaVila.shtml

Bay of Biscay, France
Surfing in Europe might seem an oxymoron to many, but with a wetsuit, it's a great destination year-round. The deep-water trench in this bay helps build waves recorded with faces as high as 50 feet. And what could be a better break than hanging ten in such "dream surf locations" as Biarritz, Hossegor, and Lacanau, then living it up in town?

Lahinch, County Clare, Ireland
First surfed in 2005, Aileen (named after *Aill na Searrach* head-land above it) is "the most awesome big wave to be discovered in recent surfing history." Surfers must be towed in to below the west coast's Cliffs of Moher by Jet Ski. But after a bracing ride, the Emerald Isle's "beautiful, craggy western coast" offers as many "hidden gems" to explore on land as in the water. Bring your wet suit, gloves, and boots, as the "water's a bit cold."
surf-forecast.com/breaks/lahinch

10 great places to exercise your sense of adventure

Keeping your New Year's fitness resolutions doesn't have to be a long and lonely trip on the treadmill. Men's Health *editor in chief David Zinczenko shares his top places to make the world your gym.*

Lake Tahoe, Nevada
If you find yourself sick of the slopes but still craving some serious cardio, try snowshoeing. A good place to begin would be the miles of groomed trails in the Sierra Nevada near Lake Tahoe. "We may not realize it, but our lives have become increasingly noisy between the TVs, computers, and politicians. Snowshoeing is the perfect way to plug into the serenity and silence your mind is craving, with the exception of an owl now and then." *bluelaketahoe.com*

Cozumel, Mexico
Jacques Cousteau put the Palancar Reef on the map more than 50 years ago when he declared it a scuba hot spot. This island off Mexico is surrounded by coral, which makes it a reef-seeker's refuge. Grab your oxygen tank and swim your way into shape. *islacozumel.com.mx*

Koh Tao, Thailand
It's not called Thai-boxing for nothing. Pack a punch against calories by training with skilled professional fighters on this remote island in Thailand. "If you're not feeling challenged by your current workout, having a guy square off against you intending bodily harm is plenty of motivation." Show off your leaner physique and regain your strength by spending your afternoons beachside. *tourismthailand.org/attraction/suratthani-84-5415-1.html*

Whistler Blackcomb, British Columbia, Canada
Hit the slopes of our northern neighbor and brace yourself for a workout you're sure to feel après-ski. Consistently ranked one of the top ski destinations in the world, Whistler Blackcomb offers something for everyone—from advanced backcountry skiers to snowplowers in ski school. "The problem with skiing in the United States is that there are so many people. Canada doesn't have nearly

the population of skiers, so you don't spend your time waiting in lift lines when you can be on the hill." *whistlerblackcomb.com*

Lake District, Argentina

"Cycle your way from Chile to Argentina in the (northern Patagonia) Lake District, a natural treasure featuring picturesque volcanoes, dazzling lakes, and a national parks preserve. It's the antidote to the big bus tour…a great fitness boost, and it allows you to slow down and meet the people and see the country." *www.turismo.gov.ar/eng/menu.htm*

County Wicklow, Ireland

"You'll be hard-pressed to find a greener spot for golfing than Ireland, where overall the courses are more difficult than even Scotland's." Head to County Wicklow, just south of Dublin. The area, home to the Wicklow Mountains National Park and the backdrop of the film *Braveheart,* offers more than a dozen courses, many overlooking the Irish Sea. *visitwicklow.ie*

Goa, India

"Take a yoga retreat in this Portuguese colony known for gorgeous beaches and a temperate climate along the Arabian Sea. In stressful times, we can all use new ways to unwind. It's a destination where you're taking in your surroundings and connecting with nature in a way that you can't on a mat in a gym." *goaindiatourism.com*

Rio Chiriqui Viejo, Panama

Channel your inner Indiana Jones on the rapids of Rio Chiriqui Viejo in southwest Panama near the Costa Rican border. "Paddle alongside the region's lush jungle, enjoying scenic views of wildlife, vegetation, and waterfalls. Is there anything more primal and exciting than rafting through a jungle?" *visitpanama.com*

Grajagan Bay, East Java, Indonesia

This Indonesian bay is a treasure trove for surfers looking for the ultimate in catching waves. "Die-hard surfers consider Grajagan Bay in East Java, northwest of Bali, to be the best surfing spot in Asia, if not the world." If you're a beginner, start off with smaller surf breaks like Tiger Tracks and Chicken, where the break is about half the size of those at the hang-ten haven of G-Land Bay. *eastjava.com*

Caribbean National Forest, Puerto Rico
The locals call it El Yunque, but to vacationers, the Caribbean National Forest is a hiker's haven. The 28,000-acre reserve offers countless trails for exploration of the country's vast array of vegetation and wildlife. "People think of the crowded cities in Puerto Rico, but . . . if you travel around on foot, you're bound to encounter a type of wildlife you won't see in San Juan." *topuertorico.org/reference/yunque.shtml*

10 great places to feel
the need for speed

Every Memorial Day weekend, more than 200,000 spectators crowd the Indianapolis Motor Speedway to watch the Indy 500. But that's not the only place to get your high-speed fix. Driver Danica Patrick, the first woman to win an Indy car race, spoke about the best places for speed demons.

Indianapolis Motor Speedway, Indianapolis, Indiana
The mother of all racetracks, this vast complex also includes a hotel, a museum, a golf course, and tours that offer visitors high-speed rides with real Indy 500 drivers about 100 days annually. The month leading up to race day is full of events, including a half marathon. "The Speedway is definitely No. 1. The race is exciting, and the museum gives you a good feel for how the cars have changed over the years." *indianapolismotorspeedway.com*

Long Beach, California
Laid out through the city rather than on a track, the Toyota Grand Prix of Long Beach is the oldest major street race in North America, held in April since 1975. For fans, there is "lots going on. It's a good party, and you have the pro/celebrity race, which draws in a lot of celebrities." *gplb.com*

Richmond International Raceway, Richmond, Virginia
A favorite of race fans, with less expensive tickets and tailgating

in the parking lots. "It is a
short track with huge, high
grandstands. You get that
Southern excitement for
racing—a lot of NASCAR
fans, really loud." It also gets hot
by mid-June, so night races are a welcome respite for fans. *rir.com*

Motegi Twin Ring, Motegi, Japan

Known as "the Indy of Japan," this track about 50 miles from
Tokyo is Honda's high-tech test facility. There are two tracks and a
hotel, and Twin Ring hosts the Indy Japan 300 each September—
the event where Patrick made history by winning in 2008. "I loved
going there before I won. I like the food. You get sushi and sashimi
and rice, very simple but very good." Besides the race, fans can
enjoy a large museum and high-tech interactive attractions.
www.mobilityland.co.jp/english

Honda Indy Toronto, Toronto, Ontario, Canada

"I love Canadians. They're so much fun; they're so into racing. In
downtown Toronto, there are so many good restaurants, bars, and
places to go." The route for the street race goes through downtown, making this July race logistically one of the easiest to attend,
within walking distance of major hotels. *hondaindytoronto.com*

Infineon Raceway, Sonoma, California

This track is just 30 minutes from the Golden Gate Bridge, and
you can see vineyards as you pull in. Besides the Indy Car race
each August, the track hosts five other major races, including
NASCAR and NHRA dragsters. "The whole package is great: the
location, with Napa and Sonoma; San Francisco is nearby; and for
the race, it is always beautiful and mild. You can see a lot of that
track, and there are a lot of places to watch the race from."
infineonraceway.com

Texas Motor Speedway, Fort Worth, Texas

Some tracks have few opportunities for passing, but the Texas
Motor Speedway allows cars to run side by side, adding to the
excitement. The track hosts the Bombardier Learjet 550 each
June, one of the few open-wheel races held after dark. "You can

see a lot of the action in the corners. You don't have to get up early. As a fan, it's another good party." *texasmotorspeedway.com*

Milwaukee Mile, Milwaukee, Wisconsin
May does not end with the Indy 500: It finishes a week later with the AJ Foyt 225 at the oldest continuously operating motorsports venue in the United States, the Milwaukee Mile. The unique track allows cars to race three or even four wide at times. "You can see all of the track from the stands. There is side-by-side racing, and there is a lot of passing going on. It's not uncommon for the leader to lap a lot of the positions. There are some great bars in Milwaukee, obviously. Go catch a Brewers Game." *milwaukeemile.com*

Honda Grand Prix of St. Petersburg, St. Petersburg, Florida
This April race is part of the feverish run-up to the Indy 500 and another fan-friendly Grand Prix–style street race in the heart of the city. "It's definitely not Monaco, but [the race] gives you that feel with the boats all in the water. It's a more peaceful, relaxing atmosphere, a good place to go do everything near the racing: beach, hotels, restaurants, bars, water." *gpstpete.com*

Homestead Miami Speedway, Miami, Florida
"The racing in Homestead is really good. There's lots of side-by-side racing, we're racing at night, and there's always a lot of passing going on." It's also the final event of the Indy Racing League season. *homesteadmiamispeedway.com*

Celebs and speed

Celebrities have been attending the Indy 500 for years. Clark Gable was there at least three times beginning in 1947. James Stewart went in 1965. Over the years, James Garner and Paul Newman, both of whom supported racing teams, have been in the stands, as have Gene Hackman, Michael Douglas, and Bob Hope. Celeb spottings continue today at the world's largest single-day sporting event, with recent attendees including actor Sean Penn, Aerosmith vocalist Steven Tyler, and NFL quarterback Peyton Manning.

PLACES TO STAY AWHILE

✳ ✳ ✳ ✳

SPAS AND RETREATS

10 great places where silence is truly golden

For some, vacation means adventure-packed days where you hit the ground running and don't stop until nightfall; others are looking for a bit more peace and quiet on their days off. Abbie Kozolchyk, a contributing editor at Body + Soul *magazine, shares a mix of yoga retreats, spas, learning institutes, and ecolodges where the common thread, silence, "is less a requirement than a natural result of being there."*

Esalen, Big Sur, California
"This storied epicenter of alternative healing offers specialties described as 'systems of thought and feeling that lie beyond the current constraints of mainstream academia.' So expect the esoteric and, in some cases, silence. The surroundings—mountains, streams, and an ocean—don't hurt, either." *esalen.org*

El Monte Sagrado Living Resort and Spa, Taos, New Mexico
"Totally silent meals (mindful eating) take place here. Although the traditional spa offerings at this ecoluxe retreat are serenity-inducing in their own right, try the 'special offerings,' including trauma recovery, sound and vibration therapy, and spiritual cleansing. You'll emerge calmer and happier." *elmontesagrado.com*

Tambopata Research Center, Tambopata, Peru
"This lodge-cum-Duke-University-affiliated macaw research station is an eight-hour boat ride into the Peruvian Amazon. Once

at TRC, you'll be treated to a transcendental experience: Before dawn, trek to the world's largest macaw clay lick, where silence is mandatory before the noisy macaw and parrot conclave begins. The spectacle ends in 30 minutes, birds dissipate, and visitors go on to hikes and hammock appointments."
perunature.com

Miraval Life in Balance, Tucson, Arizona
"This desert resort offers the best of massage and spa treatments, plus a dizzying number of classes in yoga, meditation, adventure, creative arts, and nutrition." *miravalresort.com*

Kripalu Center for Yoga and Health, Lenox, Massachusetts
"A Jesuit seminary turned legendary yoga retreat, the spirit here is one of self-reflection and simplicity. Accommodations range from seminarian-worthy dorm rooms to spartan private rooms. While any of the programs work wonders after the holidays, particularly appropriate offerings include two R&R healing retreats: the Serenity and the Inner Peace." *kripalu.org*

Taj Garden Retreat, Kumarakom, Kerala, India
"Though the lush setting and on-site Ayurveda center should erase any stress, an overnight, rice-boat-based trip through the region's legendary and peaceful backwaters is a euphoria-inducing experience." *tajhotels.com*

Rancho La Puerta, Tecate, Baja California, Mexico
"What began in 1940 as a bring-your-own-tent 'health camp' has grown into adobe casitas, organic gardens, winding trails, and exhaustive fitness and treatment facilities. The original cornerstones remain, however: the familial feel and the belief in 'the interdependence of mind, body, and spirit.' For true peace and quiet, choose the silent dinners." *rancholapuerta.com*

Shambhala Mountain Center, Red Feather Lakes, Colorado
"Shambhala is something of a serenity superstore. Within the property's 600 acres—home to forests, meadows, and gardens—visitors engage in 'contemplative arts programs,' including

meditation or advanced Buddhist retreats, hiking, massages, and star- and garden-gazing." *shambhalamountain.org*

Parrot Cay, Turks & Caicos

"For high-end and celebrity-studded serenity, the private-island resort of Parrot Cay is a great place to be. Though the blissful

R&R in Turks & Caicos

For the past decade, little has stopped growth on Providenciales, known as Provo. The most populated of the eight inhabited islands of the Turks & Caicos, Provo has evolved from an under-the-radar diving retreat to a luxury getaway name-dropped in celebrity magazines.

All along Grace Bay Beach—a five-mile stretch of postcard-perfect sand abutting gasp-inducing turquoise water—stroll bikinied tourists moneyed enough to pay high-season prices at the resorts that now line the shore. A nonstop flight from several U.S. cities, the island draws those searching for ease with their relaxation: English is the official language, and the currency is the U.S. dollar.

Dry, flat, and scrubby, Provo shows its beauty through its beaches—Grace Bay was noted as one of the world's best by *Condé Nast Traveler*—and through its clear waters, home to pristine coral reefs. Excellent snorkeling alongside angelfish and tang is available just steps from the beach in Princess Alexandra Marine Park. (Provo's entire shoreline is open to the public.)

For those with visions of being tropical castaways, Turks & Caicos has plenty of opportunity: The United Kingdom Overseas Territory comprises nearly 40 isles of various sizes, most uninhabited. Several Provo operators offer half- and full-day fishing and diving excursions, and it would be easy to while away a week lazily exploring outlying islands.

But first, there are conchs to catch. Turks & Caicos celebrates its native mollusk with a festival every year, and the delicacy graces menus islandwide. Masks in hand, tourists plunge into the shallow warm water.

When leaving a canopied daybed sounds like too much work for visitors, Provo's meticulously landscaped resorts provide the ultimate do-nothing escape. Many people spend their vacations enjoying the suite life, venturing off the grounds only to go to other resorts for dinner.

setting alone is a textbook tropical paradise, with secluded white sandy beaches and aqua water, the on-site spa seals the deal. The Asian treatments are extraordinary, as are the yoga and meditation offerings." *parrotcay.como.bz*

Bay of Fires Lodge, Tasmania, Australia
"You'll be doubly Down Under (on an island south of mainland Australia) on this remote and outrageously beautiful stretch of coastline. A two-day prelude awaits your arrival at the lodge, during which several guides and fellow travelers hike the coastline. Spend the first night at a beach camp within the Mount William National Park. The main lodge (featuring high tea and showers) becomes your base for meditation, inspired views, kayaking, swimming, and more hiking." *cradlehuts.com.au*

10 great places to recycle yourself

Looking for a little R&R? Help yourself and the planet by visiting a "green spa," an ecofriendly resort that doesn't harm nature as it nurtures you. "This is probably the next step in ecotravel," says Jeanie Pyun, editor of Organic Style *magazine. "It's wonderful to be able to indulge in a completely luxurious, pampered situation" without hurting Mother Nature. Pyun shares some favorite feel-good getaways.*

The Rock Spa, Fregate Island Private, Seychelles
"At this cliff-top sanctuary near the Indian Ocean, visitors can harvest ingredients for their own scrumptious spa treatments." Innovative programs "protect and increase the rare and endangered plants and birds on the island." *fregate.com*

Daintree Eco Lodge & Spa, Daintree, Queensland, Australia
Set in a rain forest, "this tree-house-style spa and lodge pampers the environment almost as lavishly as it does its guests. Skin-soothing treatments prepared from lillypilly berries, wattleseeds, and desert salts honor the indigenous Aboriginal heritage of the region. In addition to standard ecopractices, such as recycling and water conservation, the resort's entire business plan revolves around its environmental, social, and ethical impacts." *daintree-ecolodge.com.au*

Golden Door, Escondido, California

"A taste of the Orient—California style. Energy efficiency permeates this luxury spa that caters to your every whim, whether you're looking for a week of light exercise and relaxation or a full-scale fitness boot camp. Gourmet meals are prepared in your preferred portion size using fresh ingredients from a four-acre organic garden." *goldendoor.com*

Rancho La Puerta, Tecate, Baja California

"A 'summer camp for adults' set in the high desert just four miles from the Mexican border. Scents of wild rosemary and sage waft through the windows in the evening as coyotes howl in the distance. The lush six-acre organic garden and orchard supplies the ranch with an abundance of fruits and vegetables." *rancholapuerta.com*

The Crossings, Austin, Texas

"Designed to be healthy inside and out, The Crossings features scenic pathways surrounded by native plants that transport people and supplies throughout the facility without vehicles. Windows and skylights bring the natural Texas environment indoors." *thecrossingsaustin.com*

New Age Health Spa, Neversink, New York

"Two chemical-free greenhouses and a large garden are the centerpieces of cuisine at this woodland spa. Herbs from the greenhouses also are incorporated into the spa's signature purification treatments." *newagehealthspa.com*

Spa at Sundance, Sundance, Utah

"Treatment blends of honey, cornmeal, sage, and sweet grass are a luxurious reminder of the spa's Native American roots. Buildings crafted with ecofriendly materials create a rustic, handcrafted look." *sundanceresort.com*

El Santuario, Valle de Bravo, Mexico

"Located in a 16th-century village 2-1/2 hours west of Mexico City, El Santuario is surrounded by more than 400 acres of nature preserves. When you're not indulging in the spa's organic meals or spa treatments, you can choose from a variety of ecoadventures—from hiking and biking to treetop zip-line tours." *elsantuario.com*

Sundara Inn & Spa, Wisconsin Dells, Wisconsin
Set in a forest, Sundara offers "organic cuisine prepared from ingredients grown on Midwest family farms. The sandstone body polish, containing powdered remnants of ancient Cambrian sandstone, is harvested on-site." *sundaraspa.com*

El Monte Sagrado Living Resort and Spa, Taos, New Mexico
"With every environmentally friendly detail, from fabrics to cleaning supplies to treatment ingredients, this spa was designed to go 'beyond organic.' Spa treatments are crafted from an intoxicating blend of indigenous plants, flowers, and minerals. A 'biolarium,' or giant greenhouse, contains an aquatic treatment system that filters the water." *elmontesagrado.com*

10 great places to get everything under the sun

All-inclusive resorts can be a value alternative to à la carte tropical vacations. Doug Stallings, senior editor at fodors.com/80degrees, a section of the Web site that explores warm-weather escapes, suggests some resorts that offer bang for the buck.

Almond Beach Village, Heywoods, Barbados
This 32-acre family-friendly resort set on a former 18th-century sugar plantation has a soft-sand, mile-long beach. Included in the rate: golf, sailing, waterskiing, and more, making it "one of the island's best values." *almondresorts.com*

Excellence Punta Cana, Punta Cana, Dominican Republic
"This adults-only lovers' lair exudes romance." Included in the all-suites resort is one 30-minute horseback ride per visit. "If you prefer to simply relax by the lazy-river pool or on the beautiful stretch of beach, both have waiter service. And it's not just well drinks here; premium brands are poured at the bars." *excellence-resorts.com*

Club Med Columbus Isle, San Salvador Island, Bahamas
"One of Club Med's most relaxing Caribbean resorts has excellent food, nice rooms, and a beautiful beach." Kids three and older are welcome at the all-inclusive resort. "Activities include group sailing and windsurfing lessons, fitness classes, tennis, and water sports." *clubmed.us*

Couples Swept Away, Negril, Jamaica
"The sports facilities here are among the best in the Caribbean." Rates include fitness classes, snorkeling cruises, tennis, golf, and scuba diving, plus transfers, gratuities, premium drinks, and even weddings. As its name implies, it's a couples-only resort. *couples.com*

Body Holiday at LeSport, Cariblue Beach, St. Lucia
This resort is ideal for "those who like to indulge body and soul," since spa treatments (except on arrival and departure days), along with myriad fitness classes, are included in the rate. And Tao, the resort's upscale restaurant, is "one of the island's finest." *thebodyholiday.com*

Amelia Island Plantation, Amelia Island, Florida
The golf, tennis, and spa facilities are big draws at this family-oriented resort, where accommodations range from hotel rooms to three-bedroom villas. "If the sound of waves crashing on the beach doesn't lull you to sleep, the pillow-top mattresses should. With its ancient oaks, marshes, and lagoons, it is a worthy destination for hiking, biking, and bird-watching." *aipfl.com*

Mawamba Lodge, Tortuguero, Costa Rica
"Located between the Tortuguero Canals and the Caribbean, this is also the only jungle lodge within a ten-minute walk of town. For the all-inclusive experience, buy a package tour for comfortable (hot water!) rustic rooms and garden views." Meals are served in the spacious dining room. Also included: guided tours of the jungle and canals. *grupomawamba.com*

Aventura Spa Palace, Riviera Maya, Mexico
"The stunning grounds of this adults-only resort on the Riviera Maya have a meditation pond, yoga hut, labyrinthine Zen path, and botanical gardens." Facilities include an indoor pool with sound therapy and coves for snorkeling. *palaceresorts.com*

Presidente InterContinental Los Cabos Resort, San Jose del Cabo, Mexico
"Cactus gardens surround this low-lying hotel, one of the originals along the beach." The staff caters to families, and the resort's "ground-floor rooms, which have terraces, are the best. Make sure you try Napa, the property's top restaurant." *ichotelsgroup.com/intercontinental/en/gb/locations/loscabos*

Dreams Puerto Vallarta Resort & Spa, Puerto Vallarta, Mexico
"Dramatic views of the rock-edged beach" make this resort special. Plus, "theme nights go all out—salsa dancing, reggae, and circus nights—and for sports night, ball games with hot dogs and beer. There are activities for kids and adults." *dreamsresorts.com*

10 great places to revive the spirit

Good health equates to more than just the physical— refueling your emotional and spiritual sides can do wonders for a body. Mark Ogilbee and Jana Riess, authors of American Pilgrimage: Sacred Journeys and Spiritual Destinations, *offer suggestions for spiritual retreats and getaways.*

Abbey of Gethsemani, Trappist, Kentucky
Visitors who want a taste of the Trappist monastery where American writer Thomas Merton spent most of his adult life need go no further than the gift shop to purchase the monks' famous bourbon fruitcake, fudge, or cheese. But those who want to really experience this sanctuary in rural Kentucky need to make a retreat reservation several months in advance. "Retreats are silent and self-directed, and guests are invited to participate with the brothers in praying the Psalms several times each day." *monks.org*

Community of Jesus, Orleans, Massachusetts
Guests bathe themselves in comfort as they work on their spiritual growth at this Christian community in the Benedictine monastic tradition on Cape Cod. "Soft towels, fine china, delicious food, fresh flowers—no detail is forgotten." Hear the community's world-class choir and attend daily services in the basilica-style Church of the Transfiguration. *communityofjesus.org*

National Shrine of Our Lady of the Snows, Belleville, Illinois
Maintained by Missionary Oblates of Mary Immaculate, this immensely popular outdoor shrine complex includes a church, a grotto, several spiritually themed gardens, and numerous other contemplative sites. *snows.org*

Mount Calvary Retreat House and Monastery, Santa Barbara, California
Half a dozen monks, brothers in the Order of the Holy Cross, extend gentle, unobtrusive hospitality to pilgrims and contemplative visitors in their mountainside monastery above Santa Barbara. "Delicious food, quiet atmosphere, meditative gardens, and expansive views of the Pacific Ocean invite spiritual renewal at your own pace." *www.mount-calvary.org*

Mission San Juan Capistrano, San Juan Capistrano, California
Best known for the celebrated return of the swallows on or about March 19 every year, the historic Spanish mission at San Juan Capistrano also contains the rustic Serra Chapel and its womblike shrine room dedicated to St. Peregrine, patron saint of cancer sufferers. "Petitioners light candles to the smallish but unnervingly lifelike statue of the kneeling saint, then write their prayer requests directly on the plaster walls. It is a powerfully intimate, healing space just feet from the outside world." *missionsjc.com*

Santuario de Chimayo, Chimayo, New Mexico
"A rustic adobe chapel nestled in a river valley between Santa Fe and Taos is the destination for a multitude of pilgrims who come

Talk to the Expert

DESTINATION SPAS DRAW COMMITTED GUESTS

"There are no bad spas, just bad matches," says Alan Coombs, who, with his wife, Carole, owns the family-run Green Valley Spa in St. George, Utah. Green Valley is a destination spa—that is, its primary purpose is spa services and wellness programs. Coombs discusses state-of-the-spa topics.

Q: What's the difference between resort and destination spas?

A: Destination spas are started by people who are seriously interested in their own health and well-being as well as that of others. They're former therapists or healers, or they have an epiphany, such as a serious illness, that leads to a spa stay, which inspires them. Resort spas are controlled by accountants . . . and treat you like a hotel guest. At a destination spa, you're fully enveloped by the staff, and there's a personal, hands-on feeling. The staff ratio is generally at least one-to-one, if not two-to-one.

Q: Why don't destination spas draw a larger share of vacationers?

A: Not many people know enough about destination spas to be interested. [Traditionally, they] have meant a commitment to a lifestyle change, and most vacationers don't want to get out of their comfort zones. First-time spa-goers usually come because they are hurting, physically or mentally or emotionally. They feel they need that impetus to get their lives together. Once you've been, you realize you met wonderful people and felt terrific, the food was wonderful . . . you loved the hiking and getting up in the morning, you have photos of yourself climbing a 100-foot rock wall . . . you want to return.

Q: Does that include men?

A: [Typically] men are dragged here by their wife or girlfriend. They don't know if they really want to be here, but by the end they say it was their best vacation ever. Our spa is male-oriented or, at least, unisex. We don't offer the more usual aerobic program; we have full-service golf and tennis schools . . . the most beautiful hiking trails.

seeking spiritual and physical healing from the holy dirt—yes, dirt—they scoop from *el posito,* a small hole in the ground in a sanctum off the chapel's sanctuary. Letters of gratitude, no-longer-needed crutches, even banged-up prosthetic limbs line the walls near *el posito*—a persuasive testimony."
archdiocesesantafe.org/AboutASF/Chimayo.html

Nauvoo, Illinois
The towering Mormon temple here is closed to the non-Mormon public, but there's plenty more for the nearly one million visitors who come to this restored Mississippi River village every year. "Like an 1840s version of Colonial Williamsburg, Old Nauvoo seems stranded in time to the days when (Mormon founder) Joseph Smith lived here, with more than 60 restored or re-created buildings." *beautifulnauvoo.com*

Lac Ste-Anne, near Edmonton, Alberta, Canada
Every July, tens of thousands of pilgrims flock to this lake named for St. Anne, traditionally identified as the grandmother of Jesus. The pilgrimage has its roots in Native peoples' seasonal migration patterns and received a boost when Catholic missionaries established a church at the lake in the 19th century. "The result is a unique cultural and spiritual event at the intersection of Native American ('First Nations' in Canada) and Catholic tradition—believers are known as Native Catholics."
www.dioceseofkeewatinlepas.ca/lacsteanne.htm

Chapel of the Holy Cross, Sedona, Arizona
Magnificent red-rock forma-
tions dominate the Sedona
landscape and are purport-
edly home to some half dozen
vortexes, nodes of particularly
healthy earth energy that
attract thousands of New Age
believers every year. But other
pilgrims are drawn to the

Chapel of the Holy Cross, an ecumenically minded Catholic chapel built on a red-rock formation. "Architecturally bold—a giant cross

forms part of its structure—and spiritually dynamic, the chapel is open daily for prayer and meditation within its coolly modern sanctuary." *chapeloftheholycross.com*

Dog Chapel, St. Johnsbury, Vermont
"All creeds, all breeds, no dogma allowed" is the motto of the charming Dog Chapel tucked into the rolling hills of Vermont. "Conceived and built by artist Stephen Huneck, this undersized New England village–style church is a whimsical and tasteful sanctuary where serious dog lovers can come to celebrate the spiritual connection they have with their beloved canine companions." And that's exactly what thousands do every year. *dogmt.com/dogchapel*

AND ANOTHER THING . . .

MORE PLACES TO DETOX, TUNE UP, AND CALM DOWN

Here are more North American spas that specialize in getting the body running lighter and cleaner.

- The Greenhouse Spa, Arlington, Texas (thegreenhousespa.net)
- We Care Spa, Desert Hot Springs, California (wecarespa.com)
- Hippocrates Health Institute, West Palm Beach, Florida (hippocratesinst.org)
- Elemental Embrace, Brighton, Ontario, Canada (elementalembrace.com)
- The Raj, Vedic City, Iowa (theraj.com)
- Regency Health Resort and Spa, Hallandale, Florida (regencyhealthspa.com)
- Sanoviv Medical Institute, Rosarito, Baja California, Mexico (sanoviv.com)
- Red Mountain Spa, Ivins, Utah (redmountainspa.com)
- Tree of Life Rejuvenation Center, Patagonia, Arizona (treeoflife.nu)

KID- AND PET-FRIENDLY SPOTS

10 great places to link up with your family

Tear it up this year and let the whole family enjoy tee time together with a family golf vacation. John Atwood, editor in chief of Travel + Leisure Golf *magazine, shares his selections.*

Walt Disney World Resort, Orlando, Florida
"Better known for its multitude of attractions for kids, Walt Disney World has a fine collection of golf courses, including Magnolia, a stylish Joe Lee design named for its magnificent trees. Steal an afternoon or coax the kids onto the links when they find themselves all Moused out." *disneyworld.com*

Hershey Resorts, Hershey, Pennsylvania
They call it "the sweetest place on earth." And who's to argue? On some days, you can actually smell chocolate in the air. "The grown-up parts of this family resort exude sophistication, from the 36-hole country club where Ben Hogan once served as head pro to the sleek Circular Dining Room in the Moorish-themed main hotel. The kid component is over-the-top: a theme park with more than 60 rides and 10 roller coasters. There's also a short golf course called Spring Creek for beginners." *hersheypa.com*

Wigwam Golf Resort & Spa, Litchfield Park, Arizona
"Originally a bring-the-kids desert getaway for the private use of Goodyear employees, this 54-hole golf resort retains a bit of its Eisenhower-era innocence. Sign the young ones up for the kids' program while you succumb to a treatment at the Elizabeth Arden Red Door Spa, then enjoy the water slide and lawn croquet as a family. Older children may be ready for horseback lessons or, of course, swing instruction at the Jim McLean Golf School." *wigwamresort.com*

Grand Wailea Resort Hotel & Spa, Maui, Hawaii

"Pool paradise: One is all slides, swings, and rapids; one is soothing and serene (adults only); and another is devoted to scuba. There are also six restaurants, Hawaii's largest spa, a kids' camp, and—oh, yeah—five championship golf courses within five minutes, transportation provided." *grandwailea.com*

Grand Traverse Resort & Spa, Acme, Michigan

"Golf is huge here, with courses by Jack Nicklaus and Gary Player, plus a third 18 and a Jim McLean Golf School. Book rooms in a high floor of the main tower overlooking East Bay or have the run of a resort condominium." There's also Kids' Night Out with pizza, a bonfire, tennis, and other diversions for the 6 to 12 set. They can sign up for a week's worth of fun at Camp Traverse. *grandtraverseresort.com*

Balsams Grand Resort Hotel, Dixville Notch, New Hampshire

"At this luxurious White Mountain redoubt, families are seated at one table all week to foster conversation and friendship. Surrounding the grande dame hotel is a wilderness of lakes, forests, and mountain peaks to be explored, and the resort's Donald Ross golf course is a rare mix of brawn and trickery." *thebalsams.com*

Kiawah Island Resort, Kiawah Island, South Carolina

"This award-winning resort can lodge vacationing families in a private mansion, a luxury villa, or seaview suite in the ultraswank Sanctuary Hotel. In selecting from Kiawah's five 18-hole golf courses, beware the famous Ocean Course: On a windy day, it's more than a young player can handle. Nature-loving kids will love the outdoorsy Kamp Kiawah program." *kiawahresort.com*

Casa de Campo, Dominican Republic

"If the young ones have their passports in order, then so is a trip to this Caribbean golf mecca, where the resort staff runs a family-beach Olympics, group mural painting, and open-air merengue lessons. At some point, the devoted golfer must break away to savor one of the hemisphere's top ten golf resorts: Pete Dye's famed Teeth of the Dog." *casadecampo.com.do*

Fairmont Chateau Whistler, Whistler, British Columbia, Canada
"This turreted palace at the foot of Blackcomb Mountain exerts a magnetic draw on U.S. vacationers, not least for the rugged Robert Trent Jones Jr. golf course." Everyone can polish their game at the hotel's David Leadbetter Golf Academy, a practice and learning center that offers instruction and video analysis for golfers of varying ages and skill levels. *fairmont.com/whistler*

Sunriver Resort, Sunriver, Oregon
"By the time his parents are unpacked, a young Sunriver guest can be two miles away on a mountain bike—or on a horse exploring Deschutes National Forest or on a canoe seat skimming toward distant Mount Bachelor. Golfers have their choice of three acclaimed golf courses, each of which will challenge the most sophisticated player." *sunriver-resort.com*

10 great places for a grand time with the grandkids

Forget the generation gap. Create memories and have a blast by staying at a family-friendly place. Susan Avery, senior editor at grandparents.com, an online community to help grandparents connect with their grandchildren, shares her picks.

Camp Richardson Resort, Lake Tahoe, California
"This is old Lake Tahoe. The rustic lodgings, without telephones or TVs, are reminiscent of a simpler, quiet life." Sheltered by pines on the southwestern shore of the lake, the resort offers a choice of tent campsites, cabins, RV sites, or a historic hotel. Rent boats at the marina, ride bikes together on miles of paved paths, or sit on the deck at the resort's Beacon Bar & Grill and admire the changing colors. *camprichardson.com*

River Run Canoe & Camping, Brownfield, Maine
"The calmness of the Saco River makes it an easy paddle for all different ages." It's one of the most popular recreational rivers in the

state, and the sandy bottom of the Saco is inviting for a swim. Go ashore to picnic or camp on a sandbar along the way. Bring your own equipment or have this outfitter gear you up and provide shuttle service to a starting point. *riverruncanoe.com*

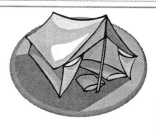

Arlington Resort Hotel & Spa, Hot Springs, Arkansas
"Go fishing. The size of a catch doesn't matter to children; what matters is bonding with their grandparents. It's about spending a few stress-free hours together in the great outdoors, side by side." Bass and crappie abound in the clean water at Lake Ouachita State Park, only half an hour from this historic downtown hotel. Tour a bathhouse, buy art, or relax on a bench and people-watch. *arlingtonhotel.com*

L'Enfant Plaza Hotel, Washington, D.C.
"This classy, family-friendly hotel is a short walk to the National Mall and the Metro (subway)." Washington, D.C., "is a great destination, but you have to know your child and make sure he or she has the right temperament, at the right age, to visit. Every bit of the trip is an educational one." Must-sees: the International Spy Museum and the U.S. Bureau of Engraving and Printing (to discover how money is made—literally). *lenfantplazahotel.com*

Camelback Inn, Scottsdale, Arizona
"New generations continue to inherit the family tradition of vacationing together at this popular 125-acre hotel." The wide-open Southwest terrain provides plenty of opportunities for bike riding or strolling the desert landscape known for its stunning light. The big complex of pools has something for everybody, and there's a golf course surrounded by desert wildlife and plants. Hopalong College, the program for children ages 6 to 12, has exploratory outdoor activities and cooking classes. *camelbackinn.com*

Paradise Guest Ranch, Buffalo, Wyoming
"The dude-ranch experience is so complete here there's no reason to ever leave." It's all about enjoying the ranch without any of the hassles of getting to museums and restaurants. Programs for kids

AND ANOTHER THING...

UNFORGETTABLE SUMMER VACATIONS

- Sandpoint, Idaho (sandpointchamber.com)
- The Big Island of Hawaii (gohawaii.com/big_island/)
- Chicago, Illinois (choosechicago.com)
- Santa Fe, New Mexico (santafe.org)
- Ocean City, New Jersey (oceancityvacation.com)
- Southwestern Utah (scenicutah.com)
- South Dakota (travelsd.com/Destinations)
- Mississippi Delta (visitthedelta.com)
- Navajo and Hopi lands, Arizona (arizonaguide.com)
- Pawleys Island, South Carolina (townofpawleysisland.com)
- Prince William Sound, Alaska (discoveryvoyages.com)
- Santa Ynez Valley, California (alisal.com)

of all ages range from pony rides to special overnight campouts. Or just sit by the pool. *paradiseranch.com*

Otesaga Resort Hotel, Cooperstown, New York
"A lot of families have come here for generations. It's like home, and the lobby is their living room." Visit the National Baseball Hall of Fame & Museum or the Farmers' Museum, where interpreters portray the occupations and rhythms of everyday living in the 19th century. There's also the Fenimore Art Museum and the world-class Glimmerglass Opera. *otesaga.com*

Hotel Le Bristol, Paris, France
"A trip to Paris is ultrahip. It's especially well suited for teens because of their appreciation level. Stay at the Bristol—it's great." In addition to seeing some of the world's greatest artworks at the Louvre, grandparents and grandkids should check out the Natural History Museum and Jardin des Plantes, the botanical garden on

the museum's grounds. Otherwise, just strolling down the streets of Paris has its own appeal. *hotel-bristol.com*

Disney's Boardwalk Resort, Lake Buena Vista, Florida
"Explore nearby Epcot from this lovely hotel. Epcot has all the excitement of a world's fair. It's like taking a trip around the world and sampling the fine food along the way. Guests walk or take boats crisscrossing Seven Seas Lagoon. Chefs come from around the world to make authentic dishes from their country. The result is absolutely top-notch." *disneyworld.com*

Hilton Hawaiian Village Beach Resort & Spa,
Oahu, Hawaii
"There's a Super Pool landscaped with lava-rock waterfalls. On the grounds near the lobby, the kids can see more than 30 species of wildlife, including super-popular penguins, ibises, flamingos, and a variety of birds and fish." Pack your grass skirt and take the children to a hula show followed by fireworks over Waikiki. *hiltonhawaiianvillage.com*

10 great places to loosen your collars

When you're ready for a getaway, don't forget the pets, says Dawn Habgood, coauthor with Robert Habgood of Pets on the Go. *"So many people treat their pets like family, and it's more accepted to travel with them. So hotels go all out, offering room service, vet-created menus, and pet concierges." Habgood shares special spots offering creature comforts for pet and owner.*

Ritz-Carlton Hotel, New York, New York
"Conveniently set next to Central Park, this ultra-luxurious hotel wows with five-star service and accommodations. The VIP (Very Important Pooch) program (for pets up to 60 pounds) provides 22-karat-gold-plated IDs, aromatherapy coat spritzes, hand-painted ceramic dinnerware, quilted travel mats, and Burberry pet raincoats." *ritzcarlton.com*

W Seattle, Seattle, Washington

"This boutique hotel offers some of the best views in the city plus the 'Whatever/ Whenever' service, enabling guests to borrow any pet item left behind. The staff lavishes attention on its four-legged guests with pet toys, treats, W tags, a full complement of services—even custom pet birthday cakes. The things that separate W from the pack are the signature beds, including those for pets." *starwoodhotels.com/whotels/index.html*

Inn by the Sea, Cape Elizabeth, Maine

"The staff at this classic inn has been rolling out the pet red carpet for more than 15 years, and they know how to please pets and their 'people.' Treats always are set out in the spacious suites (the best have ocean views), but these are just a prelude to room service's Bow Wow burgers and homemade biscuits. Expansive lawns slope down to the beach, our idea of doggie heaven." *innbythesea.com*

Woof Cottages, Nantucket, Massachusetts

"Our dogs love exploring Nantucket's stunning beaches and pristine conservation lands and snoozing on the back patio at the Even Keel Café. The cottages, set on the harbor, feature pet treats, bowls, beds, and toys to keep furry friends occupied and comfortable while you peruse the list of pet-friendly activities/restaurants. Dogs and cats are welcome with innkeeper approval." *thecottagesnantucket.com/rooms/withpets.php*

St. Regis Resort, Aspen, Colorado

"The St. Regis gets everything right. Any place that puts Frette linens on your bed (and your pet's) embodies luxury. The resort is tucked against Aspen Mountain, with easy access to both the slopes and in-town amenities. The staff will do whatever it takes to make your stay—and your pet's (80 pounds or less, please)—perfect." *stregisaspen.com*

San Ysidro Ranch, Montecito, California

"It's easy to find your well-appointed cottage here: Just look for your name, and your pet's, burned into the placard on the door. Nestled on 500 hillside acres, the elegant ranch [boasts a] privileged Pets Program, featuring 'Pawier' water, homemade treats, or gourmet items off the pet menu. Explore the 17 miles of trails, then relax with massages for you and your pet." *sanysidroranch.com*

Loews Ventana Canyon Resort, Tucson, Arizona
"The spectacular Ventana Canyon and Catalina Mountain foothills are reason enough to visit. The Loews Loves Pets program welcomes pets of all sizes and includes a pet concierge, who suggests animal-friendly eateries, shops, and scenic hikes into the canyon. The hotel provides a 'Did You Forget' closet filled with pet goodies and necessities, along with special menu items and room service." *loewshotels.com*

Paw House Inn, Killington, Vermont
"One of a handful of inns catering to travelers with dogs, the innkeepers balance the historic Vermont country inn experience with dog-themed rooms. Also featured are doggie living rooms, a doggie daycare playhouse with indoor/outdoor recreation areas, swimming areas, and a variety of dog classes. After a busy day on cross-country trails, canines can retire to their own four-poster sleigh bed or puffy Orvis dog bed." *pawhouseinn.com*

Nine Zero, Boston, Massachusetts
"Paws down, our favorite pet-friendly luxury boutique hotel wins highest marks for service. They know both you and your dog by name, and there are specially designed bowls and beds, along with information on pet-sitting, dog walks, and massage services. All are part of the In the Dog House package. While your pets sack out on super-soft beds, it's time to snuggle into your own bed, complete with Frette linens and down comforters." *ninezero.com*

Daufuskie Island Club, off Hilton Head Island, South Carolina
"If you're lucky, a pod of dolphins will escort your ferry to this laid-back island escape, rich with Southern hospitality, plantation-style

architecture, golf-cart transportation, and room for dogs to romp. Pets get good care with gourmet treats, bowls, and designer pet beds." *daufuskieresort.com*

10 great places for making a splash

Looking for a cool dip for the summer? No, we mean really, really cool. Jason Harper, a luxury travel trend watcher for more than a decade and now executive editor of concierge.com, a Web site affiliated with Condé Nast Traveler, *directs us to hotels nationwide with the hippest swimming pools.*

The Raleigh, Miami, Florida
"Things change so quickly in Miami—but the Raleigh's pool is 100 percent classic. These are the same waters where Esther Williams paddled about in the 1950s." Sandwiched between the ocean and the Art Deco high-rise building, the pool has a scalloped design and famous waterfall that are unmistakable. *raleighhotel.com*

Amangani, Jackson, Wyoming
"Pools by the beach are one thing, but sitting in a pool at 7,000 feet in the mountains is simply incomparable." Amangani is on the edge of a butte in the grand splendor of Jackson Hole. While being catered to by the staff—there are two staffers for every guest—visitors are likely to see deer or elk feeding nearby. "There's nothing like being at this heated pool in the middle of winter, surrounded by snow." *amanresorts.com*

Four Seasons Hualalai, Ka'upulehu, Hawaii (Big Island)
If you're on the splendid Kona Coast, you might wonder why you'd need a pool amid all the natural wonder (and stellar beaches). But the King's Pond at the Four Seasons is a freshwater and seawater pool carved out of lava rock. And it's right next to the sea. "The property actually stocks the pool with tons of

vividly colored fish and gives the guests snorkel gear. It's the next best thing to diving in the ocean, but you don't have to worry about strong currents. Or, you know, sharks." *fourseasons.com/hualalai*

The Beverly Hills Hotel, Beverly Hills, California

"The kind of place you'd expect to find George Hamilton sunning himself. When people imagine a Hollywood pool, they're imagining the Pink Palace." The classic hotel, located on Sunset Boulevard, is often host to big Hollywood parties. "The palms around the pool give off a sense of privacy, but it's the cabanas where the real action takes place." *beverlyhillshotel.com*

Mandalay Bay, Las Vegas, Nevada

It doesn't get more Vegas than this. Mandalay Bay calls its pool a beach and carted in the sand to prove it. The 11-acre expanse includes a wave pool that produces swells big enough to bodyboard on. And just when you think you've seen it all, head to the Moorea Beach Club—the exclusive adult section. "You have to pay a cover to get in—but guests will get better service, good cocktails, and the chance to partake in what the resort refers to as 'European bathing' (i.e., tops optional)." *mandalaybay.com*

Hotel Gansevoort, New York, New York

The 45-foot roof-deck pool with 360-degree views has become the place that defines the Meatpacking District, one of the city's hottest neighborhoods. "A see-and-be-seen setting. During the day, bathing beauties take advantage of the free paperbacks and the DJ music piped underwater." *hotelgansevoort.com*

JW Marriott Desert Ridge Resort & Spa, Phoenix, Arizona

This four-acre pool is heaven for children and a haven for adults. The heat of the Sonoran Desert is quenched with a lazy river and slide and a massive center fountain. "It has many of the Vegas elements without any of Vegas's R-rated antics." A bonus: no charge for inner tubes. *jwdesertridgeresort.com*

The Breakers, Palm Beach, Florida

This storied resort has been around for more than a century, but the two main pools are sparkling new after a $15 million renovation. The 2,200-square-foot Relaxation infinity pool is for adults only and outlaws cell phones; the slightly larger Activity pool welcomes kids. "This is a classic resort pool experience. The Breakers [staff] know their clientele, who return year after year, generation after generation." *thebreakers.com*

Post Ranch Inn, Big Sur, California
California's Big Sur coastline is known as a dramatically beautiful drive, but it's hard to find a place to take a time out on the narrow roads. The cliffside Post Ranch Inn, with its circular, infinity "basking" pool, is the perfect answer. It's kept at an invigorating 104 degrees and is too small for laps. But lean over its western edge to get a thrilling look at the Pacific Ocean. "You'd be hard-pressed to find a better poolside view in the entire world." *postranchinn.com*

The Colonnade, Boston, Massachusetts
In summer, the best place to escape Boston's humidity is the Colonnade s rooftop pool, 11 stories up. "Expect lots of poolside champagne and Red Sox and Patriots players mixing it up with the Virgin Atlantic flight attendants who stay there. It's a great scene— if you can get in." *colonnadehotel.com*

OFF THE BEATEN PATH

10 great endangered places to see while you can

It's good to be reminded of just how beautiful—and fragile—our planet is. To help, Peter Frank, editor in chief of concierge.com, offers a list of some of the world's most threatened sites that travelers should see while they still have the chance.

Bosson Glacier, Chamonix, France
Glaciers worldwide are melting at a rapid pace. "In the Alps, the glacial retreat is particularly noticeable, so now is the time to see

them. One of the most beautiful is Bosson Glacier, situated above the town of Chamonix, the famous ski resort near the Swiss border." Travelers to Chamonix can hit the ski slopes in winter or hike Alpine trails in summer. *chamonix.com*

Mount Kilimanjaro, Tanzania

"Scientists don't agree on why, but the snows of Kilimanjaro—the only one of the Seven Summits (the highest peaks on each continent) that can be climbed by everyday Joes—are rapidly disappearing. People are rushing to climb Kilimanjaro now, while the snow

Kilimanjaro's famous icy peaks are thawing fast

According to many scientists, climate change could cause the legendary snow and ice atop Mount Kilimanjaro to disappear within the next 25 years. For the first time in almost 12,000 years (based on ice-core analysis), Africa's highest peak probably will be ice-free as early as 2022 or as late as 2033, says glaciologist Lonnie Thompson of Ohio State University.

"Of the ice cover present in 1912," Thompson and his colleagues wrote in a recent study, "85 percent has disappeared, and 26 percent of that present in 2000 is now gone."

Thompson's team examined the volume of ice loss, not just surface coverage. They found that the ice not only is shrinking in size but also is thinning rapidly. "Nearly equivalent ice volumes are now being lost to thinning and lateral shrinking," the team reported in the study.

The researchers combined measurements of ice area from aerial photographs and ground changes in ice thickness to determine how fast the ice is disappearing. Analyses of other tropical glaciers in South America, Asia, and Oceania have revealed similar loss of glacial ice, Thompson says.

The study findings also make clear that although rising temperatures play a part in the glaciers' retreat, drier and less cloudy conditions than in the past—partly the result of human-caused climate change—also are contributing to "sublimation" and melting of the glaciers atop the mountain. (Sublimation is the evaporation of ice directly into the atmosphere.)

is still there." The Marangu Hotel, in the nearby town of Moshi, offers beautiful views of the mountain. "They'll also organize your Kilimanjaro trek—either fully equipped, or 'the hard way.' " *tanzaniaparks.com/kili.html*; *maranguhotel.com*

Kruger National Park, South Africa lion habitat, South Africa
"In 2006, it was estimated that fewer than 50,000 lions remained on the entire African continent. Factors ranging from habitat loss and hunting to disease and inbreeding have decimated the lion population. To see this endangered species in the wild, visit South Africa's Kruger National Park and stay at one of the lodges there, such as Singita Game Reserve. Personalized game drives will have you staring wide-eyed at Africa's beautiful landscape populated with elephants; giraffes; hyenas; and, of course, the king of beasts." *sanparks.org/parks/kruger*; *krugerpark.co.za*

Monteverde Cloud Forest Reserve, Costa Rica
Strolling through this forest preserve has been likened to walking inside a grandiose green cathedral. "Those impressed by natural beauty will be awed by the sheer scale and lushness of this Central American landscape, which is deteriorating because of climate change and deforestation." Several hiking trails and guided tours are available, including a "sky walk" featuring six suspended bridges through and above the forest canopy. *monteverdeinfo.com/monteverde.htm*

The Everglades, South Florida
"The 'River of Grass' is a fraction of its former size, thanks to farming and development draining water away from the ecosystem. Despite a federal restoration program begun in 2000, the Everglades—home to many important animals and birds and a place of stark beauty and intense serenity—is disappearing before our eyes. See it while you still can." *nps.gov/ever*

Tanjung Puting National Park, Indonesia
The orangutans and other wildlife inhabiting Borneo—an island shared by Indonesia, Malaysia, and Brunei—are threatened by the

loss of their rain-forest habitat as a consequence of logging and farming. "The biodiversity on this third-largest island in the world is amazing. For optimal wildlife viewing, visit Tanjung Puting National Park, a wildlife preserve on the south coast of the island. Rimba Lodge, adjacent to the park, is a great place to stay." *lombokmarine.com/tanjung-puting-national-park.htm*

Taj Mahal, Agra, India

The Taj Mahal was built in the 17th century by the emperor Shah Jahan to honor the memory of his favorite wife, who died in childbirth. The Taj Mahal is a "do before you die" sight on many people's travel lists. "But due to emissions from more than 200 iron foundries in the Agra region, the world's most famous mausoleum is under serious threat from soot, particulates,  and acid rain. See it sooner rather than later." To truly appreciate the Taj Mahal's beauty, the best time to visit is early morning, when the rising sun paints the shrine in shades of pink. *tajmahalagra.com*

Hudson Bay Polar Bear Habitat, Churchill, Manitoba, Canada

"The polar bears of Canada and Alaska live on sea ice, but global warming is rapidly melting that ice and shrinking the habitat of these magnificent animals. To see polar bears in the wild, visit northern Manitoba's coast (along Hudson Bay) in the fall, when the bears are preparing to hunt seals." Polar bear viewing tours into Wapusk National Park depart from the nearby town of Churchill. *pc.gc.ca/pn-np/mb/wapusk/index_e.asp*

Great Barrier Reef, Australia

Australia's top tourist attraction, the Great Barrier Reef is the only living thing visible from space. But the reef is slowly dying because of the global rise in water temperatures and acidity. "Some scientists believe the reef may be dead in as little as 20 years. A great place to experience this natural wonder is the ecofriendly Hinchinbrook Island Wilderness Lodge, located in a national park

that's surrounded by the Barrier Reef. Canoes, fishing gear, and snorkeling equipment are available for guests."
gbrmpa.gov.au; hinchinbrookresort.com.au

Atchafalaya Basin, Louisiana
"The coastal salt marshes of Louisiana and Mississippi act as a buffer, protecting New Orleans and other coastal towns from hurricanes and their storm surges. But Louisiana is losing over 25 square miles of Delta wetlands to the sea each year." The town of Lafayette is an ideal jumping-off point to visit the Atchafalaya Basin, in south-central Louisiana. "This is the bayou as you've always dreamed of it—cypress swamps, gators, and some of the best fishing (and cuisine) in America."
lacoast.gov/landchange/basins/at/index.asp; lafayettetravel.com

10 great places that veer off the beaten path

Does everything seem a bit blah, a little "been there, done that"? Shannon Stowell, president of the Adventure Travel Trade Association and coauthor of Riding the Hulahula to the Arctic Ocean: A Guide to 50 Extraordinary Adventures for the Seasoned Traveler, *may have the cure. Here, he shares his favorite off-the-beaten-path destinations.*

Channel Islands National Park, California
Just a short boat ride from the coastal town of Ventura, Southern California's Channel Islands are home to more than 2,000 species of plants and animals—and the waters around them teem with life as well. "Kayakers can view thousands of sea birds, dolphins, sea lions, and even spouting whales." The islands also feature hiking trails, diving and snorkeling coves, and tide pools.
nps.gov/chis

Jalapão region, Brazil
Located in the northern heartland of Brazil, the Jalapão region is one of South America's "hidden gems. I love this area for its incredible scenery, friendly people, and diverse flora and fauna. Here you can take guided excursions through the jungle wilderness—a land where panthers, anacondas, and capybaras (the largest living rodent in the world) roam free—starting or ending with a stay at a comfortable safari camp." *braziltourism.org*

Yukon River, Yukon, Canada
If you read Jack London as a kid and never quite got it out of your system, this may be just the destination for you. "Boarding a custom-designed riverboat in Whitehorse, you can cruise through more than 370 miles of Yukon wilderness to Dawson City. It's a great opportunity to view wildlife, meet locals, and explore historical and geological sites." *travelyukon.com*

Ancient African ruins, Kenya
The islands off Kenya's north coast feature some of Africa's most ancient historical sites. "A visit here will give you wonderful insight into that history. You can sail to the islands in a traditional *dhow* (sailing vessel) and explore the ruins up close." Tours can include kayaking through lush mangroves, visiting a turtle-breeding project, snorkeling pristine coral reefs, and kicking back on palm-fringed beaches, with nights spent in comfortable safari-style camps. *magicalkenya.com*

Alpine trails, Switzerland
"A country that's well known for efficient transport, Switzerland has again raised the bar—this time for adventure travelers. The alpine nation now boasts a brand-new national trail system supported by detailed route guides. There are more than 12,000 miles of interconnected hiking, cycling, canoeing, and mountain-bike trails, with accessibility from more than 18,000 stops on Switzerland's public transport network." A wide range of accommodations are available, as well as luggage transportation and sports equipment rental. *switzerlandmobility.ch*

Comedic travels

Comedian and actor Jeff Foxworthy has been to every state, but he calls Bigfork, Montana, "about as pretty as any place in the world." Here, he offers travel highlights and tips.

Q: Where have you been recently that you liked or were surprised by?

A: [In 2009] I went to New Zealand. It was my wife's 50th birthday present to me because I had always wanted to go. She sent me and a buddy over there for nine days, fishing and bow hunting and hiking. The people were very friendly and laid-back. It was one of those unspoiled places. There were times I kept expecting a *T. rex* to step out. It was like *Jurassic Park.* There are no predators at all on the island and no snakes—just animals everywhere.

Q: What is the best place you've ever visited and why?

A: We went to Italy [in 2008] and I just loved it. They know how to do life there. They take their time, enjoy their meals, and they take a nap in the afternoon. We went to Rome, Sicily, and Naples.

Q: What is the most surprising/unexpected place you've ever visited and why?

A: Probably Africa, in that I didn't know it was going to touch my heart the way it did. The first time I went was [in 2005]. Ten guys in our church took my oldest kid (and other children) and went over to work in AIDS orphanages for a week. I initially did it because I want my kids to understand that we're really blessed the way we live.... But I had no idea that I'd be going back and helping build an orphanage in the slums in Nairobi. I just really fell in love with the people.

Q: Can you offer a tip or recommendation for your favorite vacation place?

A: If you go to Kenya, you have to go up to the Masai Mara (park reserve), and you have to do the hot-air balloon ride at daylight. I was kind of scared of a hot-air balloon. My daughter said, "Dad, we're here. We'll never have another chance." I recommend doing the one at sunrise, not in the middle of the day. When you're taking off, it's dark, and then you go up and the sun is peeking over. Then you look down and say, "Oh, my gosh! There are five giraffes below us."

Yellowstone National Park, Wyoming

Okay, so Yellowstone isn't exactly off the beaten path. Each year, thousands of tourists visit the oldest national park in the United States. But most of them drive to the major tourist sites, emerging from their cars only for short strolls. Experiencing the park's grandeur by bicycle gives visitors a whole new perspective—not to mention saving all that gas money. "Just imagine riding alongside beautiful Yellowstone Lake, with bald eagles soaring overhead and elk grazing nearby." *nps.gov/yell*

Spitsbergen Island, Norway

This is a great jumping-off point for exploring the Arctic. Catch an ice-breaking ship in the town of Longyearbyen on the Norwegian island of Svalbard (just south of the Arctic Circle), then circumnavigate the island of Spitsbergen. "You'll see breathtaking fjords, jagged peaks, and huge glaciers—not to mention whales, polar bears, seals, and thousands of seabirds." *visitnorway.com*

Lawrence of Arabia trail, Jordan

You've seen the movie—now you can trace the steps of the real-life T. E. Lawrence via camel and jeep and on foot. "Begin your tour in Jordan's Eastern Desert, where you can visit castles that Lawrence stayed in. You can follow his route through the Wadi Rum desert sands on an all-day camel ride, overnight in authentic Bedouin tents, and then hike through the Beidah Mountains to the ancient city of Petra." *visitjordan.com*

Choquequirao, Peru

Most vacationers have heard of the Inca Trail, which winds through the Andes to the awe-inspiring archaeological site of Machu Picchu. But there are many other breathtaking mountain treks to discover in Peru. "One of the best is a three-day hike to Choquequirao, Machu Picchu's sister site, which is still being excavated. The site overlooks the Apurimac River and offers

unbeatable 360-degree views of the surrounding mountain ranges."
peru.info

Mongolia
"The legacy of Genghis Khan is nearly palpable in this seldom-visited, remote corner of the world. Exploring this extraordinary land on horseback is a unique way to connect with that past." Guided horseback trips include a visit to Karakorum, the legendary 13th-century capital of the Mongolian Empire. When not in the saddle, travelers can spend the evenings in lodges or traditional Mongol tent camps. *mongoliatourism.gov.mn*

10 great places to appreciate the good earth

You're not alone if you're longing for some green acres of your own, says Jack Odle, editor in chief of Progressive Farmer *magazine, which ranked the most desirable rural counties in the United States based on good schools, low crime, health care, and a clean environment, as well as some intangibles such as "community." This "rural renaissance" is compelling "many people to move to the country because they want their own piece of land," he says. "It's much easier to live in a rural area—there's less crime, less pollution and, of course, there's the scenic aspect." Odle shares some alluring places perfect for laid-back country visits.*

Oconee County, Georgia
"A transitional county that retains its rural flavor, Oconee is a short drive to Atlanta." Tourists can hike in pine woods at nearby Oconee National Forest or enjoy the scenic Apalachee and Oconee rivers. "Low pollution, low crime, and excellent schools" make it a viable spot to live or linger. *oconeechamber.org*

Callaway County, Missouri
"Close to St. Louis and Kansas City, this county is scenic, with fertile plains in the north and bluffs bordering the Missouri River at its southern border." Named after Captain Callaway, the grandson of Daniel Boone, the county boasts a population of around 40,000.

Visitors to Fulton, one of Callaway's bigger communities, can tour the Winston Churchill Memorial and Library, which features Churchill memorabilia. *callawaychamber.com*

Fauquier County, Virginia

"About an hour west of Washington, D.C., this county is the home of wineries and equestrian activities, including the Upperville Colt & Horse Show, one of the oldest horse shows in the country." The Blue Ridge Mountains cater to joggers, bikers, and hikers who can pick up the Appalachian Trail at Sky Meadows State Park or the G. W. Thompson Wildlife Management Area. *fauquiertourism.com*

McPherson County, Kansas

"Children actually walk to school here, thanks to the low crime and small town feel." Tours at McPherson College, home of the only accredited liberal arts degree program of antique-auto restoration, offer a glimpse into the historical restorative approach. The county seat boasts the McPherson Museum, McPherson County Courthouse, and the 1888 Romanesque Revival–style Opera House. *mcphersonks.org*

Grafton County, New Hampshire

"With the White Mountain National Forest offering scenic drives, hiking trails, mountain climbing, backcountry campgrounds, and lots of skiing, overdevelopment is not an issue here. Grafton also is home to charming New England towns, Amish communities, and the Ivy League's Dartmouth College." *lebanonchamber.com*

Eagle County, Colorado

"Rocky Mountain peaks, ski resorts (including Vail), and secluded scenic valleys have made this county a playground for the rich and famous, although it still retains longtime farm families. To ensure the county remains true to its roots, the state legislature decided long ago that ranches could not be divided into parcels smaller than 35 acres." *eaglevalley.org*

Gillespie County, Texas

"An influx of newcomers—many retired from successful careers—alongside old-time ranching families create an interesting contrast. German heritage is everywhere you look on Main Street in the county seat of Fredericksburg, along with art galleries, antique shops, and an in-town winery." *fredericksburg-texas.com*

Sauk County, Wisconsin

"Sauk County boasts Parfey's Glen Natural Area, a part of Devil's Lake State Park—one of the continent's most beautiful spots—with rock formations and a glacial lake. The Nature Conservancy designated the Baraboo Bluffs region as one of its Last Great Places by virtue of unique rocks, plants, and animals. Organic herb and vegetable farms and quaint towns dot the region."
baraboo.com/chamber

Wilson County, Tennessee

"Although many residents commute to nearby Nashville, the county's small farms abound with cattle and hay, as well as small goat and sheep flocks. Starting the third week of August, the Wilson County Fair draws about 420,000 people through its nine-day run." *wilsoncountycvb.com*

Rankin County, Mississippi

"Just across the Pearl River from Jackson, Rankin is growing quickly but has kept its rural flavor. Great schools and health care exist for residents"; visitors are lured by fishing, boating, and camping at Ross Barnett Reservoir. Rankin's location offers easy access to Gulf Coast beaches; Tennessee's rolling hills; and the major metropolitan areas of Atlanta, Dallas, and New Orleans.
rankinchamber.com

We must go out and re-ally ourselves to Nature every day.

—Henry David Thoreau

10 great places to leave the beauty unspoiled

Resolved: Pick a place to visit this year that does not involve trashing the planet. Call it "geotourism," which is defined by the National Geographic Society as "tourism that sustains or enhances the geographical character of a place. It's a destination where you can have an authentic travel experience without harming the place." Jonathan Tourtellot, director of the society's Center for Sustainable Destinations, shares his list of favorites.

Grenada
"Grenada is one of the last Caribbean island countries not yet overwhelmed with huge, all-inclusive resorts. The beaches are beautiful, the forested and mountainous interior is ecologically rich, and the capital of St. George is the most attractive historic port town in the Caribbean." *grenadagrenadines.com*

Guanajuato, Mexico
Founded in 1554, Guanajuato is about 230 miles northwest of Mexico City in the country's historic silver-mining region. "This hilly, Spanish-colonial city teems with life and history. That presents a nice balance for both tourists and residents. Several of the city's historic buildings have been tastefully converted into hotels and restaurants, and the narrow streets of the city center are delightful to wander through." *guanajuatocapital.com*

Ashland, Oregon
Nestled in the foothills of the Cascades about 285 miles south of Portland, Ashland is famous for its annual Shakespeare Festival. It is also one of the most historic and appealing small towns in the United States. "Ashland's downtown area and surrounding neighborhoods are remarkably well-preserved, with charming, turn-of-the-century Queen Anne architecture. The wonderful array of boutique-type shops and restaurants attracts both tourists and locals." *ashlandchamber.com*

Isle of Skye, Scotland

If you adore Scotland, you'll love this quiet island retreat off the country's northwest coast. "Skye combines dramatic mountain and coastal scenery with a vibrant cultural and social scene. The residents maintain a strong focus on protecting the natural environment and preserving traditional Gaelic culture. There are castles to visit, tiny villages to wander through, and a wonderful food and drink festival that has become an annual event." *skye.co.uk*

Mackinac Island, Michigan

Situated in the Straits of Mackinac between Michigan's upper and lower peninsulas, Mackinac Island is a throwback to an earlier time. Homey, rural, and scenic, the island exudes authenticity and a relaxed feel. "Mackinac Island is a slice of true Americana, and the pace is kept purposefully slow. One big reason is that no cars are allowed—the only ways to get around are on foot, on bicycle, or by horse-drawn carriage." *mackinacisland.org*

A Grand vacation

If you're planning a getaway to Mackinac Island, better plan ahead: The vacation season is roughly from mid-May to early November, the dates the landmark Grand Hotel operates.

Getting to Mackinac Island is half the fun. Access is only by small plane or boat. Guests to the Grand Hotel are picked up at the dock by horse-drawn carriage. No motor vehicles are allowed on this three-mile-long island.

The pace on the island is slow. In the turn-of-the-century village, Victorian homes and shops have been restored. Fort Mackinac, more than 200 years old, is an extensive collection of buildings, artifacts, and clothing.

Although there are other accommodations on the island, the centerpiece is inarguably the 385-room Grand, with its 700-foot veranda and extensive grounds featuring gardens, a pool, a golf course, riding stables, and more. The ambience is definitely old world. *grandhotel.com*

Cape Breton Island, Nova Scotia, Canada
"Located off Nova Scotia's northeastern coast, Cape Breton is a beautiful, semiwild island where the locals are part of the experience. The aesthetic appeal is high, with scenic drives and unique fishing villages to visit. Authentic culture and history are everywhere—you'll find Celtic traditions in one village and Acadian in the next. Best of all, tourism hasn't harmed these communities; the revenue it brings in has helped preserve them." *capebretonisland.com*

Wachau Valley, Austria
With few development pressures and a keen appreciation for history, Austria has a good record for taking care of its landscapes. "In the wine-making region of the Wachau, each village tries to outdo the others in preserving and promoting local heritage. Take in the scenery from a river cruise on the Danube, sample some of the area's renowned wines, and be sure to tour the well-preserved Benedictine Abbey in the medieval town of Melk." *austria.info*

Chaco Culture National Historical Park, New Mexico
Located in the northwest corner of New Mexico, Chaco Canyon houses the remarkably well-preserved remains of what once was a huge Anasazi city called Pueblo Bonito. At its peak, around A.D. 900, the settlement was the center of Anasazi society and home to thousands of Native Americans. The site includes sports arenas, places of worship, a marketplace, and cliff dwellings up to five stories high. "A long, unpaved access road helps keep this archaeologically rich site untrampled." *nps.gov/chcu*

Northeast Kingdom, Vermont
"The three counties of the Northeast Kingdom are—in the opinion of residents and tourists alike—the real Vermont. This is rural America at its most nostalgic, enlivened by a vibrant cultural arts community and the wonderful Vermont scenery. There are scenic back roads to drive, quaint little towns to explore, wonderful hiking in the summer, and great skiing in the winter." *travelthekingdom.com*

Coastal Fjords, Norway

Rugged terrain and a cool, wet climate help keep the Norwegian coastline beautiful and unspoiled. But when the sun does shine, it's truly spectacular. "Avoid the huge summer cruise ships, which let you see the fjords but not really experience them. Instead, go for a springtime mix of driving, hiking, and short trips on the Norwegian coastal ferry line. Stay at the local inns, which serve foods unique to each fjord." *visitnorway.com*

10 places to leap into the weirdly wonderful

Take a leap of imagination and picture yourself amid the landscape of some otherworldly natural wonders. Leslie Weeden, travel director of Outside, *shares her favorite out-of-the-ordinary getaways.*

Jellyfish Lake, Palau Islands, South Pacific

The diversity of coral is the main attraction here, but it takes a leap of faith to enter Jellyfish Lake. "It's a landlocked saltwater lake in the middle of one of Palau's Rock Islands. If you've ever been mesmerized by diaphanous jellyfish in a tank at an aquarium, you can imagine what it's like to swim in a lake full of them. These are caramel-colored, softball-size, and harmless Mastigias jellyfish. Go snorkeling there with the Oceanic Society." *visit-palau.com*

Boiling Lake and the Valley of Desolation, Dominica, West Indies

Take a stroll through Dominica's primeval landscape. "Boiling Lake is a three-hour hike into the island's mountainous interior. The lake, which bubbles at 190 degrees, is surrounded by misty cliffs. You walk through dense rain forest and the Valley of Desolation, a stark place where sulfurous gas pours from vents along the way." The secluded Papillote Wilderness Retreat offers adventure packages. *dominica.dm*

Cappadocia Region, Turkey

Three-million-year-old volcanic eruptions have created a bizarre and beautiful landscape in central Turkey: the Cappadocia region, with its narrow sandstone spires called fairy chimneys, and other unusual rock formations. "Aside from the gorgeous spires and chimneys and sandstone valleys, what's really amazing about this place is its underground cities, cave hotels, and rock-hewn dwellings. It would not seem out of place to find the sand people from *Star Wars* in this landscape." *tourismturkey.org*

Wrangell–St. Elias National Park & Preserve, Alaska

Climbers are starting to explore the "moulins," or pits, up to 300 feet deep in the glaciated areas of the Wrangell–St. Elias in southeast Alaska. The sport is called "moulineering" and involves ice axes and crampons. "Go with St. Elias Alpine Guides to rappel down into one of these frozen pits that lead to surreal ice passages and caves. Waterfalls crash down some of them, forming icy pools at the bottom." *nps.gov/wrst*

White Sands National Monument, New Mexico

"This unusual landscape in southern New Mexico is 275 square miles of glimmering white sand dunes. It is different from Great Sand Dunes National Park farther north, because the sand here is stark white. For maximum otherworldly effect, backpackers can camp out in the park during a full moon." *nps.gov/whsa*

The Blue Lagoon, Grindavik, Iceland

The Blue Lagoon, about 20 minutes from Reykjavik, is 53,820 square feet of mineral-rich geothermal seawater. "This is

Frozen in time

Viking descendants aren't Iceland's only breathtaking attractions. This island the size of Kentucky boasts mountains, glaciers, geysers, hot springs, and waterfalls—as well as small but sturdy horses that sure-footedly carry vacationers across the volcanic landscape.

But one of Iceland's most visited places is manmade. The Blue Lagoon, a mammoth pool of approximately 100-degree seawater and silica near Reykjavik, lures more than 400,000 visitors each year.

a surreal spa experience, bathing in the milky, steamy turquoise waters surrounded by hills of black lava. The lagoon's white silica mud is reputed to be healthy and revitalizing for the skin." Stay at the renovated Art Deco Hotel Borg in Reykjavik, and visit the Blue Lagoon for a natural high: a steam bath in a lava cave or a waterfall massage. *bluelagoon.com*

River caves, Belize

You can float on an inner tube for seven miles along underground rivers in the jungle of Belize. "In the beam of your headlamp, you'll see stalagmites and stalactites and underground waterfalls as you float past." *travelbelize.org*

Atacama Desert, Chile

Running for about 600 miles between the Pacific Ocean and the Andes in northern Chile, the Atacama Desert is the driest patch on the planet, with a sculptural and surreal landscape. "The Atacama is a series of salt flats with no vegetation. Then there's the stark, moonlike Valle de la Luna and the highest geyser field in the world." *sernatur.cl*

El Rosario Monarch Butterfly Sanctuary, Angangueo, Mexico

Every November, some 250 million monarch butterflies migrate from Canada and the northeastern United States to the volcanic highlands of central Mexico. "You hike in forests of oyamel trees, which are just plastered with the orange-and-black monarchs, and see them fluttering around like millions of falling leaves. El Rosario Monarch Butterfly Sanctuary is close to the town of Angangueo in Michoacan. Natural Habitat Adventures runs trips from January through March." *visitmexico.com*

Gobi Desert, Mongolia

Go camel-trekking, hike to petroglyphs, and visit with nomadic families passing through the desert. Make the Three Camel Lodge, an eco-outpost in the Gobi's Gurvansaikhan National Park, your base camp. It has 30 *gers,* or traditional felt tents, with wood stoves and solar-powered electricity. "Talk about Big Sky country. This relatively luxurious camp is in one of the most remote spots on earth, which makes it particularly great for stargazing." *mongoliatourism.gov.mn*

10 great places to check into movie-hotel history

They may not receive any awards at Oscar time, but real hotels are often used as "supporting players" in notable films. Tony Reeves, author of The Worldwide Guide to Movie Locations, *nominates ten of his favorite silver-screen hotels.*

Millennium Biltmore, Los Angeles, California
Opened in 1923, downtown L.A.'s grand hostelry has been associated with moviedom for decades. In the 1930s and '40s, its ornate ballroom played host to the Academy Awards ceremonies. "The Biltmore has also been a familiar screen presence over the years. Among other roles, it served as the 'Beverly Palms' in Eddie Murphy's blockbuster *Beverly Hills Cop* and became New York's 'Sedgewick' in *Ghostbusters.* The Biltmore is also where Michelle Pfeiffer vamps it up in *The Fabulous Baker Boys.*"
millenniumhotels.com/millenniumlosangeles

San Domenico Palace, Taormina, Sicily, Italy
Built on the site of a 15th-century monastery and incorporating some of its original structure, the luxurious San Domenico sits on a bluff overlooking the Mediterranean. "It's a gorgeous setting that's featured in Michelangelo Antonioni's classic 1960 film *L'Avventura.* The film ends with a famous scene on the hotel's terrace, with the peak of Mount Etna visible on the horizon."
sandomenicopalace.hotelsinsicily.it

Hotel Alfonso XIII, Seville, Spain
"This palatial hotel's courtyard stands in for the 'Cairo Officers Club' in David Lean's 1962 epic *Lawrence of Arabia. Star Wars*

San Francisco's still dizzy over *Vertigo*

When Alfred Hitchcock's movie *Vertigo* premiered here more than 50 years ago, audiences and critics were unimpressed by the tale of a former San Francisco cop who falls for the mysterious blonde her husband hires him to follow. But decades later, Hitchcock's off-kilter love letter to the City by the Bay hovers near the top of every best movies list. And it continues to spark pilgrimages and tributes.

The moody thriller captured "the heart, soul, and pace of the city at midcentury," and Hitchcock—born in England but a longtime resident of the Bay Area—"incorporated San Francisco as if it were a leading character in the film," says Aaron Leventhal, coauthor of *Footsteps in the Fog: Alfred Hitchcock's San Francisco*. The movie stars Jimmy Stewart as Scottie Ferguson, an obsessive detective with a fear of heights, and Kim Novak as both Madeleine Elster—a socialite who believes she is possessed by the spirit of an ancestor—and a Madeleine look-alike, Judy Barton.

Some of *Vertigo*'s featured locations are now demolished or closed, including Ernie's restaurant, a longtime local favorite where Scottie first spotted Madeleine. But the city's tony Nob Hill neighborhood, where Madeleine's apartment building, the Brocklebank, still sports a signature beige awning, has "maintained its old-world San Francisco feel," notes Leventhal.

At Fort Point National Historic Site, where Madeleine plunged into the bay with the Golden Gate Bridge looming above her, "we always get people asking, 'where did she jump?' " says tour guide Ed McDaneld. (Don't try to angle for the same view: Post-9/11 security fences block public access.)

No *Vertigo* fan should miss the two-hour drive south to sleepy San Juan Bautista, where the largest of California's 21 Spanish missions served as the setting for the film's dizzying finale. The church welcomes visitors, but the tall bell tower that terrified Scottie was added to the real mission via special effects. So far, the town hasn't done much to exploit its celluloid connections, but that could be changing: In 2007, San Juan Bautista held a party to celebrate the 50th anniversary of *Vertigo*'s filming there. And in 2009, the mission opened a new museum that includes an exhibit with film-related memorabilia—celebrating the enduring magic of the master of suspense.

fans will also recognize the Alfonso as the exterior of Princess Amidala's 'Naboo Palace' in *Star Wars, Episode II: Attack of the Clones." hotel-alfonsoxiii.com*

Hotel Vertigo, San Francisco, California
Located in the heart of San Francisco a few blocks from Union Square, "the hotel is now much grander than it appeared in the 1958 Alfred Hitchcock suspense classic *Vertigo.* As the 'Hotel Empire,' the Hotel Vertigo is where—in the eerie green glow of its illuminated sign—Kim Novak was transformed into the 'dead' Madeleine in the film." *hotelvertigosf.com/index.html*

Sidi Driss, Matmata, Tunisia
" 'Iconic' is an overused word when it comes to film locations, but if any place deserves the term, it's the Sidi Driss." The unusual sunken hotel—a traditional Berber underground structure of "cave rooms" radiating from a large central pit—was used by George Lucas in the *Star Wars* saga. "Most memorably, the Sidi Driss served as Luke Skywalker's subterranean home on the desert planet of Tatooine."

The Plaza, New York, New York
Overlooking Central Park, the distinctive Plaza—built in 1907—is a familiar movie star. "Paul Hogan as Crocodile Dundee figured out the function of the bidet here, and Dudley Moore entertained working girls in the hotel's famous Oak Bar in *Arthur.* But my favorite Plaza scene is the abduction of Cary Grant from the hotel's lobby in Alfred Hitchcock's classic *North by Northwest." fairmont.com/theplaza*

Columns Hotel, New Orleans, Louisiana
Built by a New Orleans cigar magnate as his palatial home in 1883, the Columns is in the Garden District—a short streetcar ride from the historic French Quarter. "The splendid interior of this grand structure became the elegant bordello in Louis Malle's controversial 1978 drama *Pretty Baby.* This is the film in which a young Brooke Shields shot to stardom." *thecolumns.com*

Timberline Lodge, Mount Hood, Oregon
Nestled on the flanks of Oregon's spectacular Mount Hood, Timberline Lodge was built by unemployed craftsmen hired by the federal Works Progress Administration in 1937. Fashioned from mammoth timbers and native stone, the lodge was designated a National Historic Landmark in 1978. "The Timberline is an ideal place for a stressed writer to get away from it all. But if you've seen Stanley Kubrick's *The Shining,* you'll remember that Jack Nicholson's relaxing winter break goes somewhat awry there." *timberlinelodge.com*

Cardozo Hotel, Miami Beach, Florida
Owned by singer Gloria Estefan and her husband, the Cardozo sits amid the shops, restaurants, and nightclubs of Miami's vibrant South Beach area. "It's an Art Deco gem with great ocean views, and it's been employed in a host of notable films." Among them: *The Birdcage* with Robin Williams and Nathan Lane; Oliver Stone's *Any Given Sunday* with Al Pacino and Jamie Foxx; and Frank Capra's 1959 comedy *A Hole in the Head,* starring Frank Sinatra. "The Cardozo is also Ben Stiller's hotel in the raunchy comedy *There's Something About Mary.*" *cardozohotel.com*

Oakley Court, Windsor, England
Set on 35 acres of landscaped gardens on the bank of the River Thames, the Oakley Court was built in 1859 as an estate for a British nobleman. The Victorian Gothic country house was transformed into a hotel in 1981, but during much of the 1960s and '70s it stood vacant. "Right next door was Bray Studios, where many classic British horror films of that era were made. The Oakley was used regularly as the lair of Dracula, Frankenstein, and various Cornish zombies. In 1975, it achieved screen immortality as the castle of Frank-N-Furter in the cult classic *Rocky Horror Picture Show.*" *www.principal-hayley.com/venues-and-hotels/the-oakley-court*

SPECIFIC CITIES, STATES & OTHER SPOTS

10 great places to discover the hidden Florida

When visiting Florida, many of us head for Latin-flavored Miami, theme parks, or the tourist-magnet beaches. Palm trees and pools, glitzy shopping, and nightlife by the sea shape our fantasies. But there's much to discover in the "unspoiled" areas, as veteran traveler and author of Highway A1A: Florida at the Edge *Herb Hiller explains. Visitflorida.com has information for all these places, plus links to more specific sites.*

The Panhandle
This region of northern Florida is "typified by State Road 2, aka Hog and Hominy Road." You'll see old, steam-driven grist mills and "still-operating general stores where you can buy county newspapers no one [has] ever heard of." Among its highlights is the old Chautauqua town of DeFuniak Springs, with its Victorian architecture. In Falling Waters State Park, the state's highest waterfall pours upside down into a sinkhole: "You stand and look down at it, not up."

The Big Bend, four northern counties

Big Bend is being marketed as the Nature Coast, and its four northern counties (Levy, Cedar Key, Dixie, and Taylor) are distinguished by "an absence of tourist features [but] the best nature touring. Levy is horse country, and it has some of the most beautiful unknown beaches… on islands off Cedar Key, a hip artists' town." In Dixie, you can hike or bike along "exquisite canopied trails" in the winter, when migrating birds pass through. Taylor, known for scalloping in the late summer, offers "Steinhatchee, an old fishing town" where shrimp boats still tie up. Taylor and neighboring Wakulla contain part of the 68,000-acre St. Marks National Wildlife Refuge, with 274 bird species. *naturecoastcoalition.com*

Gainesville and towns south

Within half an hour of "the most sophisticated small city in Florida"—home to the University of Florida—lies a crescent of "exceptionally attractive" small towns. Micanopy, known for its antiques, also has "the best antiquarian bookstore in the state." Not quite as "spiffed up" is Cross Creek, where Marjorie Kinnan Rawlings wrote *The Yearling.* Evinston is "a jewel. Nothing's there except the family-run 1906 Wood & Swink General Store," which contains one of few remaining in-store post offices. *visitgainesville.com*

Highway A1A through Nassau and Duval counties

This part of the long, north-to-south road, "largely in view of the sea, salt marsh, or both," traverses three state parks. "All you see are folks fishing on old stumps." If you walk along paths that cut through the sand dunes to the salt marsh inlets, you'll see "manatees in the winter and beaches chockablock with driftwood." *visitjacksonville.com*

DeLand, Lake Helen, Cassadaga

On the St. Johns River, just 30 minutes west of Daytona Beach, is DeLand, home of Stetson University. The town has three historic districts and "great regard for the arts." On the west side of town, "the hub of houseboating, they have two large fleets that cruise alongside Ocala National Forest." In the tiny, undeveloped Lake Helen, "the Florida Bicycle Association is working to open a year-round, adult, bike-touring program." In Cassadaga, home of the Southern Cassadaga Spiritualist Camp, "the mediums live in small-scale, charming houses and do readings throughout the year." *riveroflakesheritagecorridor.com*

Lakeland

The grocery-store chain Publix is based in Lakeland, and its "philanthropic-minded" contributions include Hollis Gardens, which "reproduces botanically every part of the state." There's Lake Mirror, the "town's jewel, with a gorgeously ornamented lakefront from the '20s, with a walkway all the way around." Fans of Frank Lloyd Wright shouldn't miss the campus of Florida Southern College, the architect's "largest single installation in the world." *lakelandchamber.com*

Stuart

Here's an island town that's "not only attractive, it works. It came back in the '60s, when lots of people left Miami." When it

A playground you live in

Miami Beach has been one of the nation's preeminent waterfront resorts for nearly a century, earning nicknames such as The World's Playground, America's Riviera, and The Beach.

Independent from Miami, the city of Miami Beach occupies a barrier island in Miami's harbor. Though small, it boasts seven miles of beaches and more than 20 public parks. The island has long been a second-home choice for the rich and famous, first with waterfront mansions and, more recently, luxury condos.

In particular, South Beach, with its Art Deco architecture, has become well-known for its nightlife and dining and its crowd of models and fashion designers. On Collins Avenue, restaurants offer outdoor seating for people-watching.

Best for...

—Night clubbers, foodies, and people-watchers.

Claim to fame...

—The Miami Beach Architectural District, with its Art Deco structures, is a National Historic Landmark.

Don't miss...

—The original Joe's Stone Crab in the SoFi neighborhood of South Beach made the South Florida shellfish world famous.

rebounded, Stuart became "the avatar of 'yesteryear' town planning and the 'new urbanism.' " At its northernmost part is St. Lucie Inlet State Park. "You either have to walk seven miles up the beach or rent a boat to reach it. I saw only one or two sets of footprints when I kayaked there." *stuartmartinchamber.org*

Pinellas County

Six small towns in the county that contains St. Pete/Clearwater are distinctive destinations. The "hip" town of Pass-a-Grille, "literally an appendage" of St. Petersburg, is topped by the old Don Cesar Hotel, one of the few remaining "pink palaces in the state . . . like a big sand castle on the water." Gulfport, to the east, has "become a cool hangout, in a quiet way." Safety Harbor, famed for its eponymous spa, "is a wonderful town for walking around." To the north, Dunedin's old railroad bed has been turned into the nearly 40-mile Pinellas Trail, used by one million people a year. The "sane, small-scale" Indian Rocks Beach is "the best beach town" of all. Finally, the trail leads up to Tarpon Springs, an "old Greek fishing community" still "redolent with character." *floridasbeach.com*

The Redland

In this agricultural area, "people from Cuba and Mexico came up and planted exotic" blooms, so it's rife with "bromeliad farms, rare palms, orchid farms, and specialized nurseries."
tropicaleverglades.com

Calusa Blueway paddling trail

On the west coast, "adjacent to the best-known beaches—Fort Myers, Sanibel, and Captiva"—this trail is "a world apart. The biggest intrusion might be at low tide, when a sandbar pops up." Lee County residents and civic leaders who want to keep the area "almost pristine have created something that also works for tourists" seeking an environmental getaway.
fortmyers-sanibel.com

10 great places to discover Midwest charm

Attention, summer-vacation snobs: If you think the Midwest exists merely as "Flyover Country"—one big flat cornfield on the way to someplace more exciting—Dan Kaercher wants to reeducate you. From big-city excitement to sandy beaches to back-road towns and farms, "the Midwest truly is a microcosm of the entire nation," says Kaercher, editor in chief of Midwest Living *magazine and author of* Best of the Midwest: Rediscovering America's Heartland. *"The Midwest is the nation's last travel frontier because of all the overlooked surprises that await. Plus, prices are very affordable, it's generally safe and uncrowded, and Midwesterners are nothing if not friendly and welcoming." Here, Kaercher shares his love of the land.*

Columbus, Indiana
"Find fabulous examples of modern architecture everywhere you turn in what otherwise would be an ordinary Midwest industrial town located in south-central Indiana. Columbus is one grand, landscaped park with churches and public buildings designed by the likes of Eero and Eliel Saarinen, I. M. Pei, and Richard Meier." *columbus.in.us*

Council Grove, Kansas
"Well-fed cows graze contentedly in the rolling Flint Hills grasslands, and this friendly, well-kept Great Plains ranch town is filled with sites (several in the form of historic tree stumps) that recall the legendary 900-mile Santa Fe Trail. Visitors can sample peach pie at the historic Hays House or try the roast beef over at the landmark Trail Days Bakery Cafe." *councilgrove.com*

Fulton, Missouri
"How many towns can claim to be the setting of a speech that shook the world? Winston Churchill delivered his 'Iron Curtain' call to action at Westminster College here (population 12,250) in 1946. Honoring that event, you'll find a reconstructed Christopher Wren chapel and a bona-fide section of the Berlin Wall." *callawaychamber.com*

Munising, Michigan

"Here in this Upper Peninsula community, perched along a sweeping Lake Superior bay, are the breathtaking waterfalls and cliffs of 42-mile-long Pictured Rocks National Lakeshore. Visitors and locals come for the lakes, hiking trails, beaches, and lighthouses, not to mention the views." *algercounty.org*

Dubuque, Iowa

"If you love rivers and river towns, you've got to stop at the new National Mississippi River Museum and Aquarium in the Port of Dubuque. For a bird's-eye view of the city and the river, rumble up to the top of the venerable Fenelon Place Elevator, an elevated railway circa 1882." *dubuquechamber.com*

Springfield, Illinois

"The inspiring saga of Abraham Lincoln really does come to life here, when you see his home, law office, and the library and museum." Illinois' friendly capital city is replete with "ornate and carefully maintained Victorian storefronts." *gscc.org*

Washington Island, Wisconsin

"Many travelers know and love Door County, the 'Cape Cod of the Midwest.' This island, a short ferry ride beyond the tip of the peninsula, is an even more unspoiled vacation haven, with attractions as varied as a reconstructed Norwegian *stavekirke* (church), a renowned fiber arts school, and pint-sized Icelandic horses." *washingtonisland.com*

Keystone, South Dakota

"Sure, you've got to see Mount Rushmore, just 15 miles from here. But don't miss Crazy Horse Monument, an ongoing work, now being continued by the descendants of bigger-than-life sculptor Korczak Ziolkowski. It dwarfs Rushmore in size, if not also vision." *keystonechamber.com*

Lincoln, Nebraska

"Fans everywhere know Lincoln for its proud University of Nebraska football tradition. But I love the one-of-a-kind state

Lakota warrior holds family's fascination

On June 3, 1948, Korczak Ziolkowski, a gifted portrait artist, began a project that was to consume half his life: carving the image of a Lakota warrior who never let anyone take his picture. Ziolkowski used an entire South Dakota mountain as his canvas and spent 35 years blasting away at rock, having children (ten), looking wild and woolly, and drawing skeptics. When he died in 1982 at age 74, his work was so raw it looked like nothing. Many called him a fraud, and he was buried in a tomb of his own design, with a huge doorknocker on the inside.

"He had a sense of humor," says his widow, Ruth Ziolkowski.

Each year, about one million people visit Ziolkowski's mountain, now known simply as the Crazy Horse Memorial. And these days no one thinks he was a fraud.

More than seven million tons of granite had been blasted away by the artist and, while unfinished, his sculpture was largely ready for detail work. After he died, Ruth and the children took over. Working from the sculptor's model of an Indian warrior on horseback, they began shaping the warrior's face, which has since been completed.

The Lakota chief, who was bayoneted by U.S. soldiers after his surrender, was perhaps the most famous Native American resistance fighter, leading the charge against General Custer and much of the 7th Cavalry at Little Bighorn in 1876. When Lakota chiefs saw the presidential faces of nearby Mount Rushmore emerge from the Black Hills in the 1930s, they asked Ziolkowski, then an award-winning sculptor who worked for a short time on Mount Rushmore, to do a carving that would show how "the red man has great heroes too."

Ziolkowski pondered it for seven years before agreeing. "He was always for the underdog," Ruth says. The fact that no one really knows what the famous Lakota chief looked like was never a problem. "He (Korczak) was tickled to death that there were no pictures," she says. This allowed "artistic license," Ruth says, to fashion a bold, handsome face for Crazy Horse. Who, after all, would complain?

When finished (and the family still says it has no idea when that will be), the mountain will have been transformed into a 641-foot-long-by-563-foot-high sculpture—the largest in the world, higher than the Washington Monument, and so vast that Mount Rushmore's four faces could fit inside the head of Crazy Horse.

Capitol, with its soaring tower and amazing mosaics and paintings, much of it from the Art Deco era." *lcoc.com*

Lanesboro, Minnesota
"If you're looking for a Midwest Shangri-La, this is it: an idyllic valley (Root River Valley) with a Brigadoon-like village at its heart. The main pastimes here are relaxing at the many bed-and-breakfasts, biking the riverside rail-trail system, and deciding what to try at the famous pie shop in tiny nearby Whalan (population: 64)." *lanesboro.com*

10 great sites to reach for in Denver

The Mile High City has miles of things to do and see, so how do you choose? Tamra Monahan, manager of the Tattered Cover Book Store and contributing writer for Colorado's Best: The Essential Guide to Favorite Places, *offers plenty of advice on where visitors to the Denver area should be sure to go.*

Denver Art Museum
"This museum is a work of art itself. Architect Daniel Libeskind designed the DAM's Frederic C. Hamilton Building, with the jagged peaks of the Rocky Mountains in mind, and what he created is architectural art, inside and out. The building, which resembles geometric rock crystals, features artistically designed staircases and spaces that accentuate the museum's wonderful art collection. Outside, a mixture of striking angles and complex geometry create a visual masterpiece." *denverartmuseum.org*

Trios Enoteca
"Slip into this intimate wine bar for great live music, no cover charge, and over 40 wines by the glass." There's a local following for the wood-oven pizzas and happy hour at this destination in the city's Lower Downtown. *triosenoteca.com*

Comedy Works

"Spend the night laughing at Denver's oldest and most notable spot for stand-up comedy." Many rising stars, including Jerry Seinfeld, Jay Leno, Rosie O'Donnell, Ellen DeGeneres, Tim Allen, and Roseanne Barr, honed their craft here in the '80s. The intimate basement atmosphere is a contagious place for laughter. *comedyworks.com*

Cherry Creek North

"An afternoon of shop-till-you-drop must include Cherry Creek, Denver's Rodeo Drive." This 16-square-block area has dozens of galleries, boutiques, restaurants, spas, and an adjacent mall with upscale Saks Fifth Avenue and Neiman Marcus. Round out the day with a drive to Larimer Square. "Denver's most historic block was transformed into a shoppers' paradise with local favorites." *cherrycreeknorth.com*

Coors Field

"In the world of beer, Colorado is known for Coors, so it's fitting to spend an evening at Coors Field sipping an ice-cold beer [and] watching a Colorado Rockies baseball game. This state-of-the-art baseball stadium has a view of the Rocky Mountains—and terrific ballpark food. Aside from traditional hot dogs and pretzels, feast on Blue Cheese Potato Chips and Rocky Mountain Oysters (Hint: They're not seafood)." *rockies.mlb.com*

City Park

Denver's premier park, about a mile from downtown, has Sunday concerts and postcard views of the city skyline with the Rocky Mountains as a backdrop. "You can bike along the trails, row a boat on the lake, picnic on the lawn, golf, or visit the Denver Zoo in this expansive park. Wander through dinosaur exhibits [and] moon rock and outer space displays at the Museum of Nature & Science and Gates Planetarium, also in the park." *denvergov.org/parks*

Mizuna

This is consistently ranked as the top restaurant in the city. "Chef and owner Frank Bonanno is synonymous with great food in

Denver. His other restaurants, Luca D'Italia and Osteria Marco, offer some of the best culinary experiences in the Mile High City." Bonanno cures his own pancetta, sopressata, and a variety of other Italian meats. He also makes his own burrata, a creamy mozzarella-based cheese. All the pasta, including ravioli, is homemade. *mizunadenver.com*

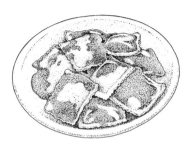

Molly Brown House Museum

"Denver's history is full of gunslingers and gold miners who tamed the Wild West. Come here for a sense of the Mile High City's rowdy past. Socialite and suffragist Molly Brown's survival of the *Titanic* voyage inspired the Broadway musical *The Unsinkable Molly Brown*." *mollybrown.org*

Denver Performing Arts Complex

"If you need a cultural fix, head here for an evening of dining and drama. Book a table at Kevin Taylor's at the Opera House, one of Denver's most elegant restaurants. After dinner, walk upstairs and take your pick of opera in the Ellie Caulkins Opera House or musical and dramatic productions at the Denver Center for Performing Arts." *artscomplex.com*

United States Mint at Denver

"The United States Mint at Denver is one of two facilities that produces our circulating coins, so take a free tour and find out how our money is made. It is located in the heart of the city, and inside this grand building you'll learn about money in the United States, production and packaging of circulating and collectible coins, and the history of the United States Mint system. Reservations are required, and tours have strict regulations." *usmint.gov*

10 great places to cool your jets at a city's airport hotel

Getting there is more than half the fun if you stay at the next generation of airport hotels, revamped to make a night near the runways more fun. Peter Greenberg, travel editor of NBC's Today *show and author of* Don't Go There! The Travel Detective's Essential Guide to Must-Miss Places of the World, *shares his favorite airport hotels.*

The Fairmont, Vancouver Airport, Vancouver, British Columbia, Canada
"The cool thing about this hotel is its location: inside the U.S. departures terminal. As an added bonus, if you're going fishing, they have a 'fish valet' to store your catch." All guest rooms have floor-to-ceiling soundproof windows. Views include the North Shore Mountains and airport runways, as well as partial views of the Pacific. *fairmont.com/vancouverairport*

Hyatt Regency Orlando International Airport, Orlando, Florida
"The cool thing about this hotel is that the bellman actually meets you at baggage claim, and you can't really get stuck in traffic on the way to the airport: You're already inside the terminal." The hotel is great for families, particularly if they have a late-night arrival or early departure. *orlandoairport.hyatt.com*

Sofitel London Heathrow, London, England
"The opening of this hotel changed the definition of what an airport hotel can be." To wit: world-class spa, fine dining, lobby bar, tea salon, and state-of-the-art rooms, including the Imperial Suite with Swarovski crystal fixtures and lights in the bathroom. The Sofitel, connected to Terminal 5 by footbridge, is also convenient to central London via Heathrow rail service. *sofitelheathrow.com*

Aloft Philadelphia Airport, Philadelphia, Pennsylvania
"If I'm going to be stuck in an airport hotel, give me a 42-inch plasma TV." Aloft adds a new twist in style to the Philly market. The lobby, which opens into a backyard patio and pool, is like a

giant living room with people using laptops, chatting, or playing pool. Grab-and-go food, from healthy meals to cheesecake from the Cheesecake Factory, is available as well.
starwoodhotels.com/alofthotels

Kempinski Hotel Airport Munchen, Munich, Germany
A soaring glass-covered atrium with towering palms greets guests as they step into the ultramodern, light-filled space of this luxurious hotel. The Fit & Fly Spa and pool are available for day-trippers as well as overnight guests. Ditto for the fine dining. Choose from the Thai-Mediterranean-inspired Safran

---

I'm No Expert But...

TO TIP OR NOT TO TIP

To try to eliminate uncertainty, we asked etiquette and hospitality experts for advice on what to tip at hotels in the United States. Their responses are inconsistent, but there's a consensus for some common tipping situations:

- Valet parking staff. Don't tip a hotel staff member who opens a guest's car door at the hotel entrance or parks the car in a valet lot. The valet who retrieves the car from the parking lot should be given $2 to $5.

- Bellhop. The common tip is $1 to $2 per bag. More can be given if the bags are heavy or the bellhop provides other services.

- Housekeeping. They should receive $1 to $5 daily. "The tip should be paid daily to ensure it goes to the person who took care of your room," says etiquette expert Patricia Rossi.

- Concierges. No tip is needed for directions, restaurant recommendations, or answers to simple questions. A $10 to $50 tip is recommended for a concierge who obtains hard-to-get event tickets or a table at a popular premier restaurant.

Despite such suggestions, hotel guests "should expect great service, and there is no obligation to tip," says Vivian Deuschl, a vice president for luxury hotel chain the Ritz-Carlton.

---

restaurant, Charles Lindbergh restaurant, or Lobby Cafe. "For once, an airport hotel in Germany that doesn't force-feed you pretzels and beer." *kempinski-airport.de/en/home/index.htm*

Grand Hyatt DFW, Dallas–Fort Worth, Texas

"Wine pairings at an airport hotel? Who knew? Even better, they've got a really decent restaurant." Dine at the Grand Met and sit at the chef's table near the show kitchen. Peruse a virtual menu with a touch screen that lists ingredients along with pictures and other information, such as chef recommendations for wine pairings. The hotel is integrated into the airport. The chic interiors, with soothing and calming color schemes, were designed to balance the stress and frenzy of plane travel. *grandhyattdfw.com*

Westin Detroit Metropolitan Airport, Detroit, Michigan

"Don't be surprised if you bump into a wedding party at this hotel—they all flew in for it. That's right, the airport hotel has become a wedding destination." Hotel guests also have entrée to shops and restaurants in the new McNamara Terminal. *starwoodhotels.com/westin*

Crystal City Marriott at Reagan National Airport, Arlington, Virginia

"If you're tired of the drama at the terminal, no problem. Across the street from this airport hotel is the Arena Stage, with great regional theater." An underground walkway connects to shops and restaurants, and a Washington, D.C., Metro (subway) stop is less than a block away to take you into the nation's capital. *marriott.com*

Hilton Chicago O'Hare Airport, Chicago, Illinois

"You don't have to be a guest to buy a day pass to the health club of this hotel and work out if your flight is delayed." Or feast at the hotel's Gaslight Club, a retro steakhouse with aged prime meat brought to the table for your selection. Allergen-free rooms with hardwood floors, pure cotton linens, and in-room air purifiers also are available. *www1.hilton.com/en_US/hi/index.do*

Radisson SAS Airport Hotel, Oslo, Norway
"Two redeeming things about this hotel: You can swing your way
through 32 virtual golf courses at the fitness center and take a day
trip into Oslo." Hop aboard the high-speed Airport Express at
the nearby train stop and get into the center of Oslo in less than
20 minutes. Or relax in the hotel's solarium, then head for the hotel
bar with its views of the runway. *radissonblu.com/hotel-osloairport*

10 great places to glam it up
in Los Angeles

Social chronicler Dominick Dunne's book, The Way We
Lived Then, *is a memoir of his years in Beverly Hills.
And if he were advising visitors today, he'd tell them not to miss the
"glitz and glamour, and that's what people who go there expect
to see." Dunne suggested the top stops to make when in town.*

Lana Turner's former home, 730 North Bedford Drive, Beverly Hills
"I know where every death house is in Los Angeles." In this big,
white colonial, Lana Turner's lover Johnny Stompanato Jr. was
stabbed to death during a heated argument in 1958. Turner's
daughter, Cheryl Crane, was freed after a jury ruled it justifiable
homicide.

Broad Beach, north end of Malibu
"More out of the way and less crowded than (southern) Malibu.
Just walking on the beach is a wonderful experience. You see great
houses and faces you recognize"—Steven Spielberg's, for one.

Hotel Bel-Air, 701 Stone Canyon Boulevard, Bel-Air
Check out "the garden at the Bel-Air Hotel for lunch." The
Terrace restaurant's heated floor makes it an eatery for all seasons.
hotelbelair.com

Book Soup, 8818 Sunset Boulevard, West Hollywood
"It's one of the great bookshops of America, and you wouldn't
expect that of L.A." Authors read from their works, and celebs
are frequent shoppers. "The staff really knows and loves books."
booksoup.com

J. Paul Getty Center, 1200 Getty Center Drive, Brentwood
"The J. Paul Getty Museum is a must. The buildings are spectacular, and so is the location"—a hilltop setting offering vistas of the Pacific Ocean and downtown L.A. Known for its collection of European, Greek, and Roman artwork, the Getty is open every day except Monday. *getty.edu*

Universal Studios Hollywood,
Universal City
"If you're in L.A., you should try to see one of the studios, as corny as it may seem, because this is Hollywood." There are tours of studio lots, demonstrations of various aspects of filmmaking, a virtual earthquake, and rides including a *Jurassic Park*–themed thriller. *universalstudioshollywood.com*

Bel-Air neighborhood, north of Sunset
Boulevard, west of Beverly Glen Boulevard
Residents of this ultra-upscale area include Hollywood moguls. "In every major city, when I'm on a book tour, when there's time, I always say, 'Take me to where the rich people live.' Because I love to look at the beautiful houses. In Bel-Air, no matter which street or lane you turn on, you will see truly beautiful homes."

Torrenueva Hair Designs, 9601 Wilshire Boulevard, Beverly Hills
"You always hear about women gossiping at the hairdresser; well, this is where you see the guys and hear all the movie news." Joe Torrenueva once worked with Jay Sebring, the hairdresser killed along with actress Sharon Tate in the 1969 Manson Family rampage. Many of his and Sebring's clients from the old days remain loyal.

Spago, 176 North Canon Drive, Beverly Hills
Hot eateries come and go, but Spago keeps on cooking. "It's to this era what Chasen's was to another. It gets the establishment of the town, and the younger people too.
wolfgangpuck.com/restaurants/fine-dining/3635

The Beverly Hills Hotel, 9641 Sunset Boulevard, Beverly Hills
"I'm a big hotel freak, and I just think the Beverly Hills Hotel is enormous fun. I have breakfast in the coffee shop. A lot of producers and directors sit at the counter, so you're not just bumping elbows with someone. You're bumping elbows with a someone with a capital *S*." *beverlyhillshotel.com*

10 great—and not great— travel surprises

There's not a one of us who hasn't been made a fool of by a vacation destination. The "perfect" vacation spot turns out to be a big disappointment, and the place we didn't expect much from turns out to be a little gem. Wendy Perrin, consumer news editor at Condé Nast Traveler *and author of* Wendy Perrin's Secrets Every Smart Traveler Should Know, *offers five "good" vacation surprises and five "bad" surprises.*

The good

Elba
"You'd think the rocky island where Napoleon was exiled before he went back to France to meet his Waterloo would be bleak or ugly. But Elba is so lovely that I'm not sure why he ever left. Besides Napoleon's hilltop villa, it's got pretty fishing ports, quaint perched villages, dramatic mountain drives."

The Sinai, Egypt
"I had pictured the Sinai as a wasteland dotted with leftover military junk, chain-link fences, 55-gallon fuel drums. But in actuality it is an unsullied mountainous terra-cotta desertscape." The best way to appreciate it "is from the summit of Mount Sinai at sunrise."

Cape Town, South Africa
"Crime rates and racial conflict were foremost in my mind when my plane landed in South Africa." But instead, Cape Town has

Global vacation values

Stretch your travel dollars around the globe and cash in on these vacation values abroad.

Riviera Nayarit, Mexico—"Designated as a new tourism destination in 2007, Riviera Nayarit (accessible from Puerto Vallarta) has been investing in hotels and infrastructure to attract visitors," says Anne Banas of SmarterTravel.com. "You can find rates at all price levels, even under $100 per night in the more laid-back villages," such as the fishing town of San Pedro. More developed Nuevo Vallarta has surfing, snorkeling, and whale watching along the white sand beaches. *rivieranayarit.com*

County Clare, Ireland—Doolin and other scenic regions outside of the major cities, where farmhouse B&Bs are plentiful, offer good deals. Visit the Cliffs of Moher and the Burren, a stunning limestone landscape. *www.county-clare.com*

Lima, Peru—"Tourism in Lima is growing rapidly, and the government is adding major funding for development," Banas says. "You can expect to find new hotels and affordable rates on ground costs." Visit colonial houses and churches in Lima's historic downtown, then pause for a Suspiro de Limeoa, a local meringue-covered dessert. *peru.info*

Vietnam—Visit Halong Bay, known locally as the eighth wonder of the world because of its thousands of limestone islands, and take an overnight boat ride. Note the floating markets, which are platforms with boats tied around them, in the bay. *vietnamtourism.com*

Vilnius, Lithuania—"Because Lithuania doesn't use the euro as its currency, it can be much more affordable than countries in Western Europe," Banas says. Go sightseeing in Old Town, known for its splendid European architecture, then sample a Lithuanian beer with local cheese. *lietuva.lt/en*

Cartagena, Colombia—"The government has been adding better security and creating tourism programs in Colombia over the past five years," Banas says. "Now intrepid travelers can come and experience colonial cities, a vibrant culture, and beaches at great values." The beach town of Cartagena has always been a favorite destination for Colombians. *cartagenainfo.com* so many "diverse sights so close to the city: the wine country, the garden route, the whale-watching towns, the penguin colony...and one of my favorite coastal drives, out to the Cape of Good Hope, where two different shades of blue, the Atlantic Ocean and the Indian Ocean, meet in the distance."

Syria

"Far from being fanatics and terrorists, Syrians are the most friendly and gracious people I have ever encountered....Best of all, Syria is a treasure trove of well-preserved Roman cities and Crusader castles that are all but devoid of tourists. It's one of the few places left where you can stumble upon a world-class ruin and feel you are the first person to have discovered it."

Anza-Borrego Desert, California

"No one ever seems to have heard of the Anza-Borrego Desert, even though it's the largest state park in California and is just two hours east of San Diego. But to this day it is my favorite state park—a geological wonderland of canyons, badlands, mesas, sand dunes, washes, and buttes—and the place where I came to understand what was meant by 'purple mountain majesties.' "

The bad

Luxor, Egypt

"The royal tombs and temples of ancient Egypt are the world's oldest tourist sites. But the grandeur of monuments like King Tut's Tomb is destroyed by the wall-to-wall tourists packed inside. And it's hard to appreciate the dignity of the Temple of Karnak when you must be herded through with hundreds of tourists as part of a painfully kitschy sound-and-light show."

Disneyland Paris (Euro Disney)

"Imagine Disney World minus the magic, the cosmetically perfect buildings, the well-oiled machinery, the smiling cast members. On the day I visited Euro Disney outside

Paris, I could have forgiven the Main Street parade not operating and the Space Mountain ride being broken. But it was hard to ignore the staff's surliness. Even the cuisine was bad!"

Yangtze River cruise

"This is supposed to be a highlight of any China trip." But instead of seeing the Three Gorges, the Yangtze's legendary 4,000-foot cliffs, and the ancient river towns, "what I saw was a thick gray haze created by the fog mixed with the pollu-  tion from the Three Gorges Dam construction (the world's largest hydroelectric project). I barely saw any villages, either: The port tours, dictated by the Chinese government, steered us toward tourist shows and gift shops instead."

Portofino, Italy

"This Italian harbor town is so famously picturesque that a poster of it hangs in hundreds of pizzerias around this country. As pretty as it is, though, what there is to see and do in Portofino is as thin as that poster and takes about an hour. Unless you want to while away an afternoon at one of the overpriced harbor-front cafés or in the even more overpriced boutiques."

Coney Island Cyclone, Brooklyn, New York

"I was not prepared for just how squalid Coney Island really is. It's Pickpocket Central; there is not one healthy bite to be found among the greasy spoons; the public restrooms are worse than rural China's; and the Cyclone (one of the country's oldest wooden roller coasters) is so bumpy that I'm still in physiotherapy for my back."

INDEX

✳ ✳ ✳ ✳